Author's Message:

NOBUYUKI ANZAI

安西信行

PRESENTS

This Babbo was also
made for me.

MÄR
Vol. 14

Story and Art by Nobuyuki Anzai

English Adaptation/Gerard Jones
Translation/Kaori Inoue
Touch-up Art & Lettering/James Gaubatz
Design/Izumi Evers
Editor/Andy Nakatani

Editor in Chief, Books/Alvin Lu
Editor in Chief, Magazines/Marc Weidenbaum
VP of Publishing Licensing/Rika Inouye
VP of Sales/Gonzalo Ferreyra
Sr. VP of Marketing/Liza Coppola
Publisher/Hyoe Narita

Printed in the U.S.A.

Published by VIZ Media, LLC
P.O. Box 77010
San Francisco, CA 94107

10 9 8 7 6 5 4 3 2

First printing, July 2007
Second printing, August 2007

www.viz.com
store.viz.com

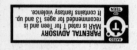

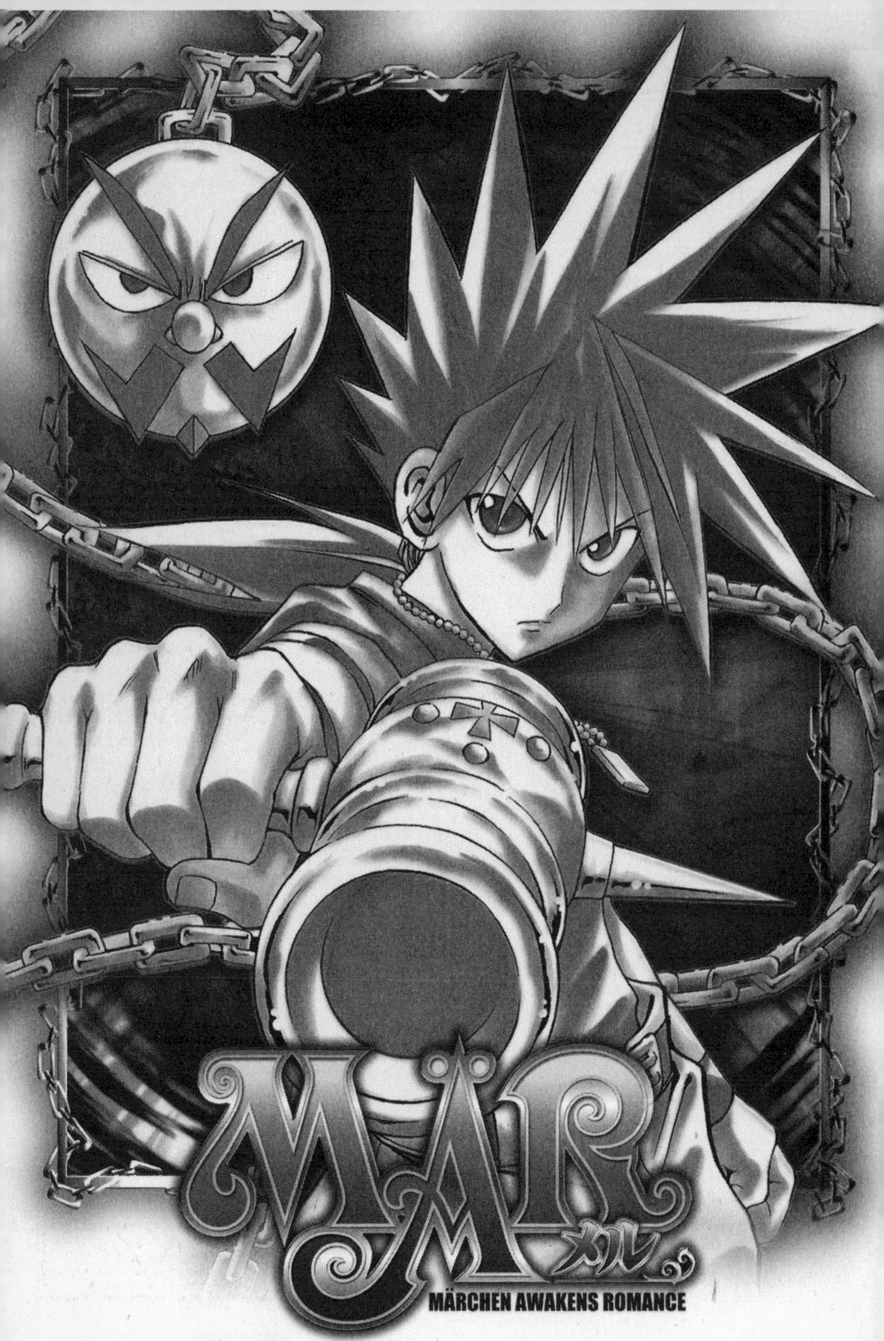
MÄR
メル
MÄRCHEN AWAKENS ROMANCE

Vol. 14

Nobuyuki Anzai

Characters

Alan

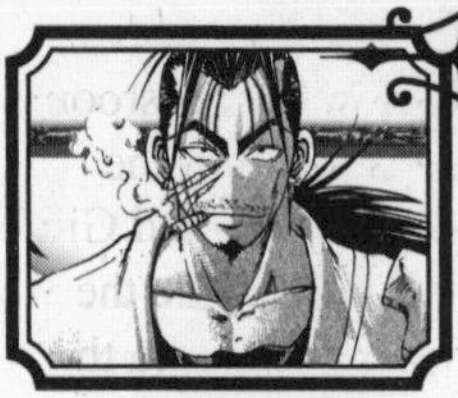

Fought in the war games six years ago alongside Ginta's father, Boss. Alan is afraid of cats.

Edward

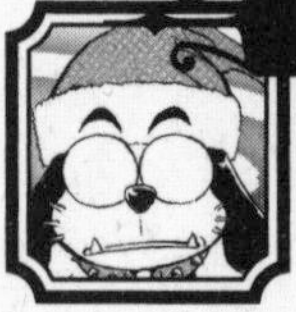

The dog who devotedly serves Princess Snow.

Snow

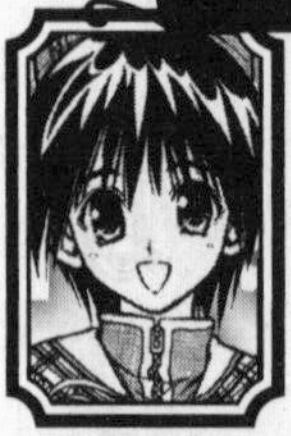

Princess of the Kingdom of Lestava. During the sixth battle, she was kidnapped on Diana's command.

Nanashi

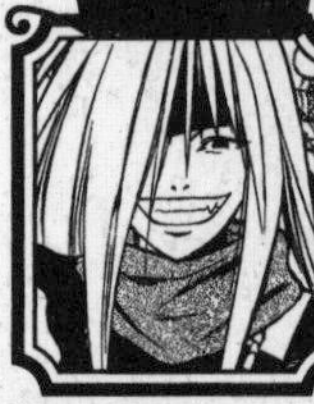

Leader of the Thieves Guild, Luberia. Detests the Chess Pieces who killed his comrades.

Alviss

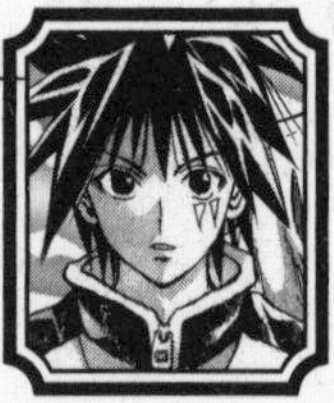

Scarred by Phantom's Zombie Tattoo in the previous War Games.

Ginta Toramizu

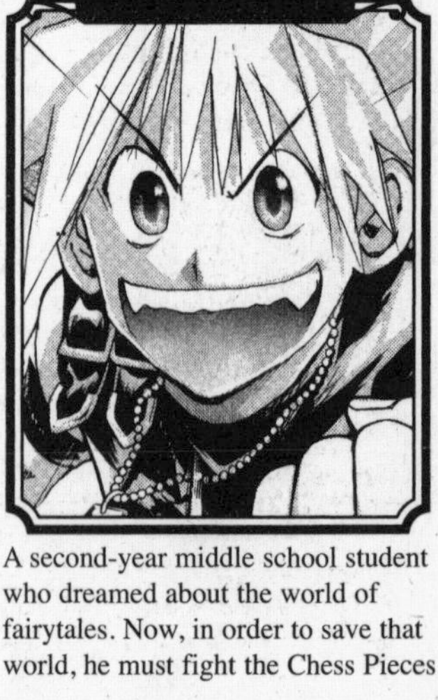

A second-year middle school student who dreamed about the world of fairytales. Now, in order to save that world, he must fight the Chess Pieces.

Babbo

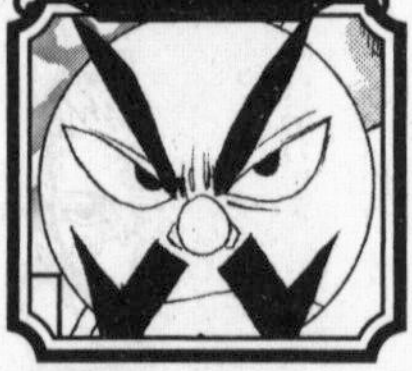

A rare talking ÄRM, who by synchronizing with Ginta is able to change shape—now up to Version 5.

Jack

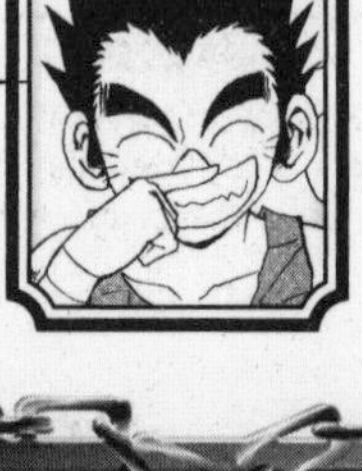

A farm boy who has left his mother and his farm to join Ginta in battle.

Previous Volume

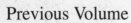

Ginta jumps through a "door" that suddenly appears in his classroom, and finds himself in the magical world of his dreams. Now, at the "request" of the Chess Pieces, the War Games have begun—and Ginta and his eight friends, calling themselves Team Mär, must battle the Chess warriors. Now the War Games have finally come down to the Final Battle. Mär has won four consecutive matches, but the fifth will by fought by Peta, the strategic planner of the Chess Pieces. For Mär, Nanashi of Luberia steps up...

Dorothy

A witch from Caldia, Kingdom of Magic. She has accepted the painful duty of killing the Queen of the Chess—her own sister.

Peta

A Chess Knight. Carried out a large-scale massacre of the Thieves Guild, of which Nanashi is the leader.

Phantom

A Chess Knight. The most powerful in the group and the leader of its combat force.

Diana

Queen of the Chess, Dorothy's older sister and Snow's stepmother.

Ian

Now a Knight. Detests Chimera, who turned his lover, Gido, into a strange creature.

Chimera

Another Chess Knight. Lost to Dorothy in the last battle.

CONTENTS

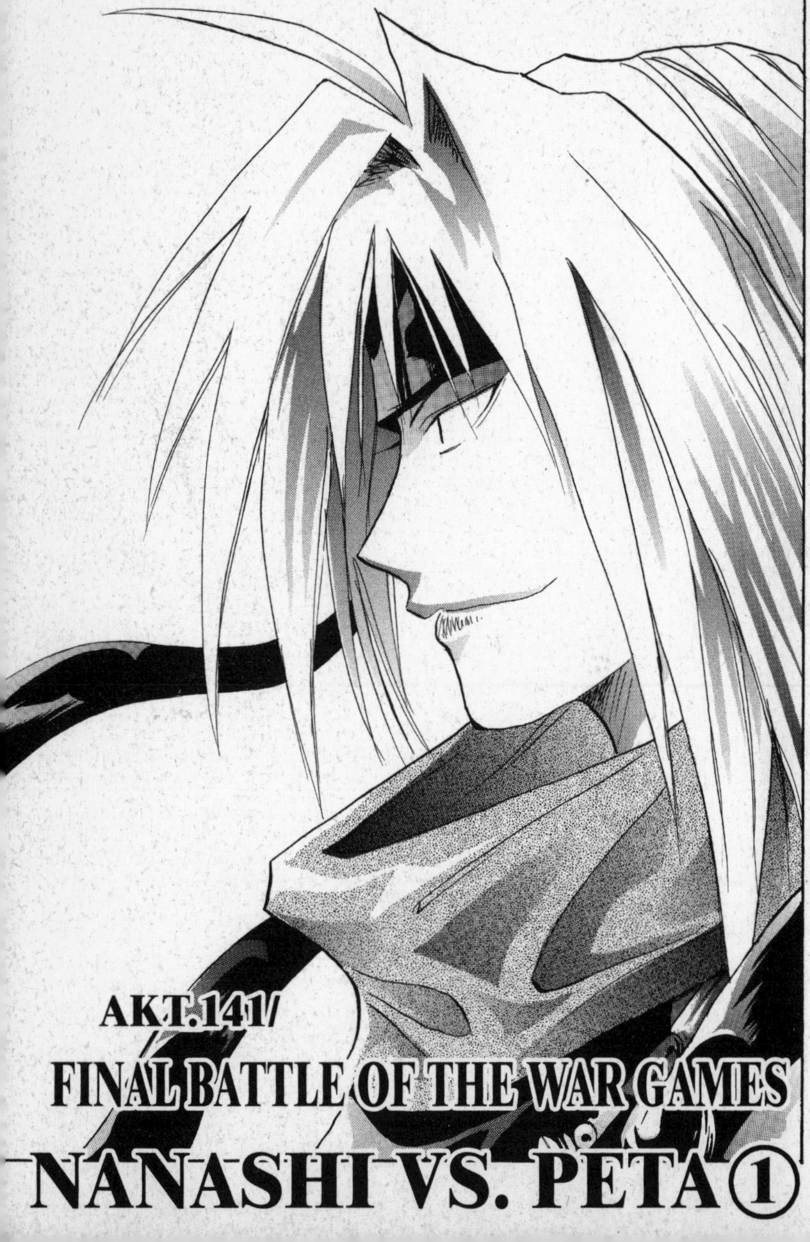

AKT.141/

FINAL BATTLE OF THE WAR GAMES NANASHI VS. PETA ①

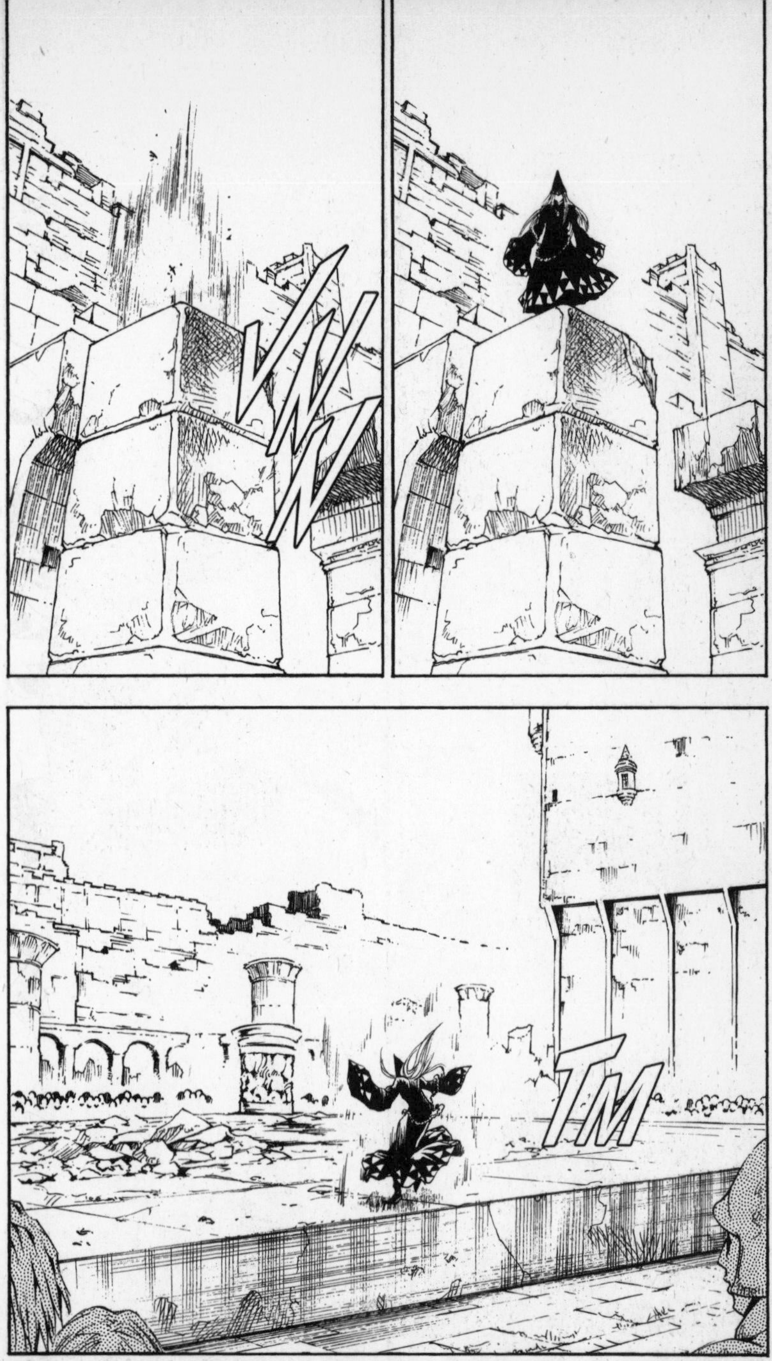
TM

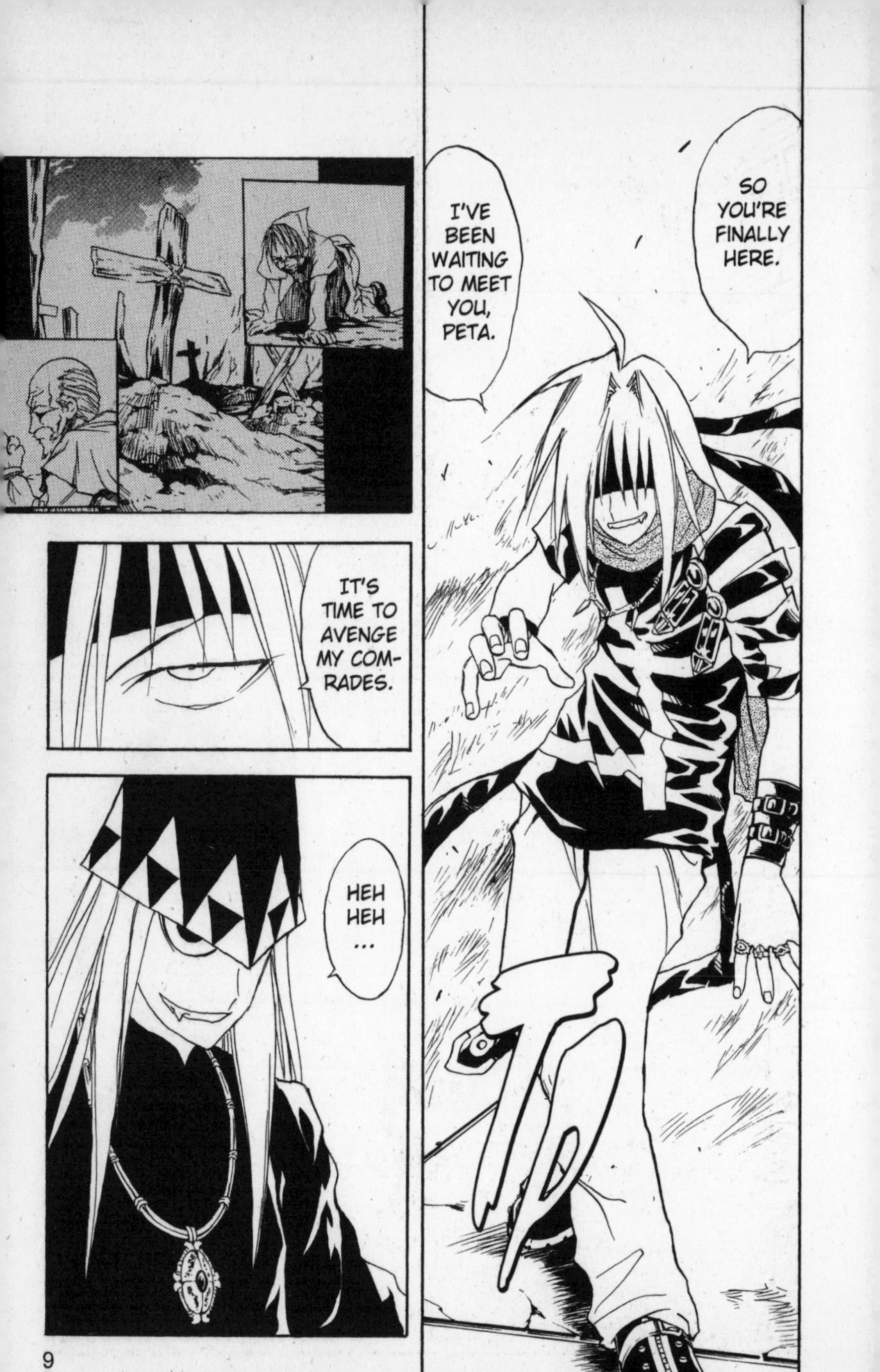
SO YOU'RE FINALLY HERE.
I'VE BEEN WAITING TO MEET YOU, PETA.
IT'S TIME TO AVENGE MY COM-RADES.
HEH HEH ...

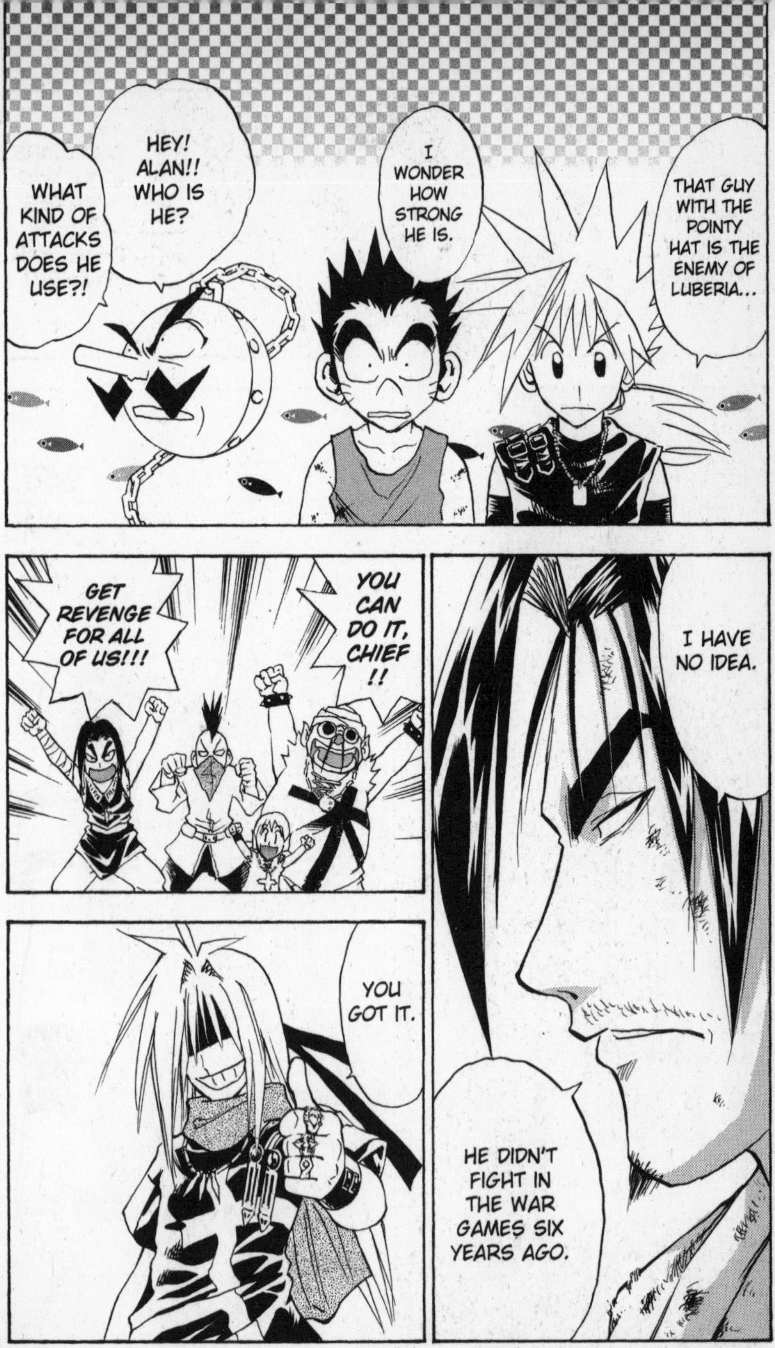
THAT GUY WITH THE POINTY HAT IS THE ENEMY OF LUBERIA...
I WONDER HOW STRONG HE IS.
HEY! ALAN!! WHO IS HE?
WHAT KIND OF ATTACKS DOES HE USE?!
I HAVE NO IDEA.
HE DIDN'T FIGHT IN THE WAR GAMES SIX YEARS AGO.
YOU CAN DO IT, CHIEF!!
GET REVENGE FOR ALL OF US!!!
YOU GOT IT.

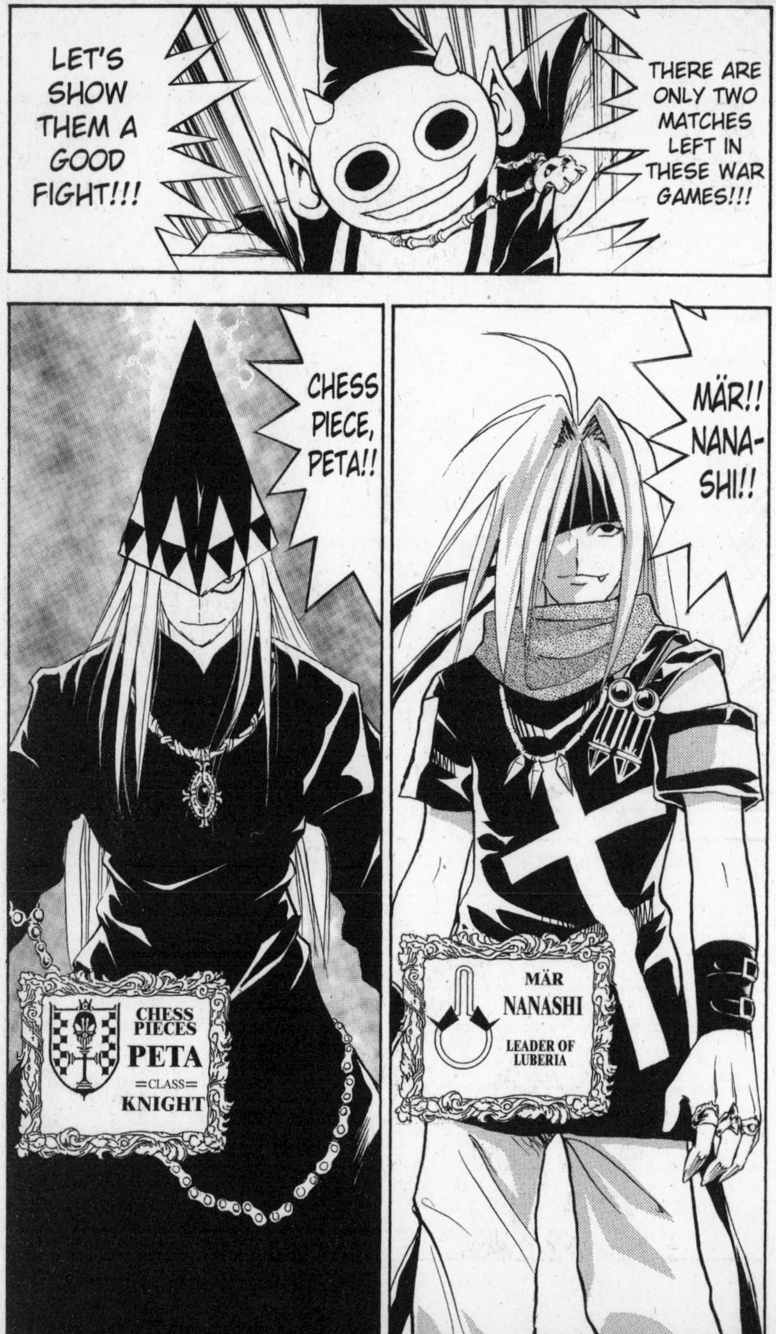
THERE ARE ONLY TWO MATCHES LEFT IN THESE WAR GAMES!!!
LET'S SHOW THEM A GOOD FIGHT!!!
MÄR!! NANA-SHI!!
MÄR
NANASHI
LEADER OF LUBERIA
CHESS PIECE, PETA!!
CHESS PIECES
PETA
=CLASS=
KNIGHT

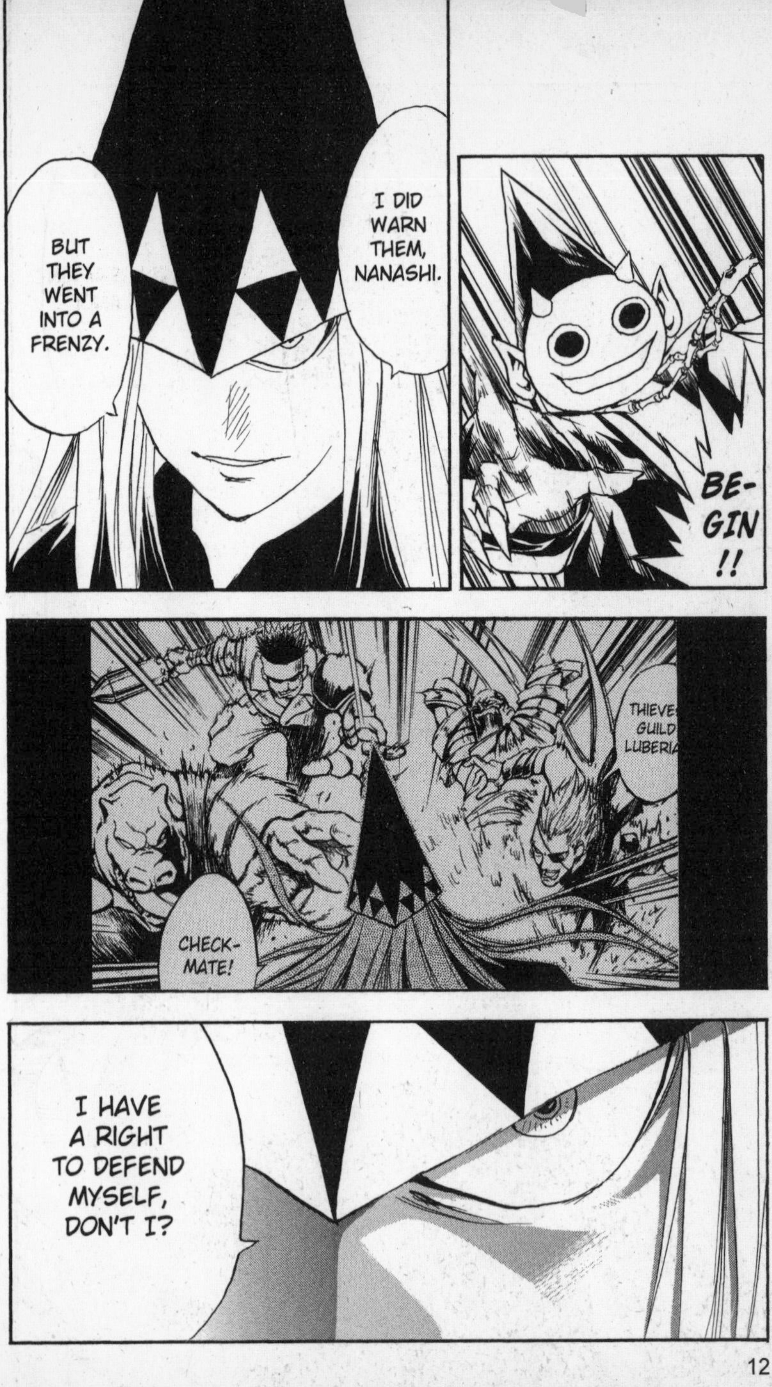
BE-GIN!!
I DID WARN THEM, NANASHI.
BUT THEY WENT INTO A FRENZY.
THIEVES GUILD LUBERIA
CHECK-MATE!
I HAVE A RIGHT TO DEFEND MYSELF, DON'T I?

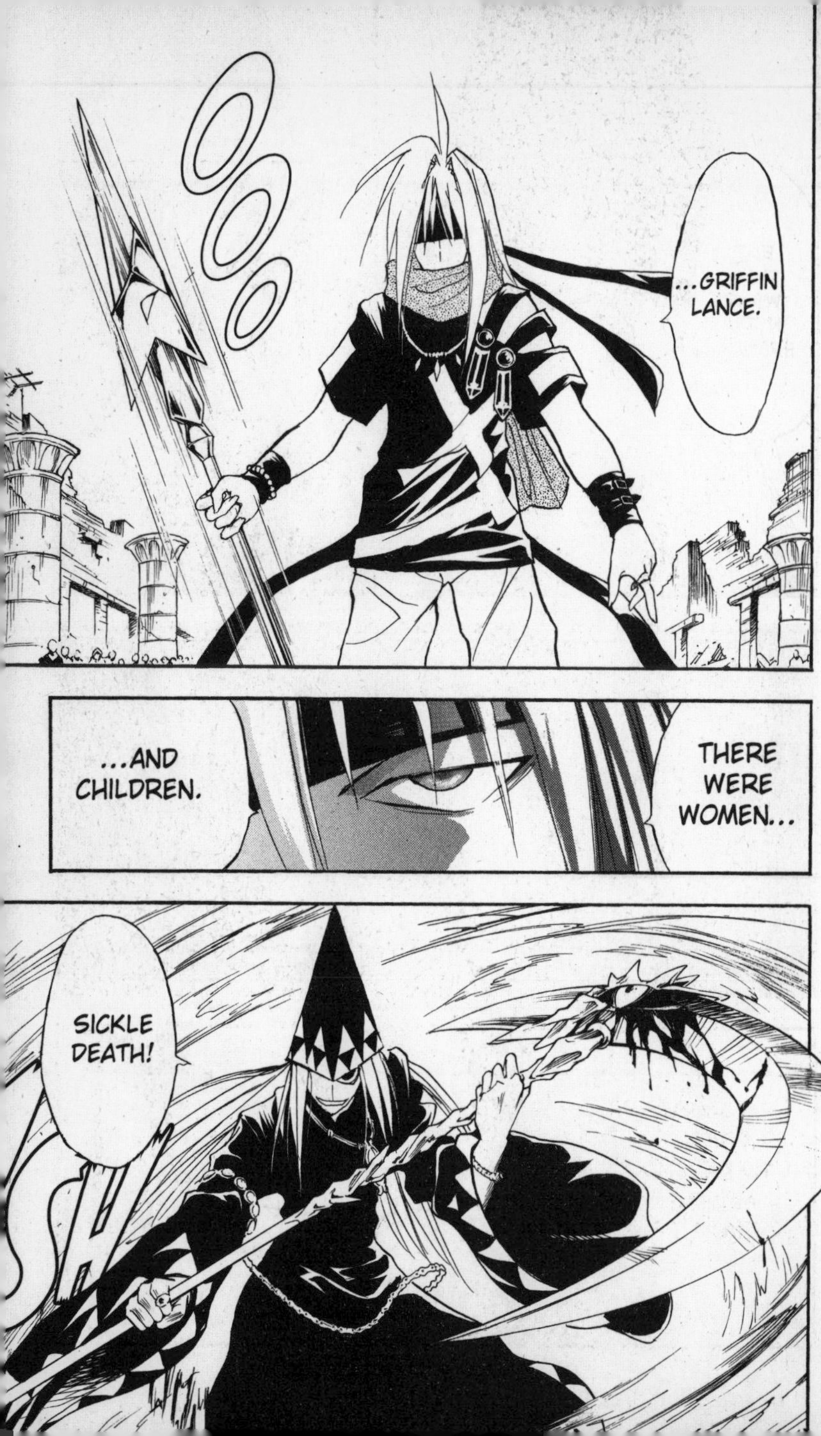
...GRIFFIN LANCE.
THERE WERE WOMEN...
...AND CHILDREN.
SICKLE DEATH!

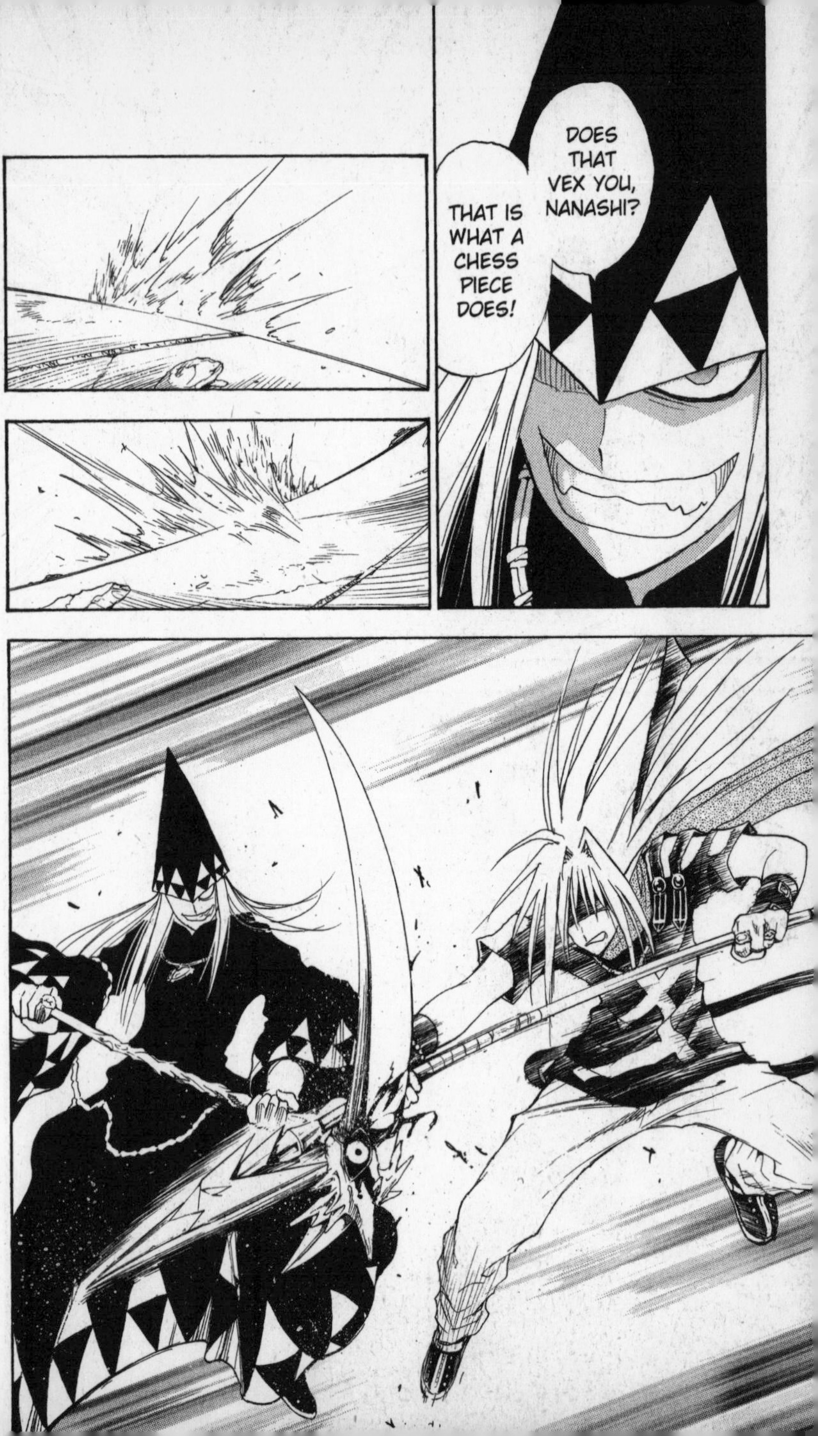
DOES THAT VEX YOU, NANASHI?
THAT IS WHAT A CHESS PIECE DOES!

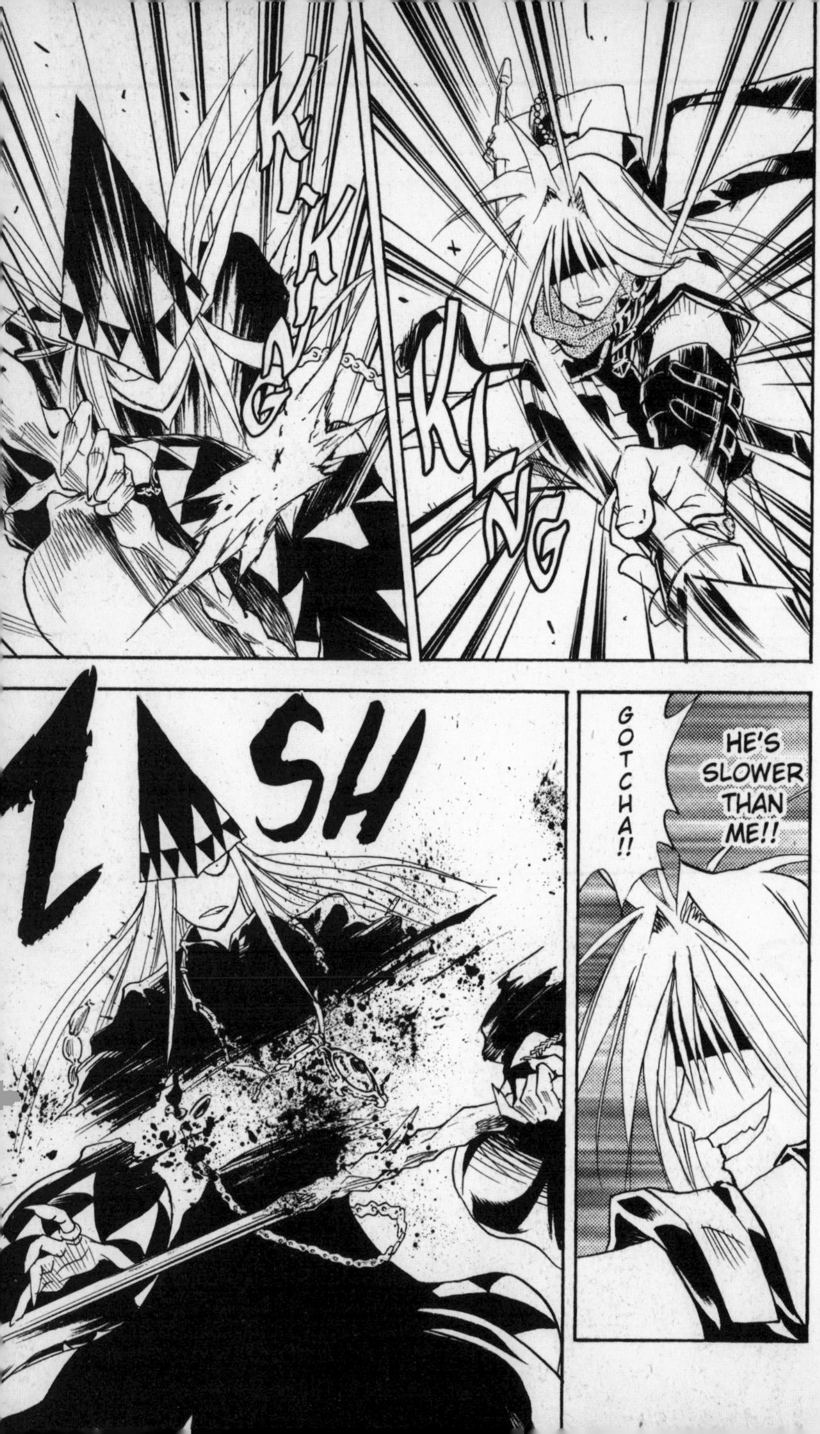
KLNG
K-KAG
GOTCHA!!
HE'S SLOWER THAN ME!!
ZASH

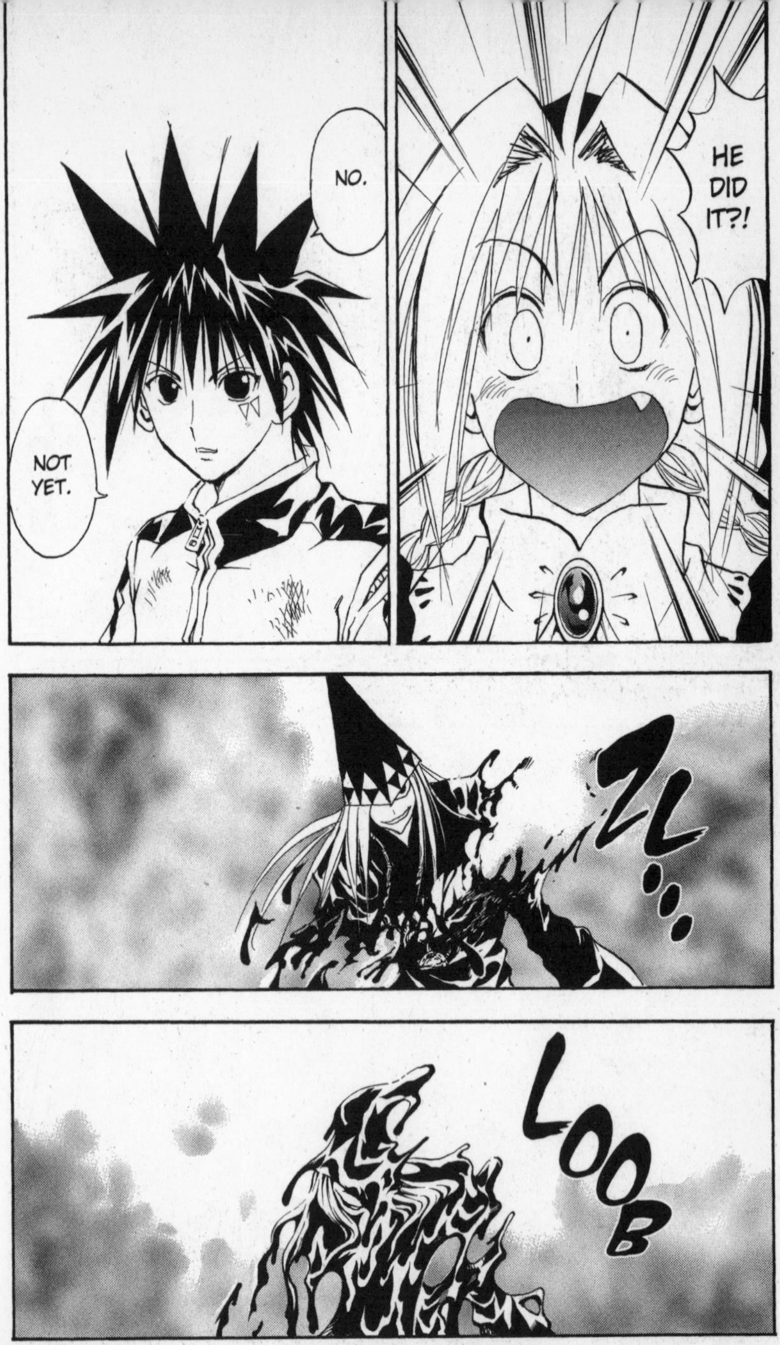
HE DID IT?!
NO.
NOT YET.
ZL...
LOOB

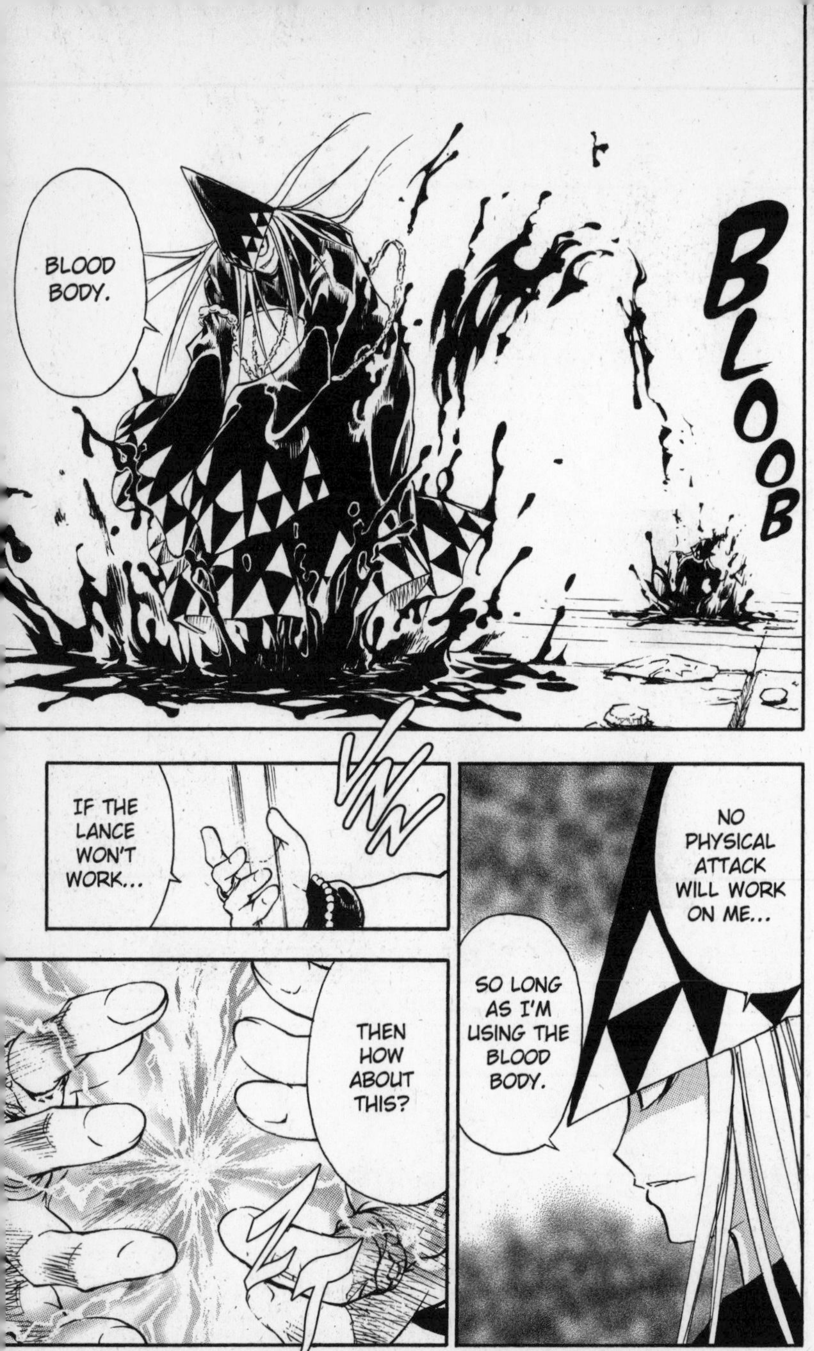
BLOOB
BLOOD BODY.
NO PHYSICAL ATTACK WILL WORK ON ME...
SO LONG AS I'M USING THE BLOOD BODY.
IF THE LANCE WON'T WORK...
THEN HOW ABOUT THIS?

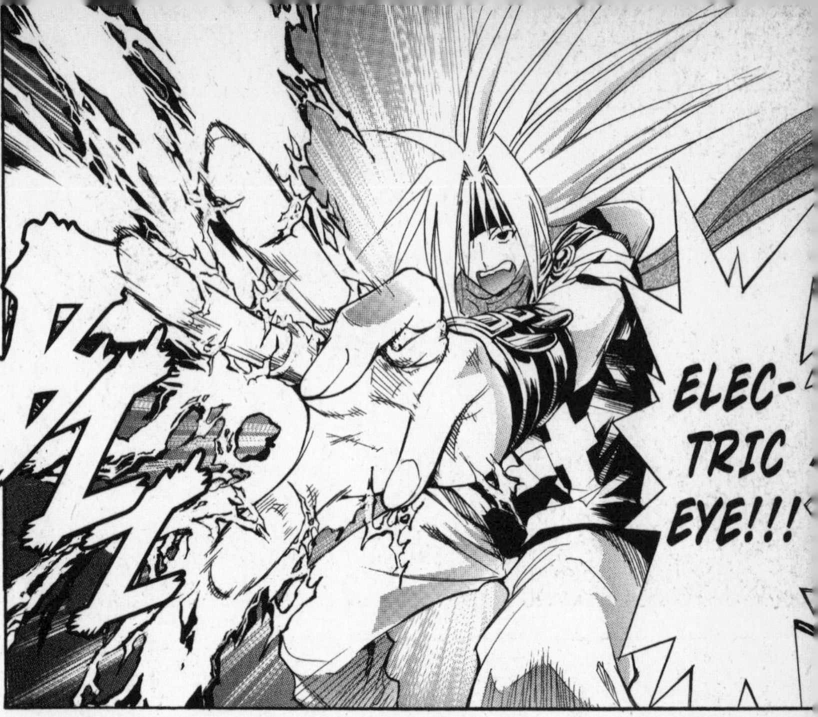
ELEC-
TRIC
EYE!!!
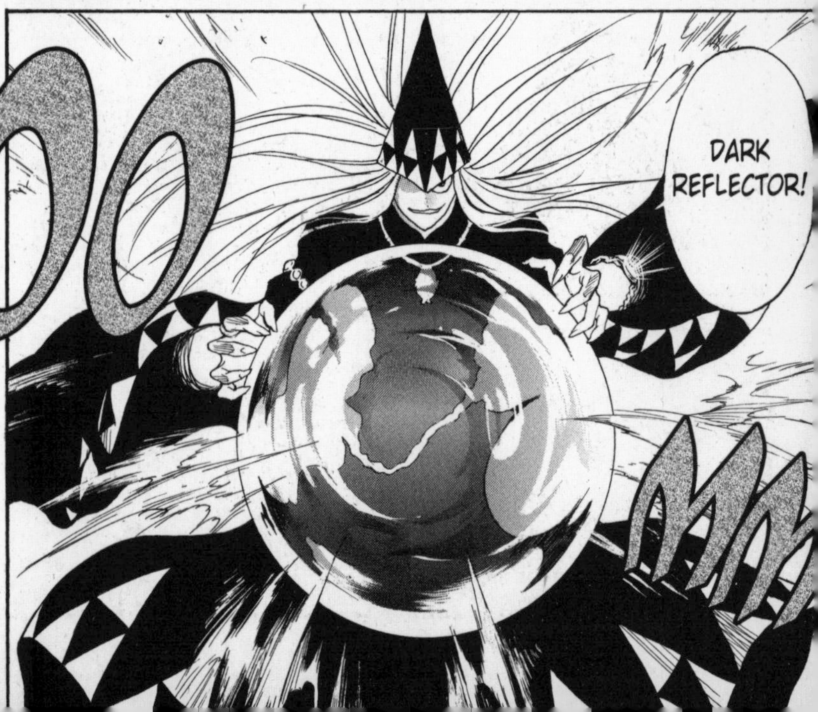
DARK
REFLECTOR!

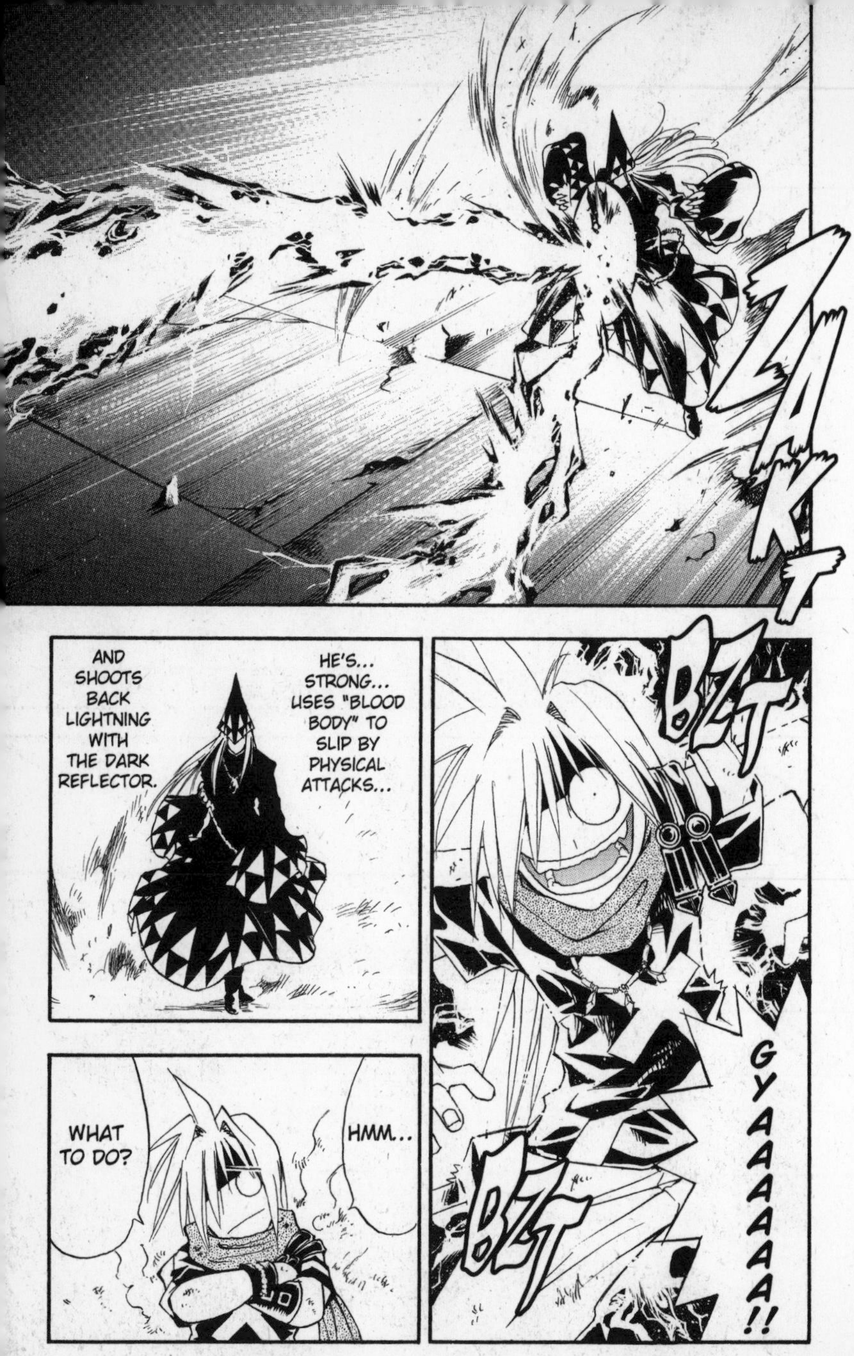
ZAKT
BZT
GYAAAAAAA!!
BZT
HE'S... STRONG... USES "BLOOD BODY" TO SLIP BY PHYSICAL ATTACKS...
AND SHOOTS BACK LIGHTNING WITH THE DARK REFLECTOR.
HMM...
WHAT TO DO?

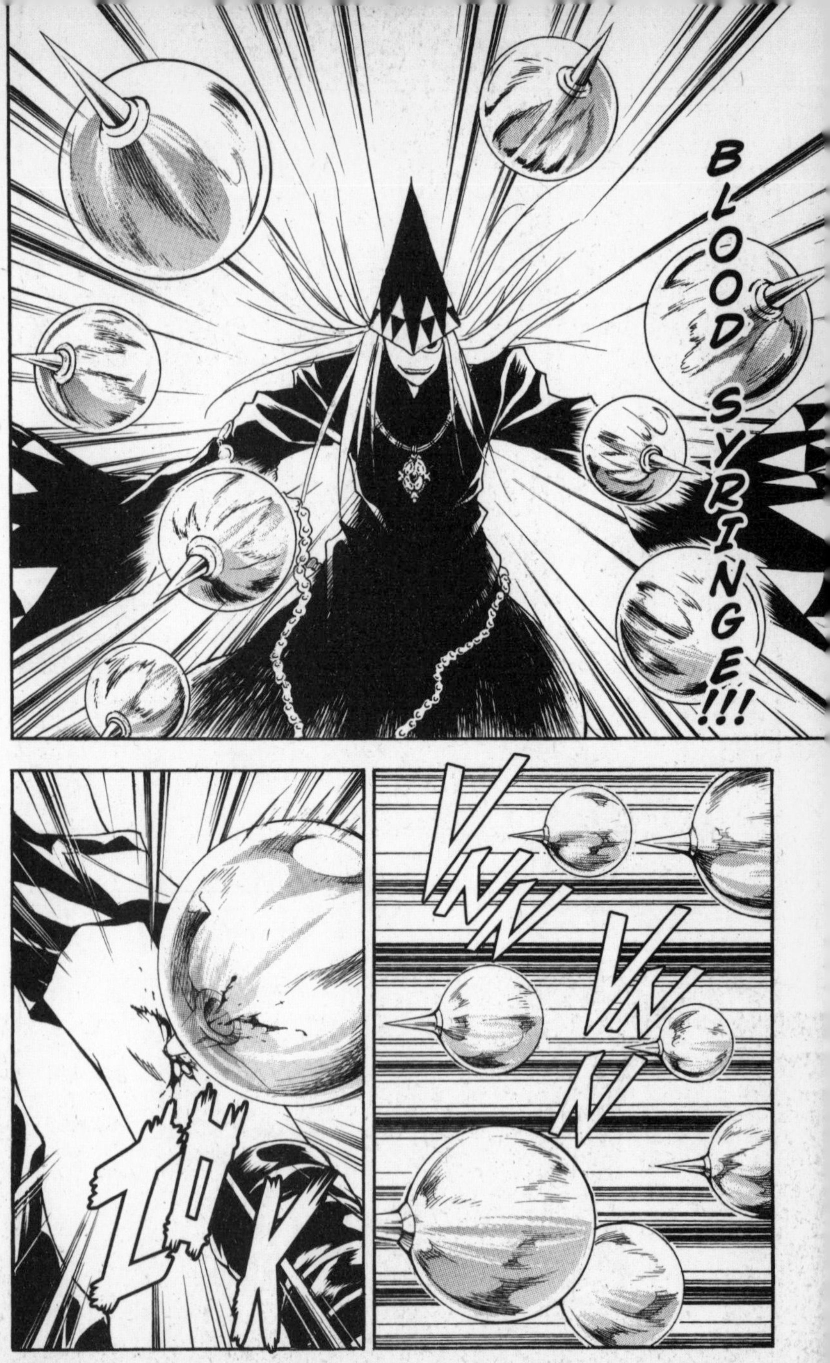
BLOOD SYRINGE!!!
VNN
VNNN
ZOK

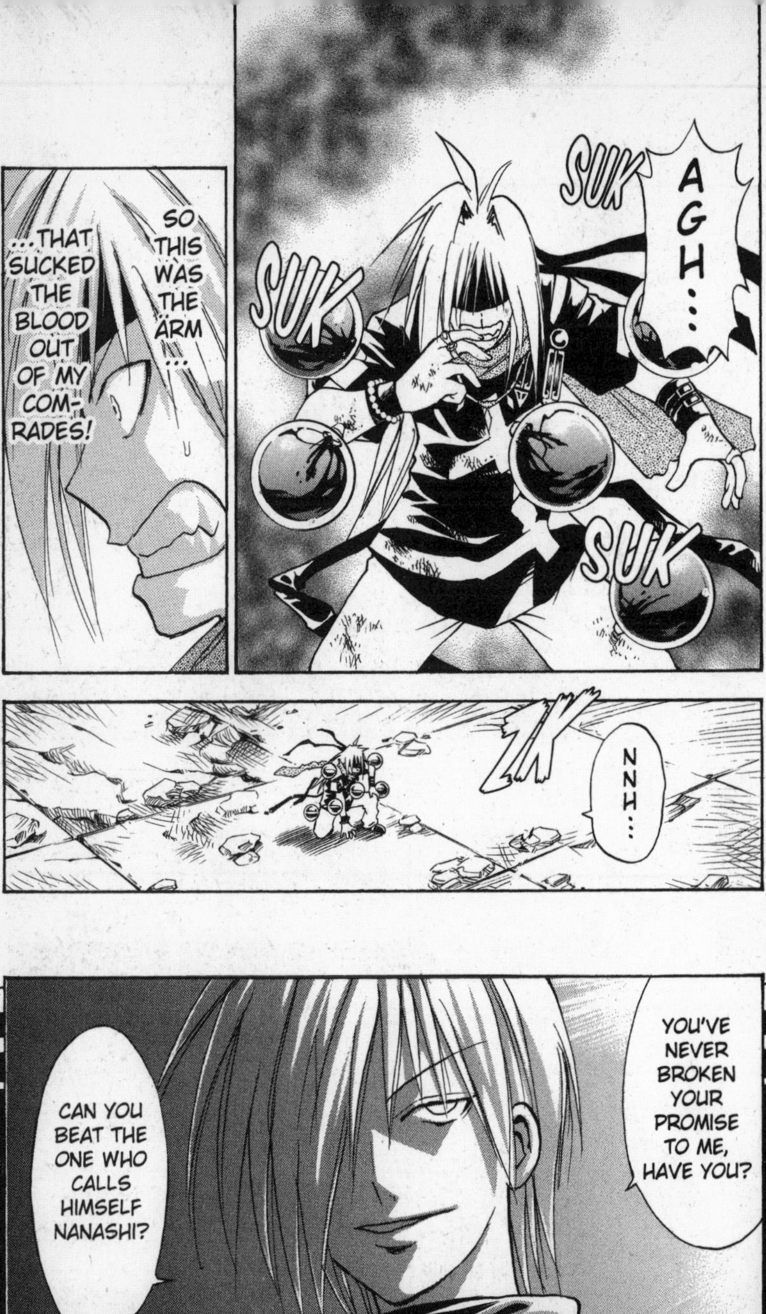
SUK
AGH...
SUK
SUK
SO THIS WAS THE ARM...
...THAT SUCKED THE BLOOD OUT OF MY COM-RADES!
NNH...
YOU'VE NEVER BROKEN YOUR PROMISE TO ME, HAVE YOU?
CAN YOU BEAT THE ONE WHO CALLS HIMSELF NANASHI?

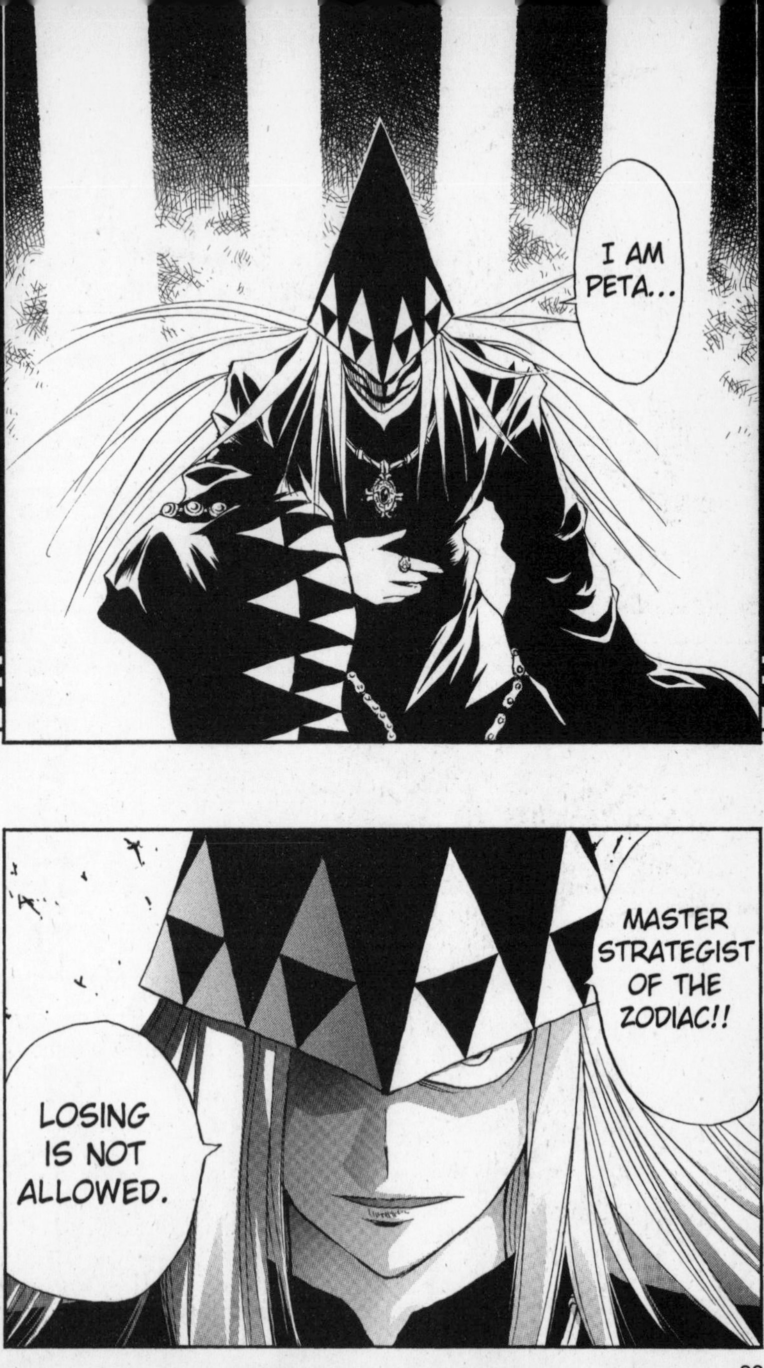
I AM PETA...
MASTER STRATEGIST OF THE ZODIAC!!
LOSING IS NOT ALLOWED.

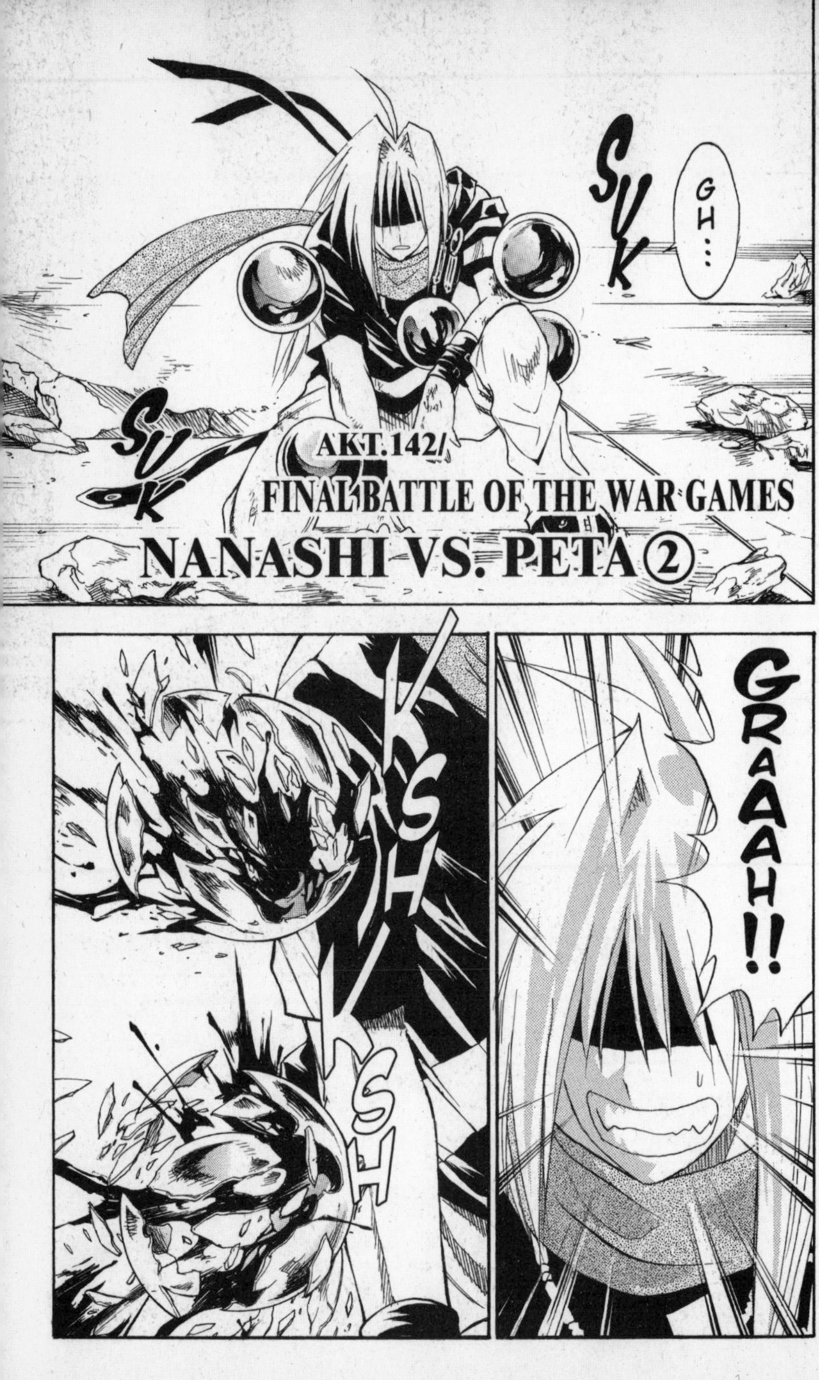
SUK
GH...
SUK
AKT.142/
FINAL BATTLE OF THE WAR GAMES
NANASHI VS. PETA ②
GRAAAH!!
KSHH
KSHH

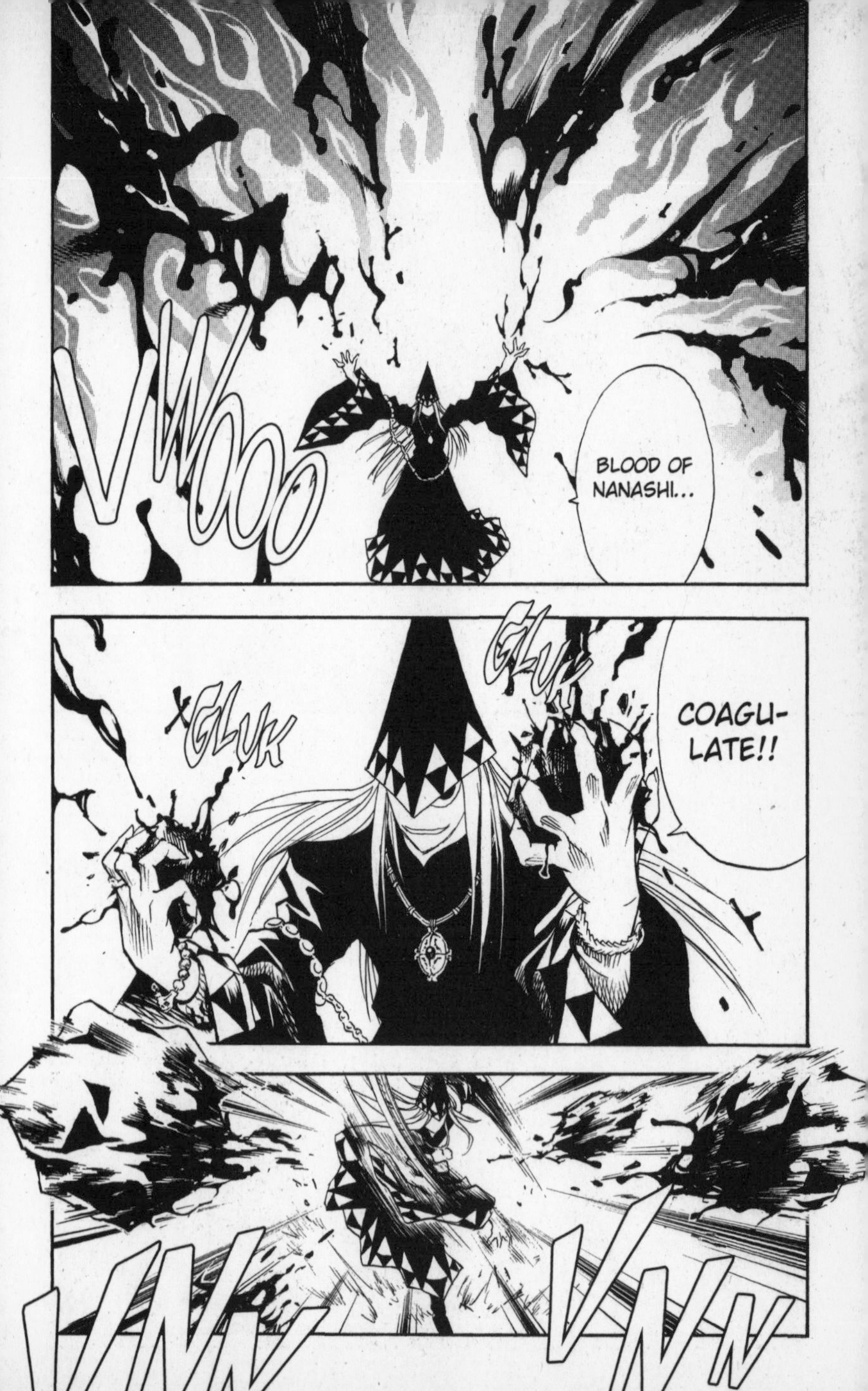
BLOOD OF NANASHI...
VWOOO
COAGU-LATE!!
GLUK
GLUK
VNN
VNN

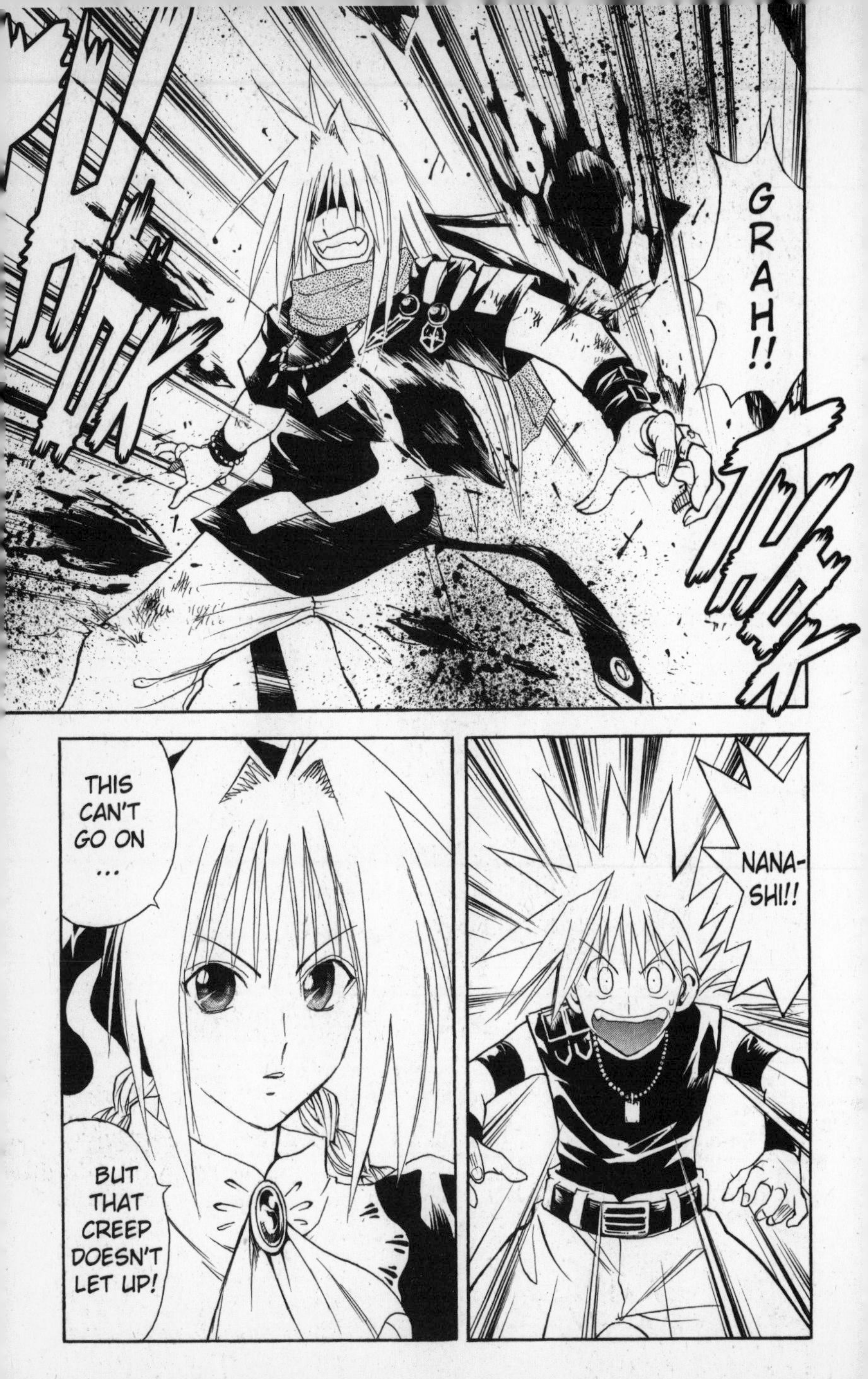
GRAH!!
NANA-SHI!!
THIS CAN'T GO ON ...
BUT THAT CREEP DOESN'T LET UP!

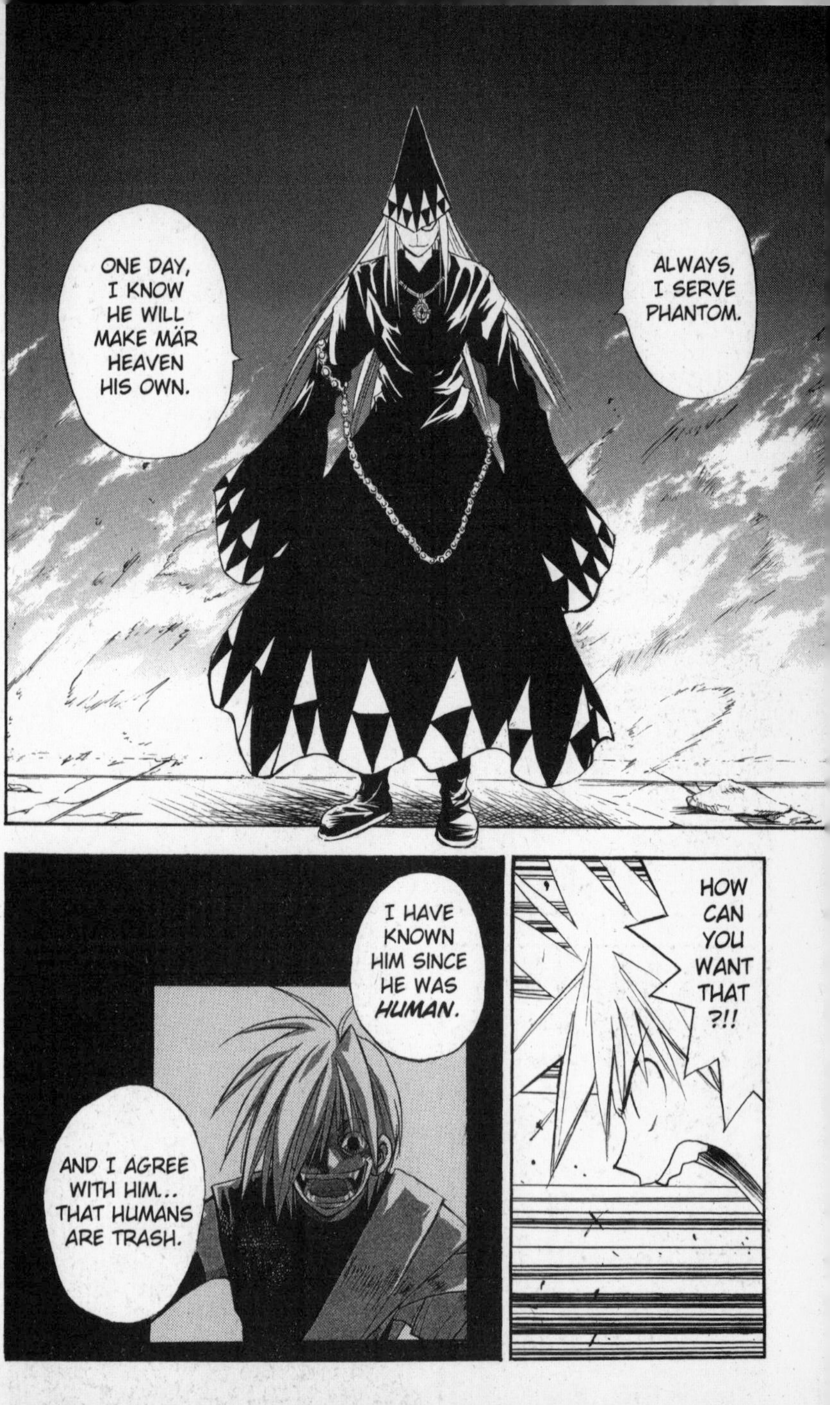
ALWAYS, I SERVE PHANTOM.
ONE DAY, I KNOW HE WILL MAKE MÄR HEAVEN HIS OWN.
HOW CAN YOU WANT THAT ?!!
I HAVE KNOWN HIM SINCE HE WAS *HUMAN*.
AND I AGREE WITH HIM... THAT HUMANS ARE TRASH.

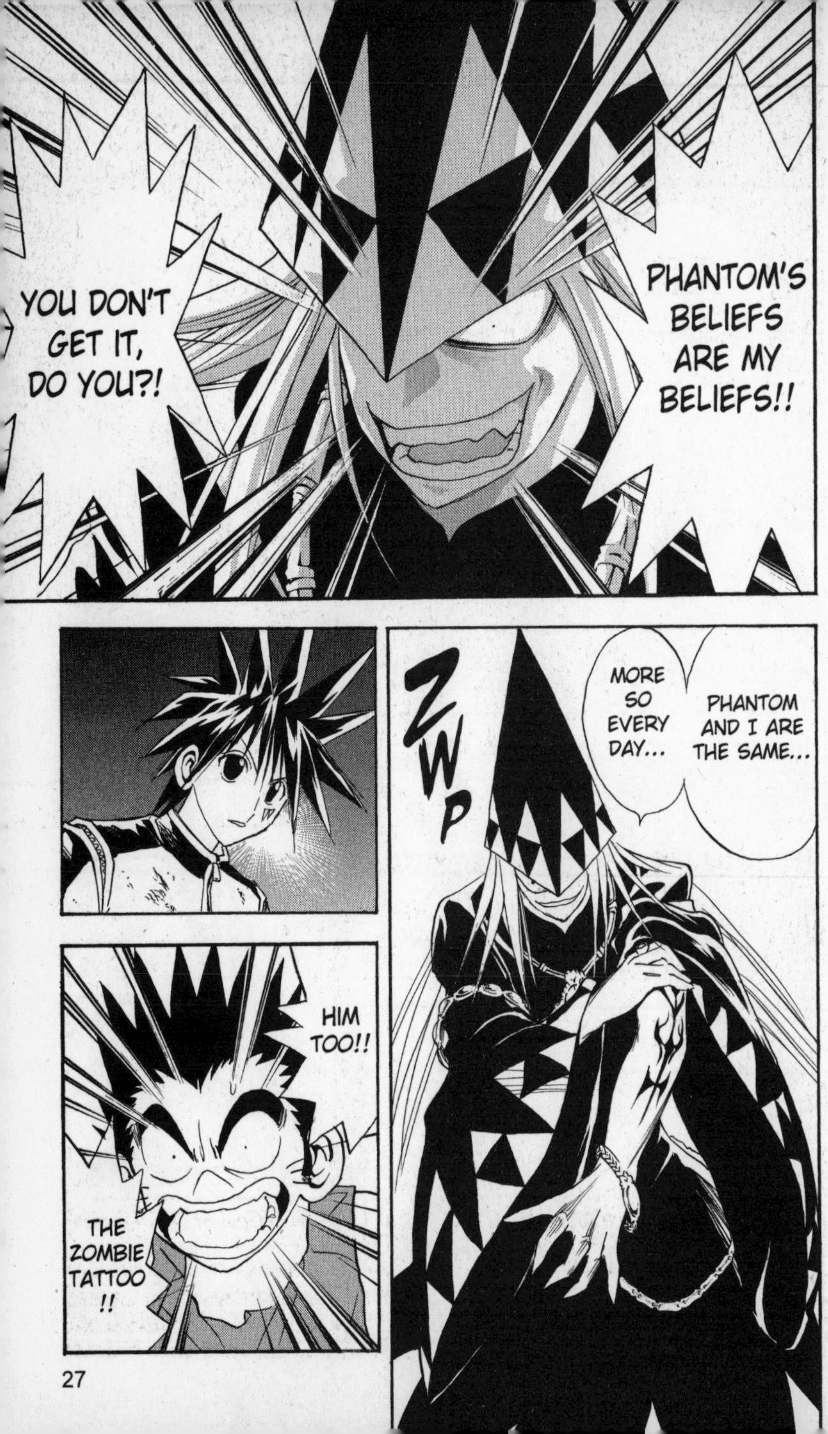
PHANTOM'S BELIEFS ARE MY BELIEFS!!
YOU DON'T GET IT, DO YOU?!
PHANTOM AND I ARE THE SAME...
MORE SO EVERY DAY...
ZWP
HIM TOO!!
THE ZOMBIE TATTOO !!

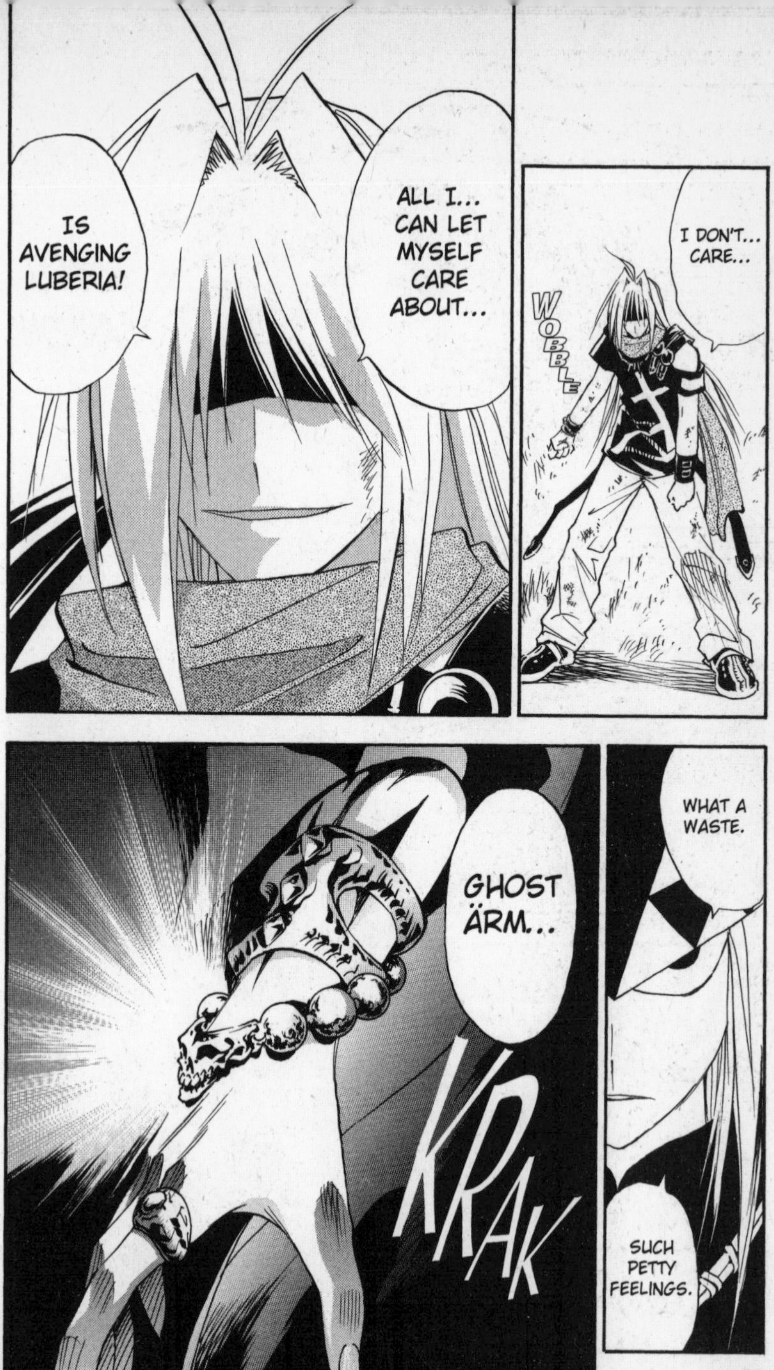

I DON'T... CARE...
WOBBLE
ALL I... CAN LET MYSELF CARE ABOUT...
IS AVENGING LUBERIA!
WHAT A WASTE.
SUCH PETTY FEELINGS.
GHOST ÄRM...
KRAK

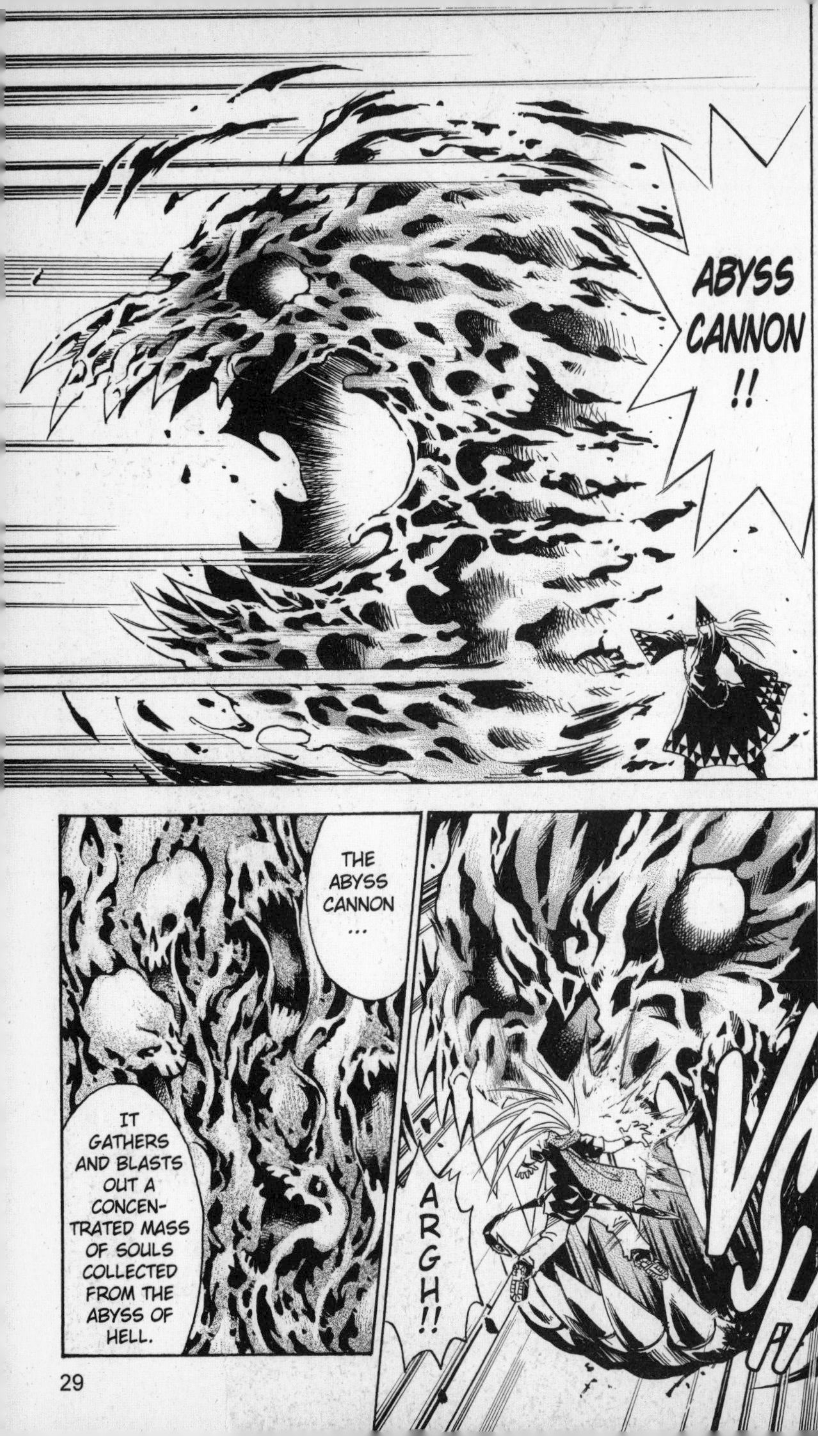
ABYSS CANNON !!
ARGH!!
THE ABYSS CANNON ...
IT GATHERS AND BLASTS OUT A CONCEN-TRATED MASS OF SOULS COLLECTED FROM THE ABYSS OF HELL.

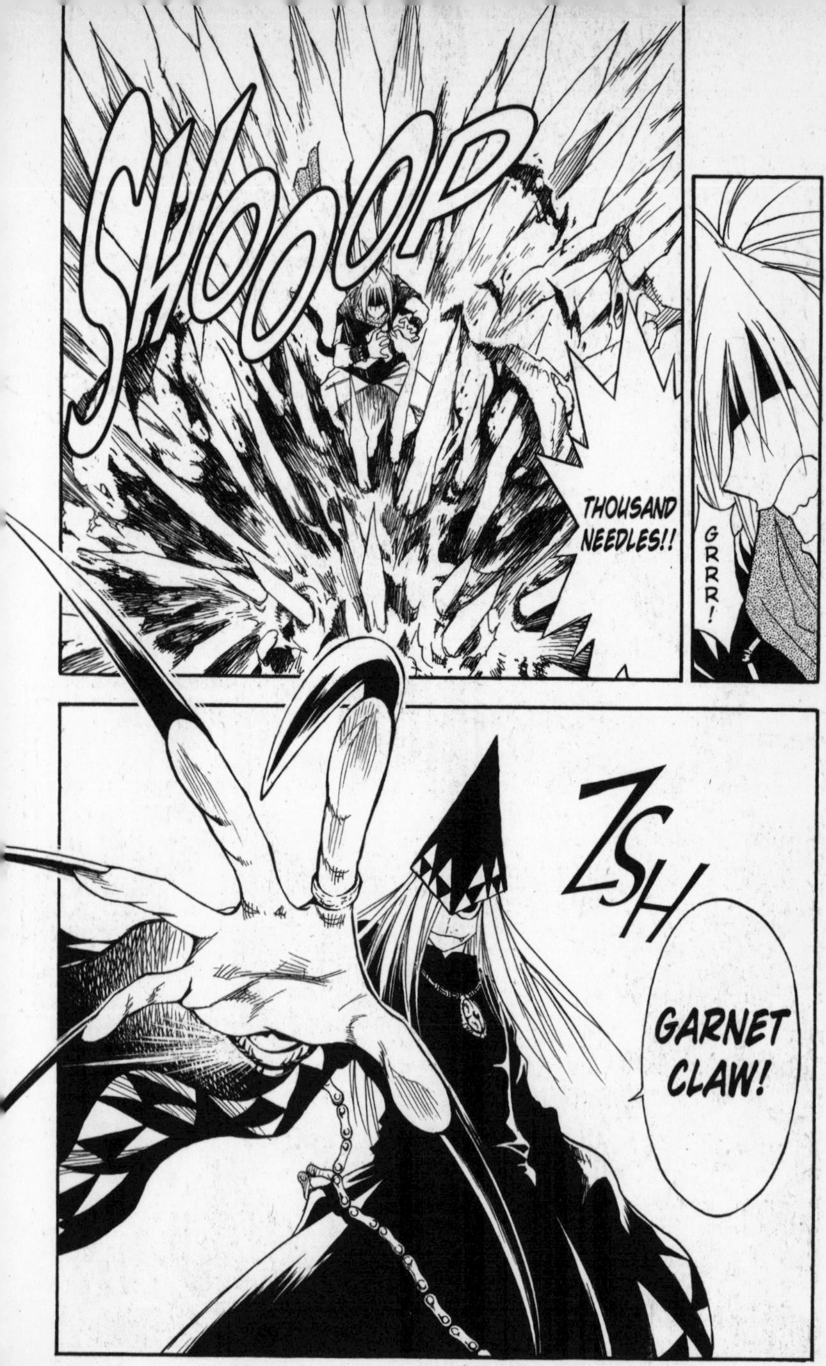
GRRR!
SHOOOP
THOUSAND NEEDLES!!
ZSH
GARNET CLAW!

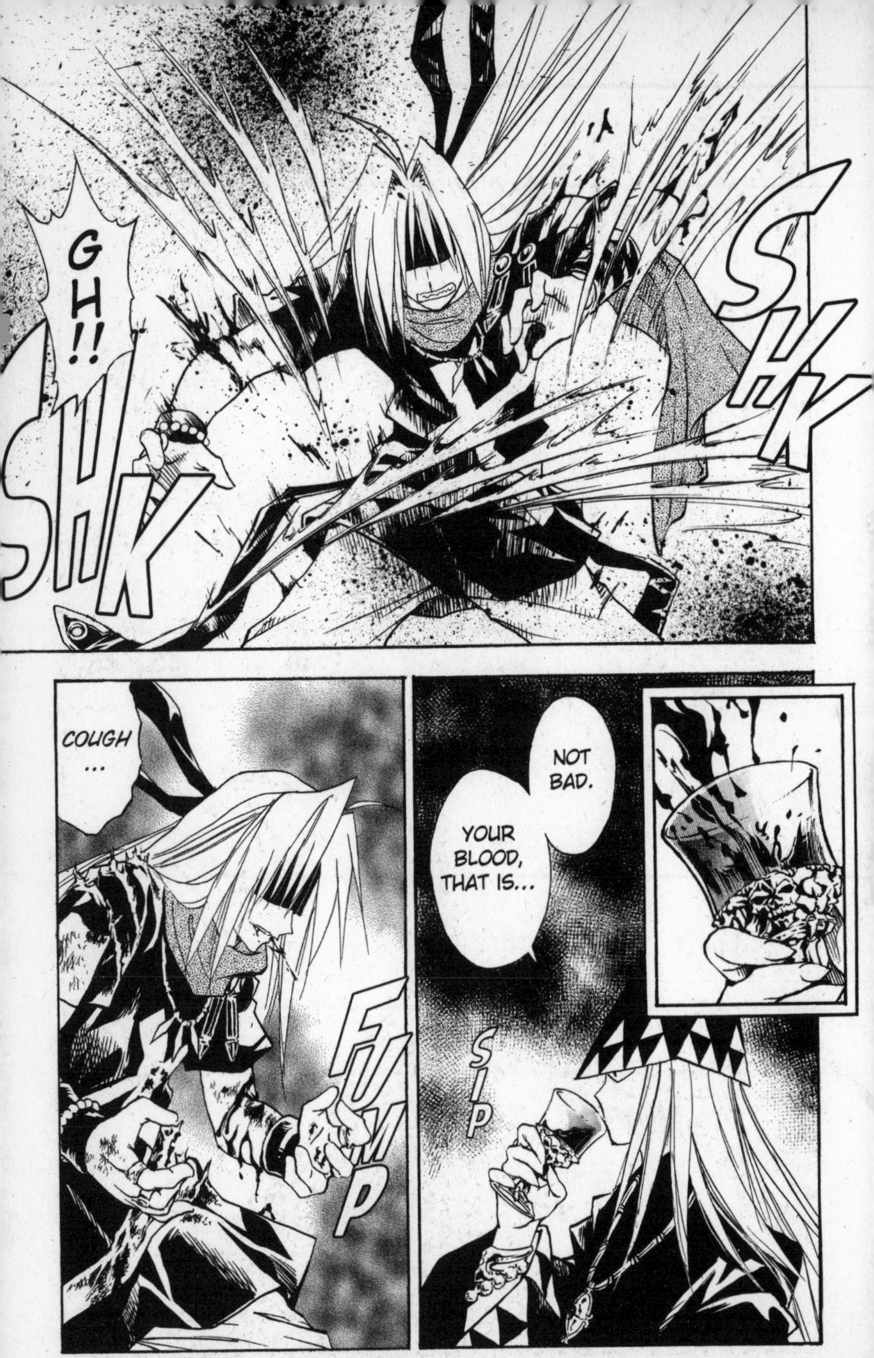
SHK
GH!!
SHK
NOT BAD.
YOUR BLOOD, THAT IS...
SIP
COUGH...
FUMP

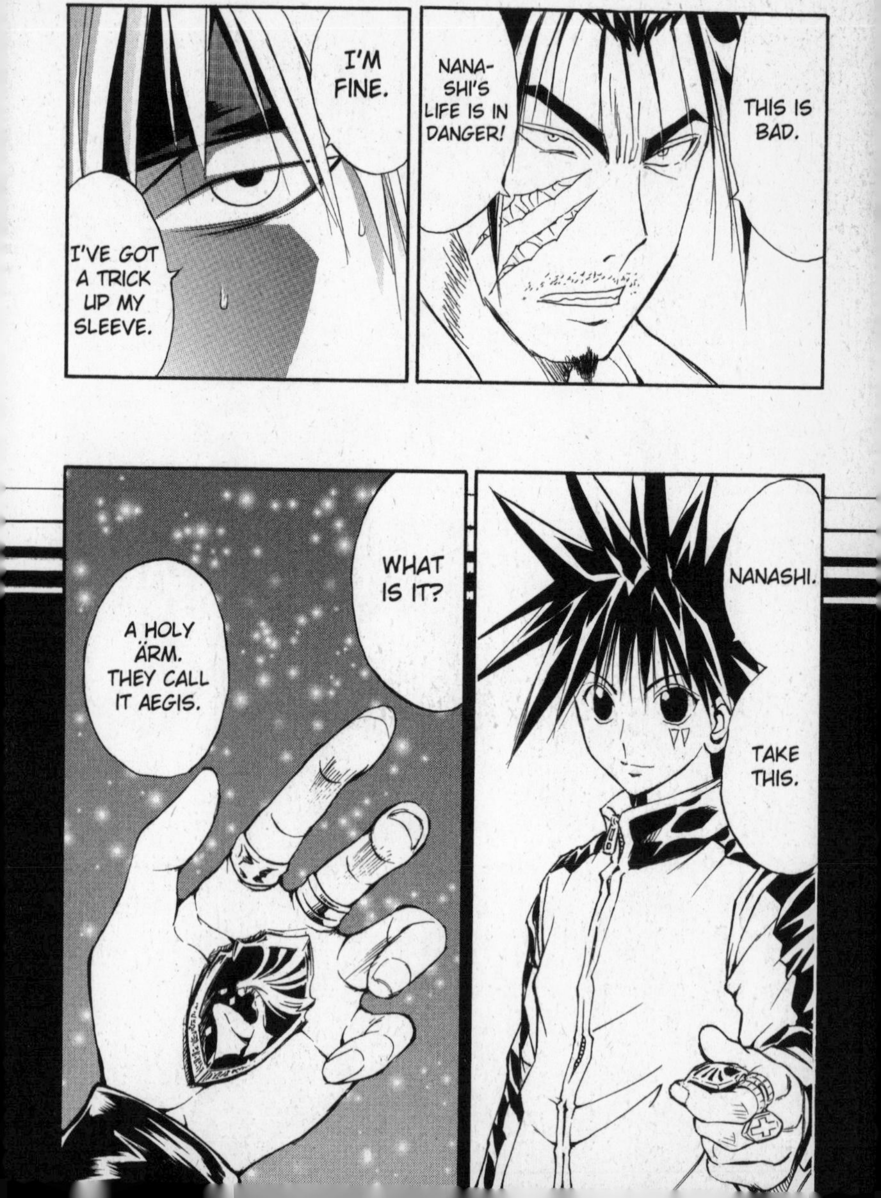
THIS IS BAD.
NANA-SHI'S LIFE IS IN DANGER!
I'M FINE.
I'VE GOT A TRICK UP MY SLEEVE.
NANASHI.
TAKE THIS.
WHAT IS IT?
A HOLY ÄRM. THEY CALL IT AEGIS.

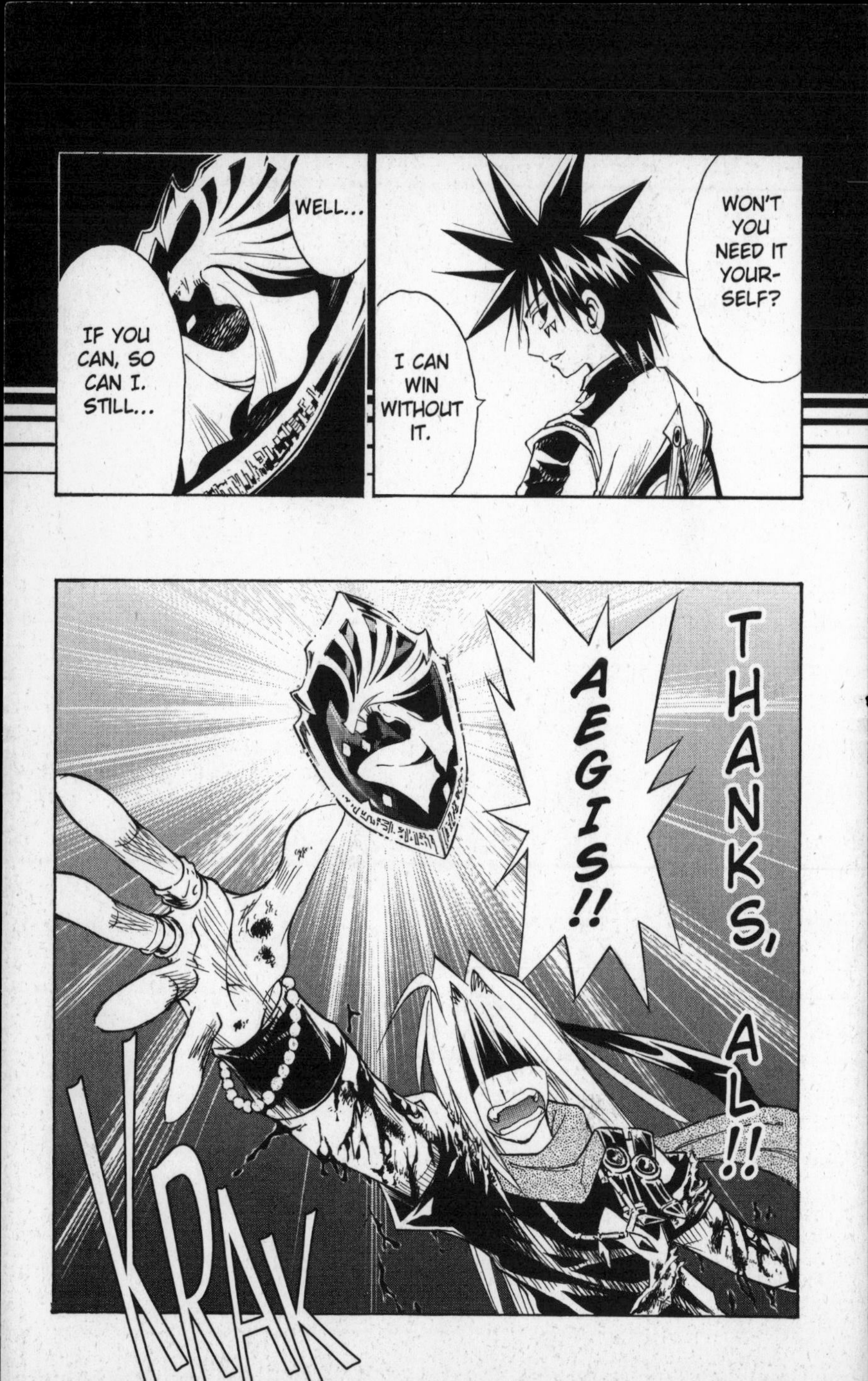

WON'T YOU NEED IT YOURSELF?
I CAN WIN WITHOUT IT.
WELL...
IF YOU CAN, SO CAN I. STILL...
THANKS, AL!!
AEGIS!!
KRAK

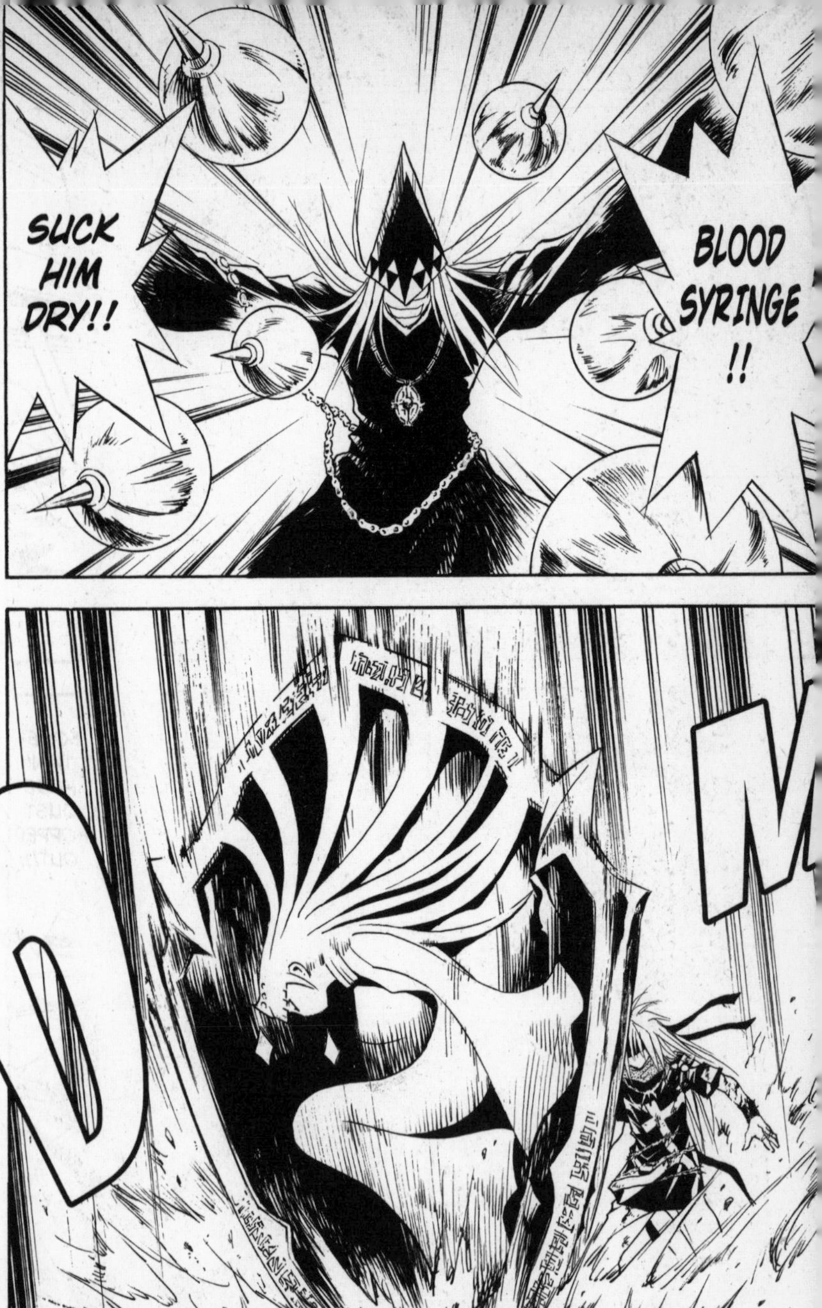
BLOOD SYRINGE!!
SUCK HIM DRY!!

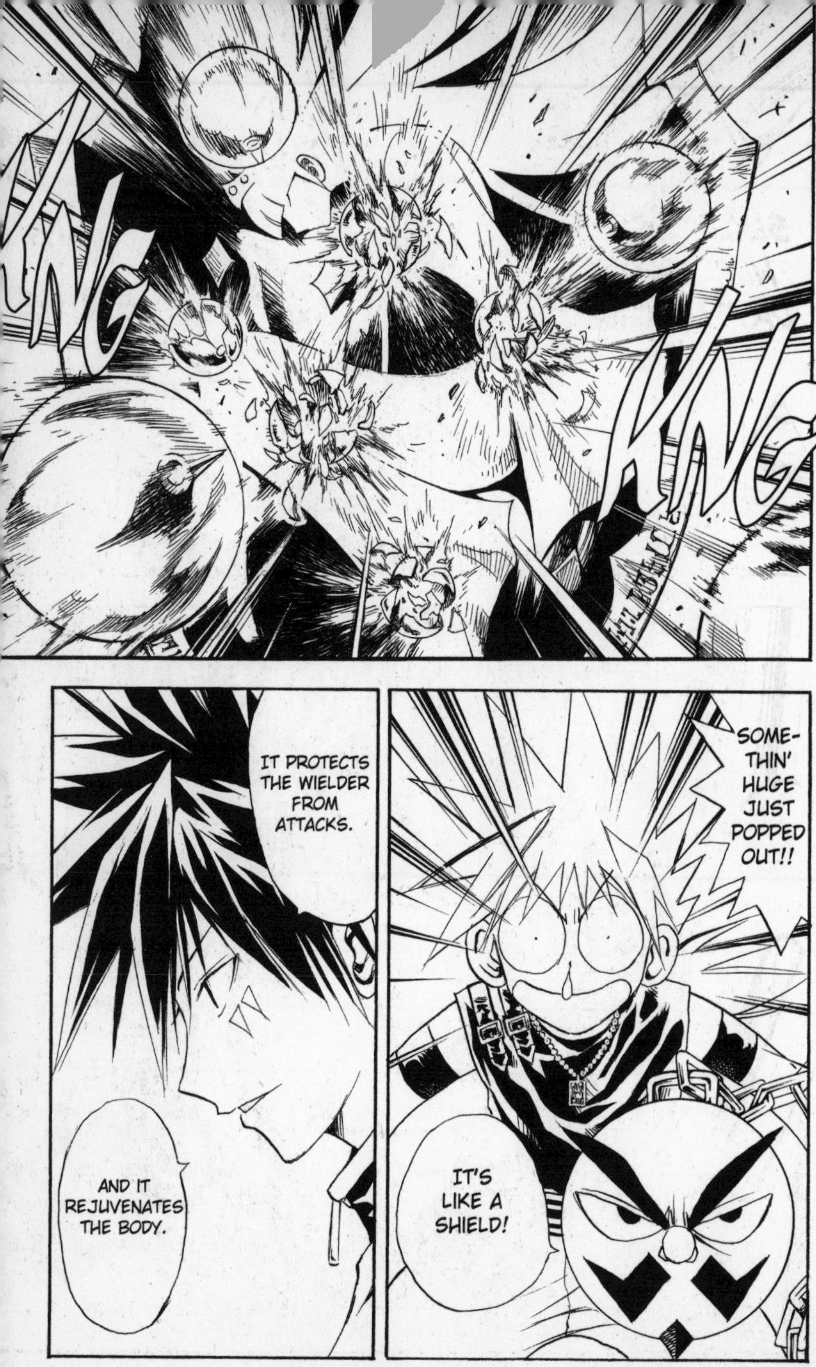
KING
KING
SOME-THIN' HUGE JUST POPPED OUT!!
IT'S LIKE A SHIELD!
IT PROTECTS THE WIELDER FROM ATTACKS.
AND IT REJUVENATES THE BODY.

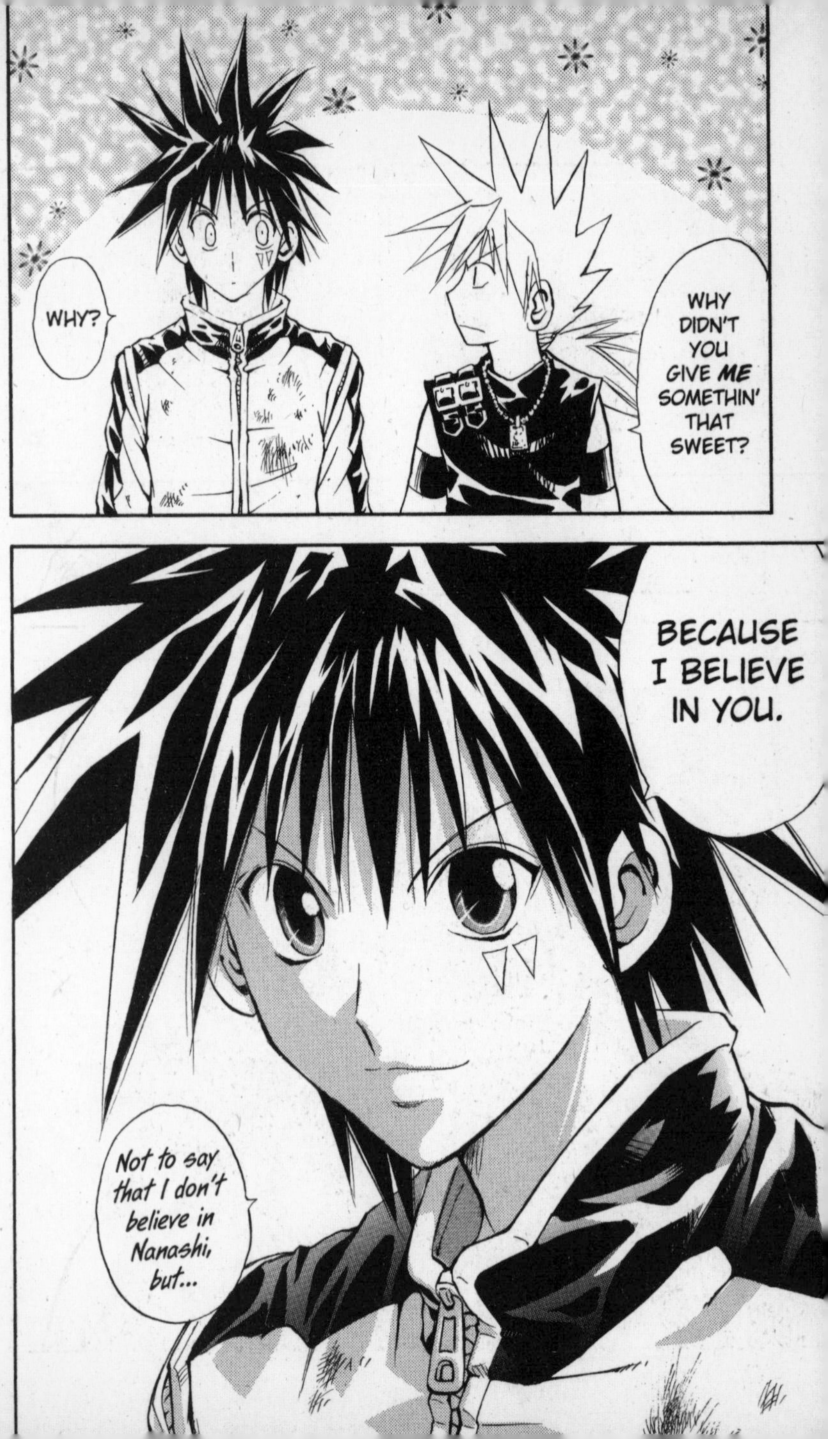
WHY DIDN'T YOU GIVE **ME** SOMETHIN' THAT SWEET?
WHY?
BECAUSE I BELIEVE IN YOU.
Not to say that I don't believe in Nanashi, but...

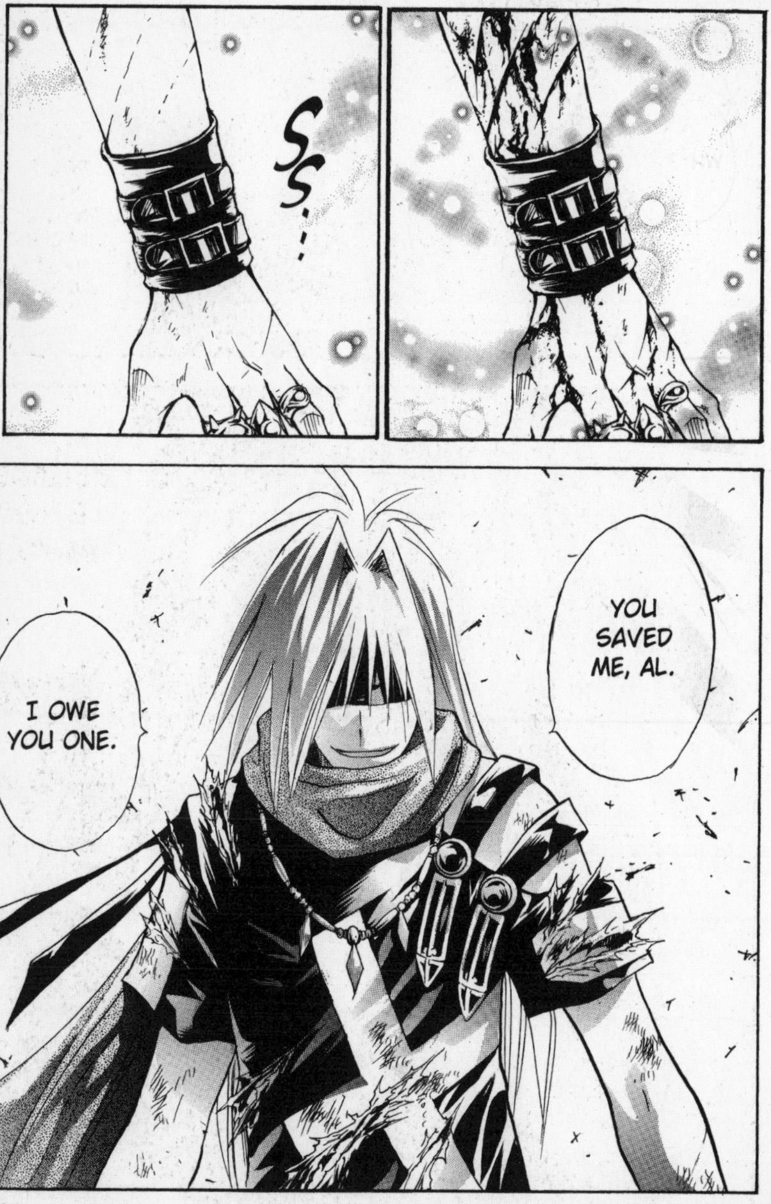
SS...
YOU SAVED ME, AL.
I OWE YOU ONE.

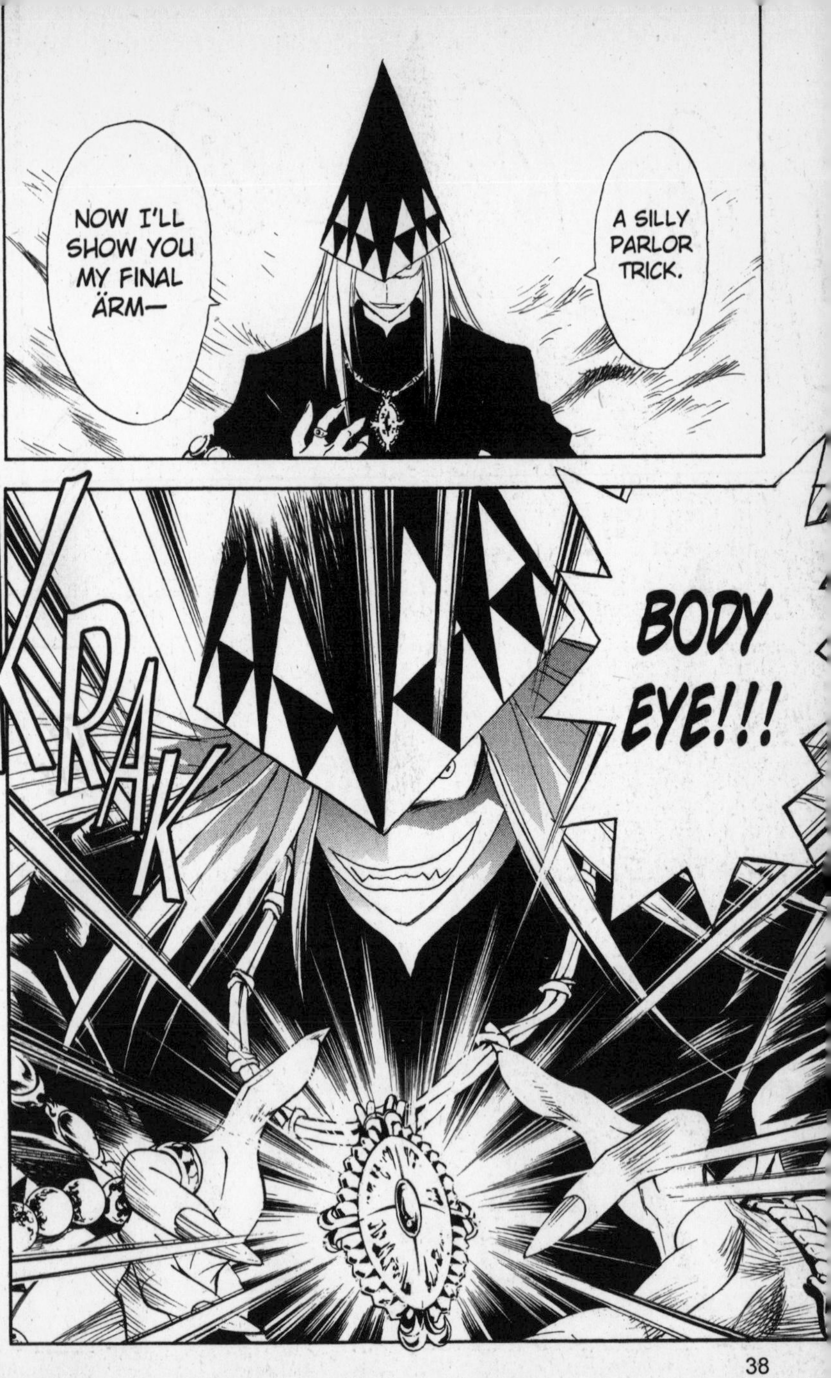
A SILLY PARLOR TRICK.
NOW I'LL SHOW YOU MY FINAL ÄRM—
BODY EYE!!!
KRAK

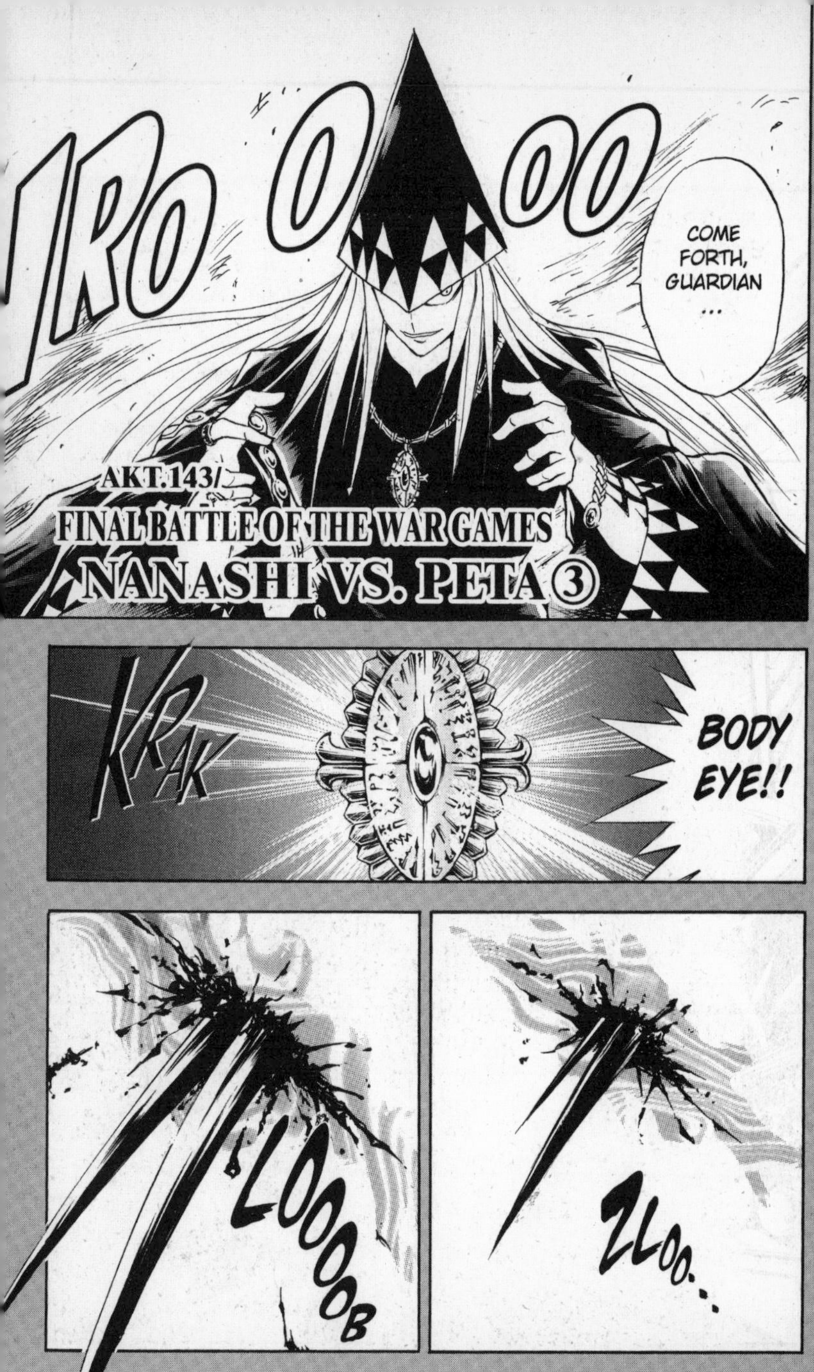
COME FORTH, GUARDIAN ...
IROOOOO
AKT.143/
FINAL BATTLE OF THE WAR GAMES
NANASHI VS. PETA ③
BODY EYE!!
KRAK
ZLOO...
LOOOOOB

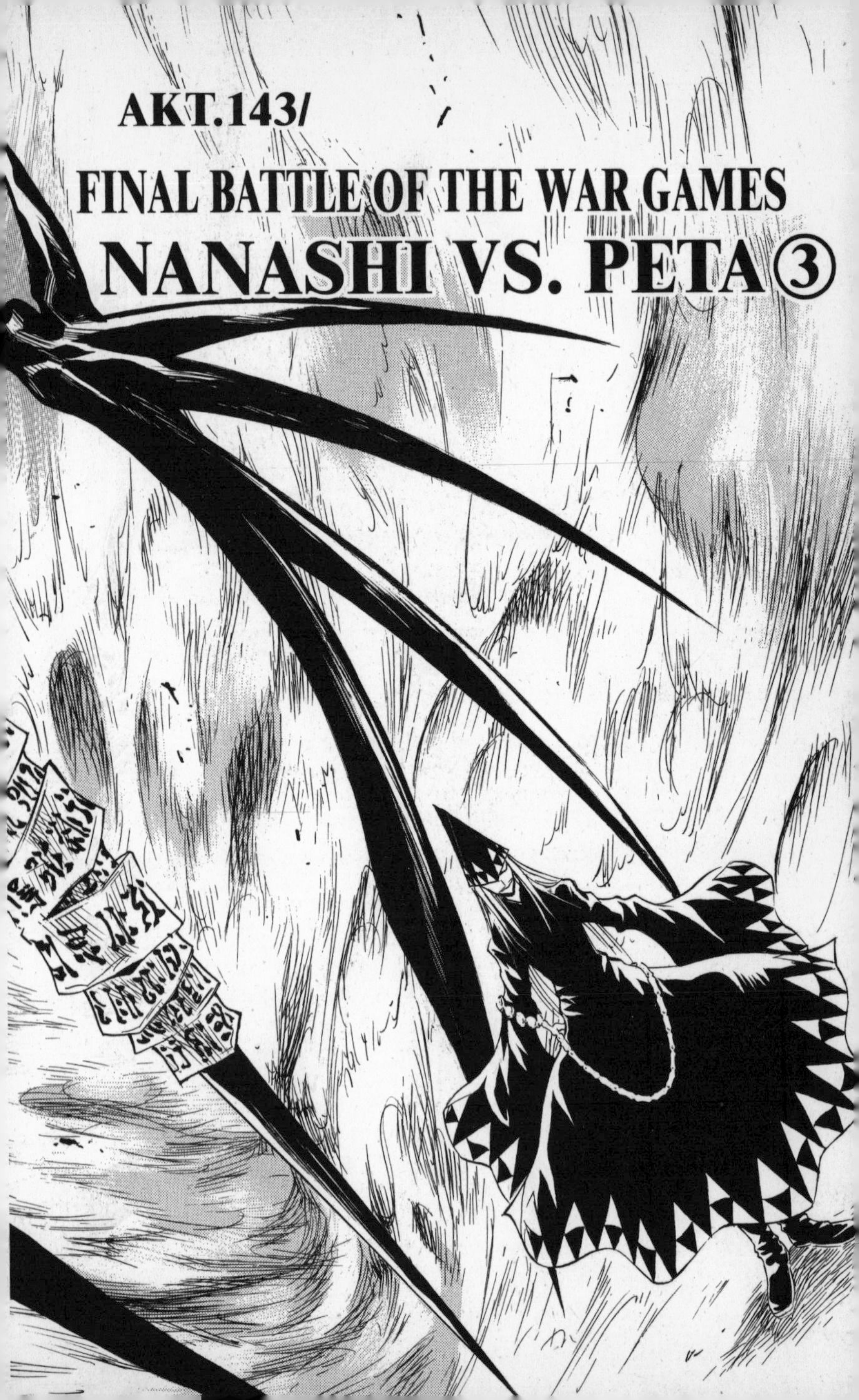
AKT.143/
FINAL BATTLE OF THE WAR GAMES
NANASHI VS. PETA ③

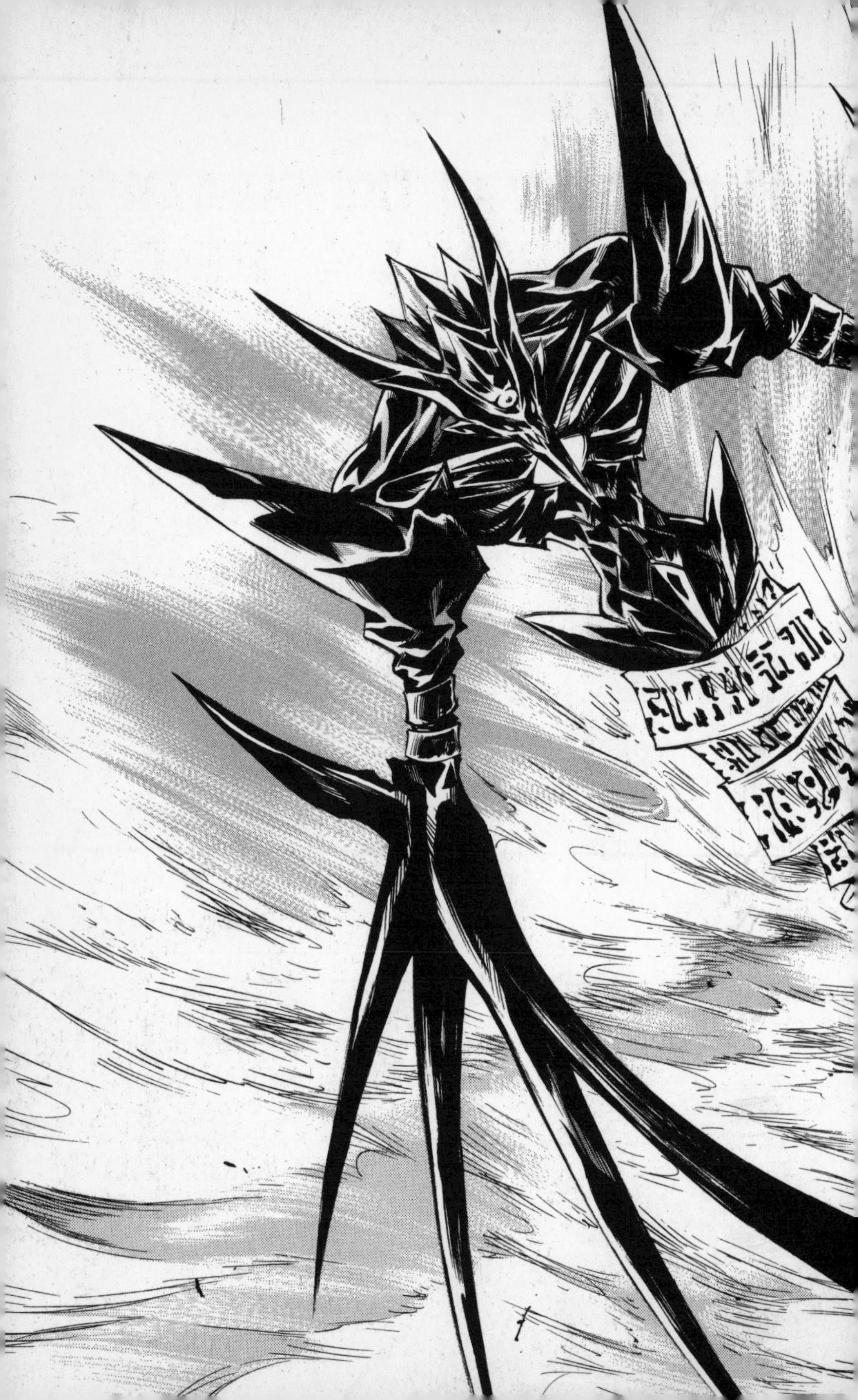

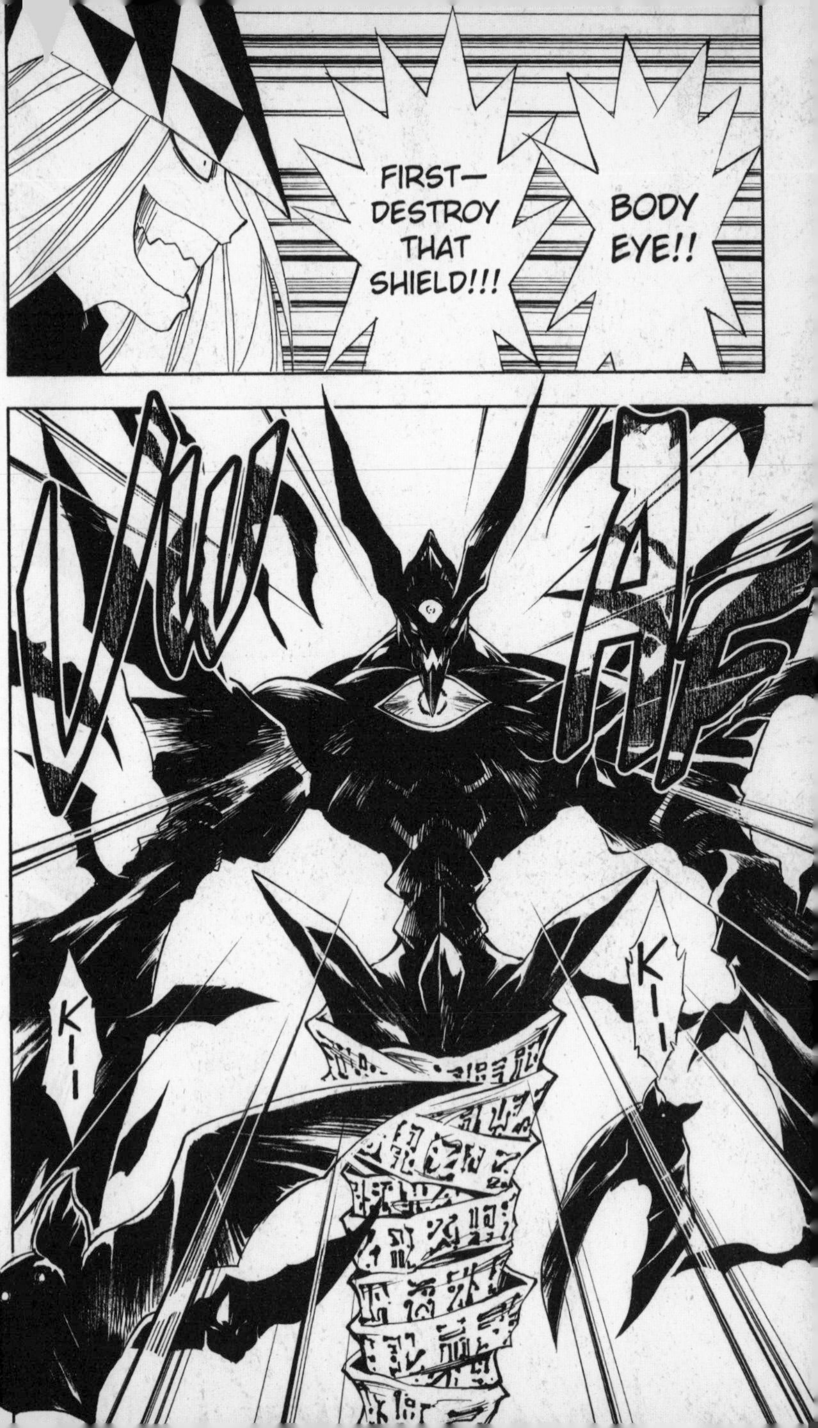
BODY EYE!!
FIRST—DESTROY THAT SHIELD!!!
KII
KII

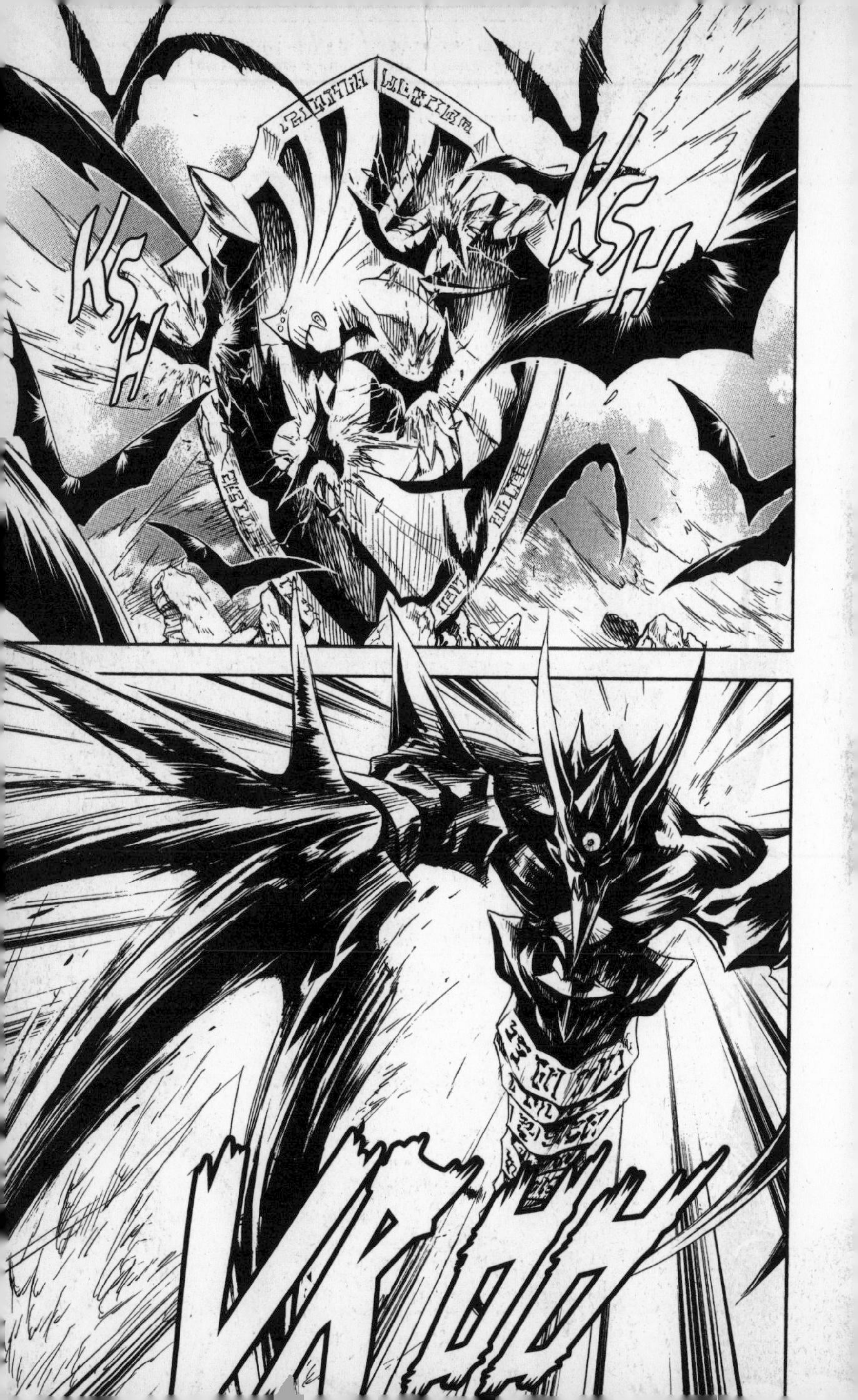
KSH
KSH

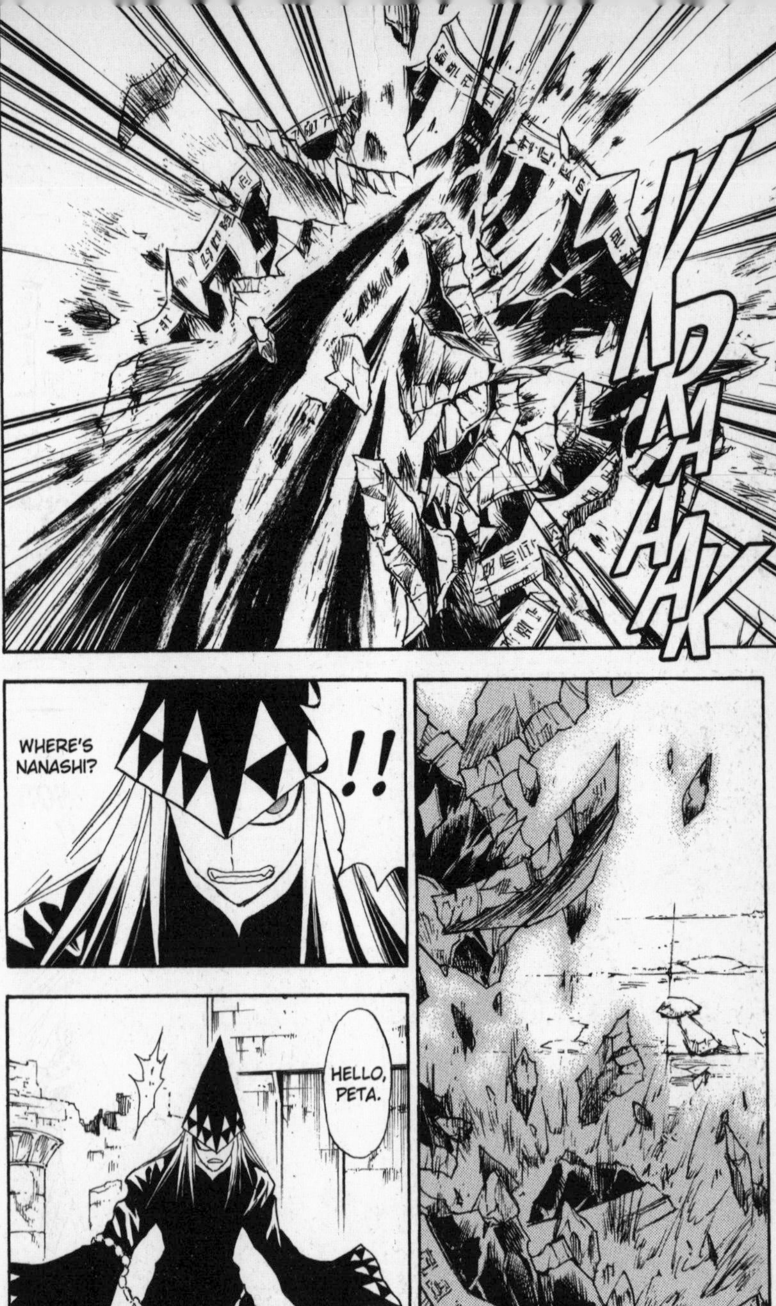
KRAAAK
!!
WHERE'S NANASHI?
HELLO, PETA.

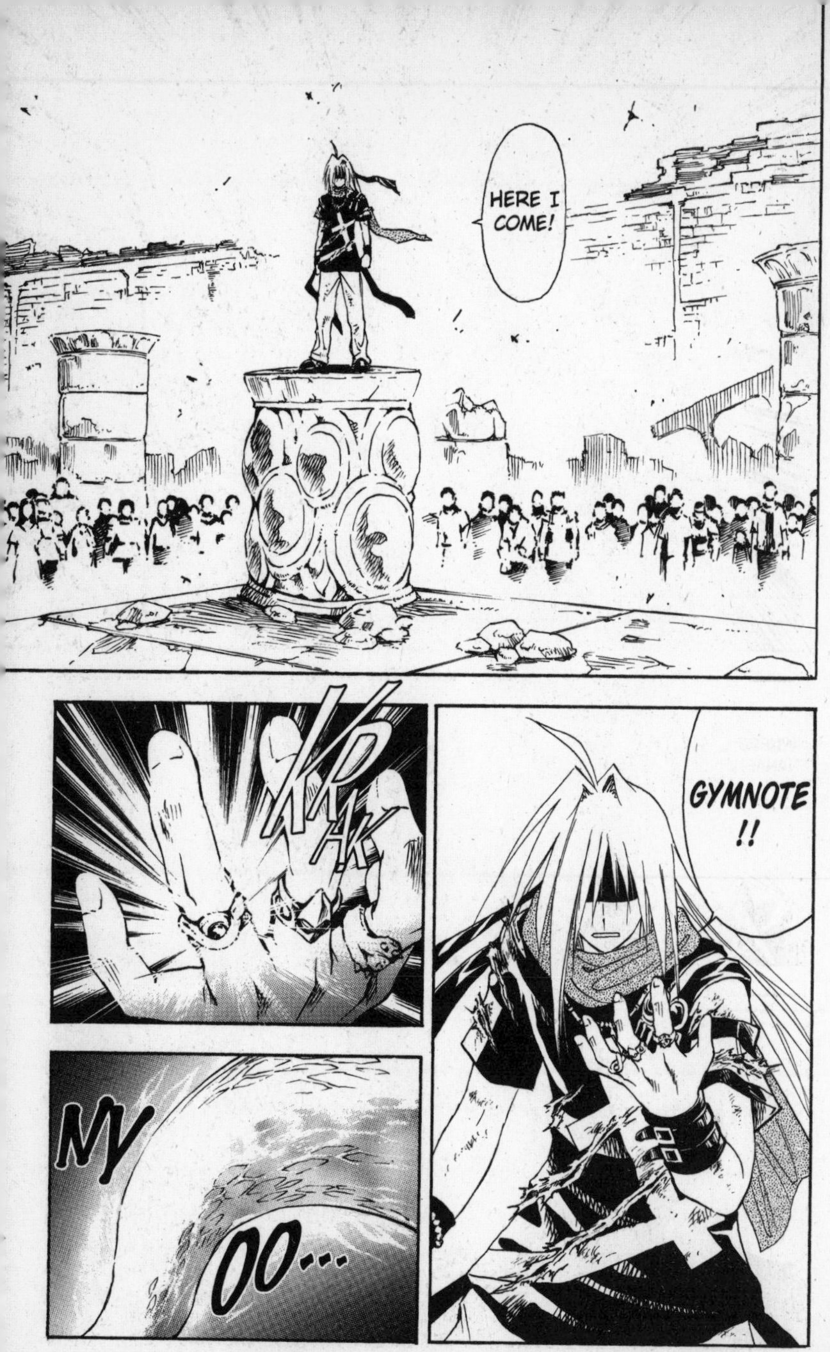
HERE I COME!
GYMNOTE !!
KRAK
NYOO...

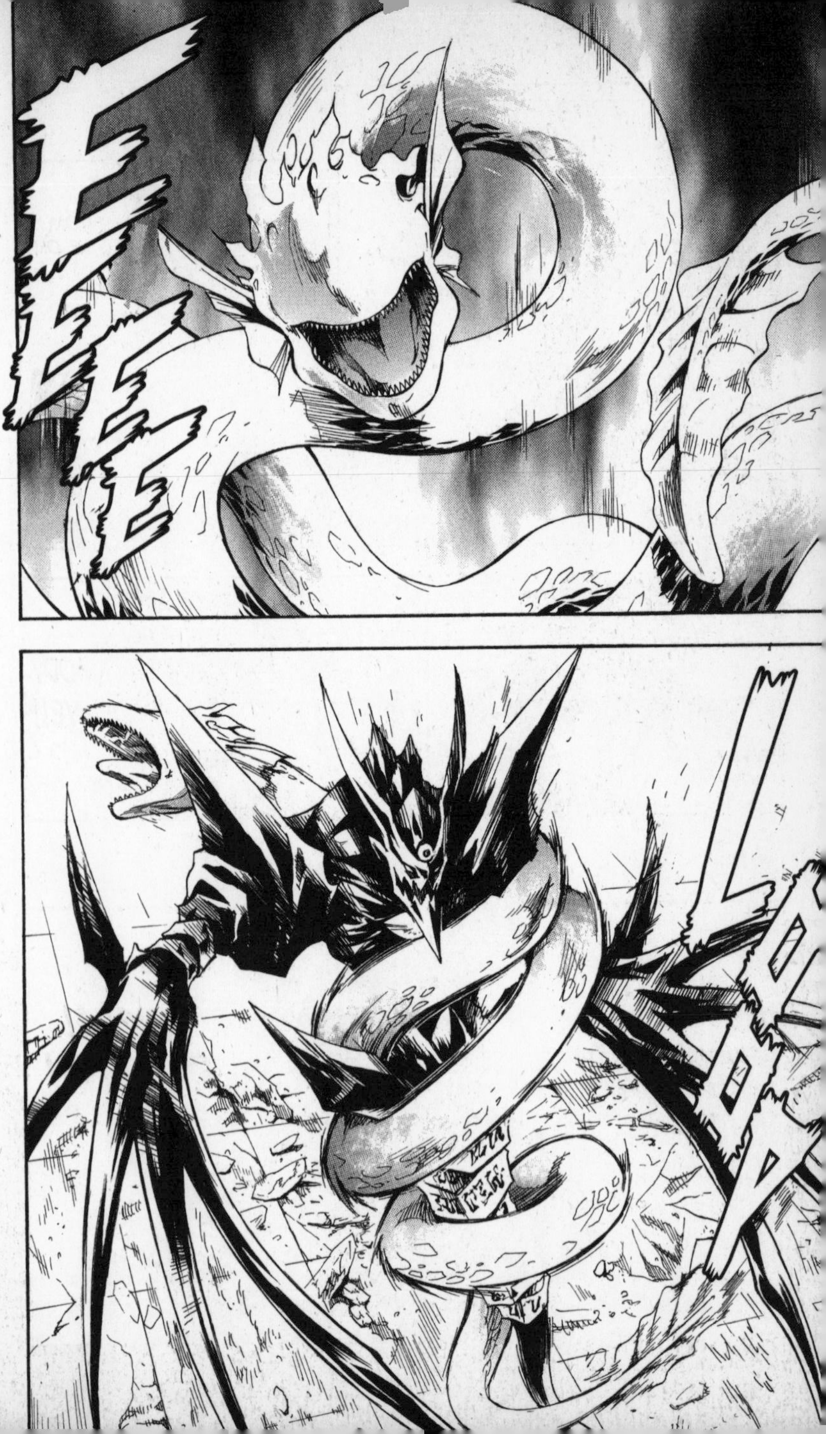
EEE

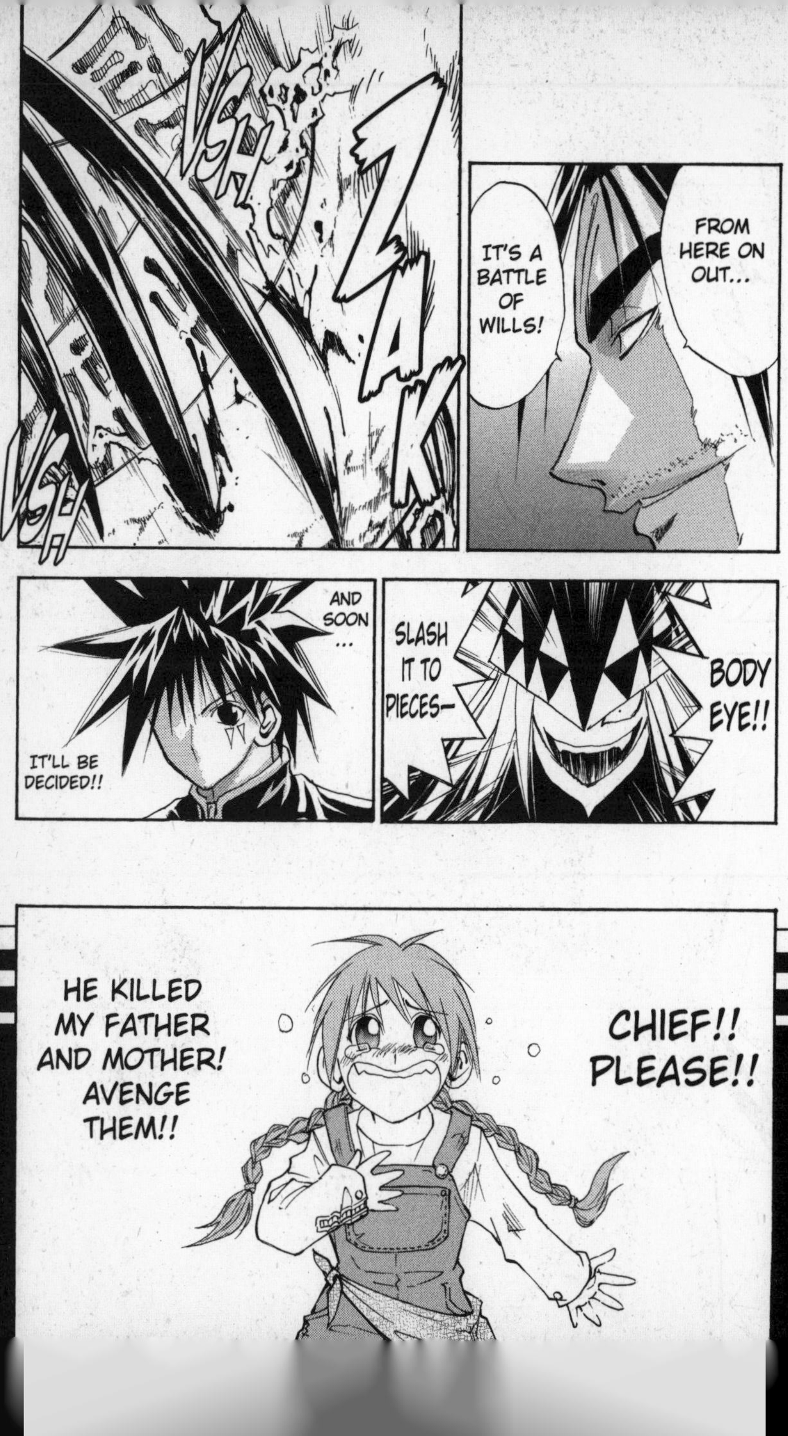
FROM HERE ON OUT...
IT'S A BATTLE OF WILLS!
VSH
ZAK
VSH
SLASH IT TO PIECES—
BODY EYE!!
AND SOON...
IT'LL BE DECIDED!!
CHIEF!! PLEASE!!
HE KILLED MY FATHER AND MOTHER! AVENGE THEM!!

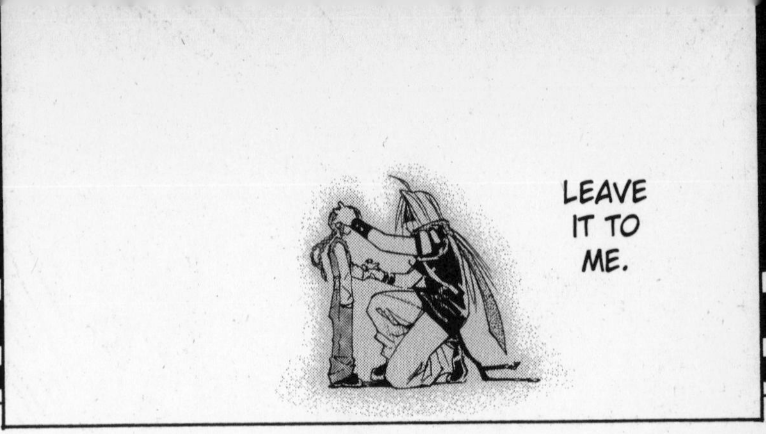
LEAVE IT TO ME.

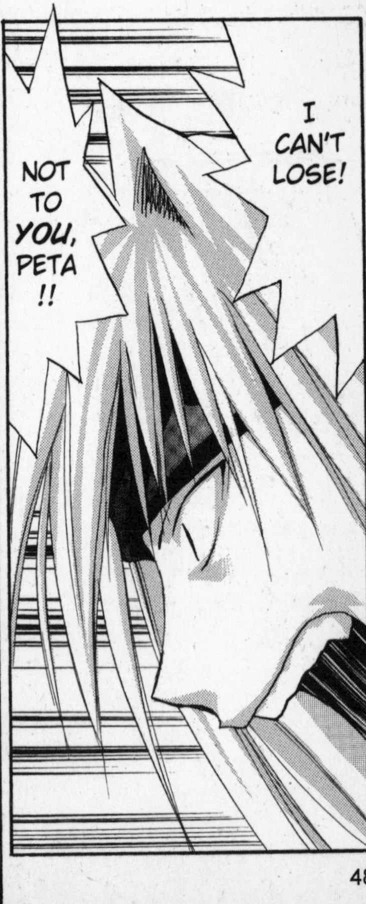
I CAN'T LOSE!
NOT TO YOU, PETA!!

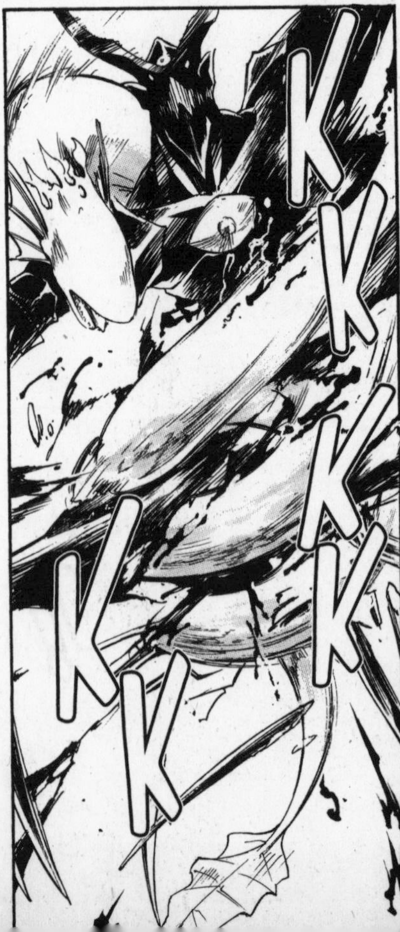
KKKKK
KK

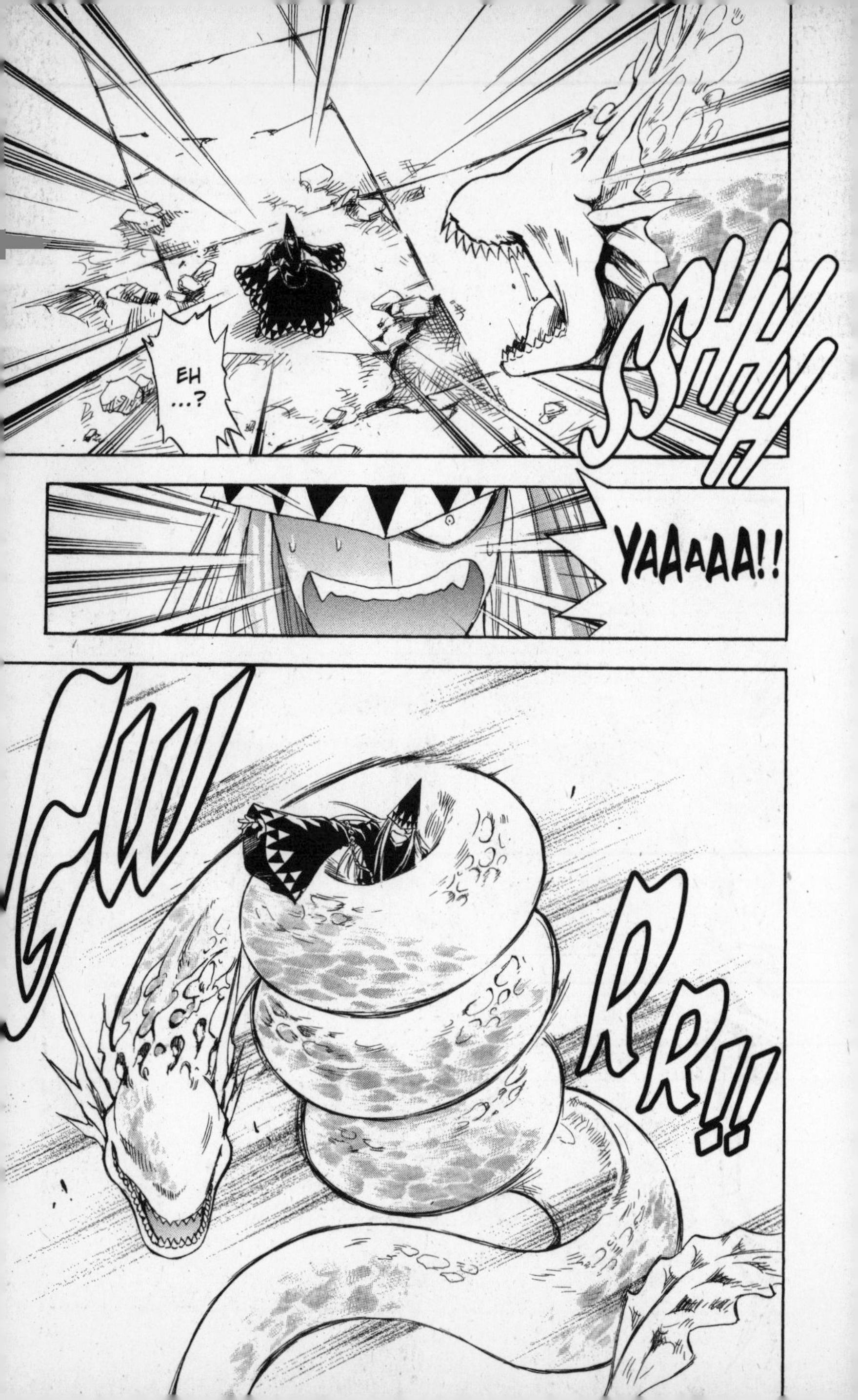
SSHH
EH ...?
YAAAAA!!
GW
RR!!

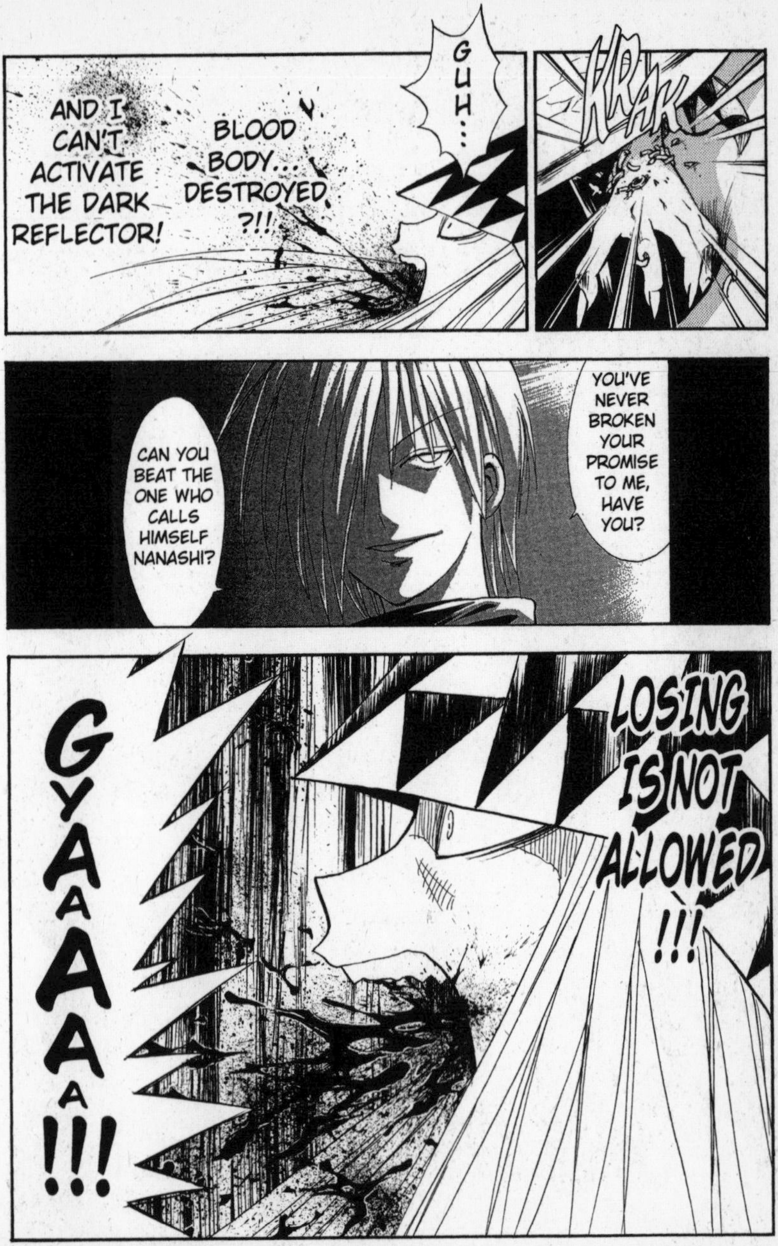
KRAK
GUH...
BLOOD BODY... DESTROYED?!!
AND I CAN'T ACTIVATE THE DARK REFLECTOR!
YOU'VE NEVER BROKEN YOUR PROMISE TO ME, HAVE YOU?
CAN YOU BEAT THE ONE WHO CALLS HIMSELF NANASHI?
LOSING IS NOT ALLOWED!!!
GYAaAAAa!!!

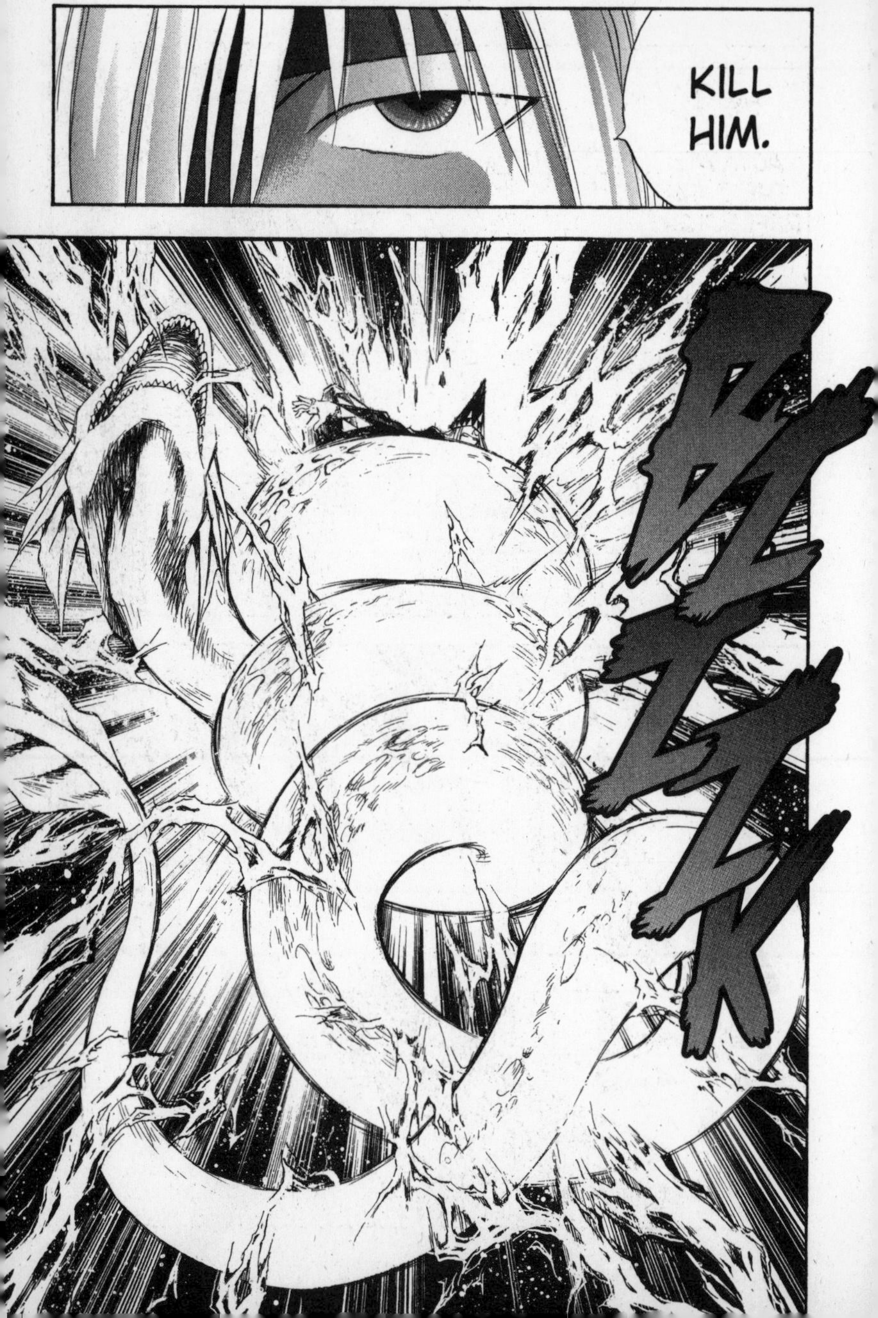
KILL HIM.
BZZZK

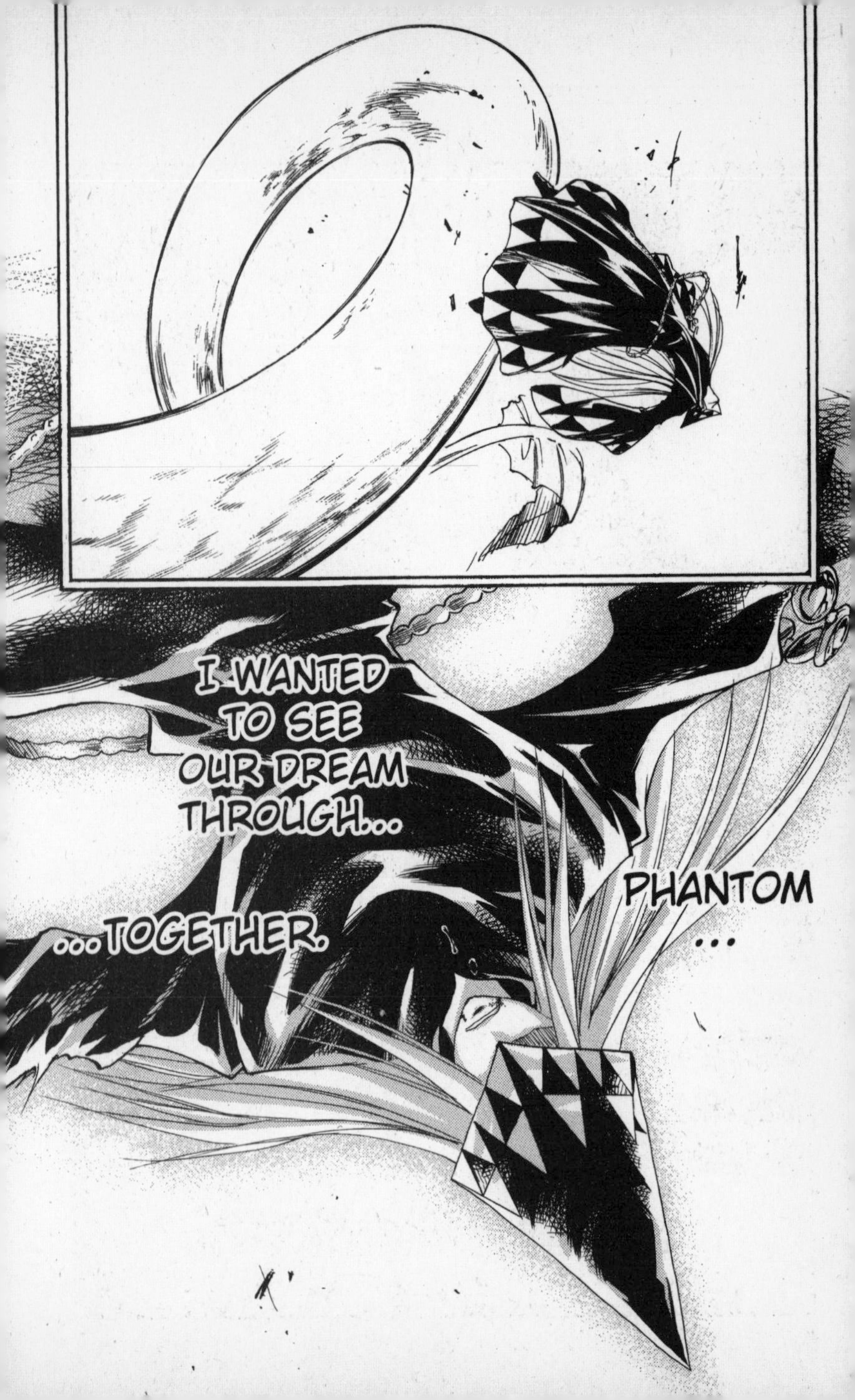

PHANTOM
...
I WANTED TO SEE OUR DREAM THROUGH...
...TOGETHER.

... DEAD ...

WUK

TM TM TM

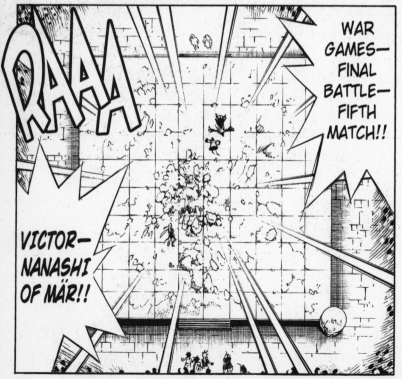

RAAA

WAR GAMES— FINAL BATTLE— FIFTH MATCH!!

VICTOR— NANASHI OF MÄR!!

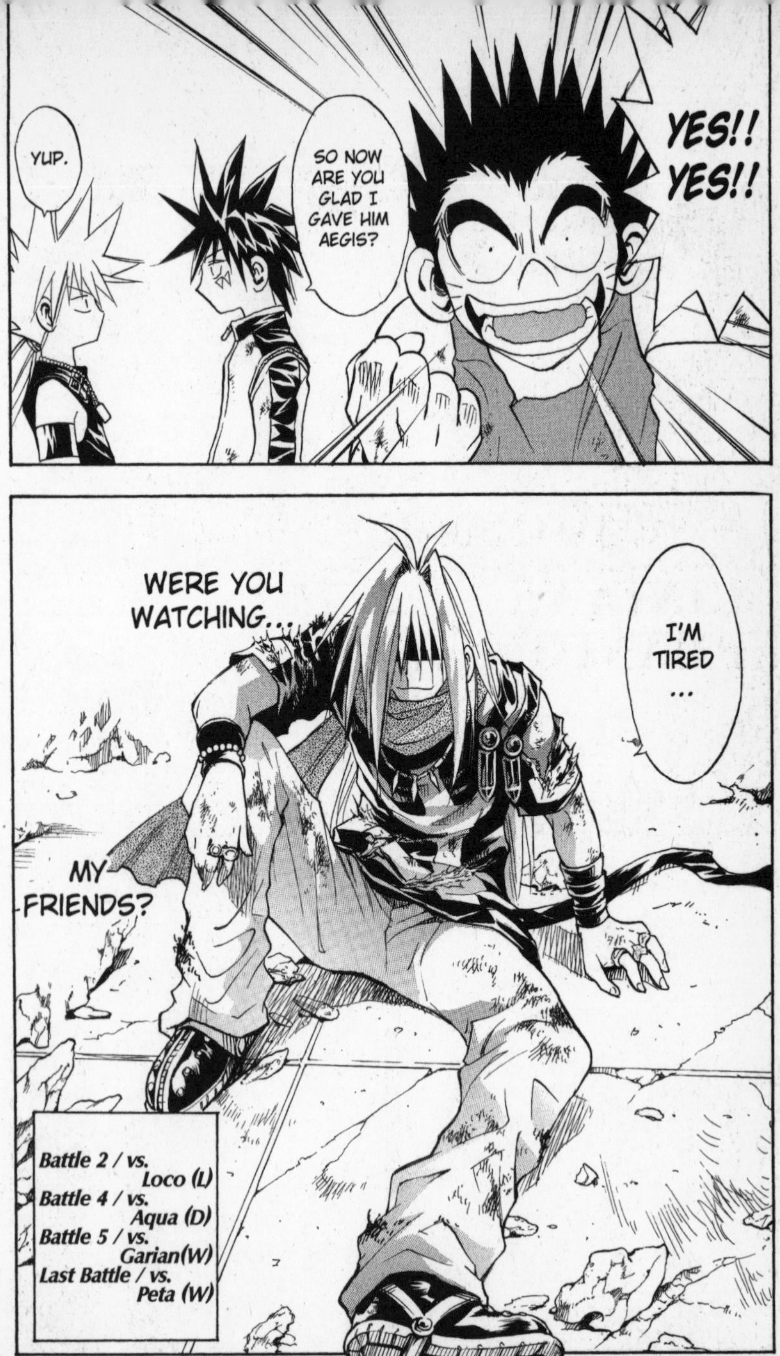
YES!! YES!!
SO NOW ARE YOU GLAD I GAVE HIM AEGIS?
YUP.
I'M TIRED ...
WERE YOU WATCHING...
MY FRIENDS?
Battle 2 / vs. Loco (L)
Battle 4 / vs. Aqua (D)
Battle 5 / vs. Garian(W)
Last Battle / vs. Peta (W)

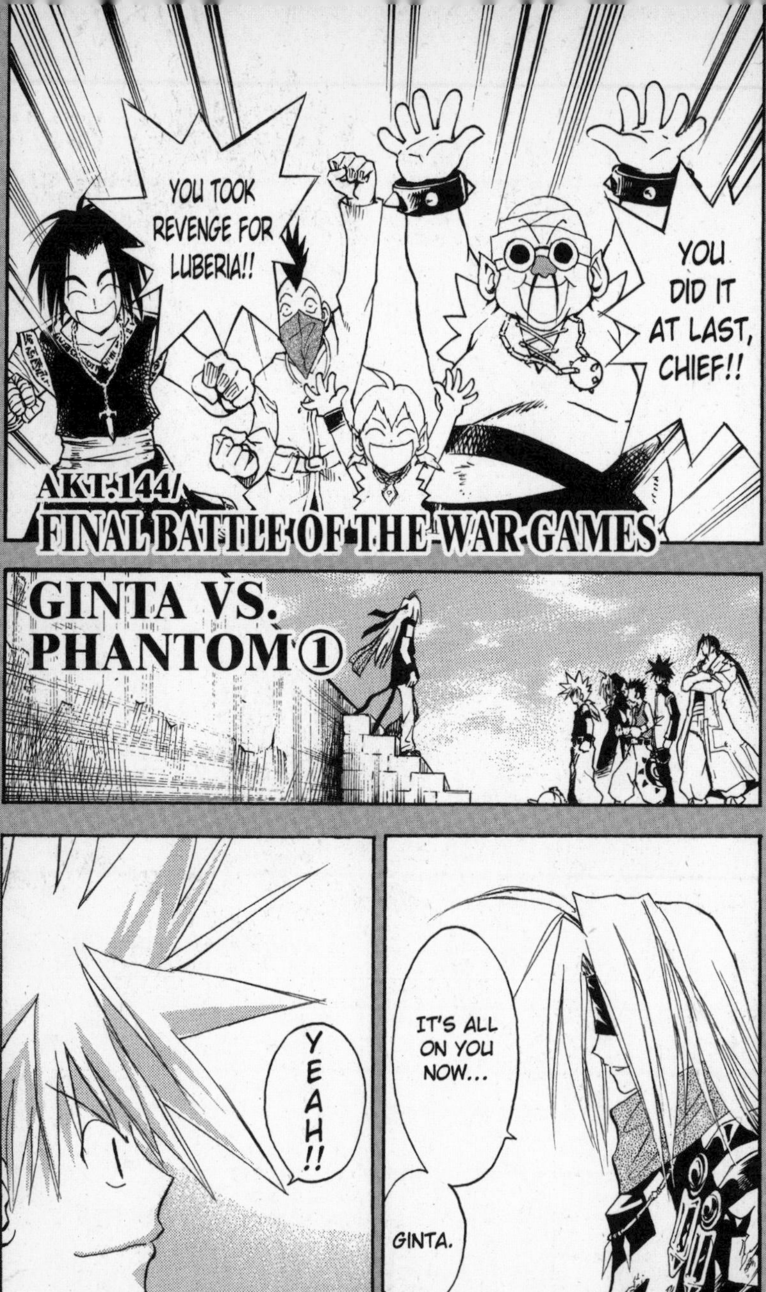
YOU DID IT AT LAST, CHIEF!!
YOU TOOK REVENGE FOR LUBERIA!!
AKT.144/
FINAL BATTLE OF THE WAR GAMES
GINTA VS. PHANTOM ①
IT'S ALL ON YOU NOW...
GINTA.
YEAH!!

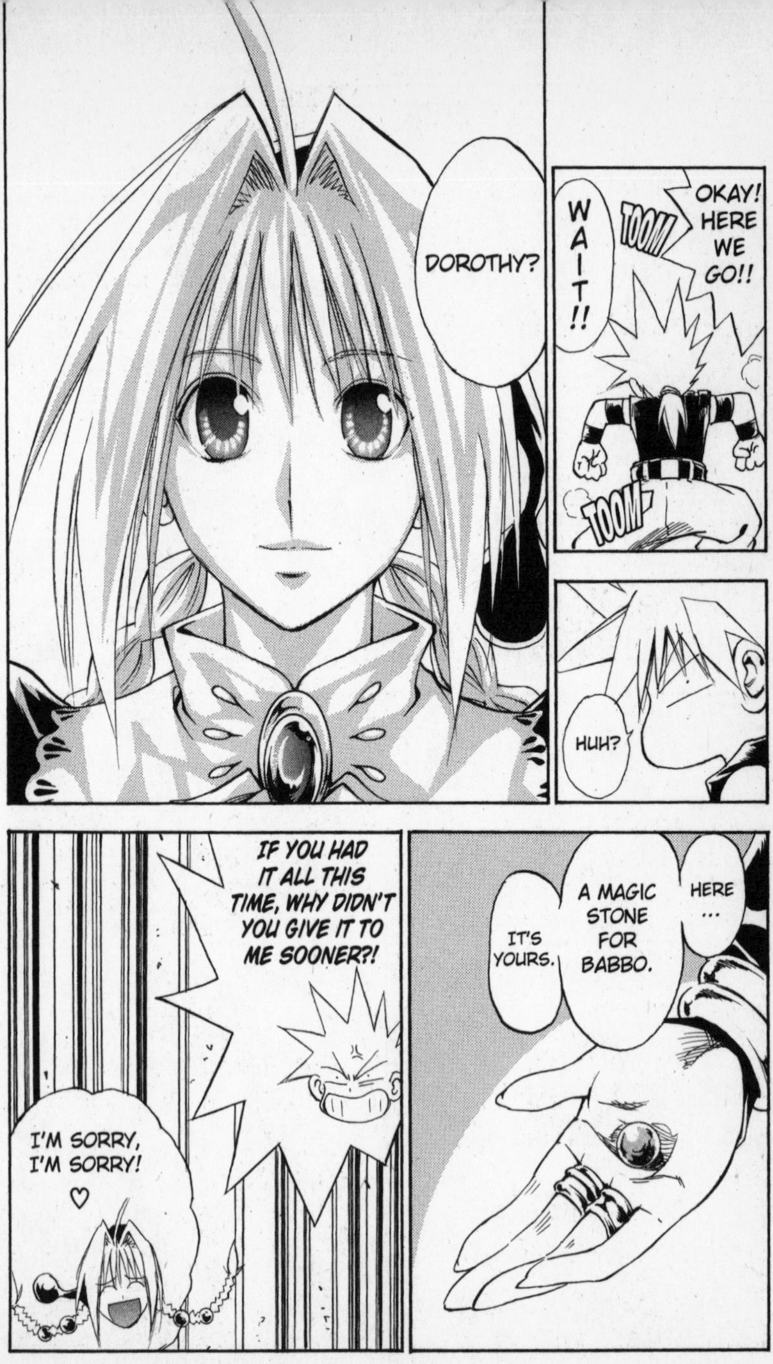
OKAY! HERE WE GO!!
TOOM
WAIT!!
TOOM
HUH?
DOROTHY?
HERE...
A MAGIC STONE FOR BABBO.
IT'S YOURS.
IF YOU HAD IT ALL THIS TIME, WHY DIDN'T YOU GIVE IT TO ME SOONER?!
I'M SORRY, I'M SORRY! ♡

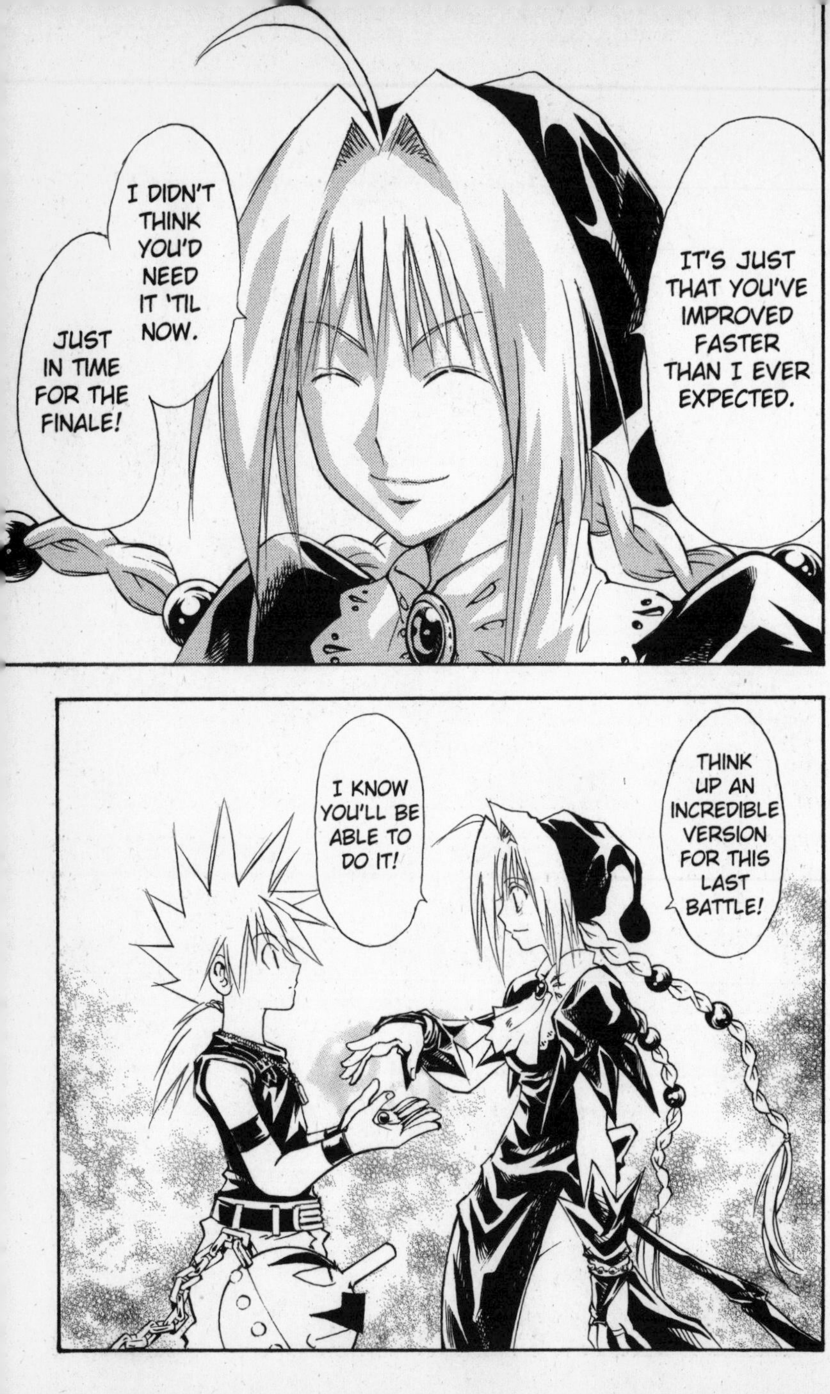
IT'S JUST THAT YOU'VE IMPROVED FASTER THAN I EVER EXPECTED.
I DIDN'T THINK YOU'D NEED IT 'TIL NOW.
JUST IN TIME FOR THE FINALE!
THINK UP AN INCREDIBLE VERSION FOR THIS LAST BATTLE!
I KNOW YOU'LL BE ABLE TO DO IT!

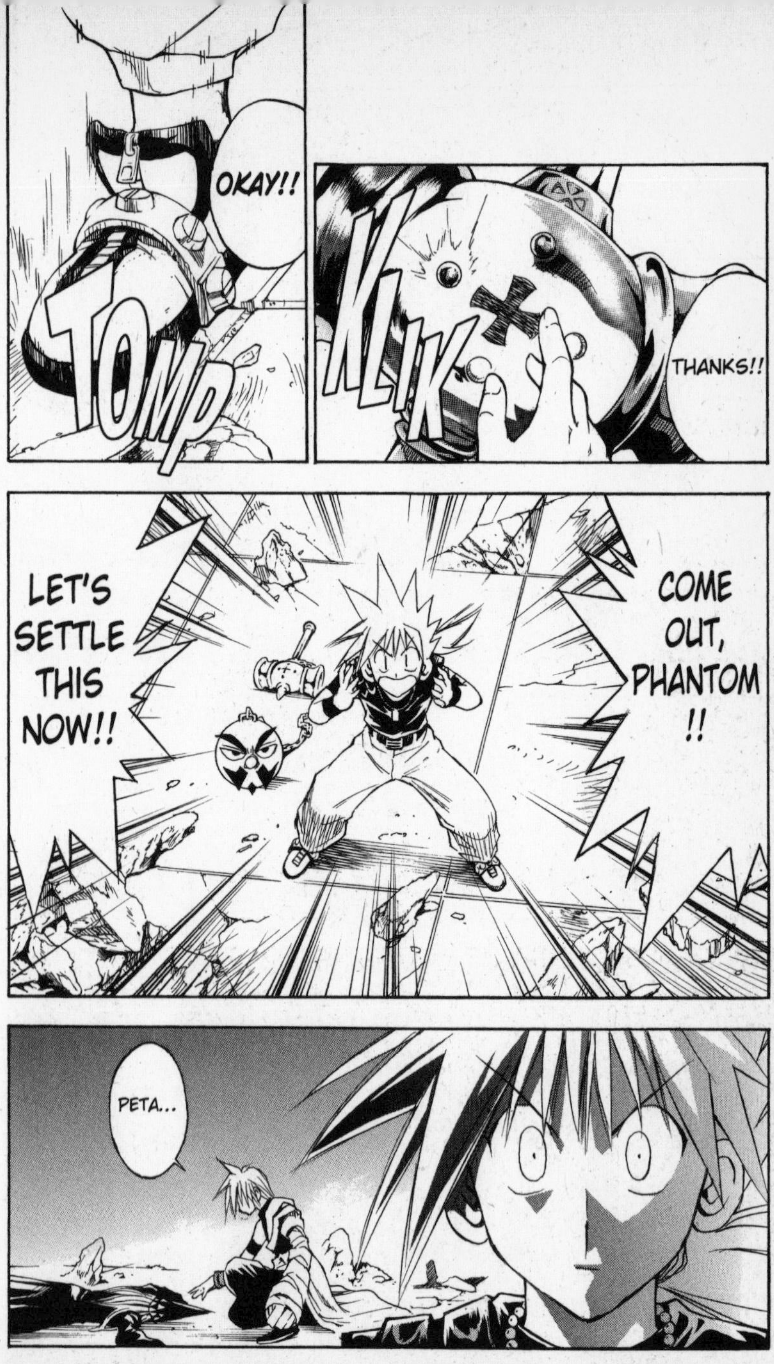
KLIK
THANKS!!
OKAY!!
TOMP
COME OUT, PHANTOM!!
LET'S SETTLE THIS NOW!!
PETA...

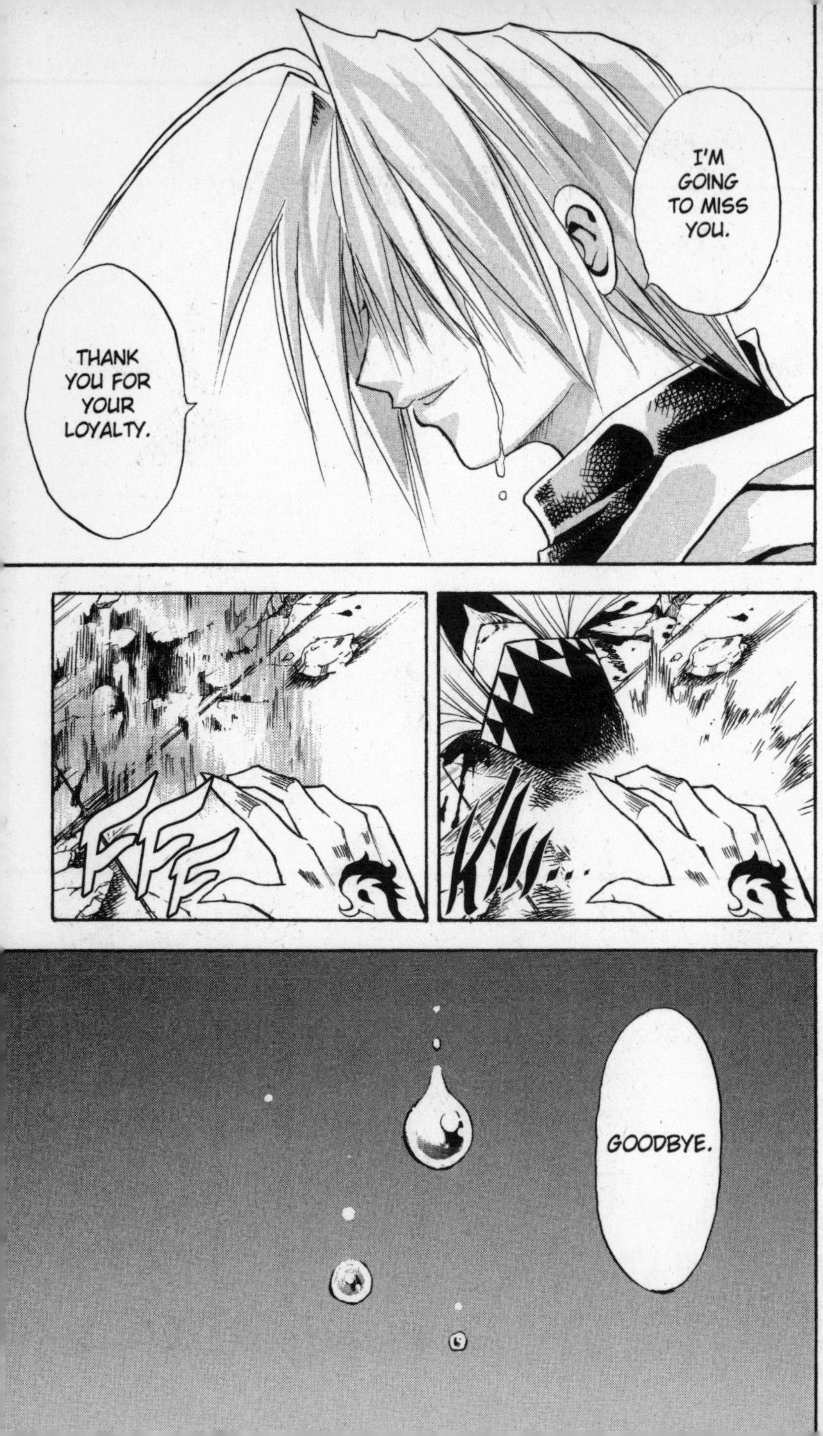
I'M GOING TO MISS YOU.
THANK YOU FOR YOUR LOYALTY.
FFF
GOODBYE.

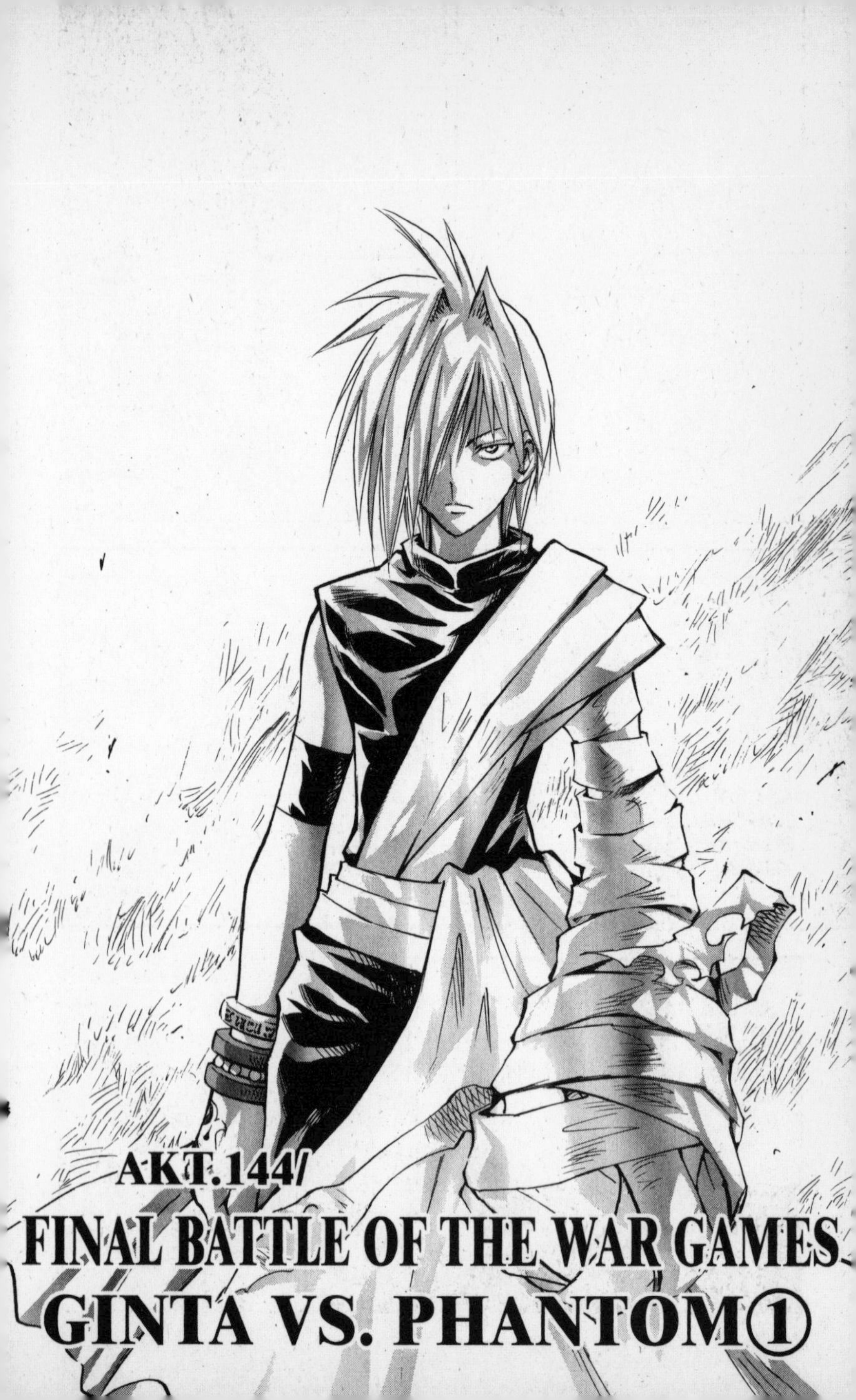
AKT.144/
FINAL BATTLE OF THE WAR GAMES
GINTA VS. PHANTOM①

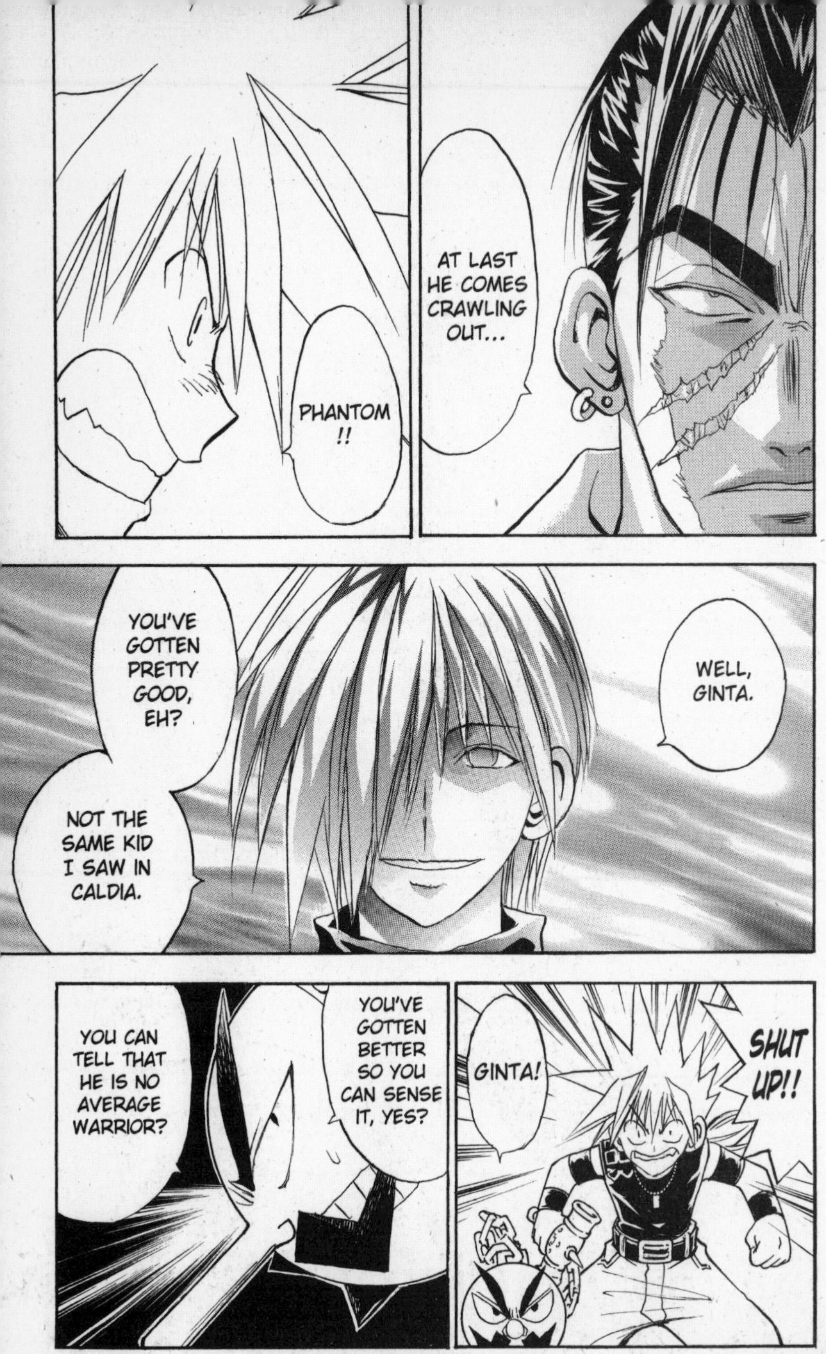
AT LAST HE COMES CRAWLING OUT...
PHANTOM!!
WELL, GINTA.
YOU'VE GOTTEN PRETTY GOOD, EH?
NOT THE SAME KID I SAW IN CALDIA.
SHUT UP!!
GINTA!
YOU'VE GOTTEN BETTER SO YOU CAN SENSE IT, YES?
YOU CAN TELL THAT HE IS NO AVERAGE WARRIOR?

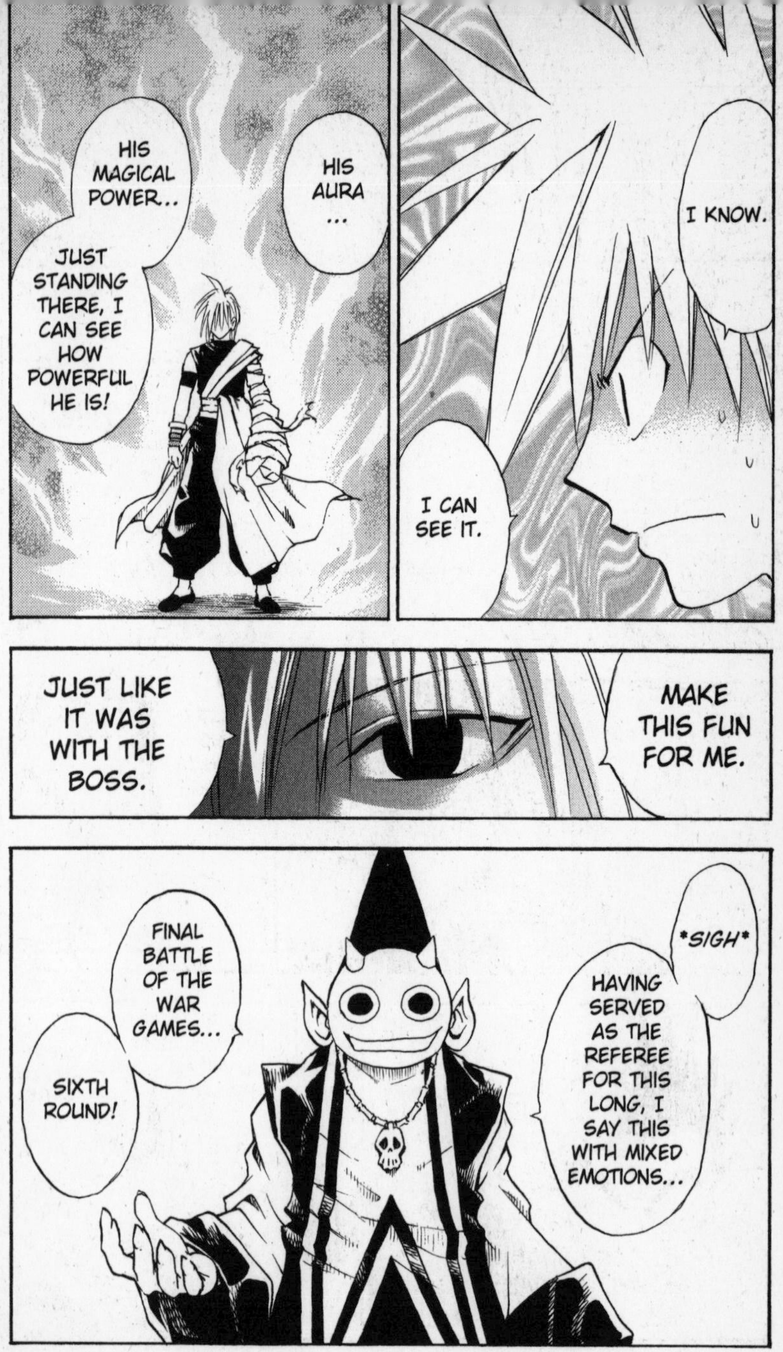
I KNOW.
I CAN SEE IT.
HIS AURA ...
HIS MAGICAL POWER...
JUST STANDING THERE, I CAN SEE HOW POWERFUL HE IS!
MAKE THIS FUN FOR ME.
JUST LIKE IT WAS WITH THE BOSS.
SIGH
HAVING SERVED AS THE REFEREE FOR THIS LONG, I SAY THIS WITH MIXED EMOTIONS...
FINAL BATTLE OF THE WAR GAMES...
SIXTH ROUND!

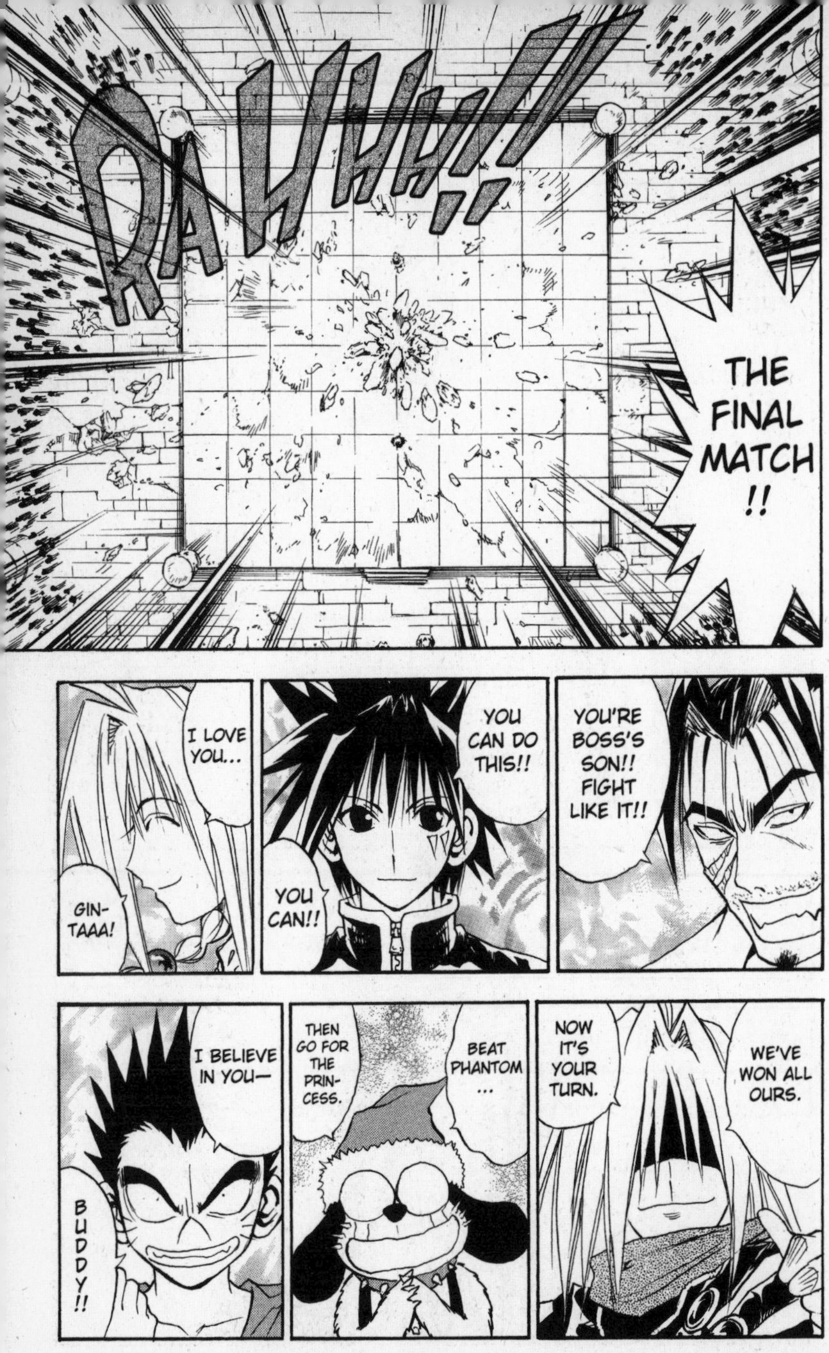
THE FINAL MATCH!!
YOU'RE BOSS'S SON!! FIGHT LIKE IT!!
YOU CAN DO THIS!!
YOU CAN!!
I LOVE YOU...
GIN-TAAA!
WE'VE WON ALL OURS.
NOW IT'S YOUR TURN.
BEAT PHANTOM...
THEN GO FOR THE PRIN-CESS.
I BELIEVE IN YOU—
BUDDY!!

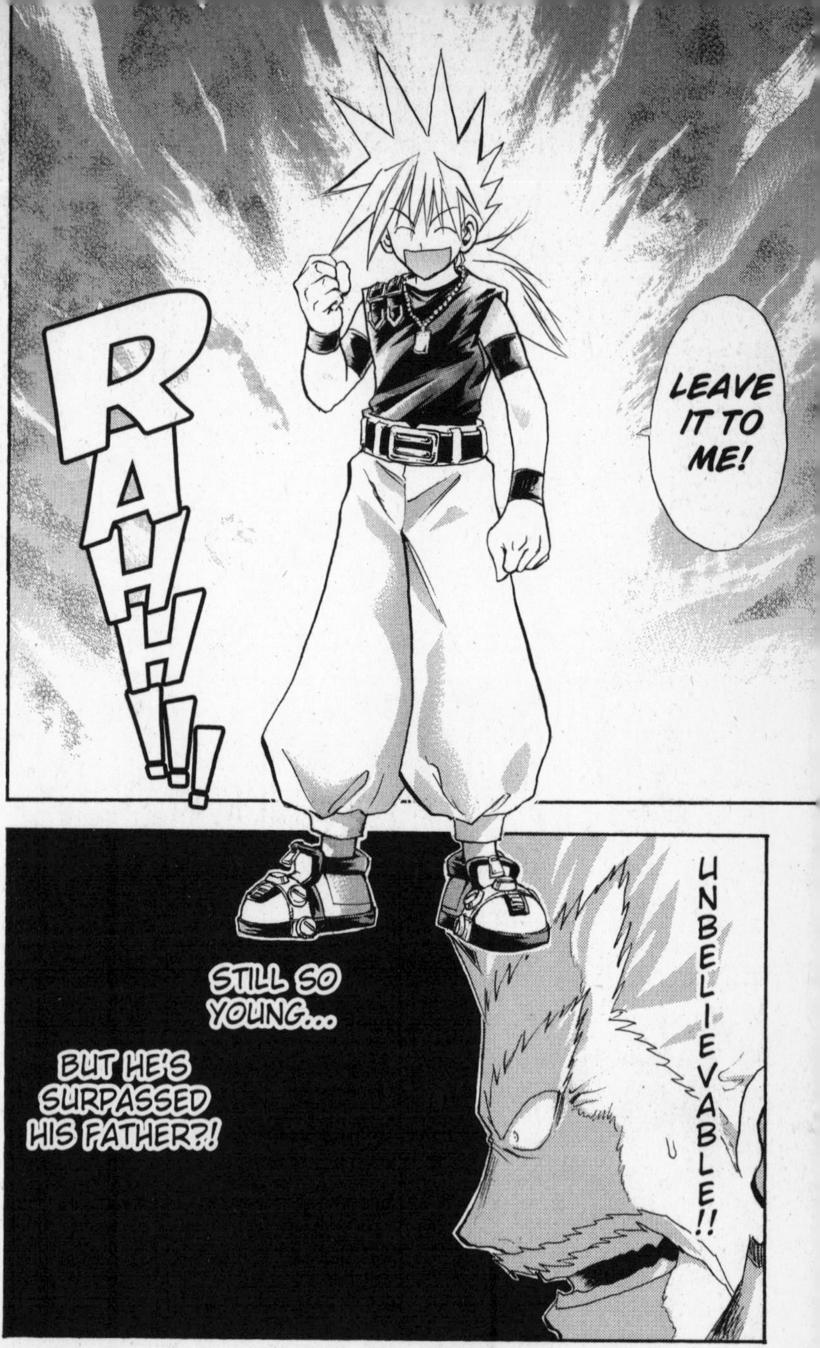
LEAVE IT TO ME!
RAHH!!!
UNBELIEVABLE!!
STILL SO YOUNG...
BUT HE'S SURPASSED HIS FATHER?!

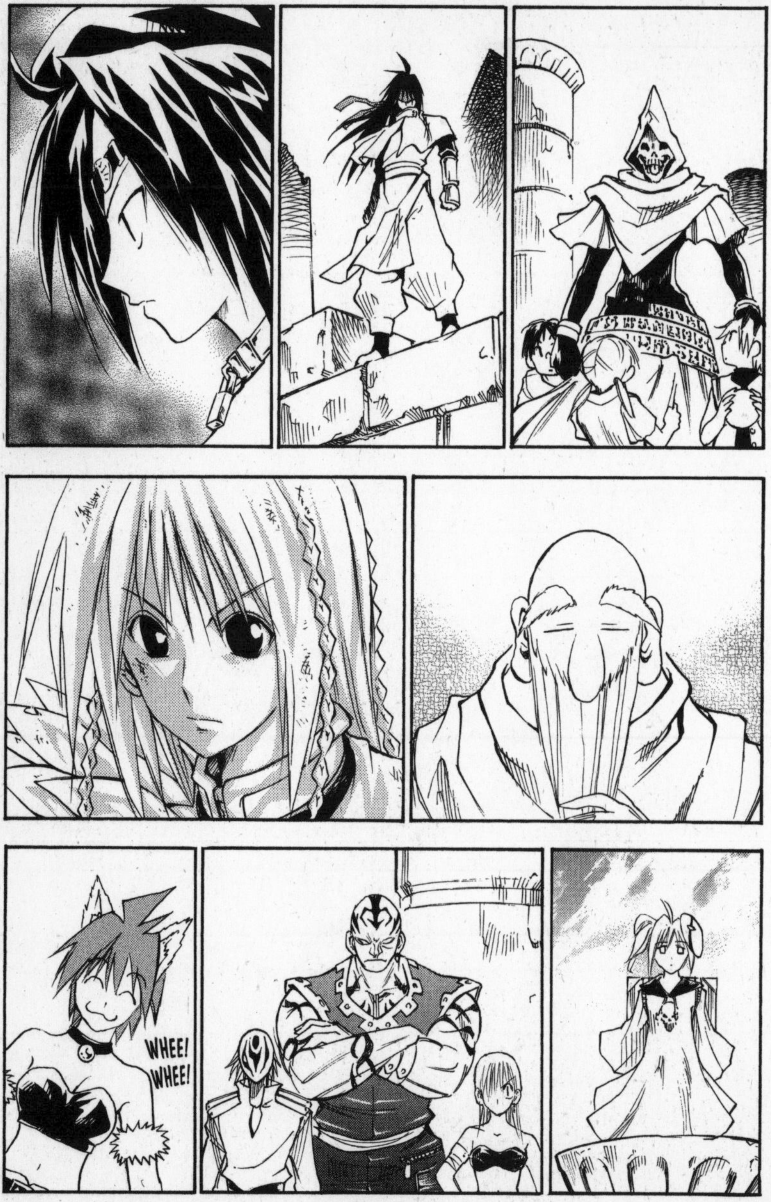
WHEE!
WHEE!

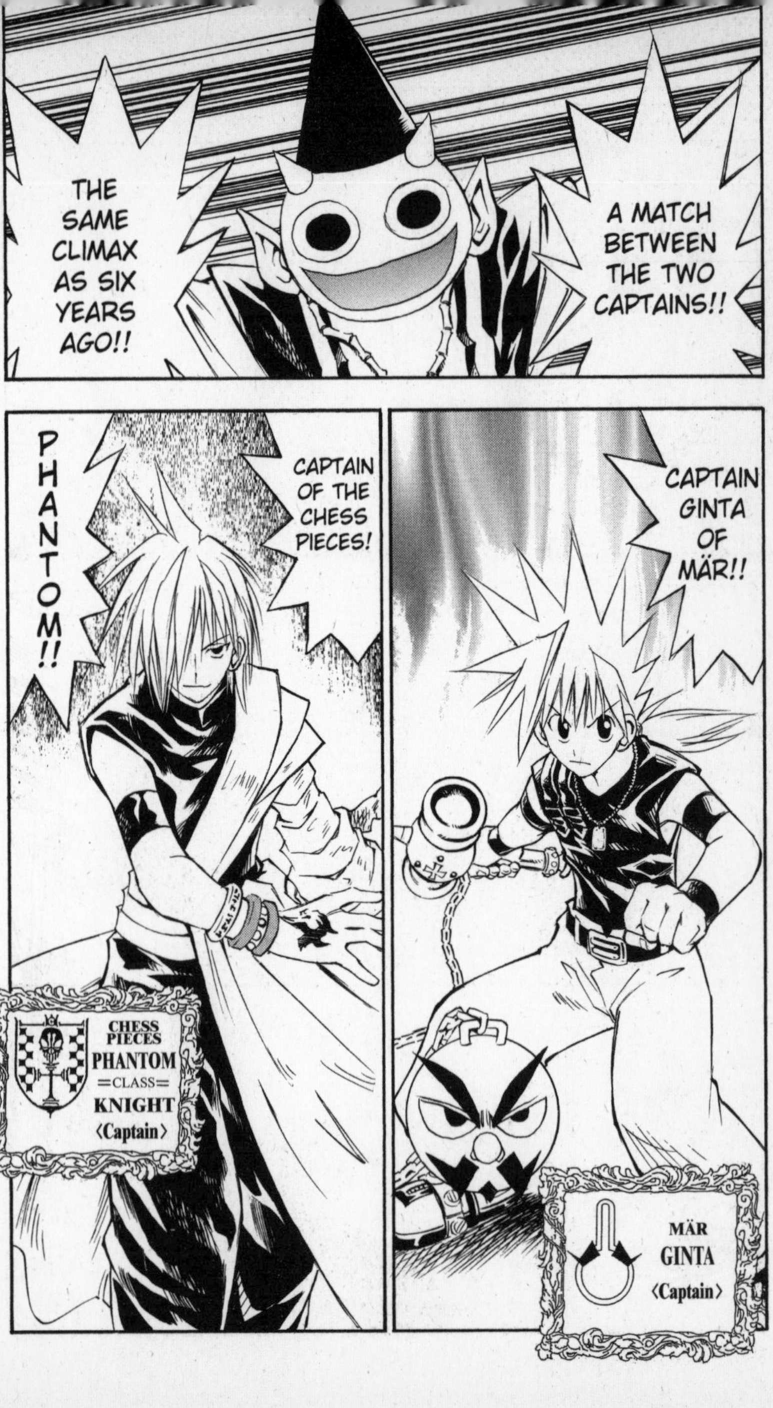
A MATCH BETWEEN THE TWO CAPTAINS!!
THE SAME CLIMAX AS SIX YEARS AGO!!
CAPTAIN GINTA OF MÄR!!
MÄR
GINTA
〈Captain〉
CAPTAIN OF THE CHESS PIECES!
PHANTOM!!
CHESS PIECES
PHANTOM
CLASS
KNIGHT
〈Captain〉

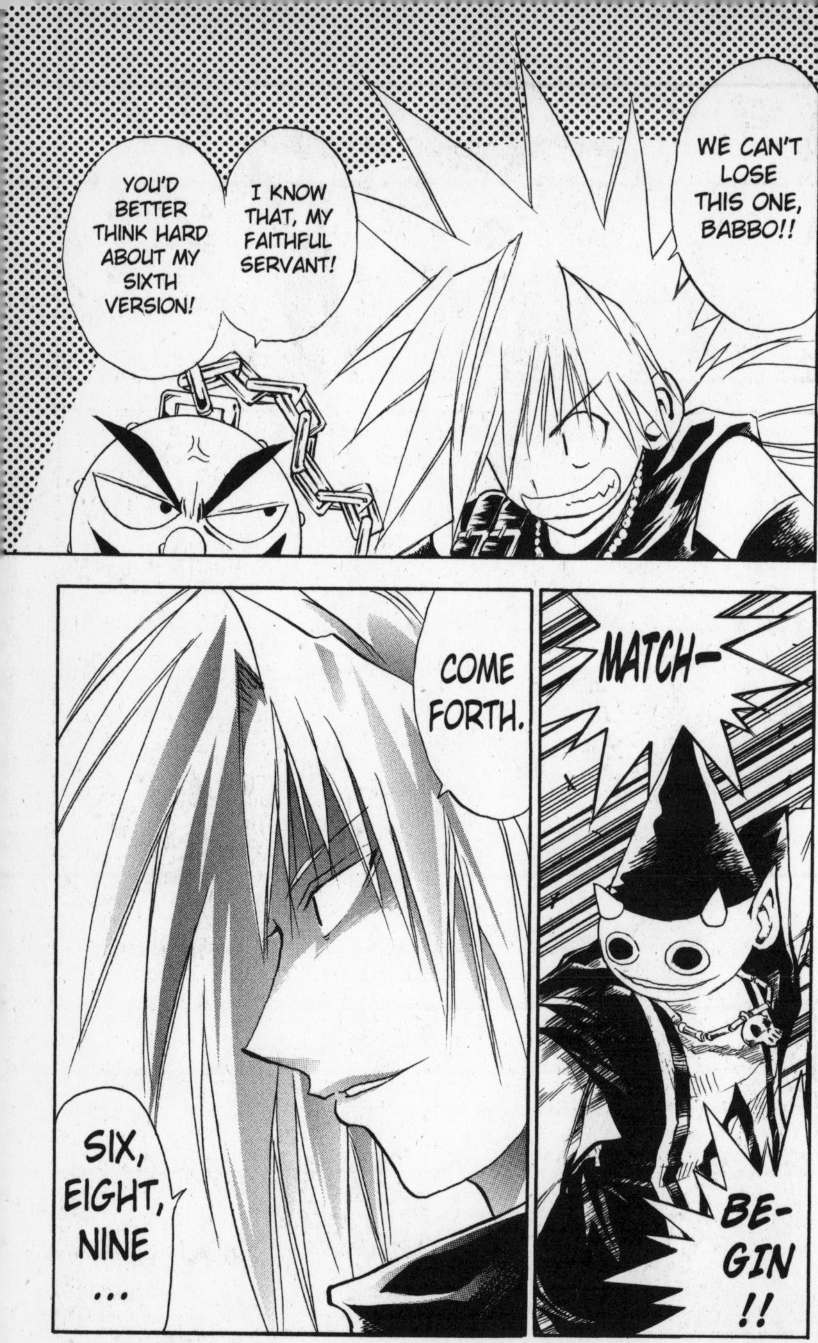
WE CAN'T LOSE THIS ONE, BABBO!!
I KNOW THAT, MY FAITHFUL SERVANT!
YOU'D BETTER THINK HARD ABOUT MY SIXTH VERSION!
MATCH-
BE-GIN!!
COME FORTH.
SIX, EIGHT, NINE ...

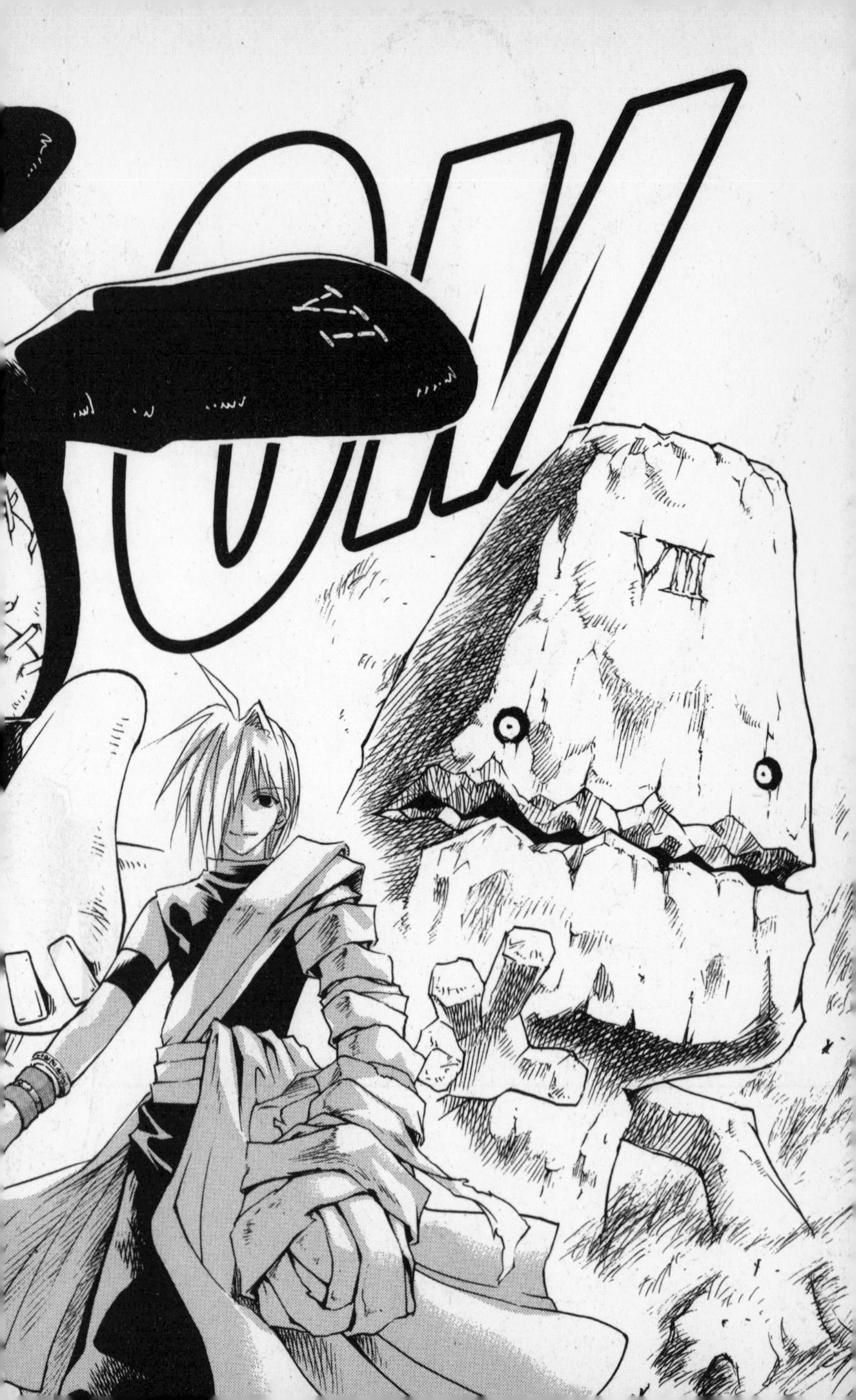
VII
VIII

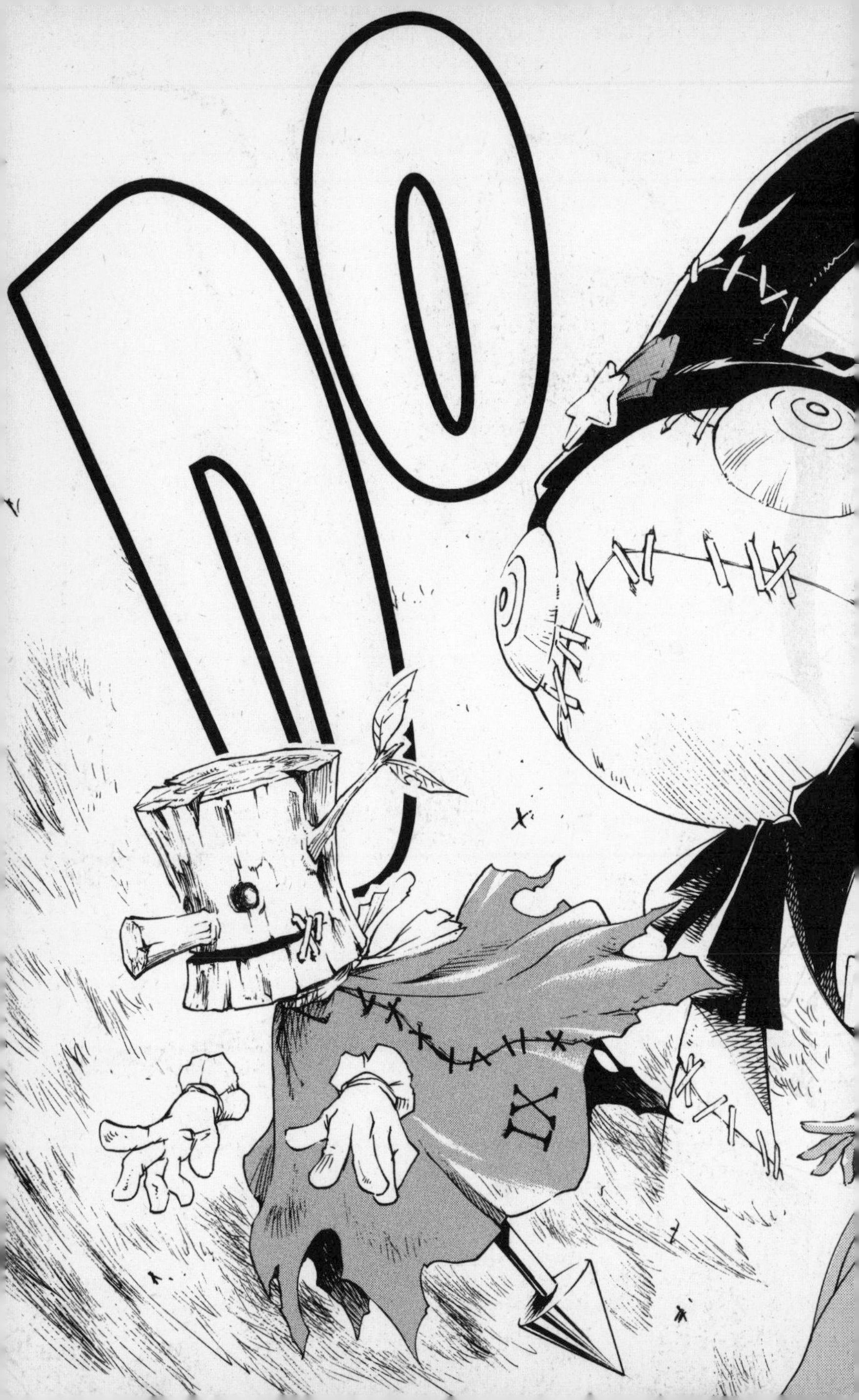
DO

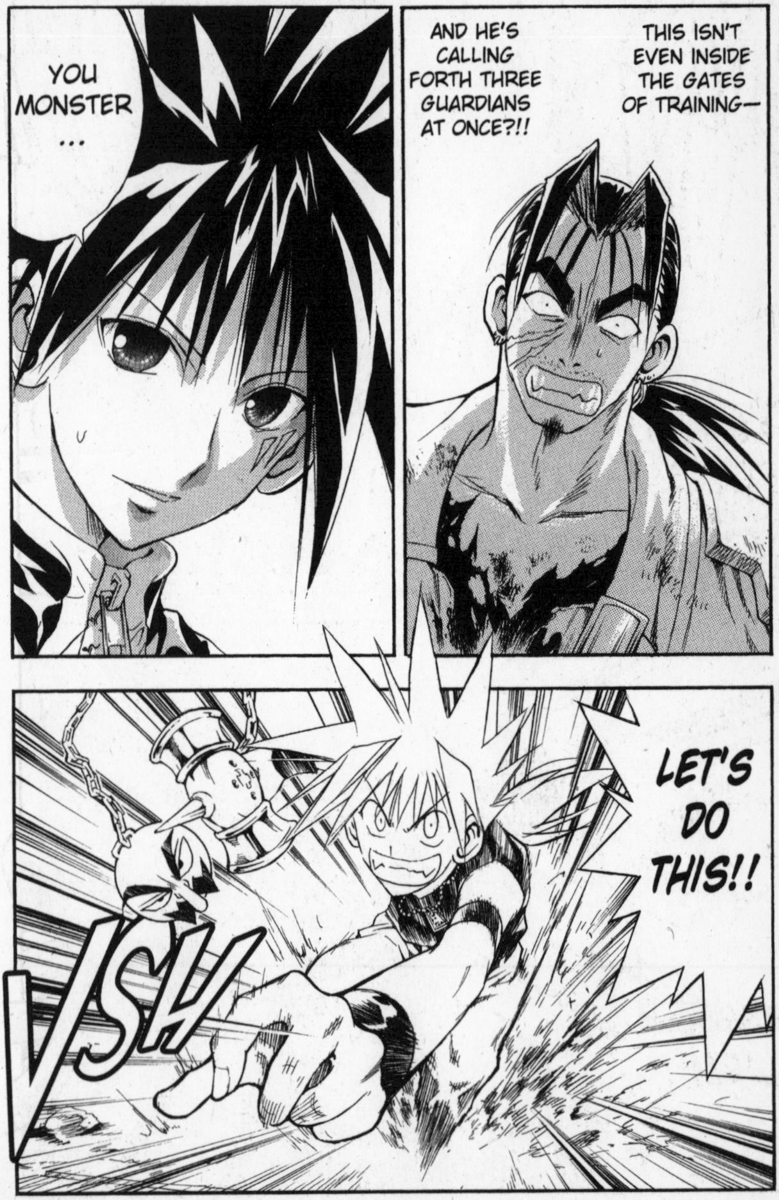
THIS ISN'T EVEN INSIDE THE GATES OF TRAINING—
AND HE'S CALLING FORTH THREE GUARDIANS AT ONCE?!!
YOU MONSTER ...
LET'S DO THIS!!
VSH

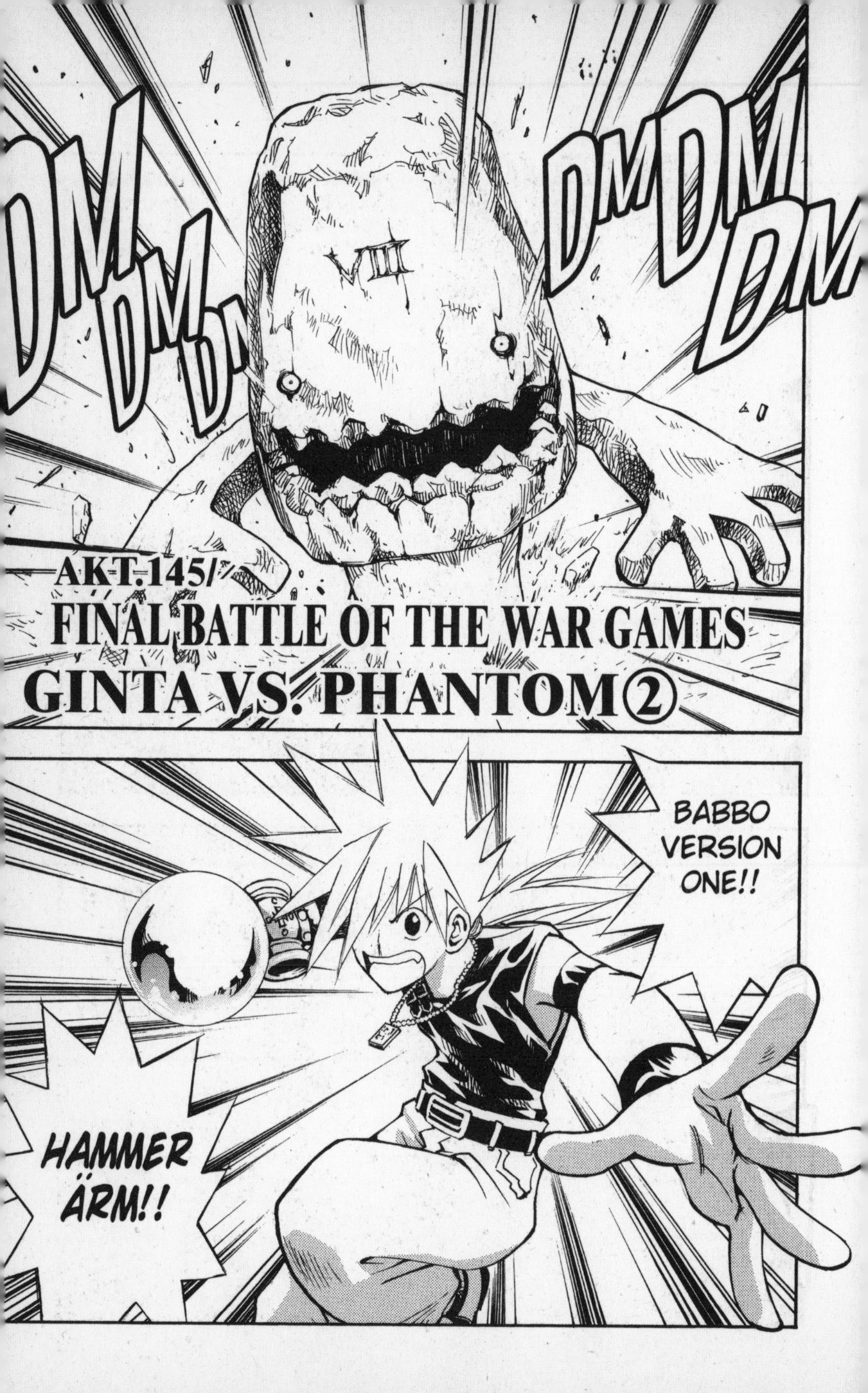
DMDMDM
AKT.145/
FINAL BATTLE OF THE WAR GAMES
GINTA VS. PHANTOM②
DMDMDM
BABBO VERSION ONE!!
HAMMER ÄRM!!

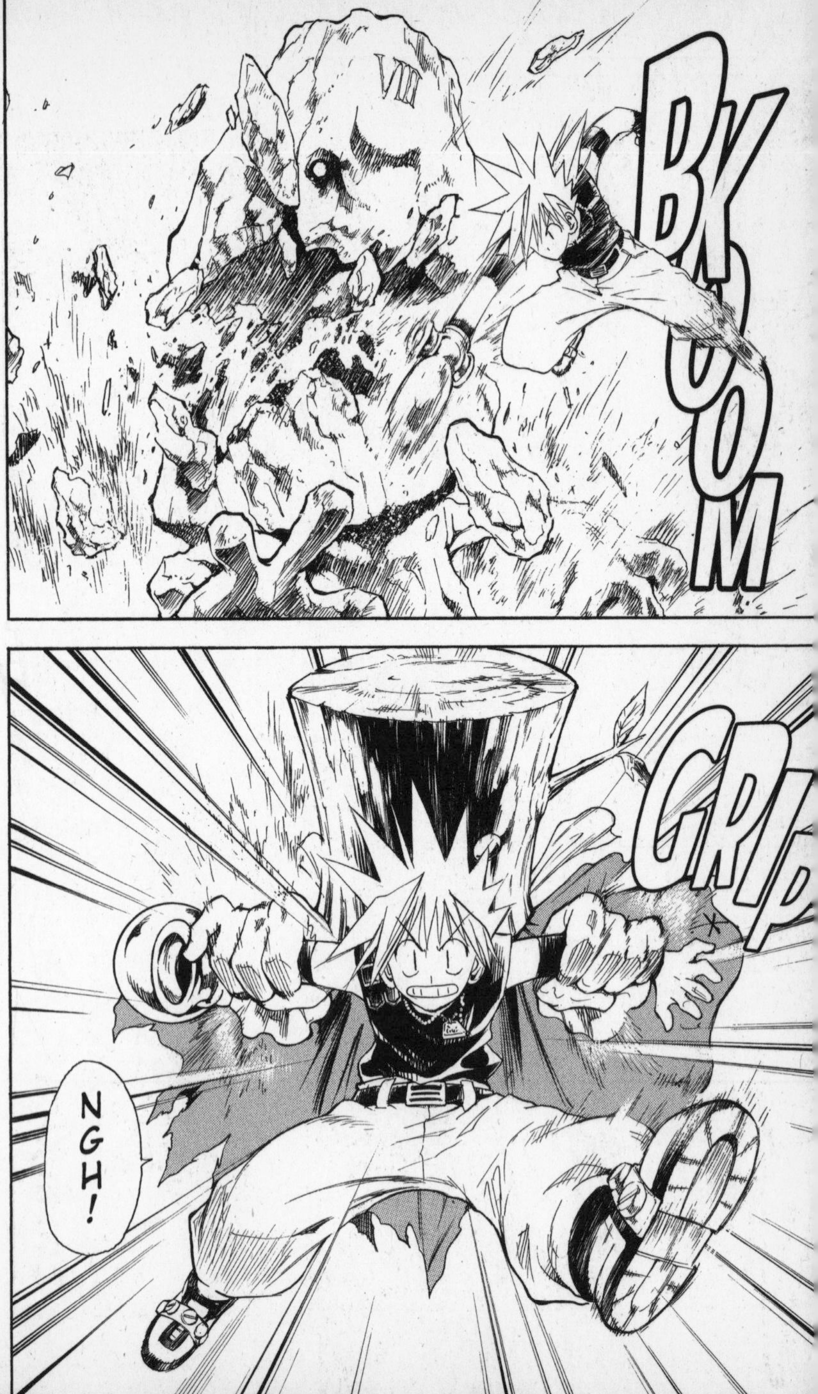
VIII
BKOOOM
GRIP
NGH!

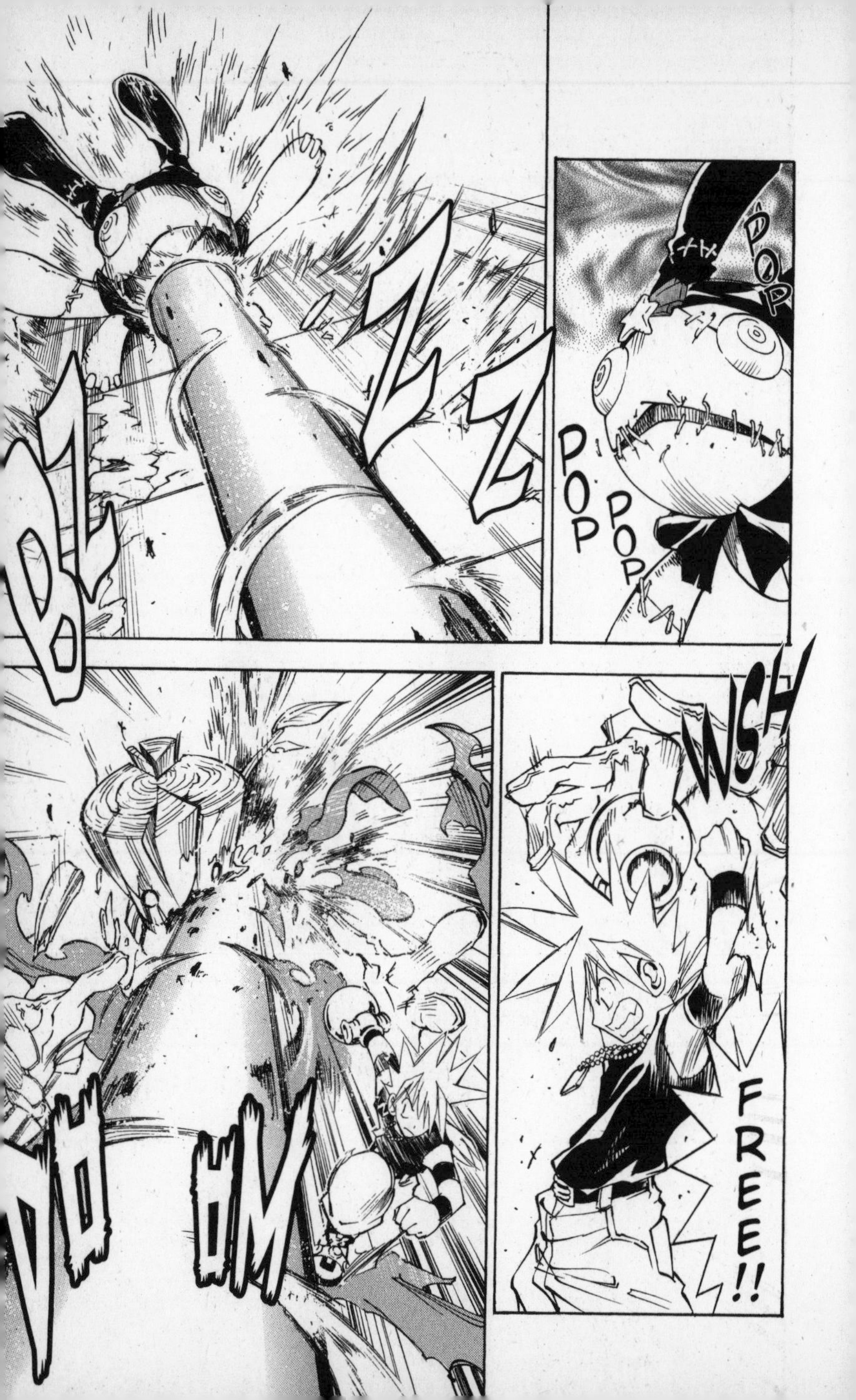
POP POP
POP POP POP
WSH
FREE!!

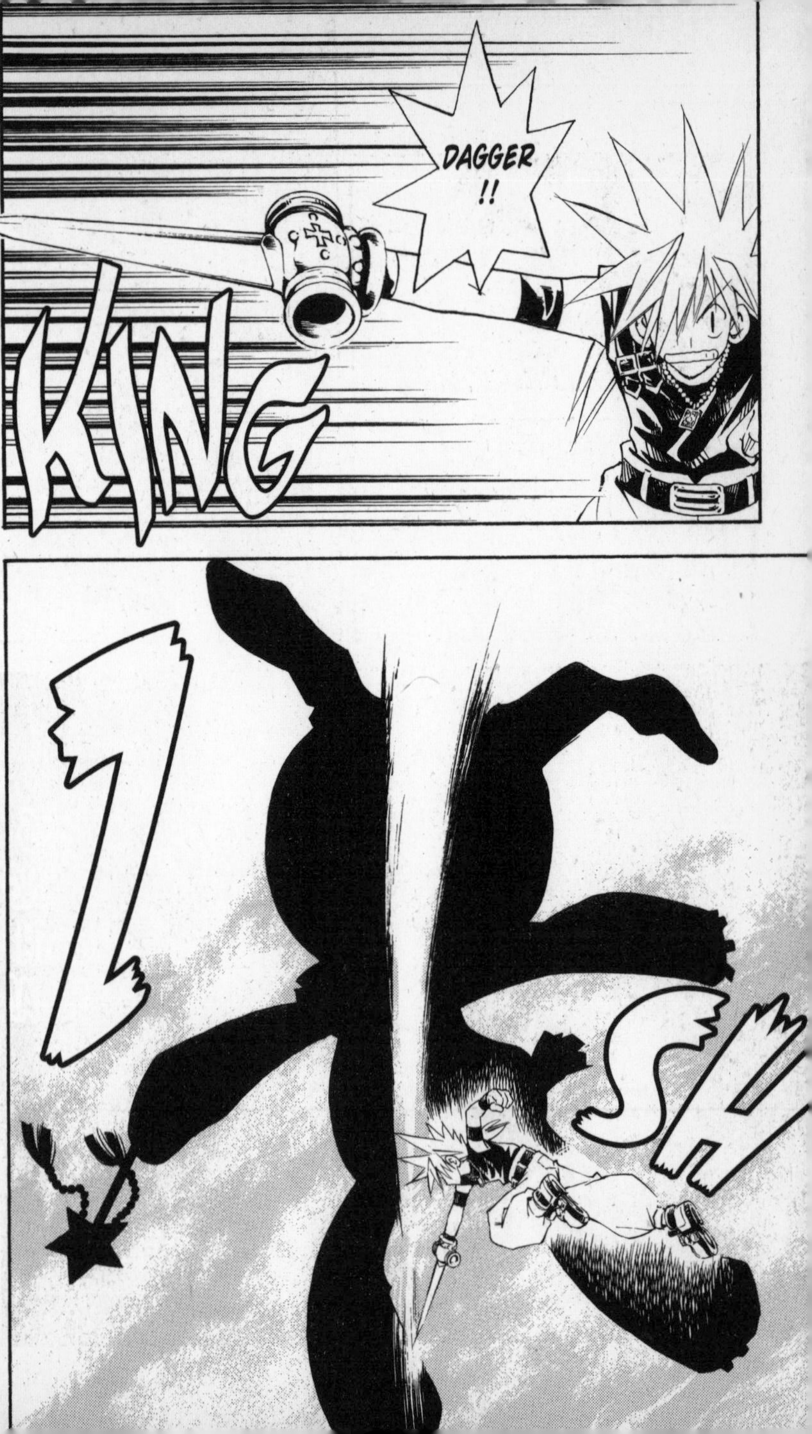
DAGGER !!
KING

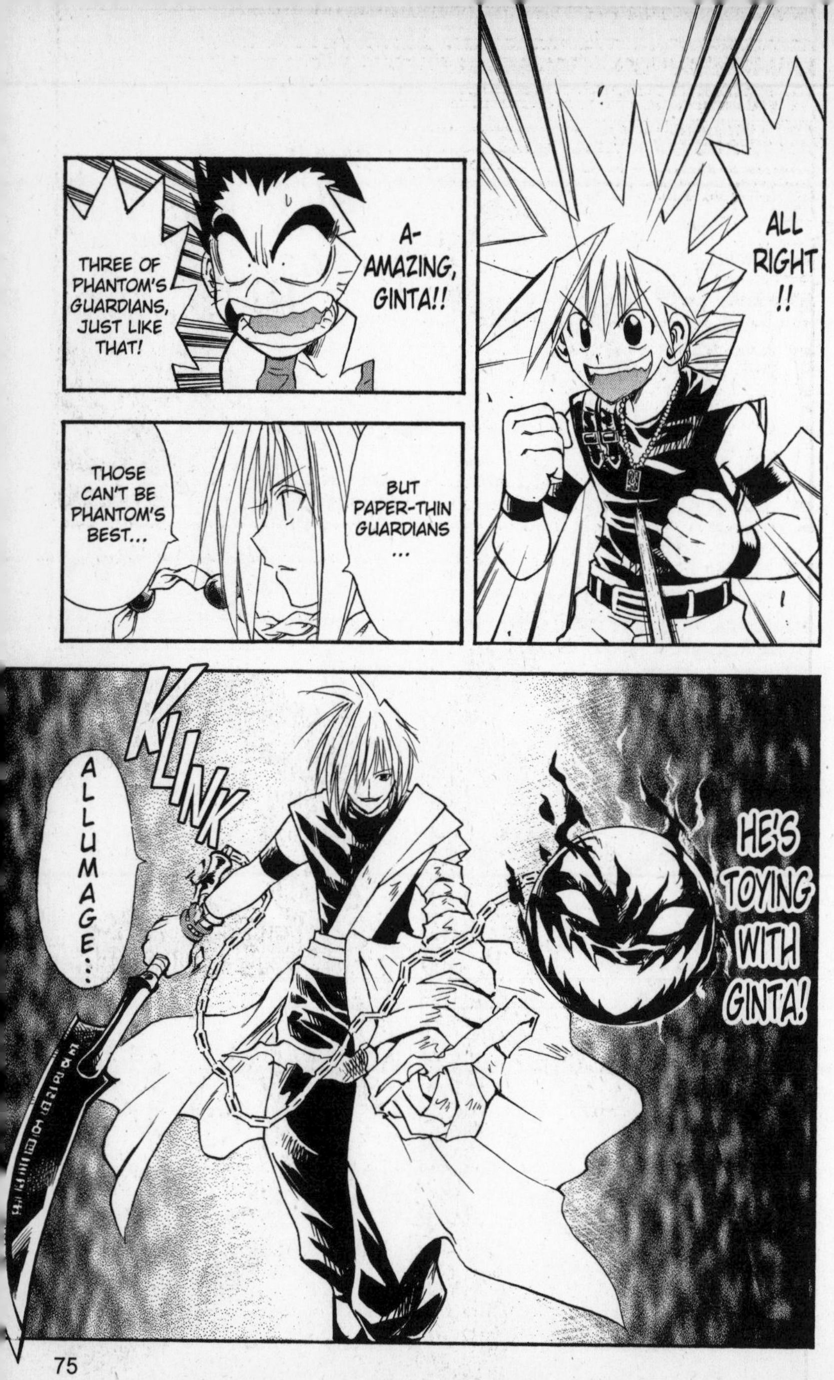
ALL RIGHT!!
A-AMAZING, GINTA!!
THREE OF PHANTOM'S GUARDIANS, JUST LIKE THAT!
BUT PAPER-THIN GUARDIANS...
THOSE CAN'T BE PHANTOM'S BEST...
HE'S TOYING WITH GINTA!
KLINK
ALLUMAGE...

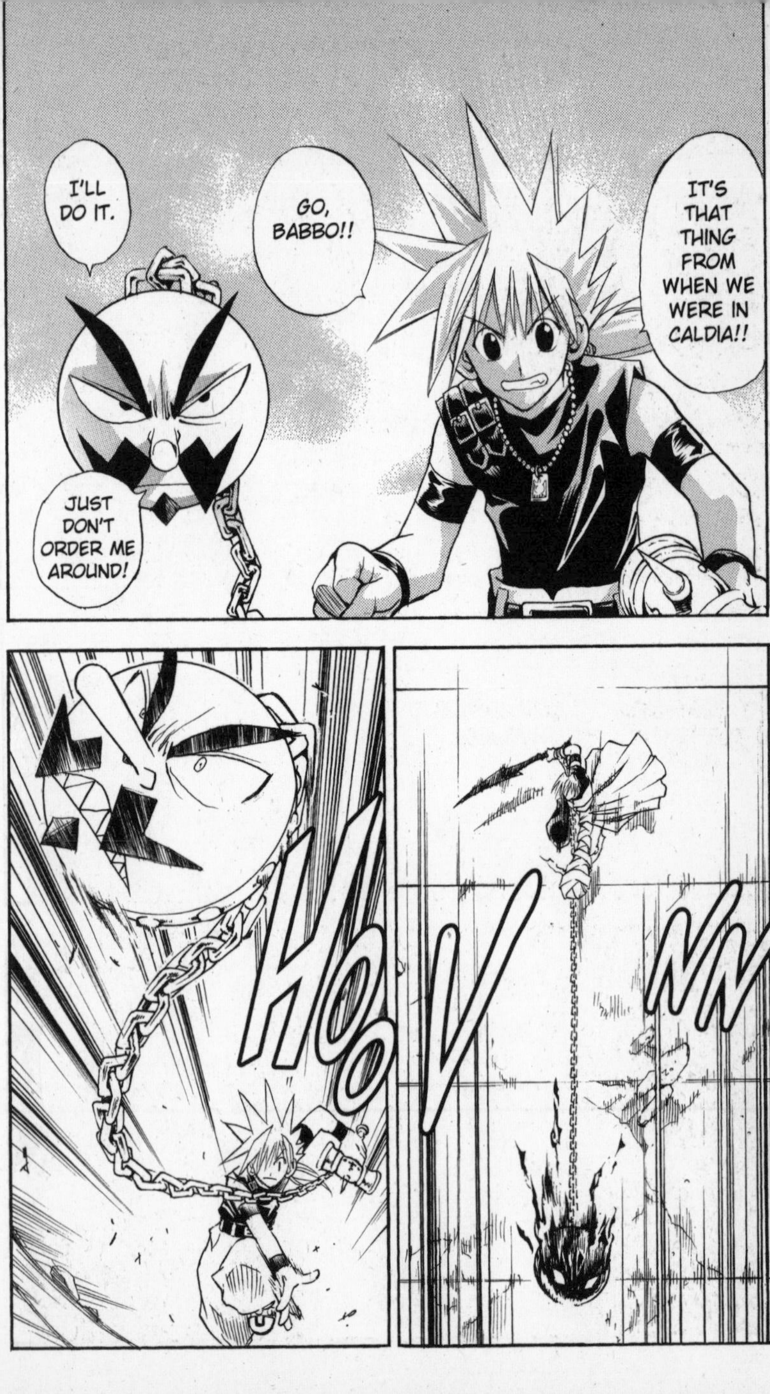
IT'S THAT THING FROM WHEN WE WERE IN CALDIA!!
GO, BABBO!!
I'LL DO IT.
JUST DON'T ORDER ME AROUND!
HOOVNN

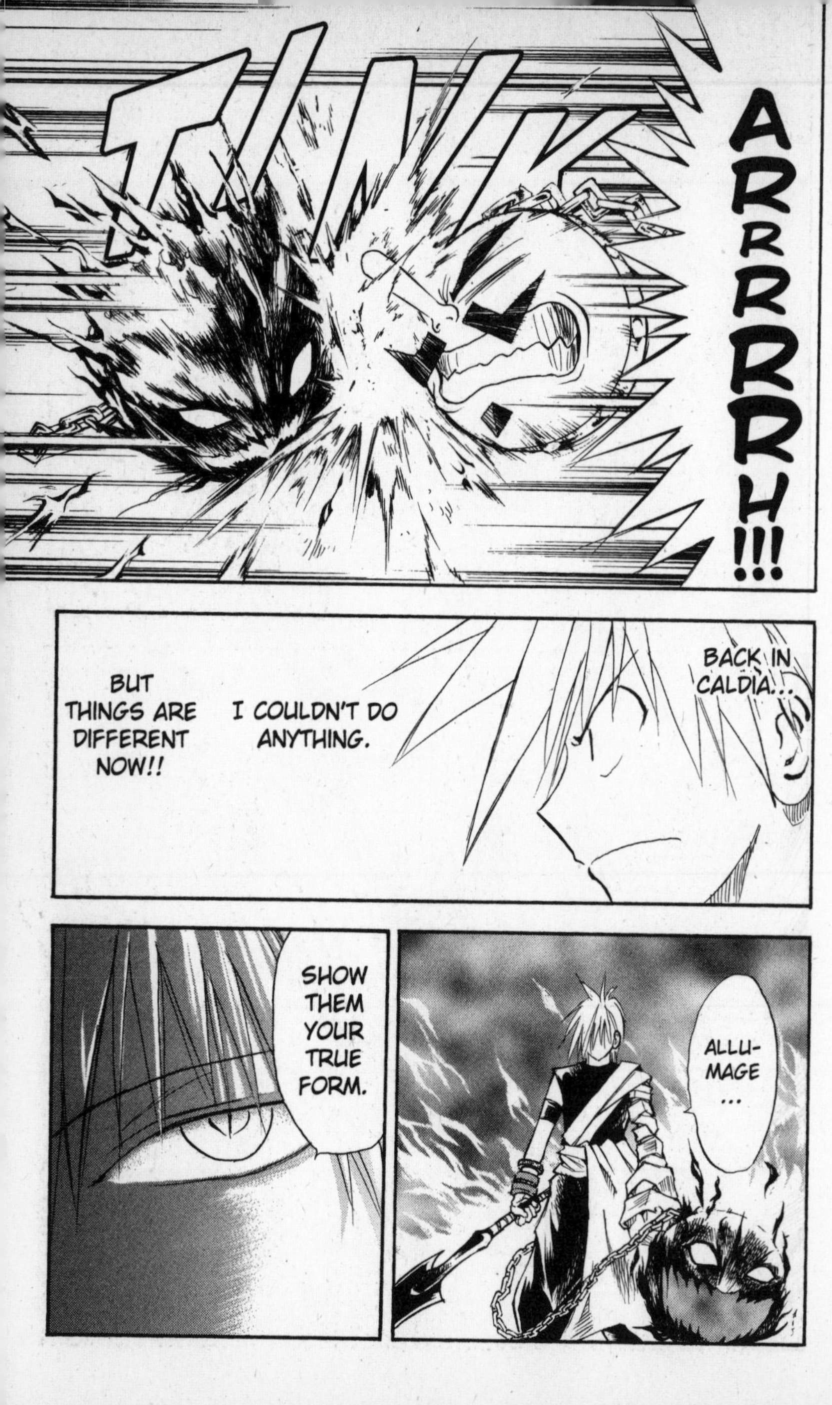
ARRRRRH!!!
BACK IN CALDIA...
I COULDN'T DO ANYTHING.
BUT THINGS ARE DIFFERENT NOW!!
ALLU-MAGE...
SHOW THEM YOUR TRUE FORM.

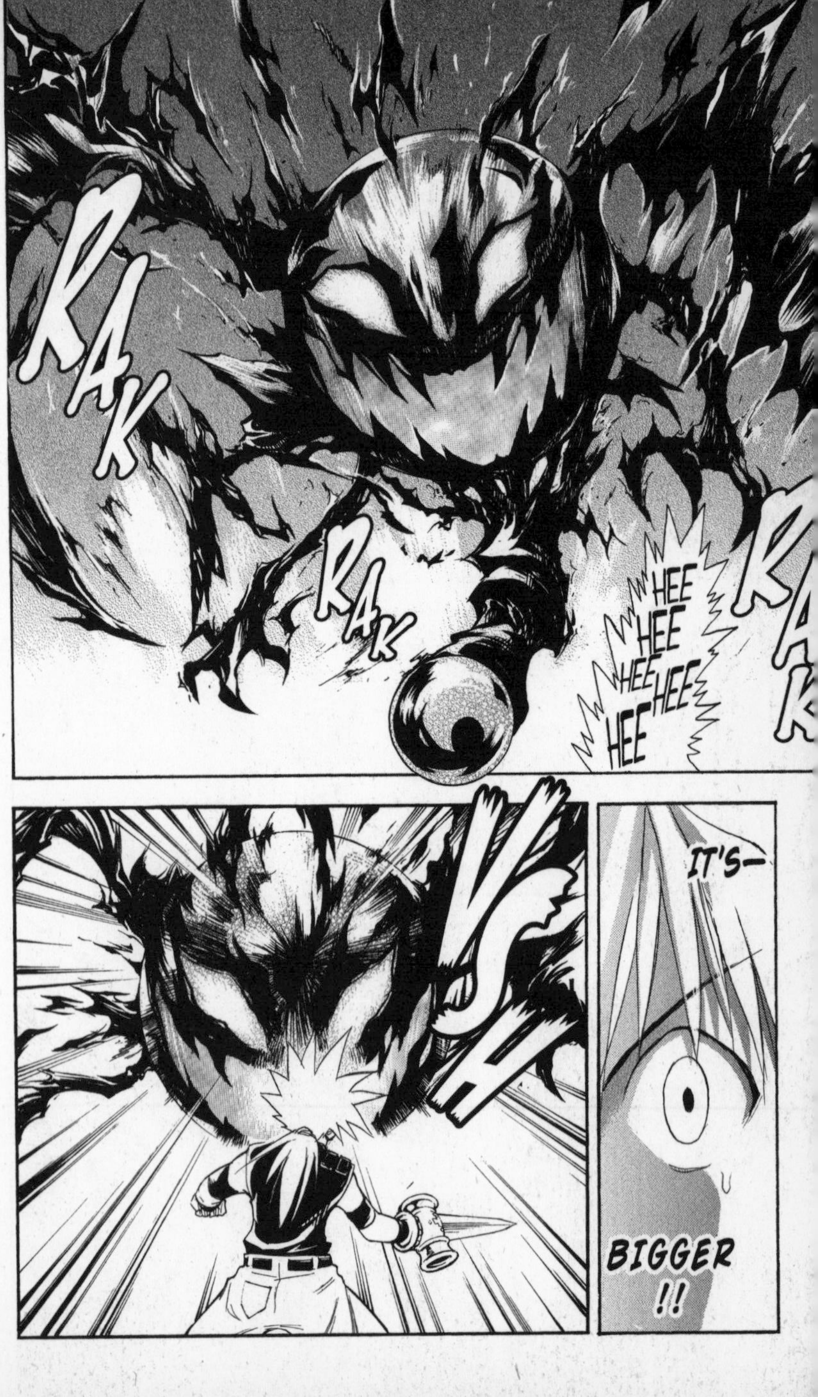
RAK
HEE HEE HEE HEE HEE HEE
RAK
RAK
IT'S—
BIGGER !!
VSH

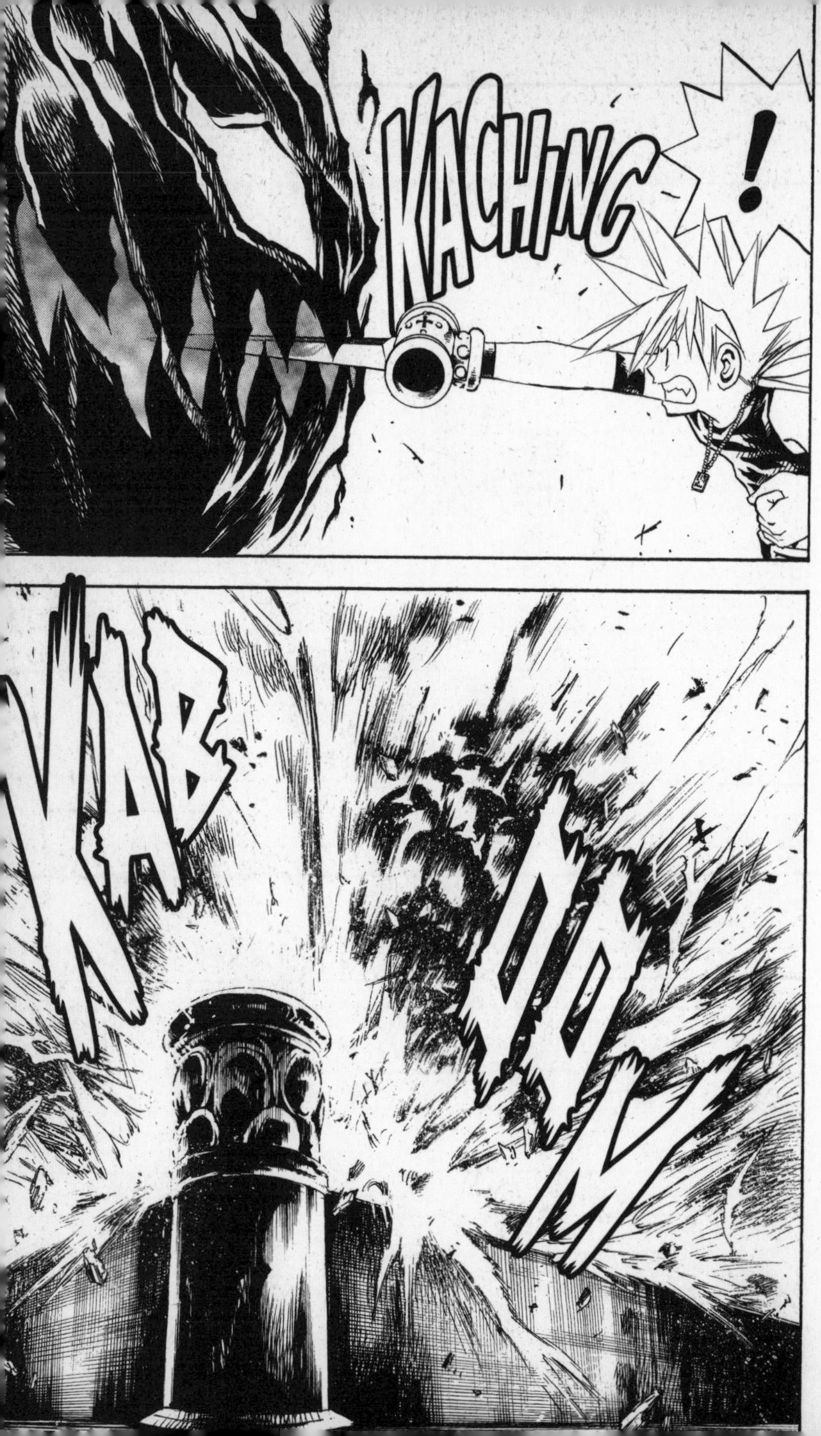
KACHING !
KAB

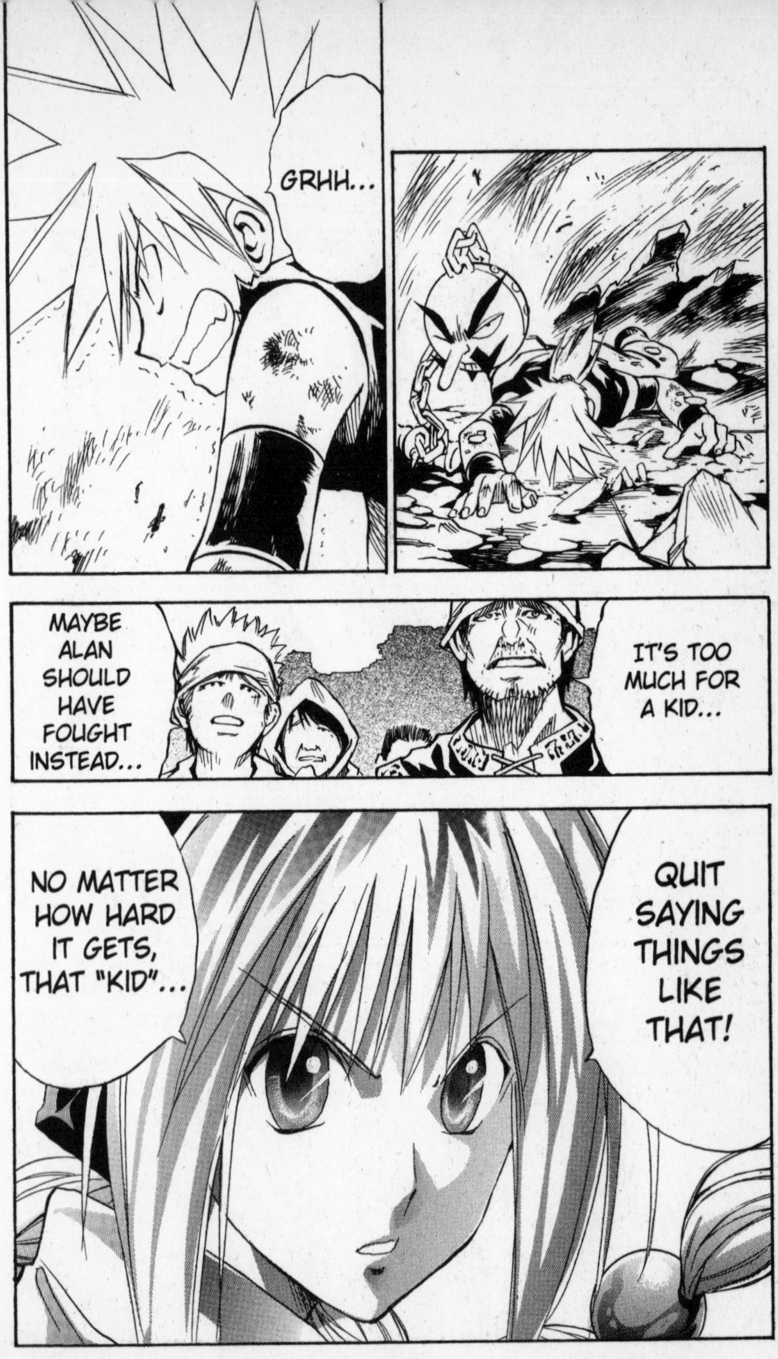
GRHH...
IT'S TOO MUCH FOR A KID...
MAYBE ALAN SHOULD HAVE FOUGHT INSTEAD...
QUIT SAYING THINGS LIKE THAT!
NO MATTER HOW HARD IT GETS, THAT "KID"...

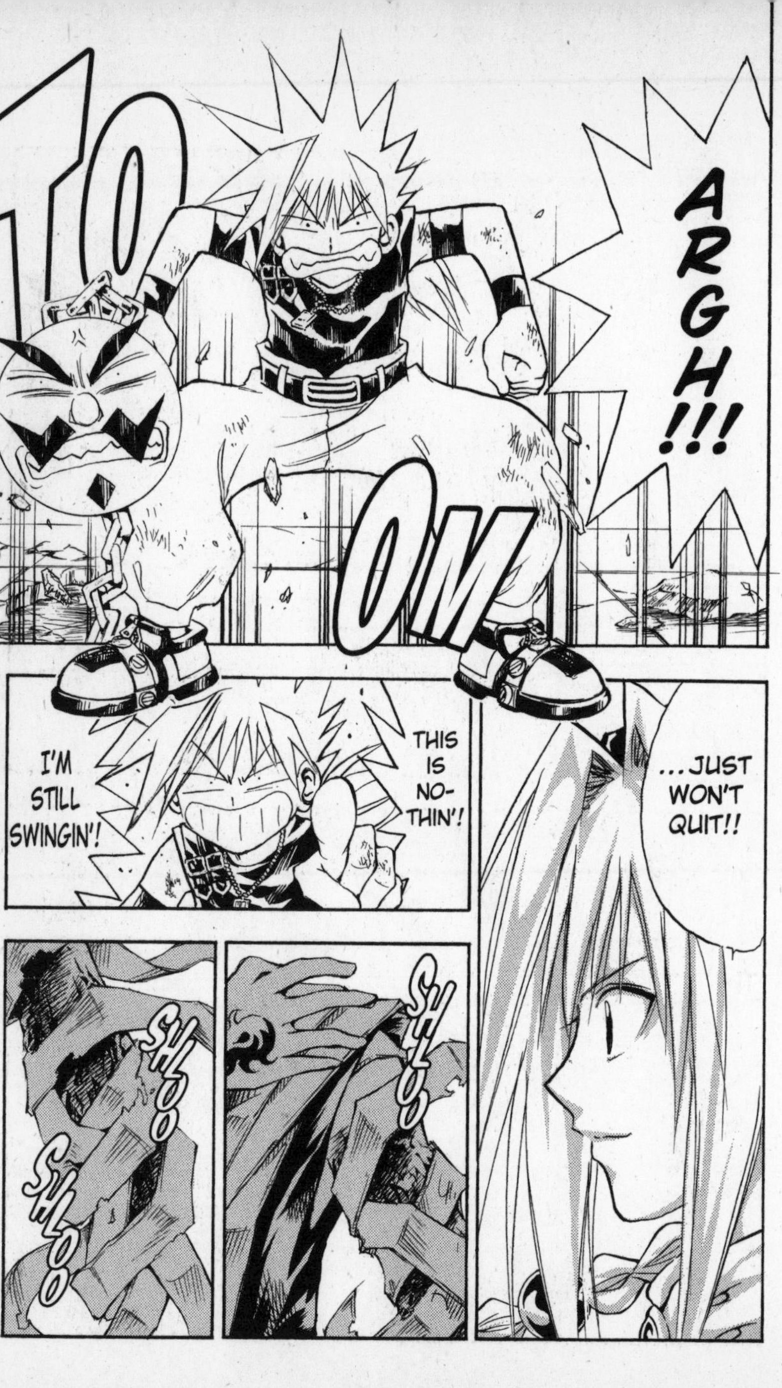
ARGH!!!
TO
OM
...JUST WON'T QUIT!!
THIS IS NO-THIN'!
I'M STILL SWINGIN'!
SHLOO
SHLOO
SHLOO

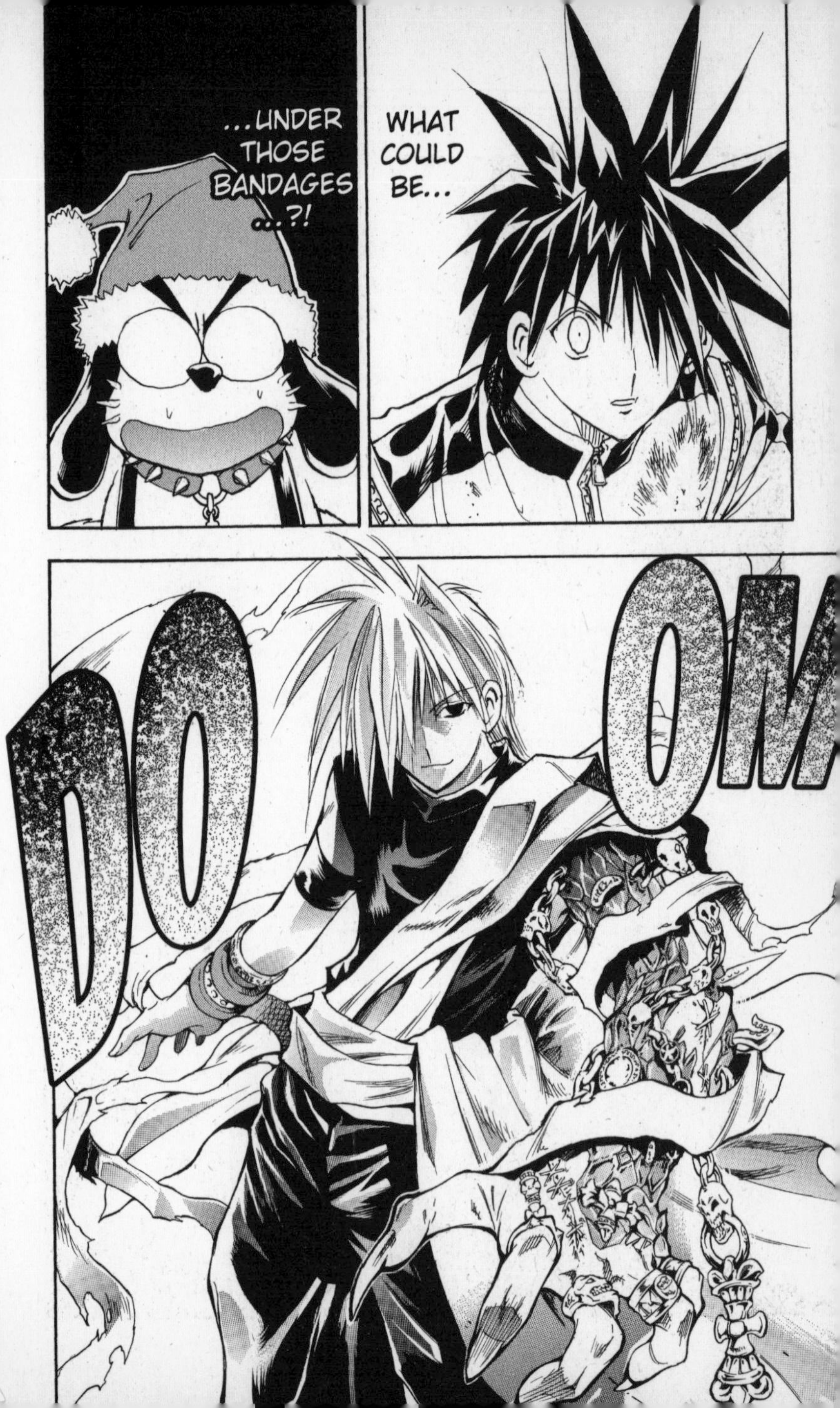
WHAT COULD BE...
...UNDER THOSE BANDAGES ...?!
DOOM

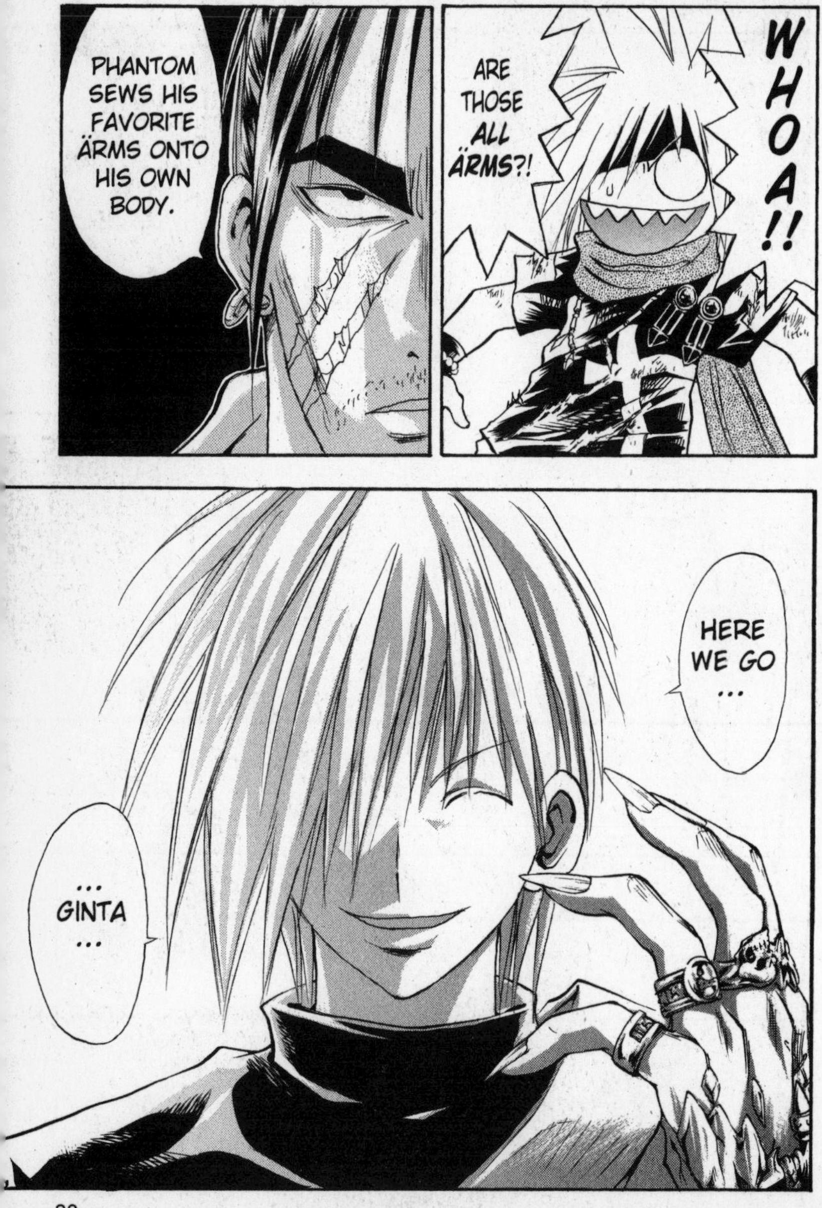
WHOA!!
ARE THOSE ALL ÄRMS?!
PHANTOM SEWS HIS FAVORITE ÄRMS ONTO HIS OWN BODY.
HERE WE GO ...
... GINTA ...

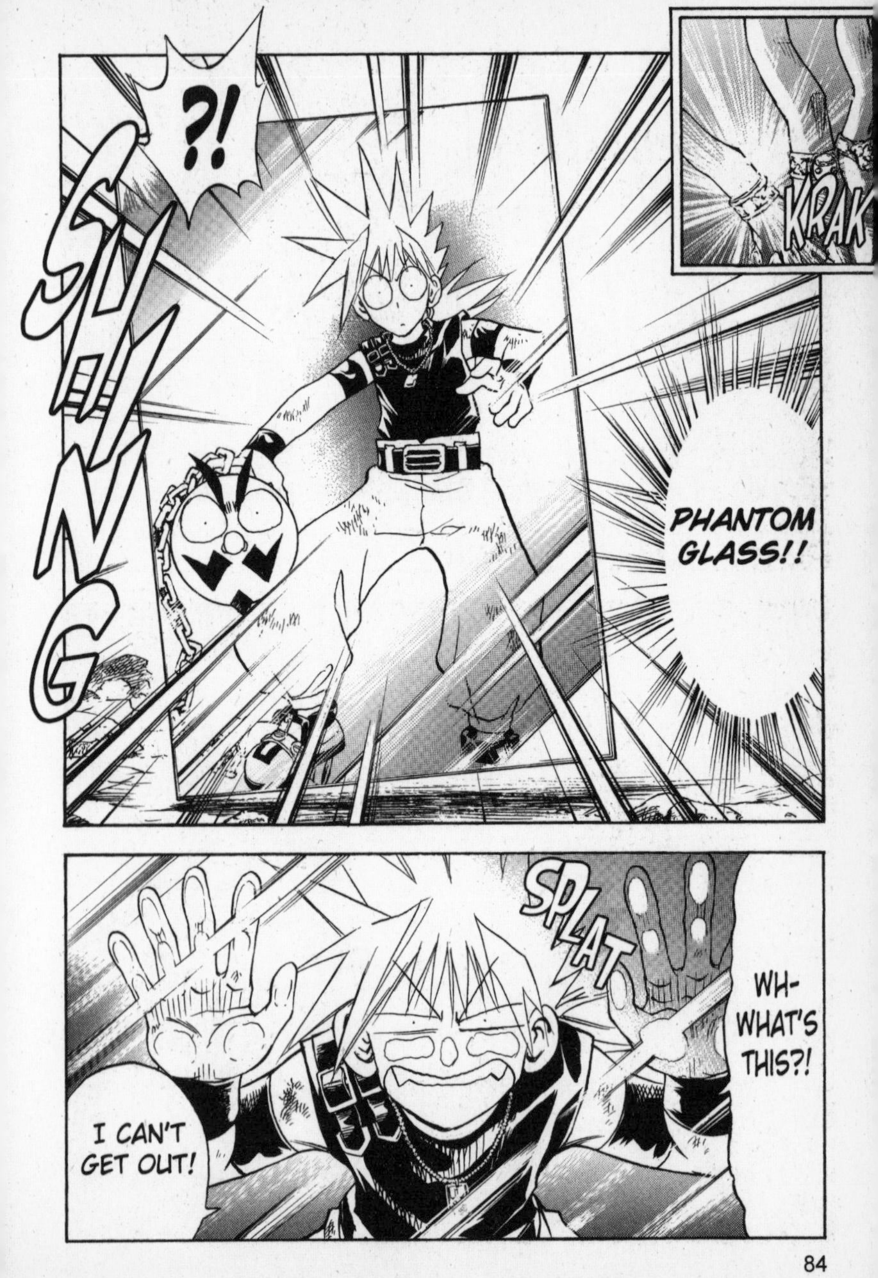
KRAK
?!
SHING
PHANTOM GLASS!!
SPLAT
WH- WHAT'S THIS?!
I CAN'T GET OUT!

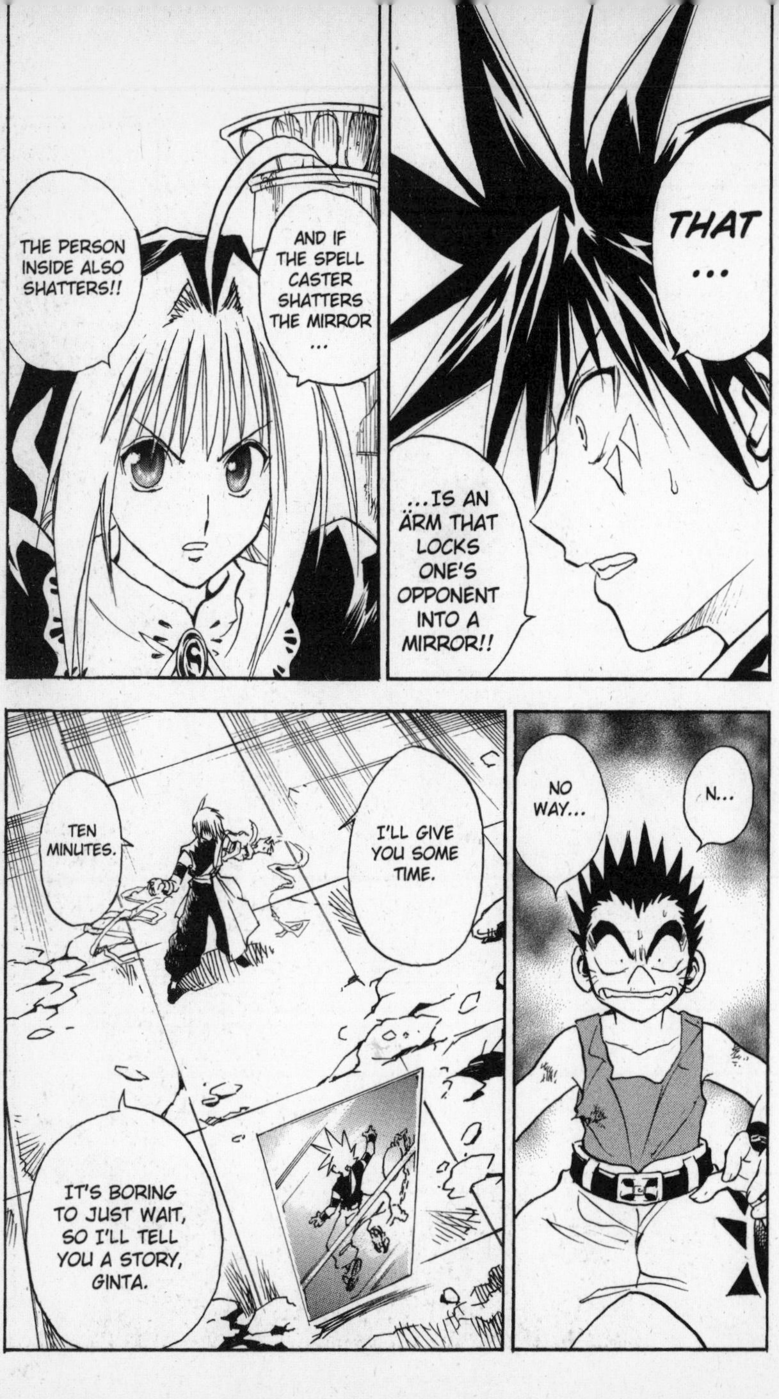
THAT ...
...IS AN ÄRM THAT LOCKS ONE'S OPPONENT INTO A MIRROR!!
AND IF THE SPELL CASTER SHATTERS THE MIRROR ...
THE PERSON INSIDE ALSO SHATTERS!!
N...
NO WAY...
I'LL GIVE YOU SOME TIME.
TEN MINUTES.
IT'S BORING TO JUST WAIT, SO I'LL TELL YOU A STORY, GINTA.

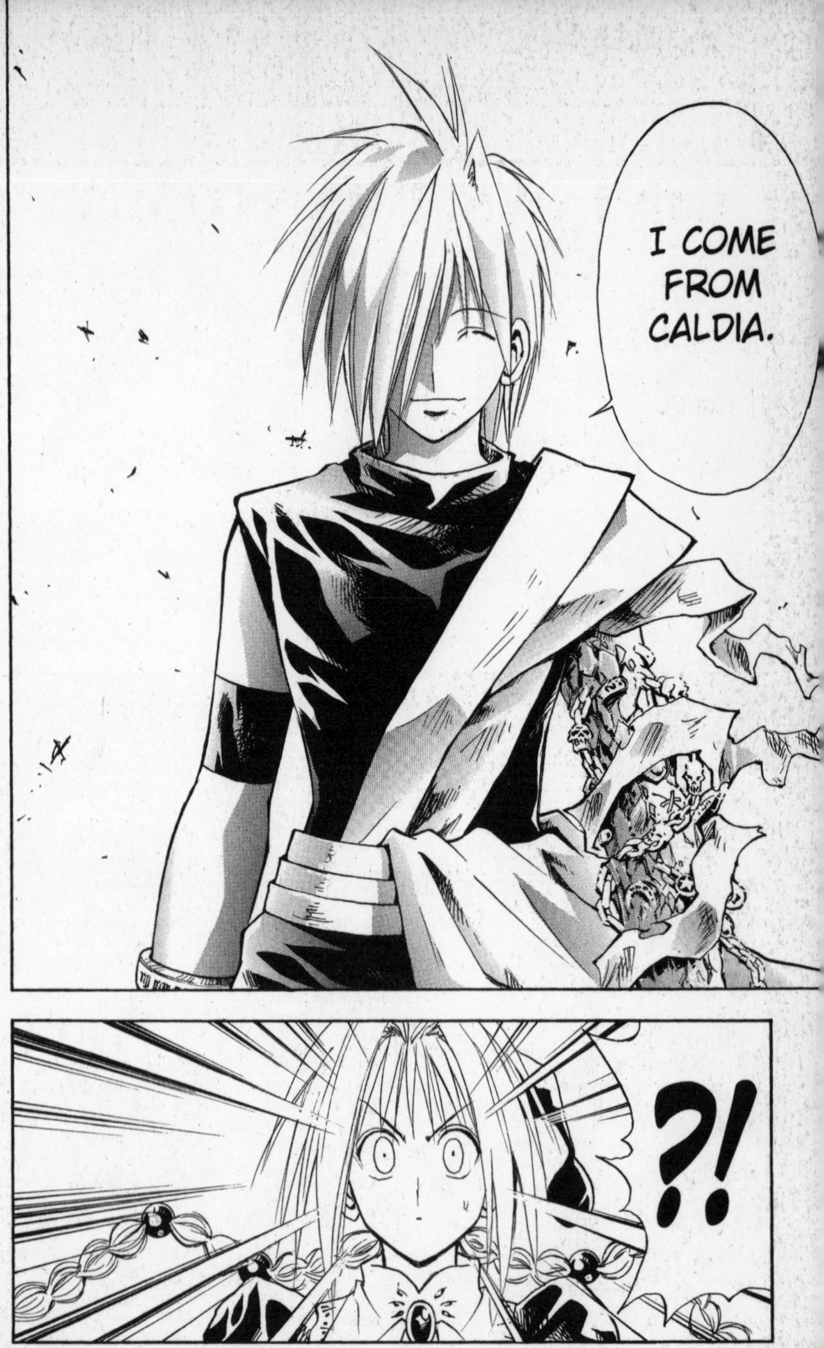
I COME FROM CALDIA.
?!

AKT.146/ FINAL BATTLE OF THE WAR GAMES

GINTA VS. PHANTOM ③

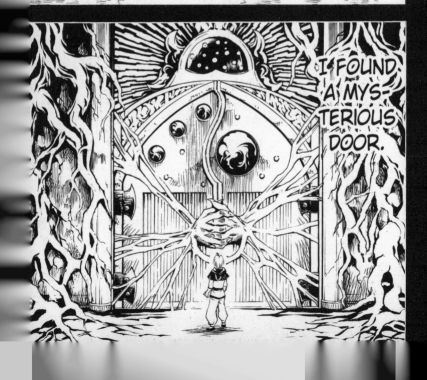

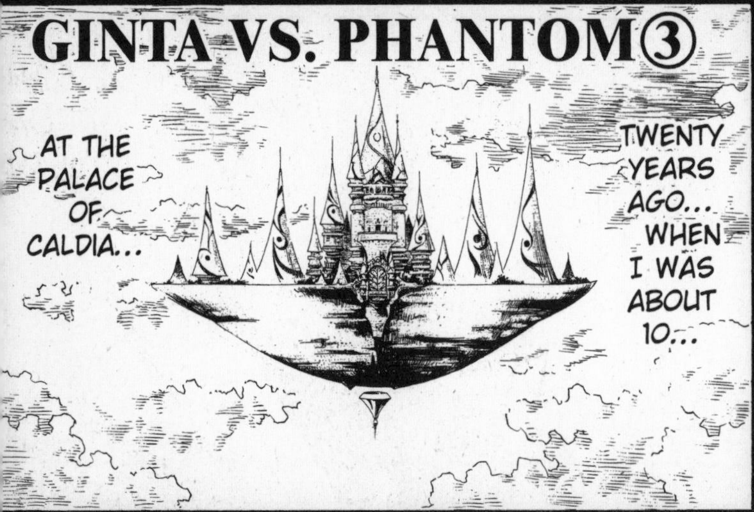
TWENTY YEARS AGO... WHEN I WAS ABOUT 10...
AT THE PALACE OF CALDIA...

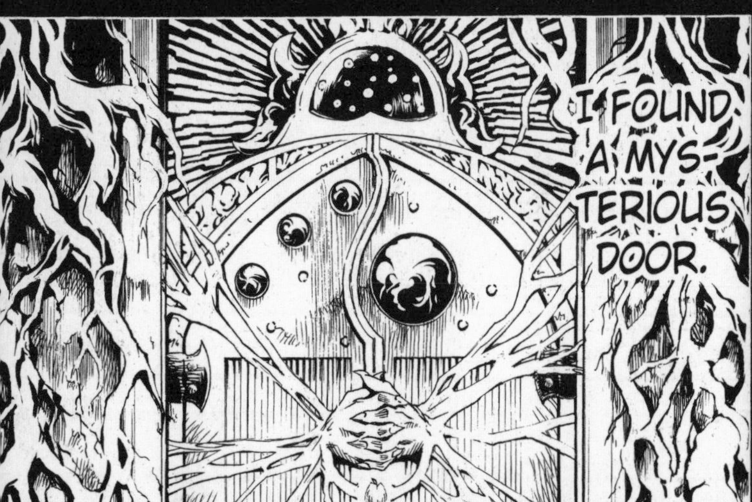
I FOUND A MYS-TERIOUS DOOR.

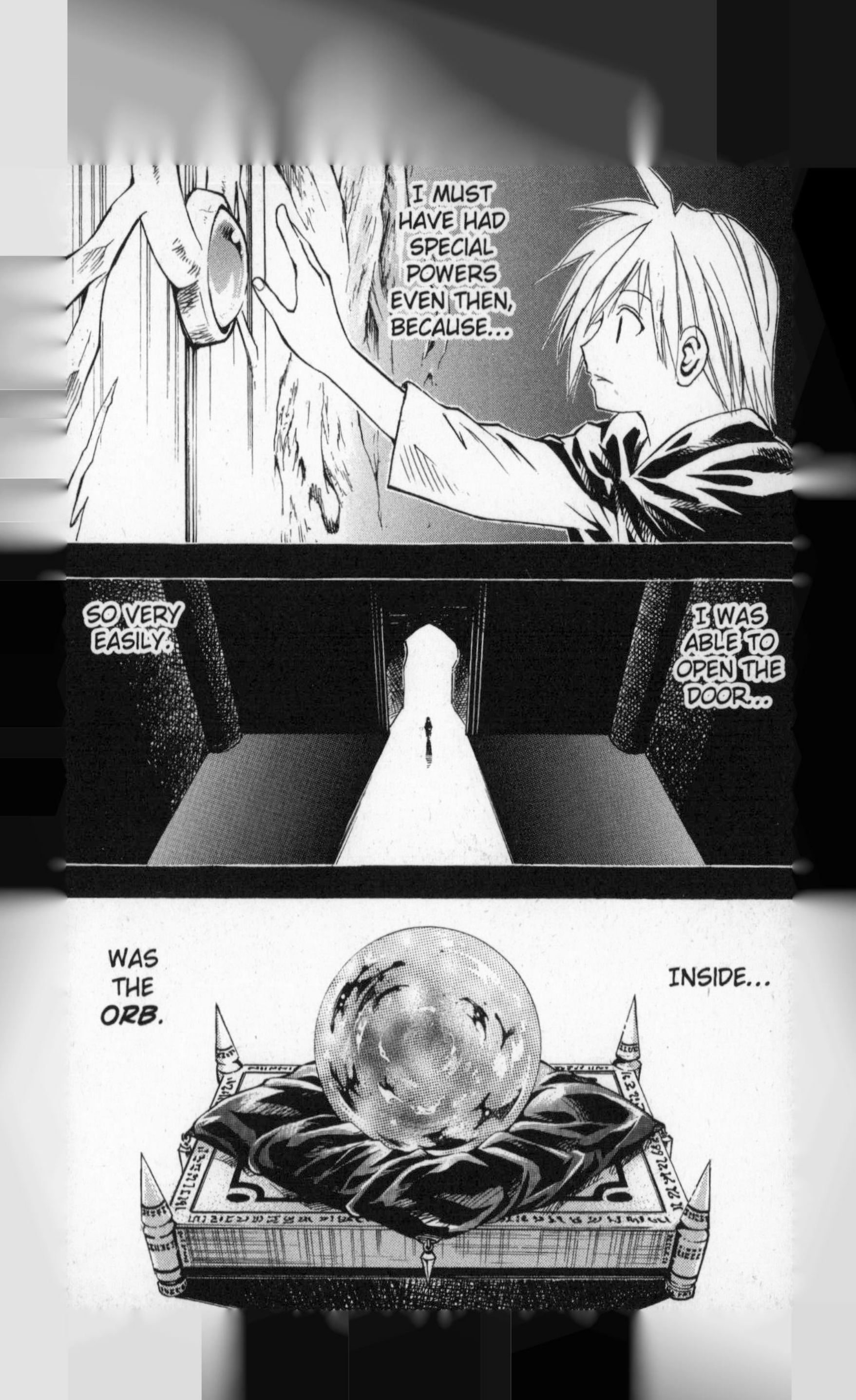
I MUST HAVE HAD SPECIAL POWERS EVEN THEN, BECAUSE...
I WAS ABLE TO OPEN THE DOOR...
SO VERY EASILY.
INSIDE...
WAS THE ORB.

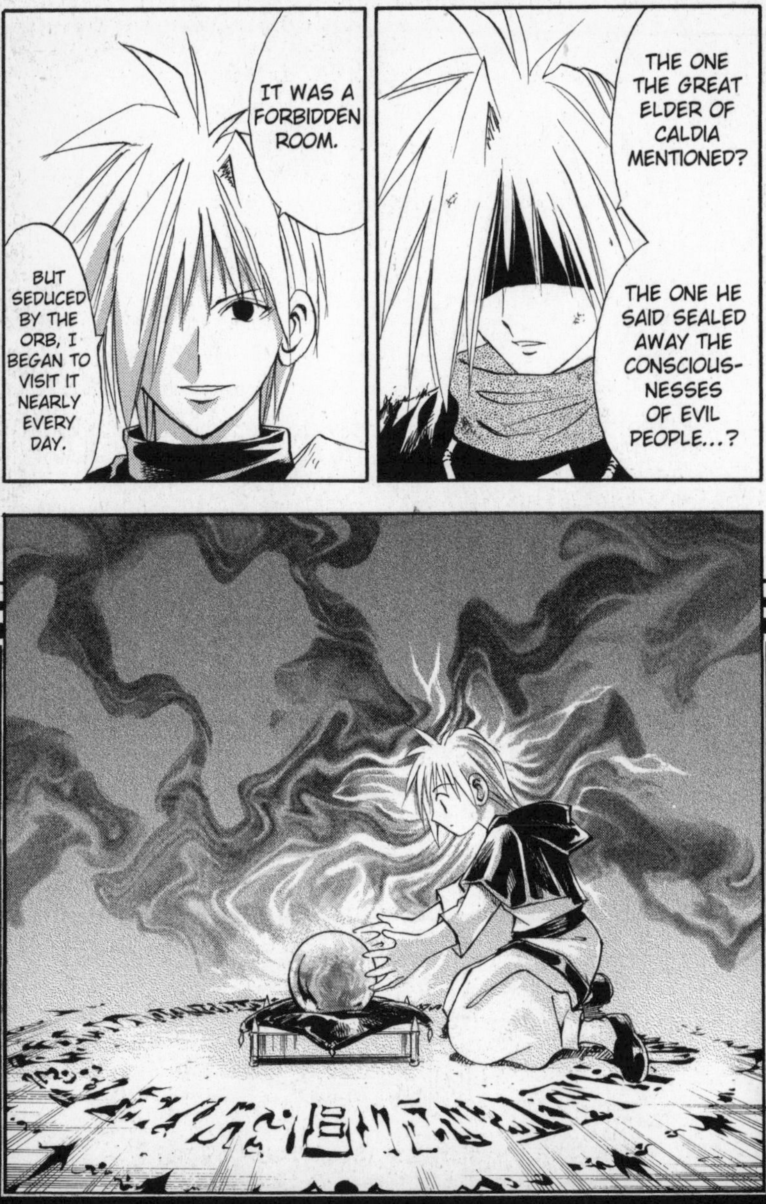
THE ONE THE GREAT ELDER OF CALDIA MENTIONED?
THE ONE HE SAID SEALED AWAY THE CONSCIOUS-NESSES OF EVIL PEOPLE...?
IT WAS A FORBIDDEN ROOM.
BUT SEDUCED BY THE ORB, I BEGAN TO VISIT IT NEARLY EVERY DAY.

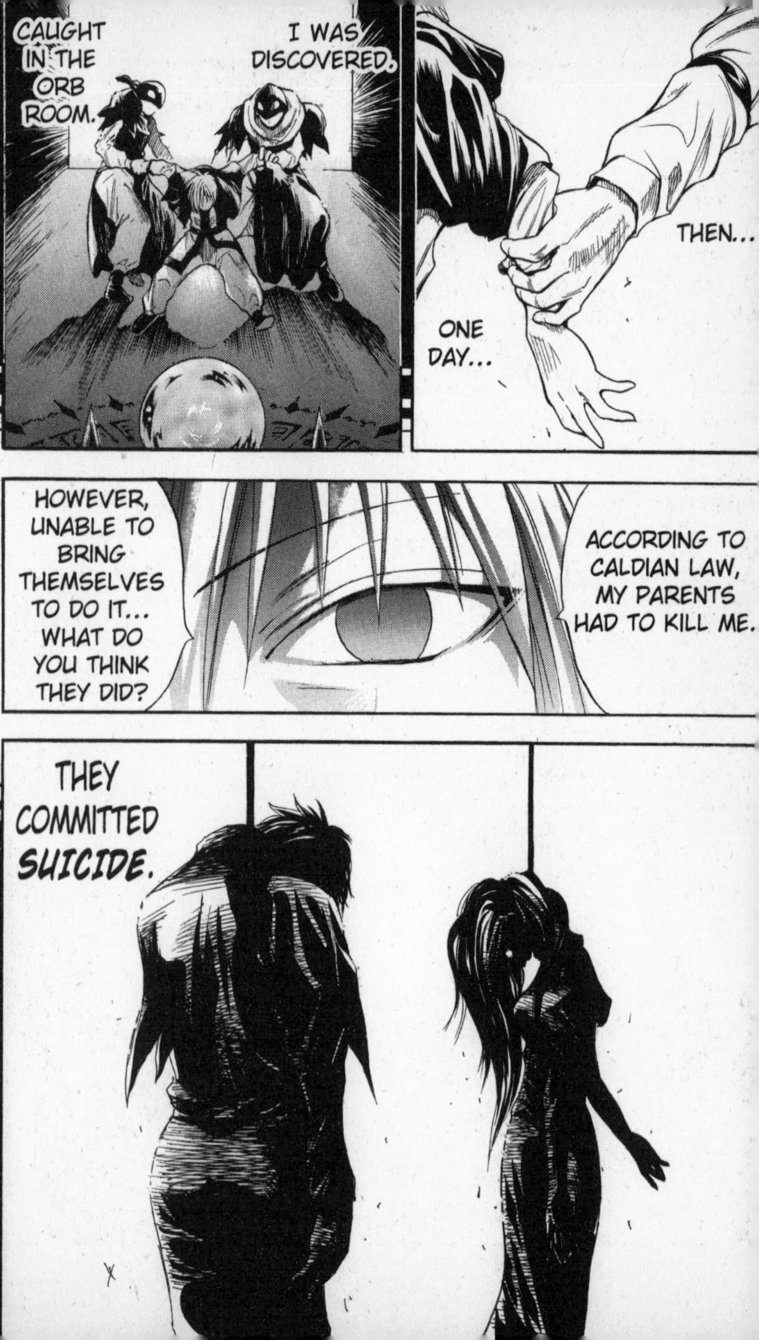
THEN...
ONE DAY...
I WAS DISCOVERED.
CAUGHT IN THE ORB ROOM.
ACCORDING TO CALDIAN LAW, MY PARENTS HAD TO KILL ME.
HOWEVER, UNABLE TO BRING THEMSELVES TO DO IT... WHAT DO YOU THINK THEY DID?
THEY COMMITTED SUICIDE.

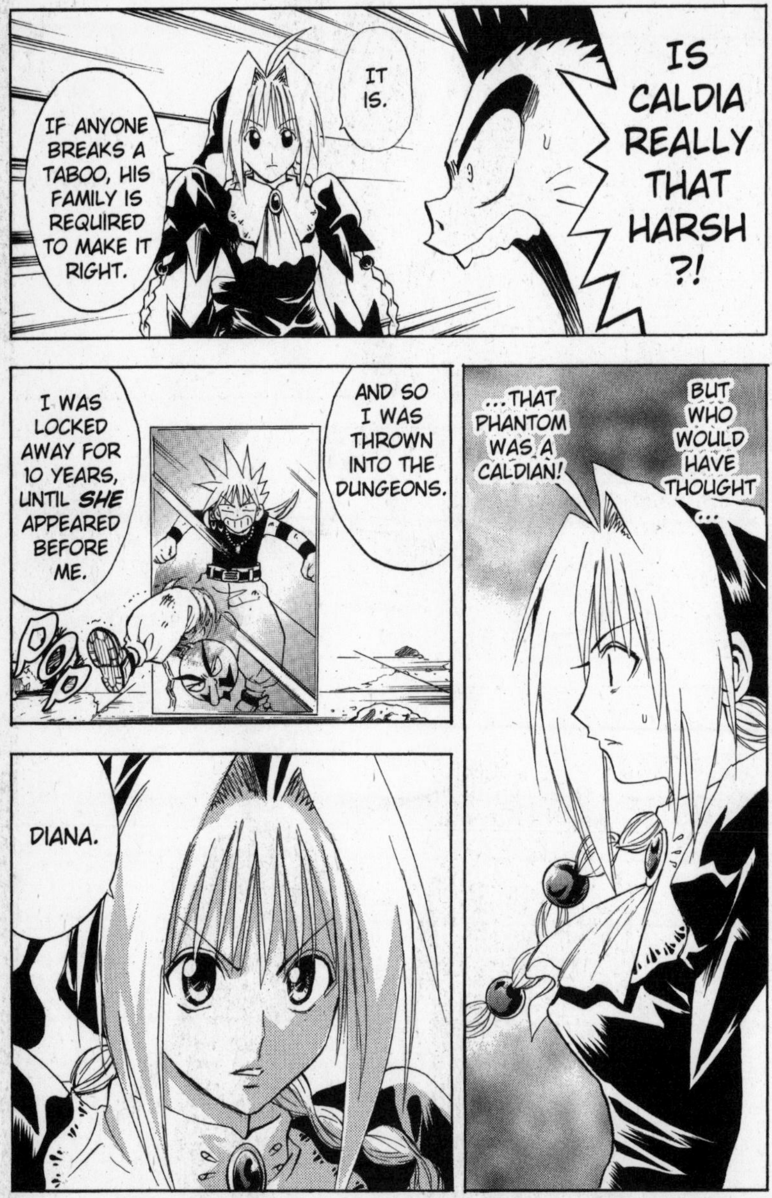
IS CALDIA REALLY THAT HARSH?!
IT IS.
IF ANYONE BREAKS A TABOO, HIS FAMILY IS REQUIRED TO MAKE IT RIGHT.
BUT WHO WOULD HAVE THOUGHT...
...THAT PHANTOM WAS A CALDIAN!
AND SO I WAS THROWN INTO THE DUNGEONS.
I WAS LOCKED AWAY FOR 10 YEARS, UNTIL *SHE* APPEARED BEFORE ME.
POP
DIANA.

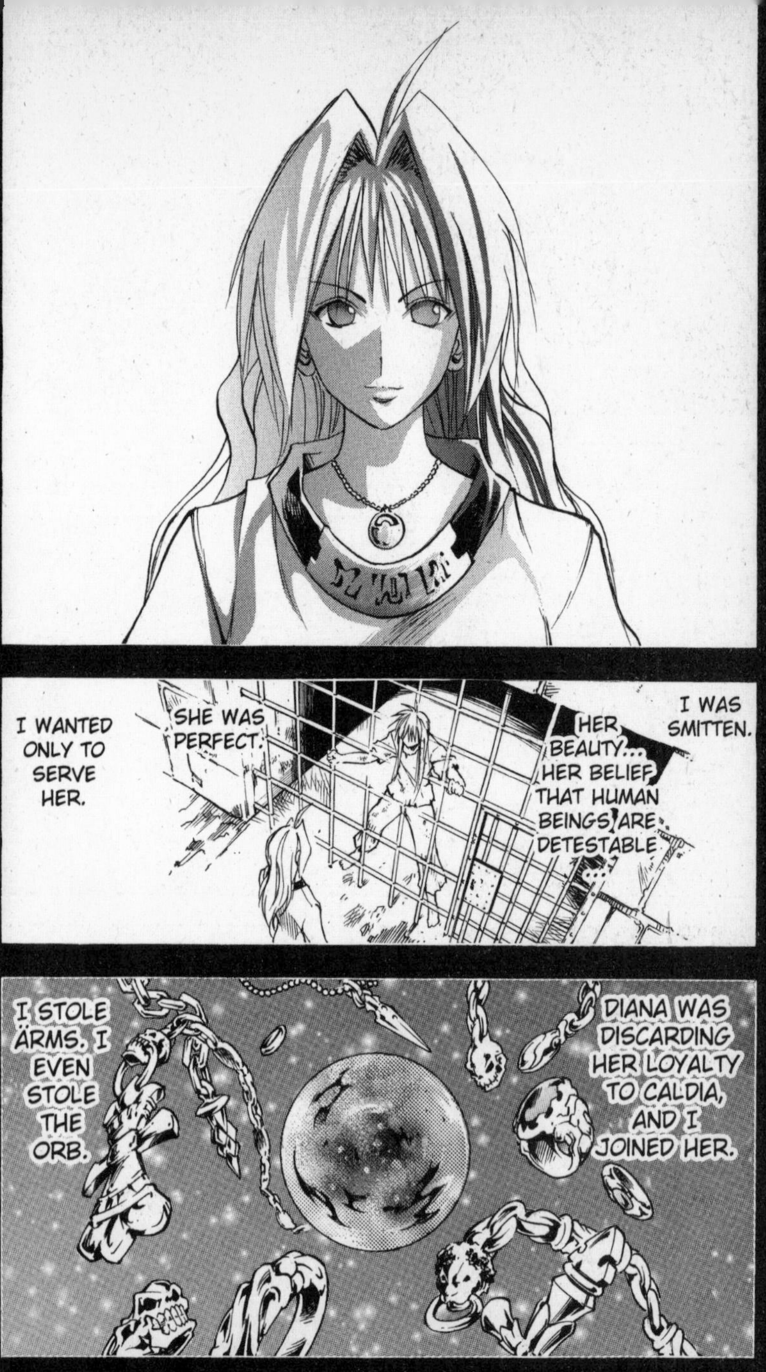
I WAS SMITTEN.
HER BEAUTY... HER BELIEF THAT HUMAN BEINGS ARE DETESTABLE...
SHE WAS PERFECT.
I WANTED ONLY TO SERVE HER.
DIANA WAS DISCARDING HER LOYALTY TO CALDIA, AND I JOINED HER.
I STOLE ÄRMS. I EVEN STOLE THE ORB.

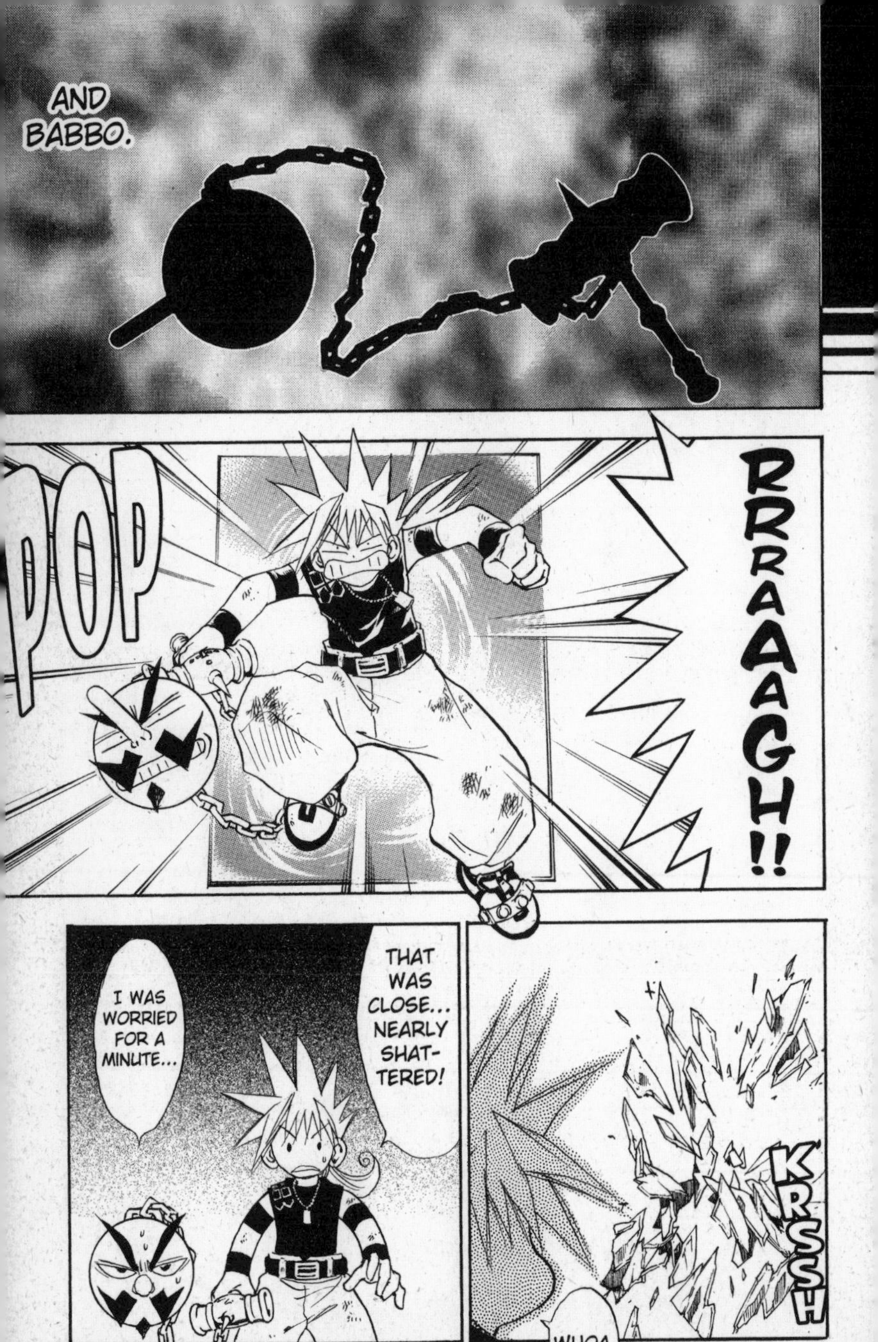
AND BABBO.
RRRAAAGH!!
POP
KRSSH
WHOA.
THAT WAS CLOSE... NEARLY SHATTERED!
I WAS WORRIED FOR A MINUTE...

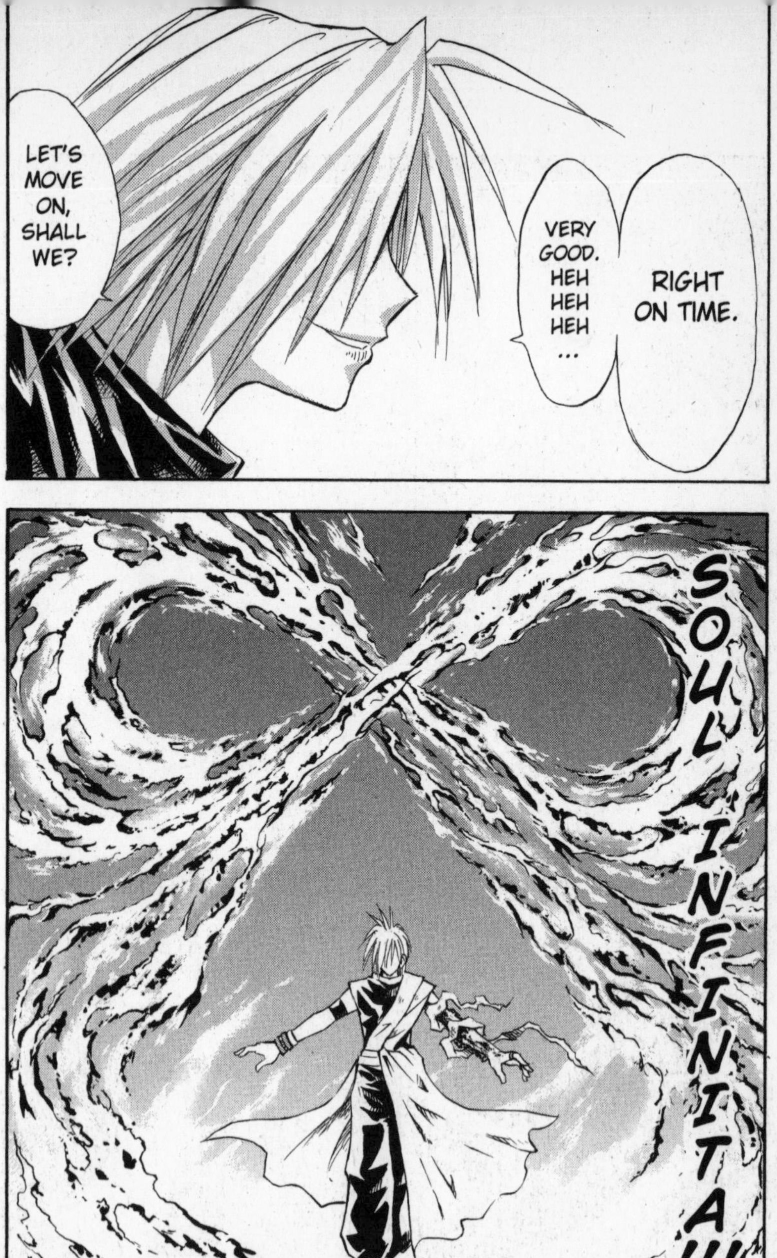
RIGHT ON TIME.
VERY GOOD. HEH HEH HEH...
LET'S MOVE ON, SHALL WE?
SOUL INFINITA!!!

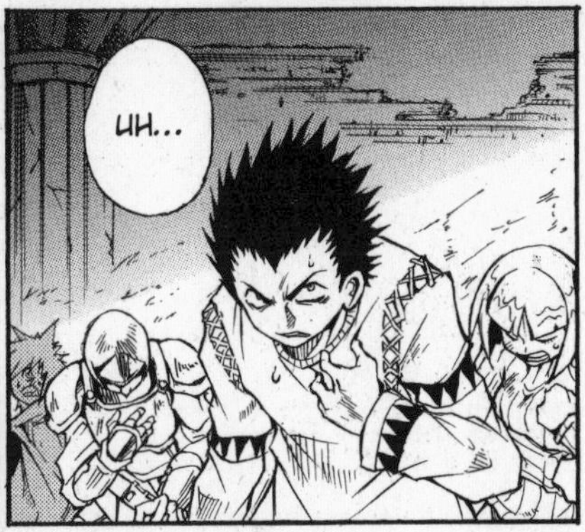
UH...

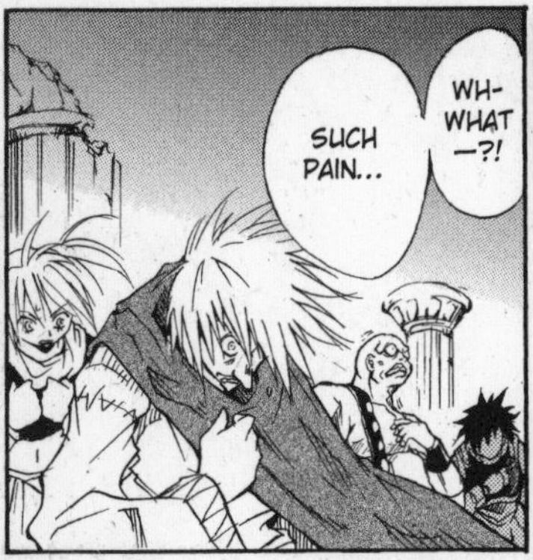
WH-WHAT—?!
SUCH PAIN...

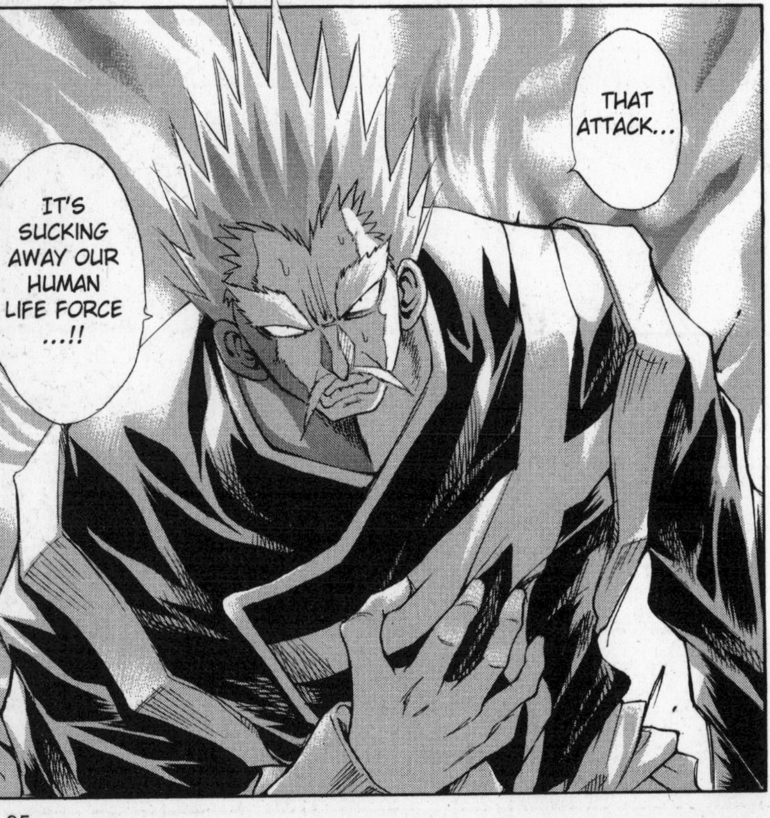
THAT ATTACK...
IT'S SUCKING AWAY OUR HUMAN LIFE FORCE ...!!

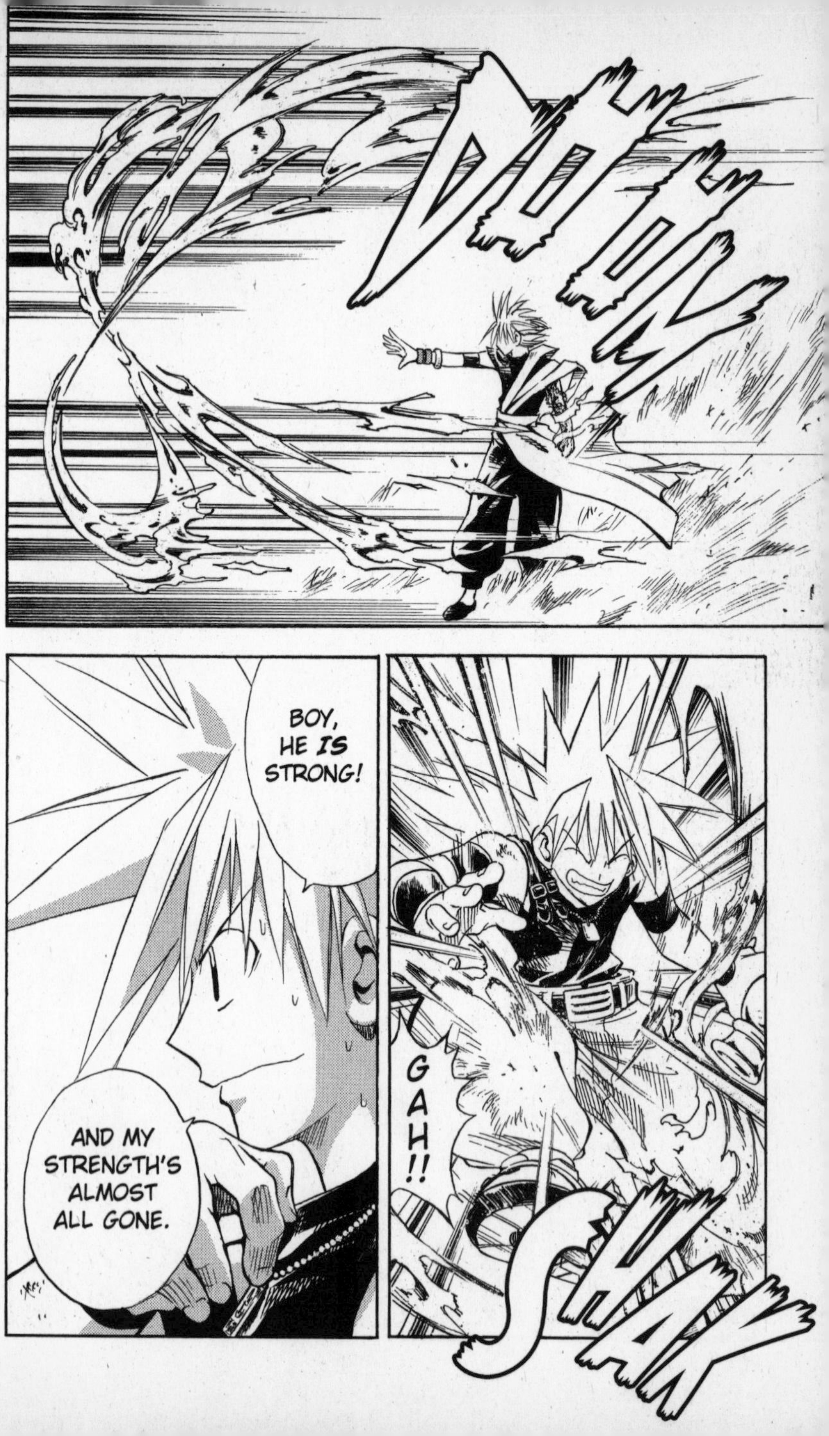
DOHN
GAH!!
SHAK
BOY, HE *IS* STRONG!
AND MY STRENGTH'S ALMOST ALL GONE.

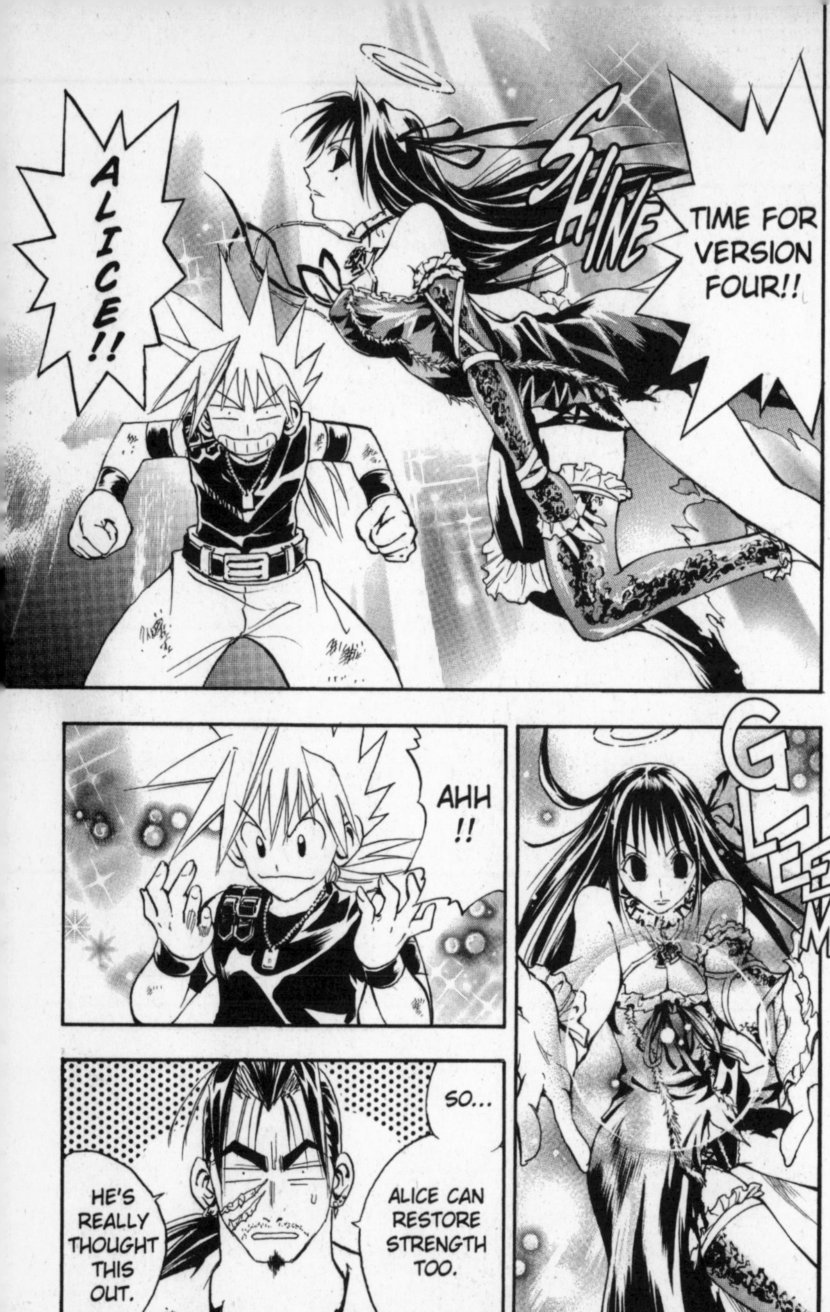
TIME FOR VERSION FOUR!!
SHINE
ALICE!!
GLEEM
AHH !!
SO...
ALICE CAN RESTORE STRENGTH TOO.
HE'S REALLY THOUGHT THIS OUT.

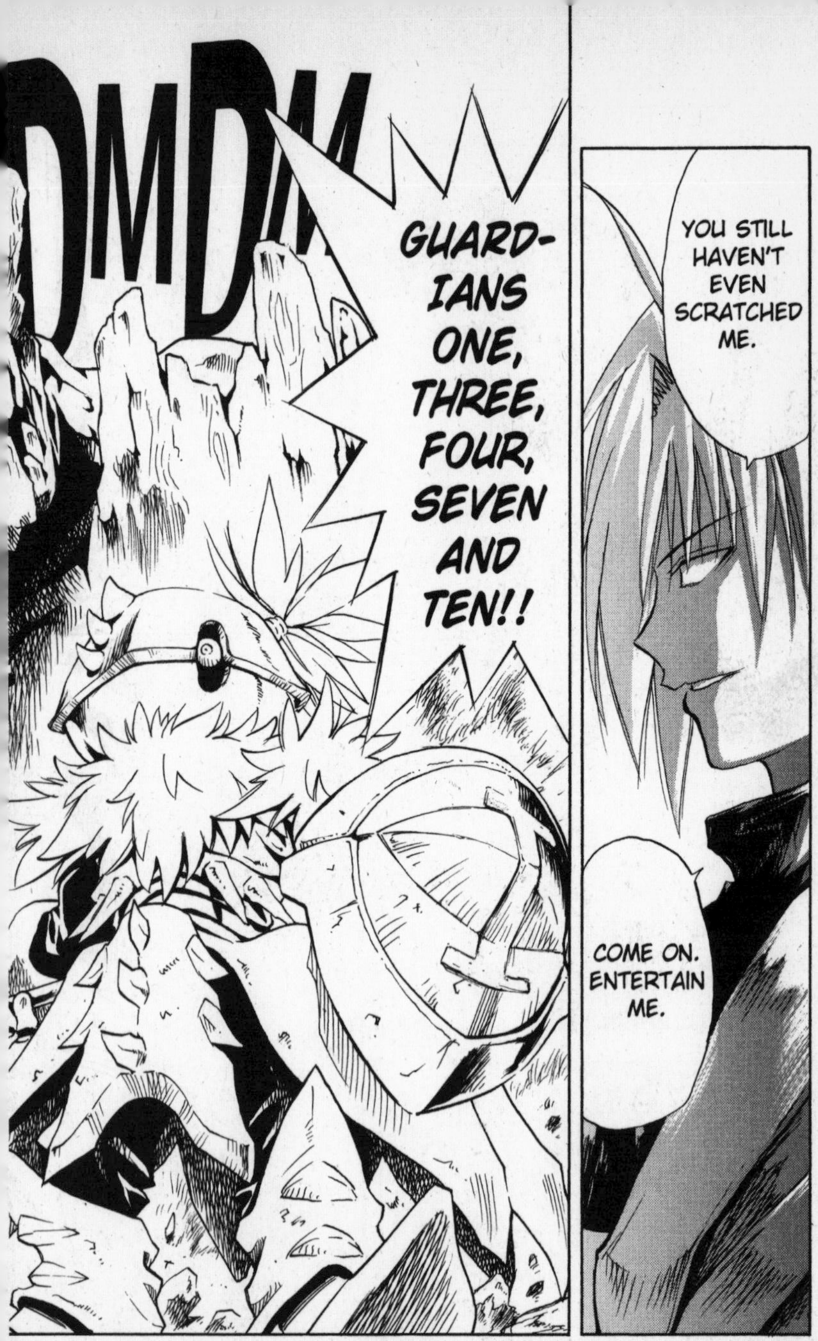
YOU STILL HAVEN'T EVEN SCRATCHED ME.
COME ON. ENTERTAIN ME.
DMDM
GUARD-IANS ONE, THREE, FOUR, SEVEN AND TEN!!

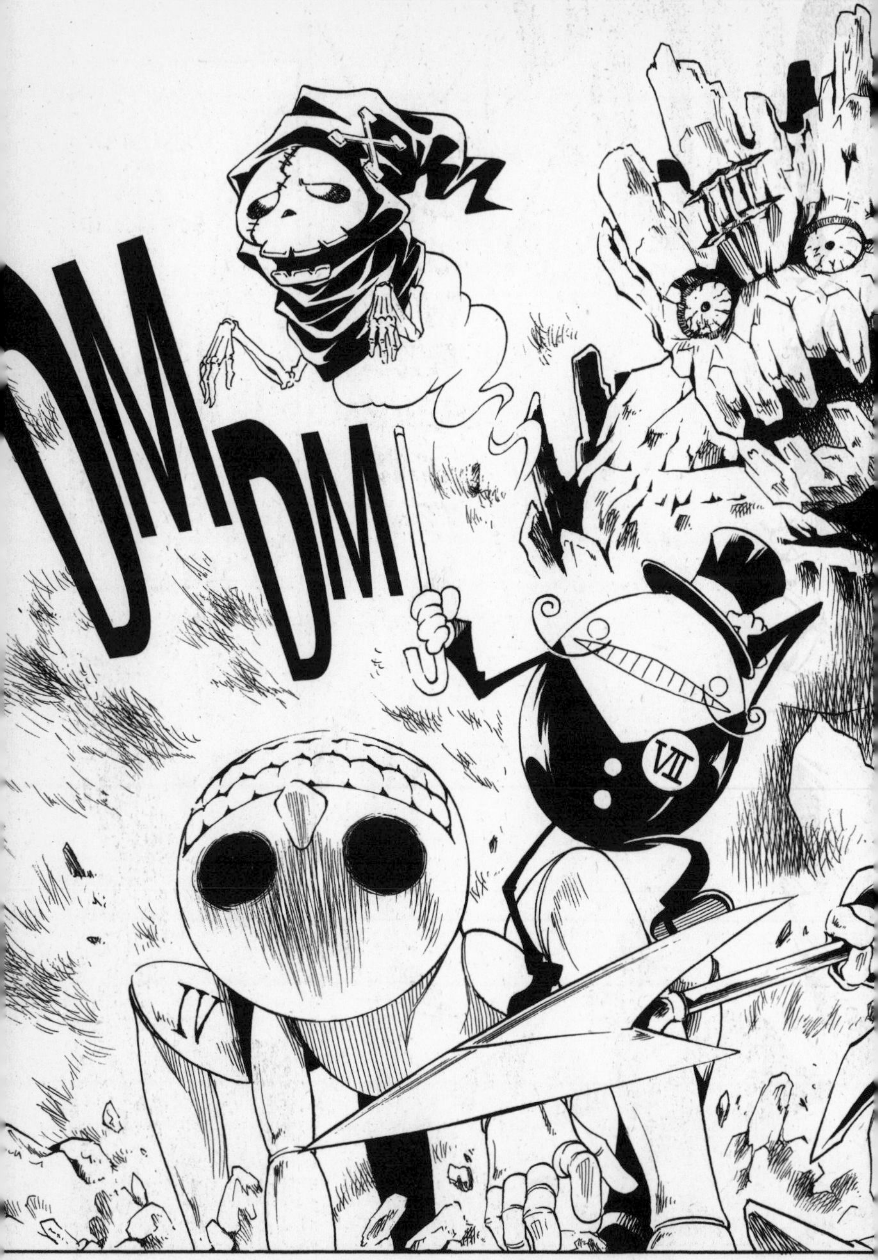
DM DM

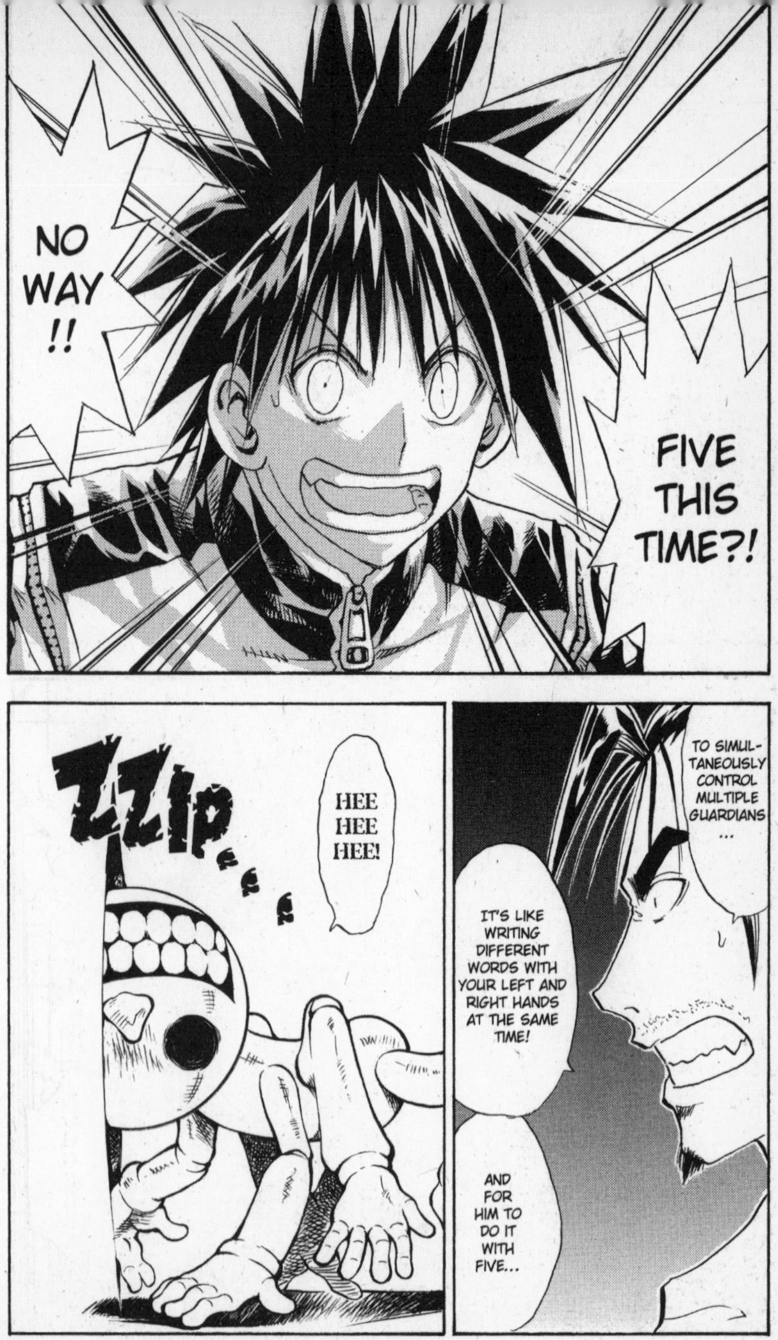
NO WAY!!
FIVE THIS TIME?!
TO SIMUL-TANEOUSLY CONTROL MULTIPLE GUARDIANS...
IT'S LIKE WRITING DIFFERENT WORDS WITH YOUR LEFT AND RIGHT HANDS AT THE SAME TIME!
AND FOR HIM TO DO IT WITH FIVE...
HEE HEE HEE!
ZZIP

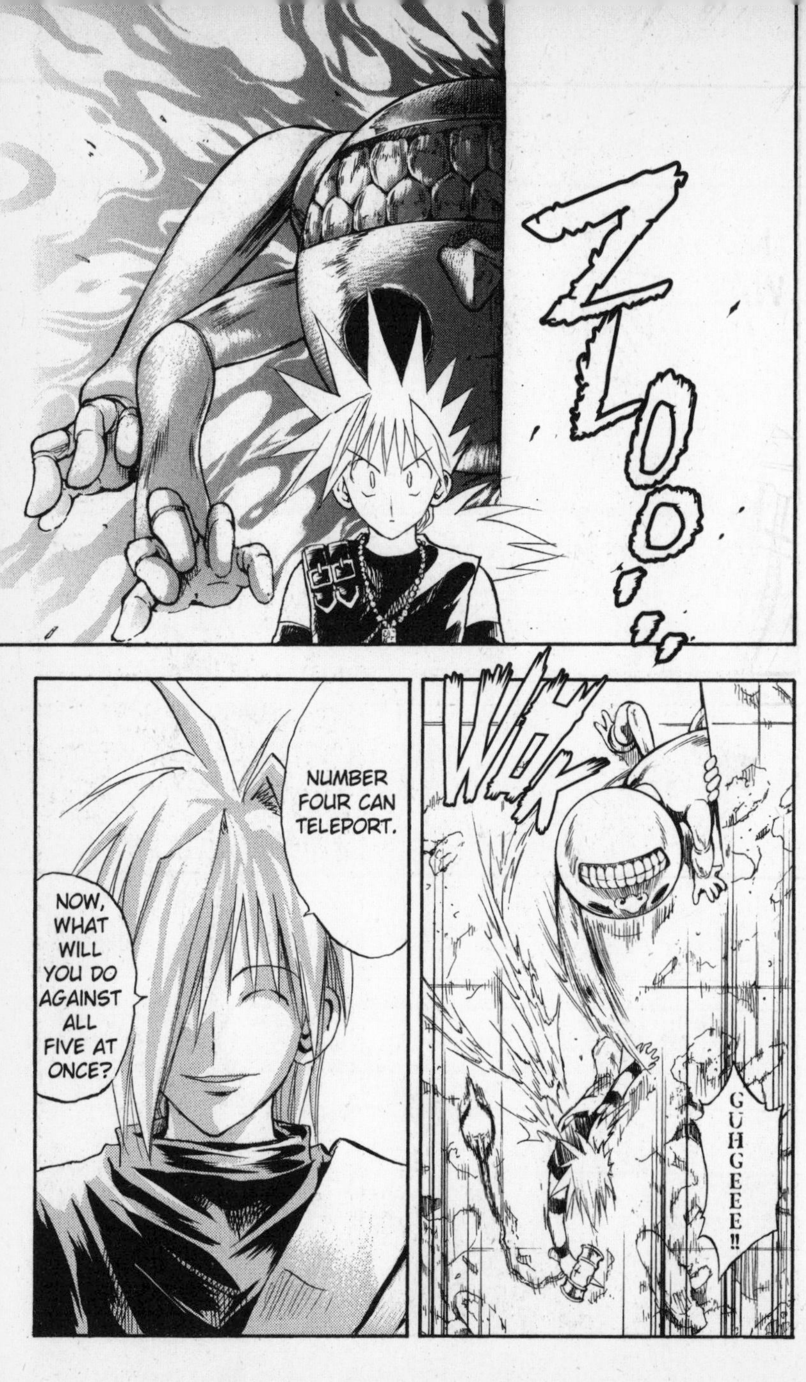
ZOOO...
WHAK
GUHGEEE!!
NUMBER FOUR CAN TELEPORT.
NOW, WHAT WILL YOU DO AGAINST ALL FIVE AT ONCE?

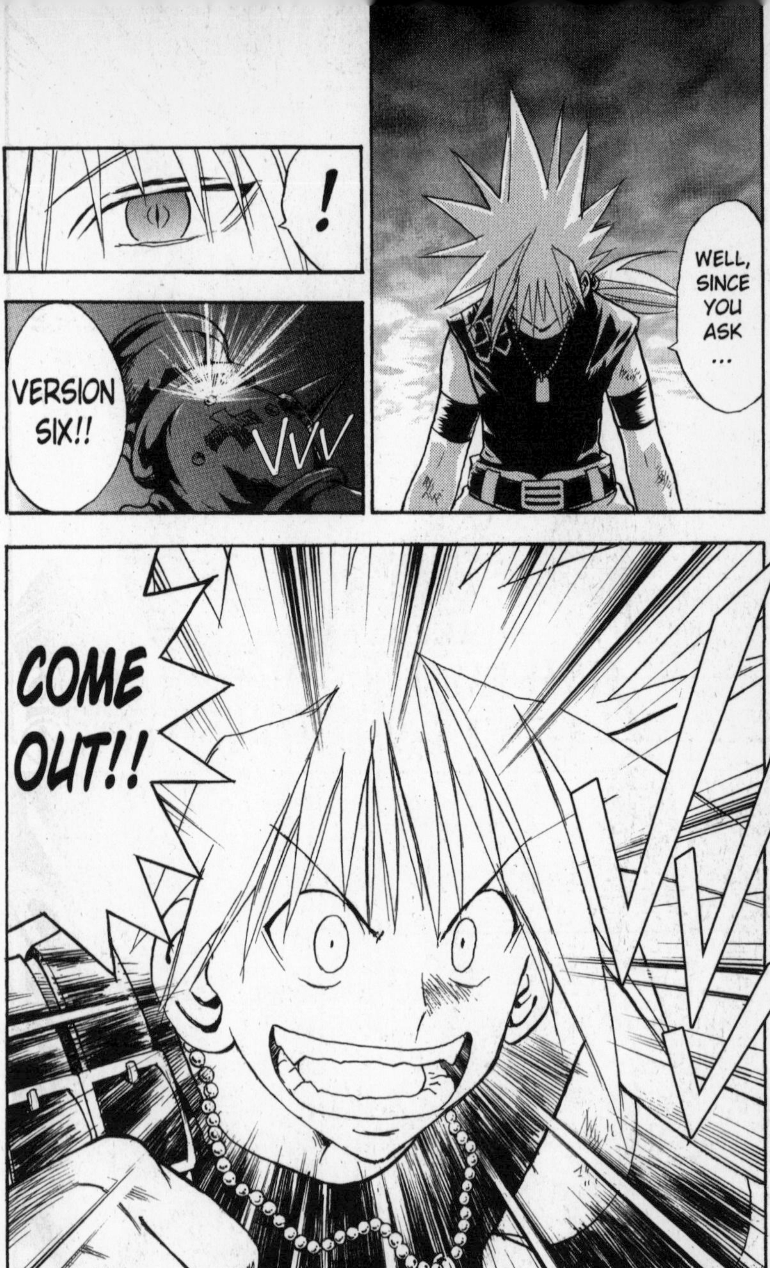
WELL, SINCE YOU ASK ...
!
VERSION SIX!!
VVV
COME OUT!!

AKT.147/ FINAL BATTLE OF THE WAR GAMES GINTA VS. PHANTOM ④

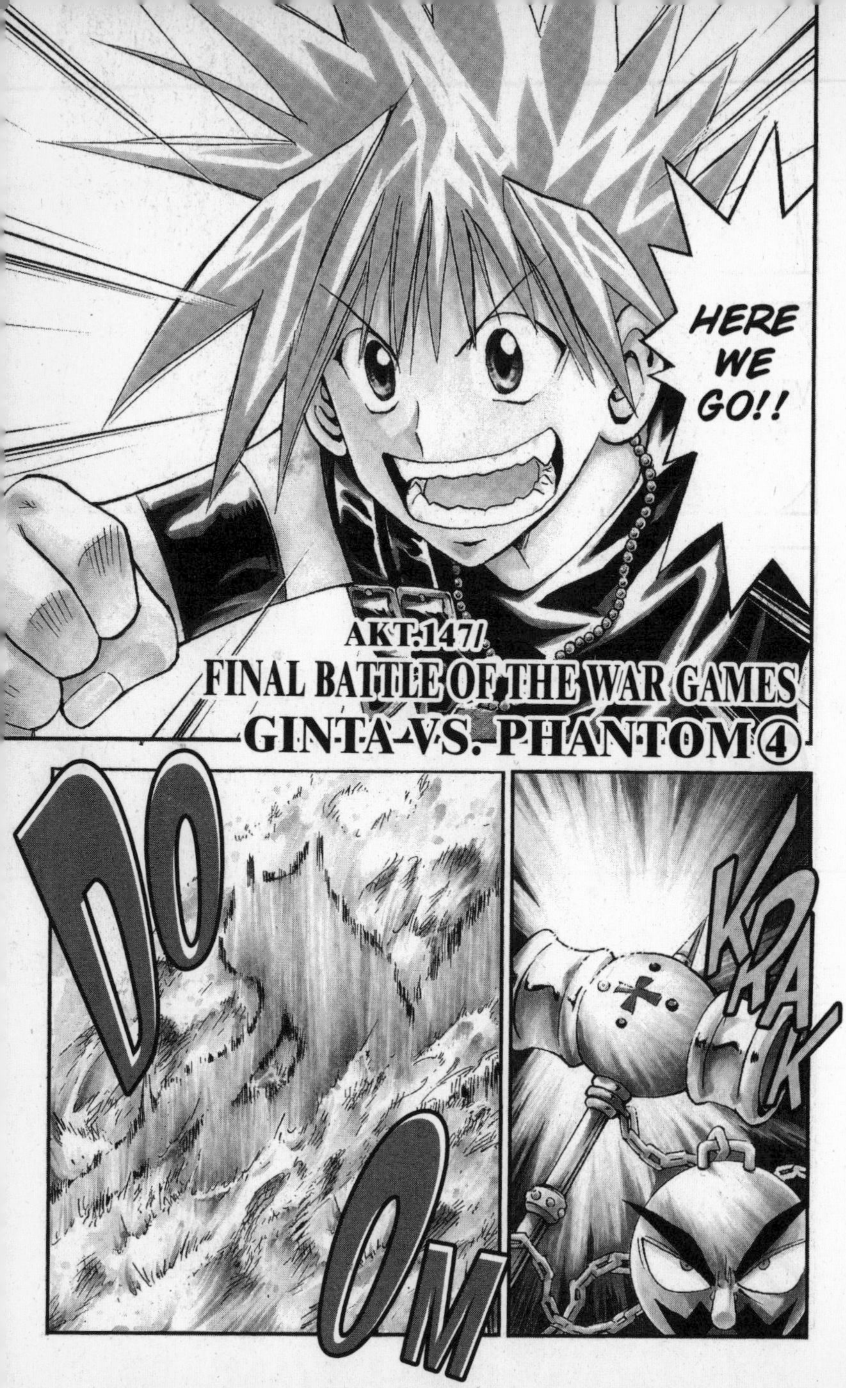
HERE WE GO!!
KRAAK
DOOM

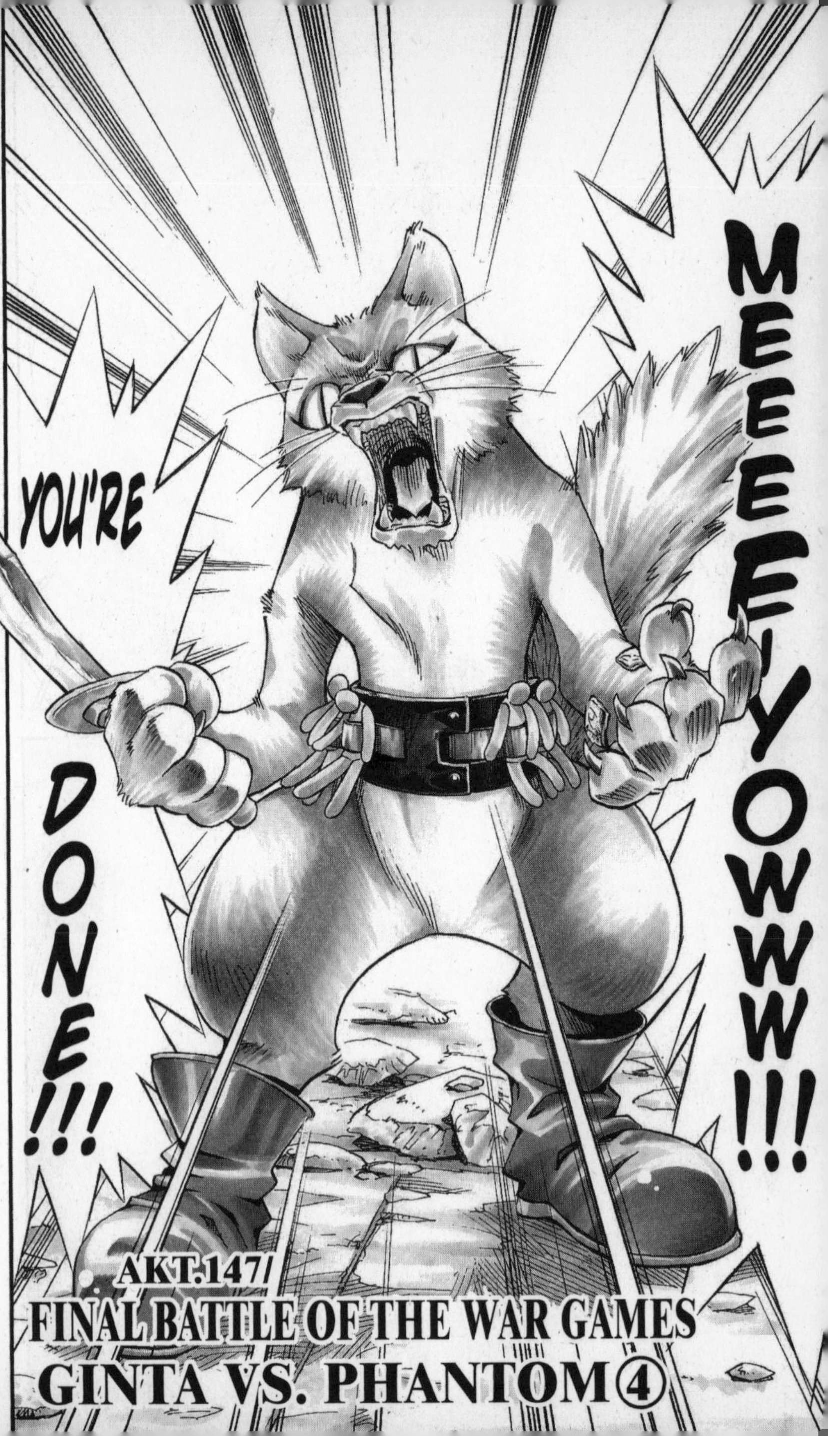
MEEEEYOWWW!!!
YOU'RE DONE!!!
AKT.147
FINAL BATTLE OF THE WAR GAMES
GINTA VS. PHANTOM ④

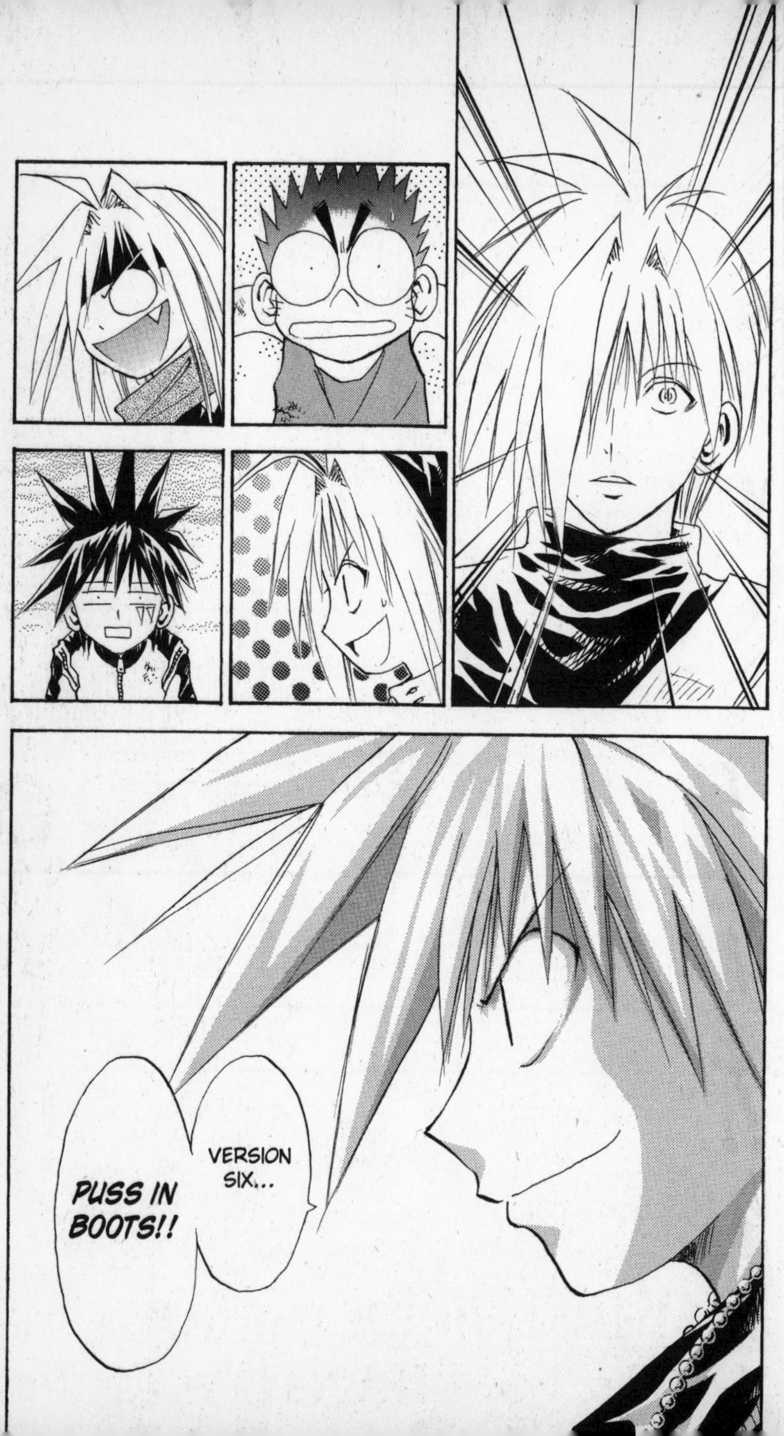
VERSION SIX...
PUSS IN BOOTS!!

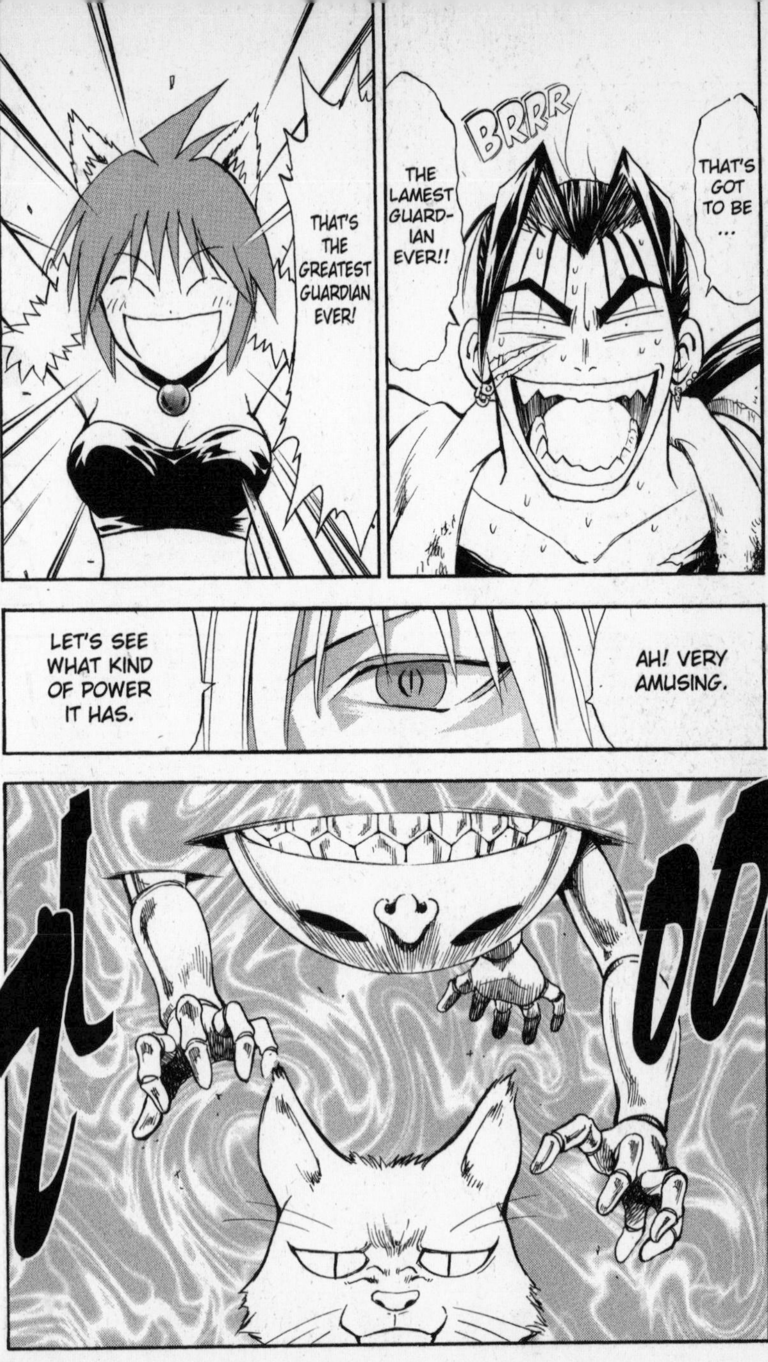

BRRR
THAT'S GOT TO BE ...
THE LAMEST GUARD-IAN EVER!!
THAT'S THE GREATEST GUARDIAN EVER!
AH! VERY AMUSING.
LET'S SEE WHAT KIND OF POWER IT HAS.

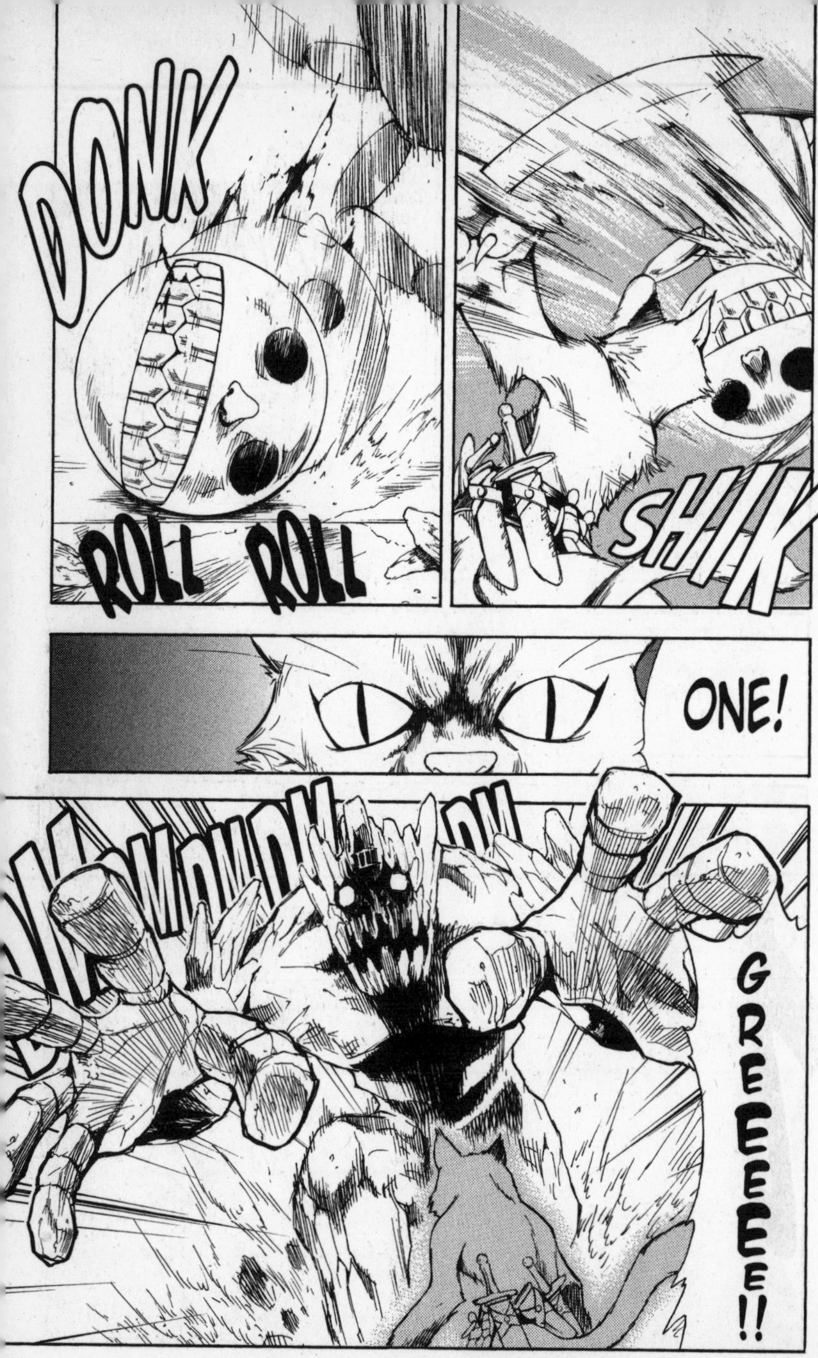
SHIK
DONK
ROLL ROLL
ONE!
GREEEEEE!!

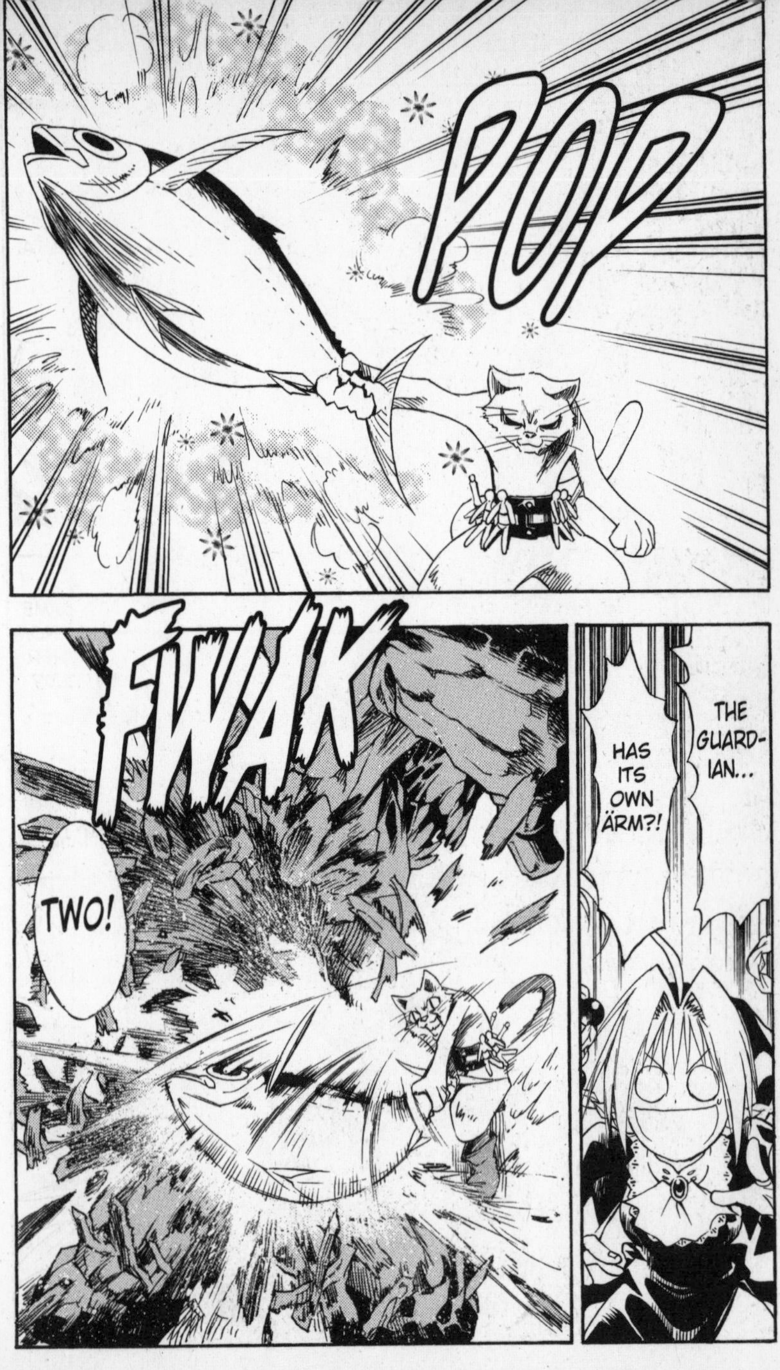
POP
THE GUARDIAN...
HAS ITS OWN ÄRM?!
FWAK
TWO!

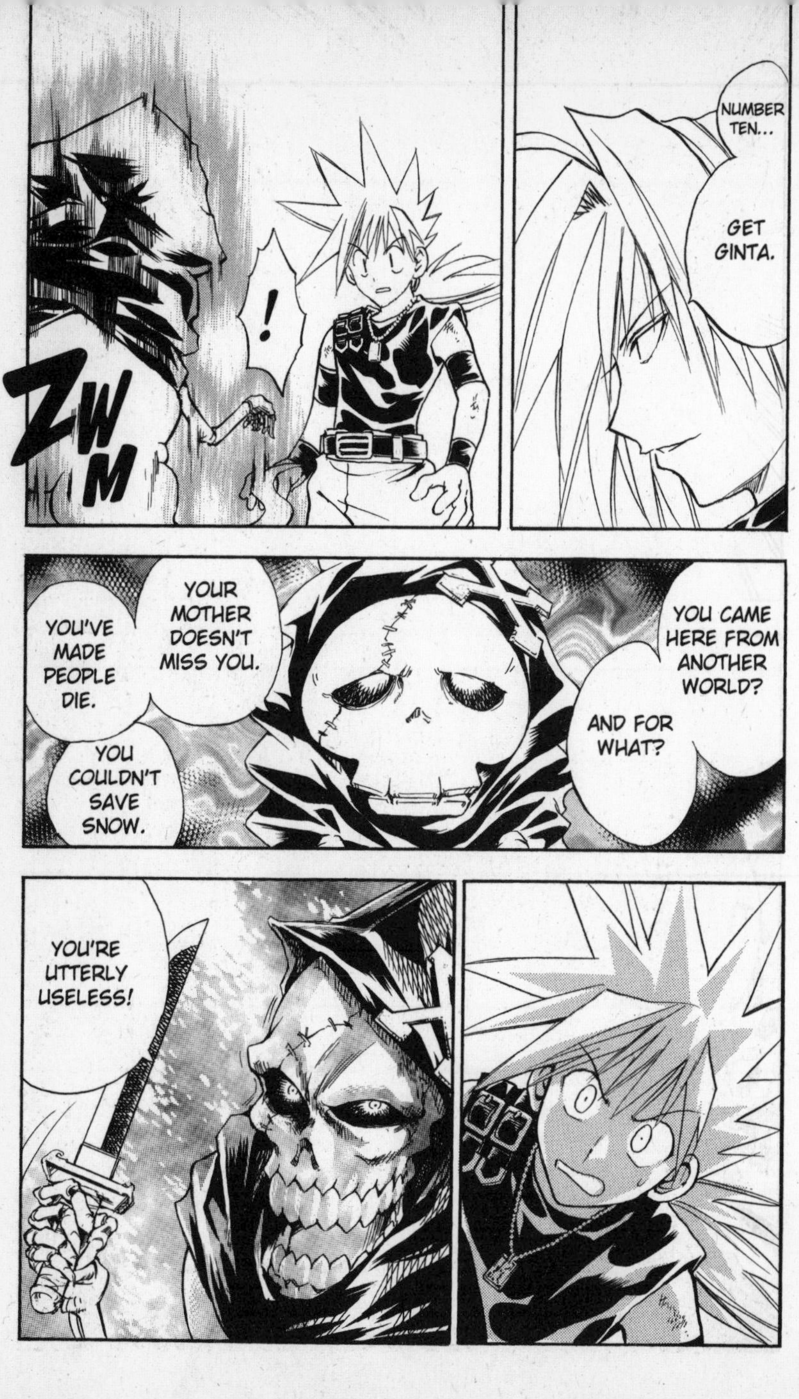
NUMBER TEN...
GET GINTA.
!
ZWM
YOU CAME HERE FROM ANOTHER WORLD?
AND FOR WHAT?
YOUR MOTHER DOESN'T MISS YOU.
YOU'VE MADE PEOPLE DIE.
YOU COULDN'T SAVE SNOW.
YOU'RE UTTERLY USELESS!

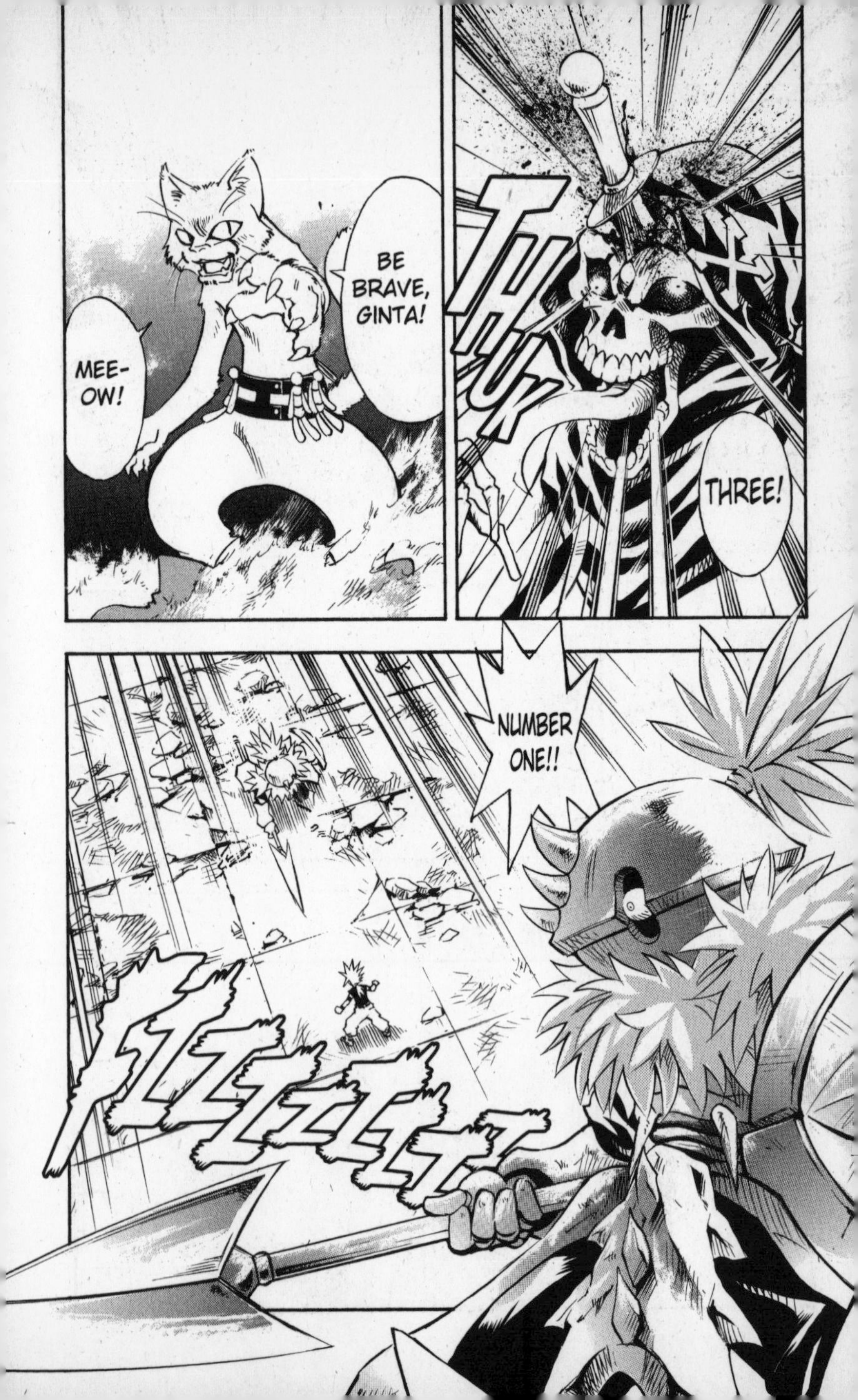
THUK
THREE!
BE BRAVE, GINTA!
MEE-OW!
NUMBER ONE!!

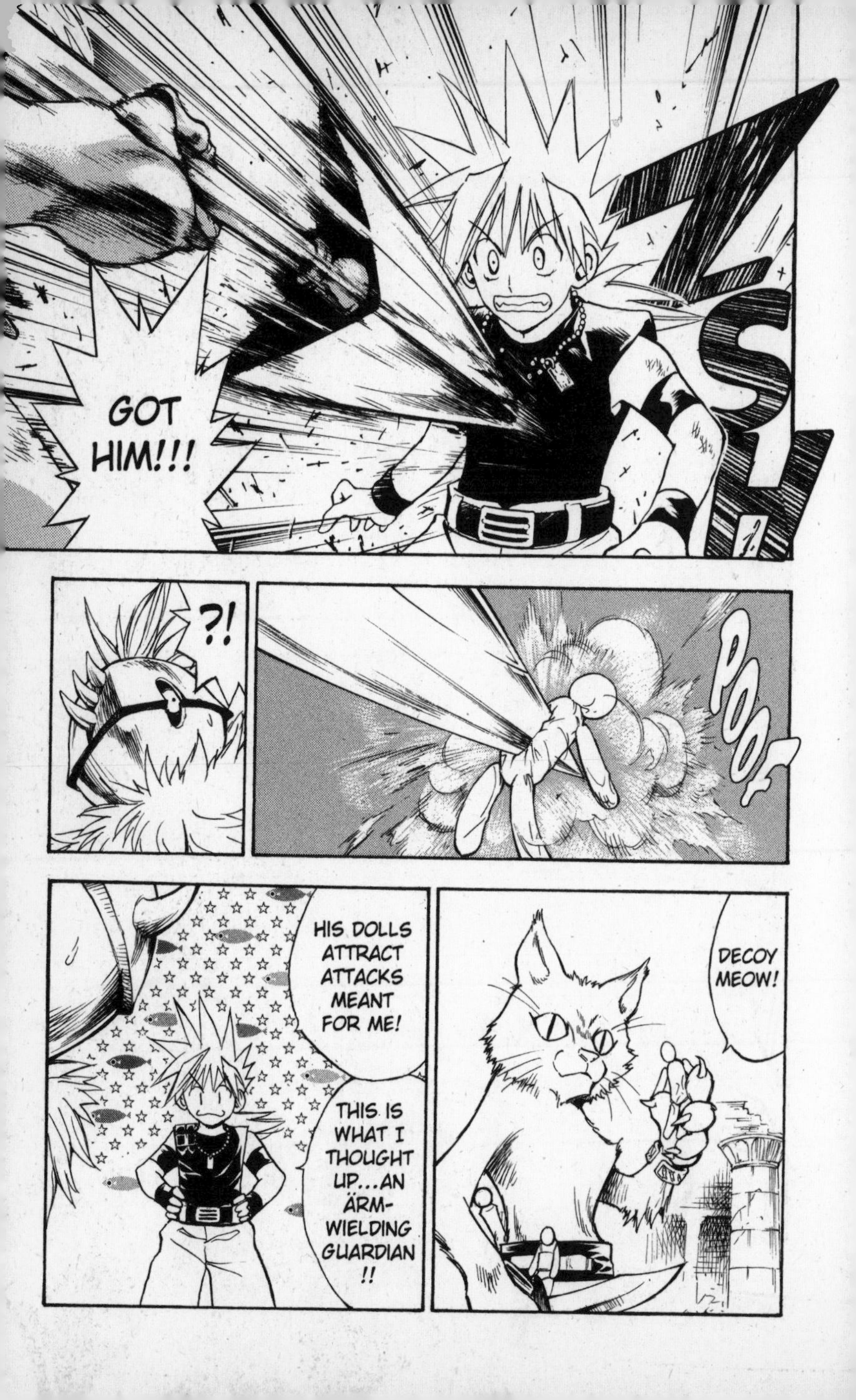
ZSH!
GOT HIM!!!
POOF
?!
HIS DOLLS ATTRACT ATTACKS MEANT FOR ME!
THIS IS WHAT I THOUGHT UP...AN ÄRM-WIELDING GUARDIAN !!
DECOY MEOW!

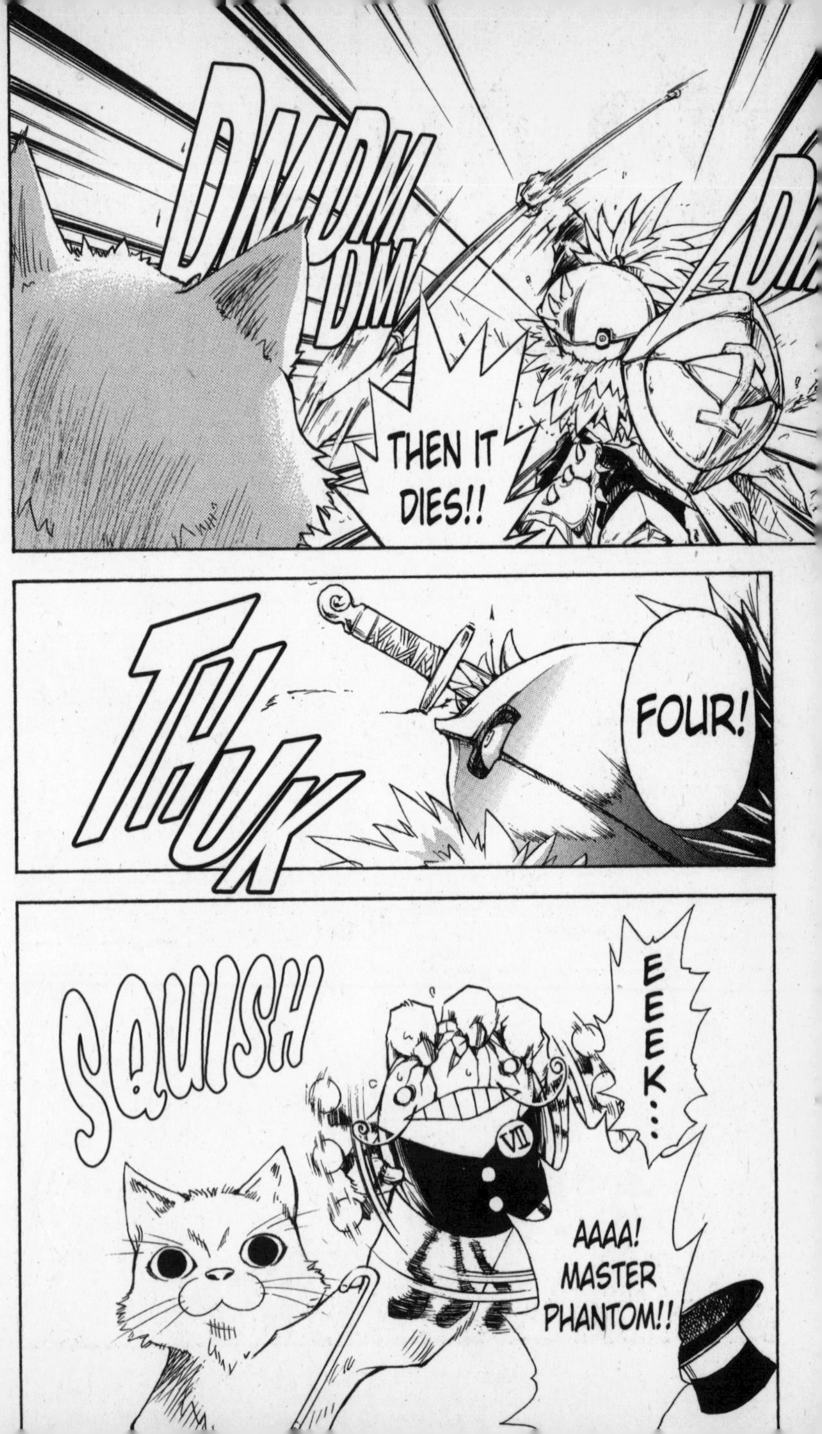
DMDM DM
DM
THEN IT DIES!!
FOUR!
THUK
EEEK...
SQUISH
AAAA! MASTER PHANTOM!!

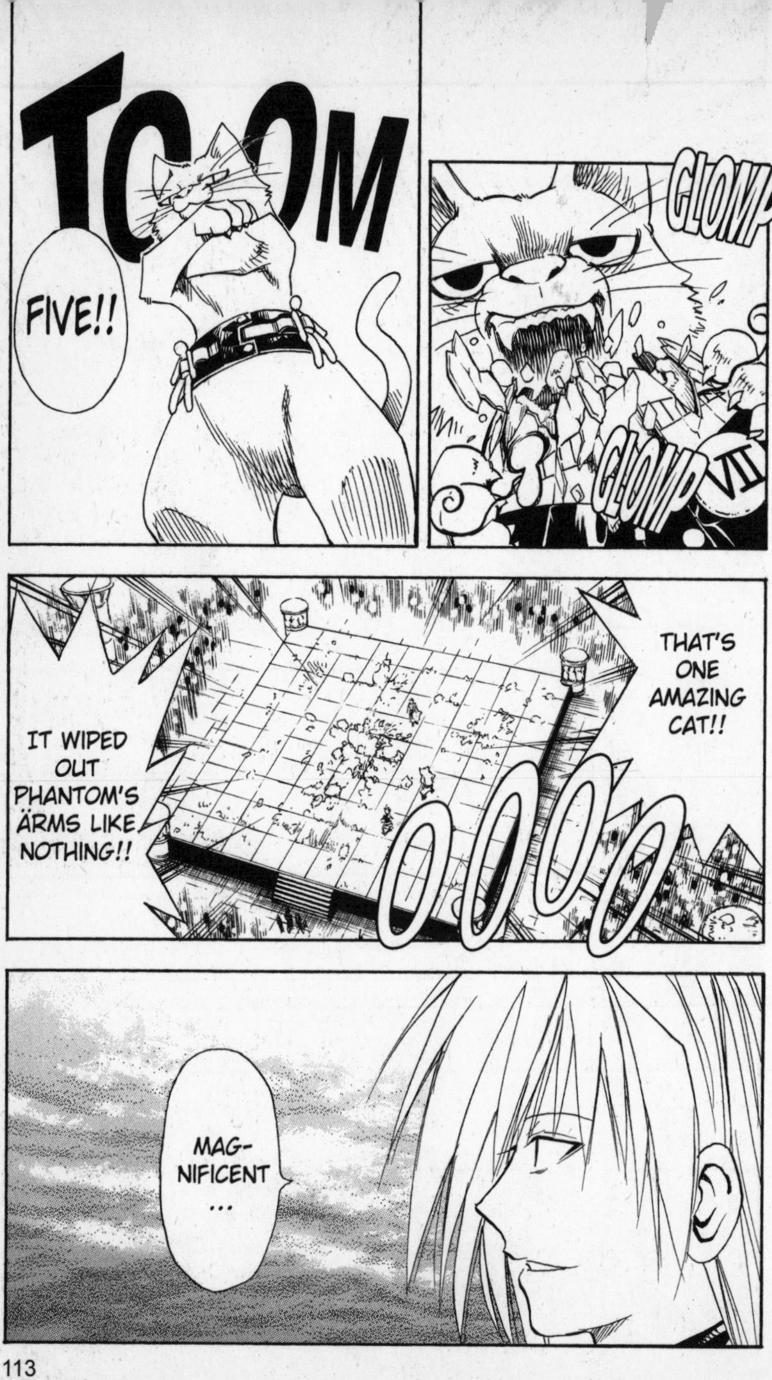
GLOMP
GLOMP
VII
TOOM
FIVE!!
THAT'S ONE AMAZING CAT!!
IT WIPED OUT PHANTOM'S ÄRMS LIKE NOTHING!!
OOOOO
MAG-NIFICENT...

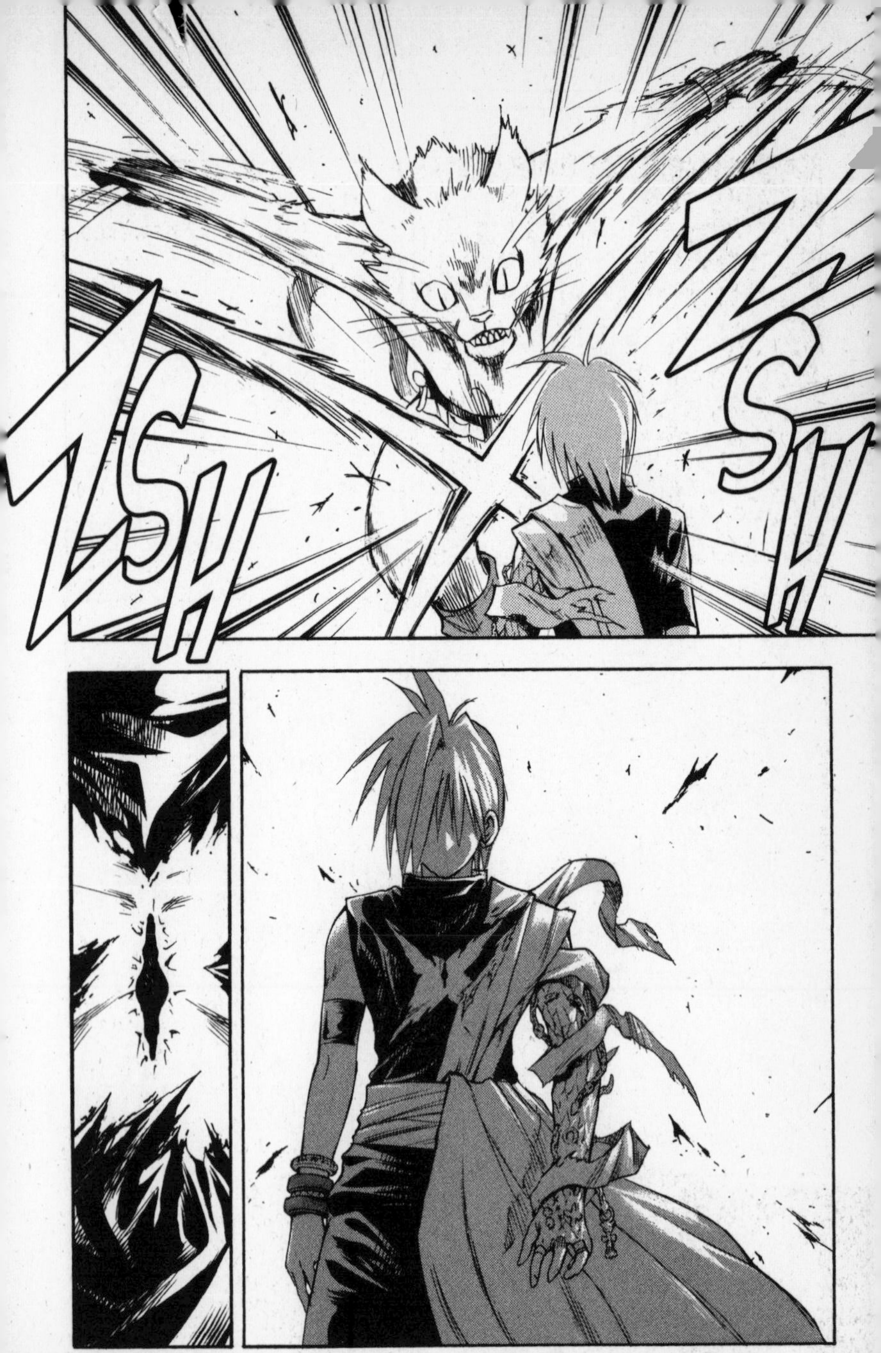
ZSH
ZSH

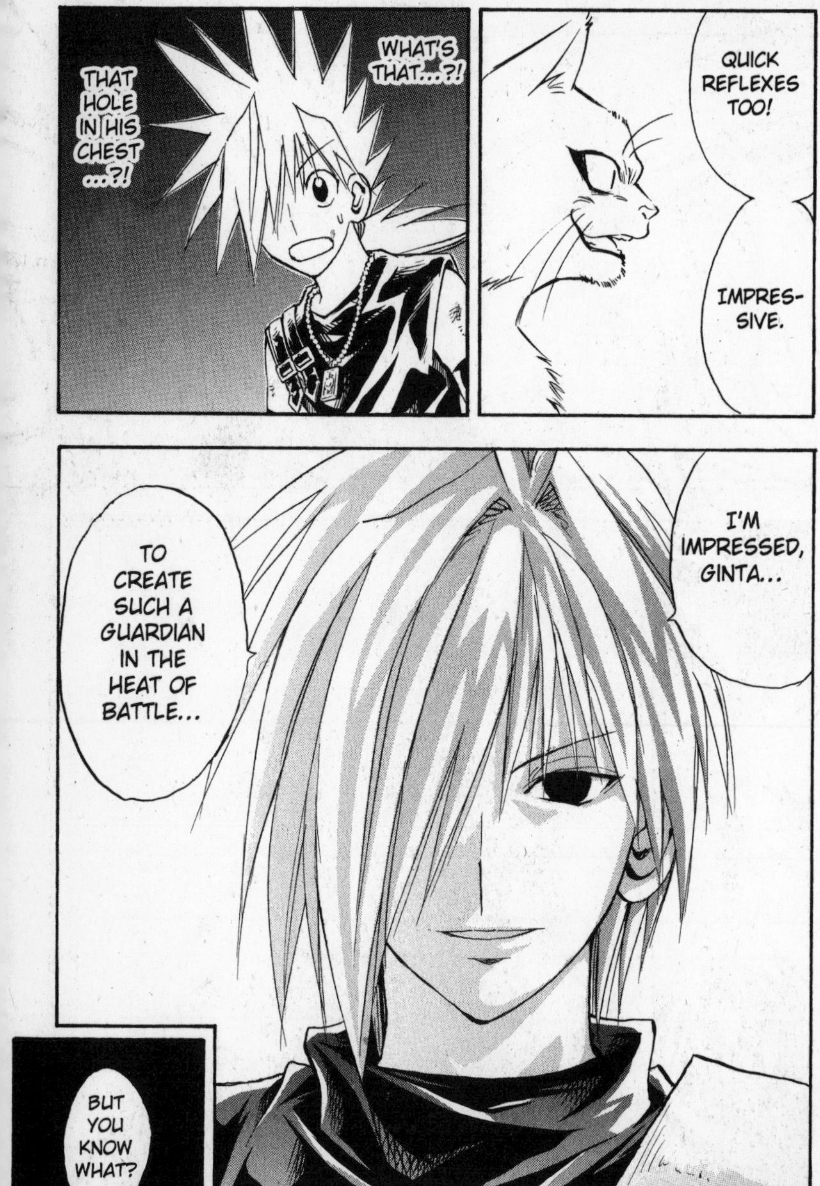
QUICK REFLEXES TOO!
IMPRES-SIVE.
WHAT'S THAT...?!
THAT HOLE IN HIS CHEST ...?!
I'M IMPRESSED, GINTA...
TO CREATE SUCH A GUARDIAN IN THE HEAT OF BATTLE...
BUT YOU KNOW WHAT?

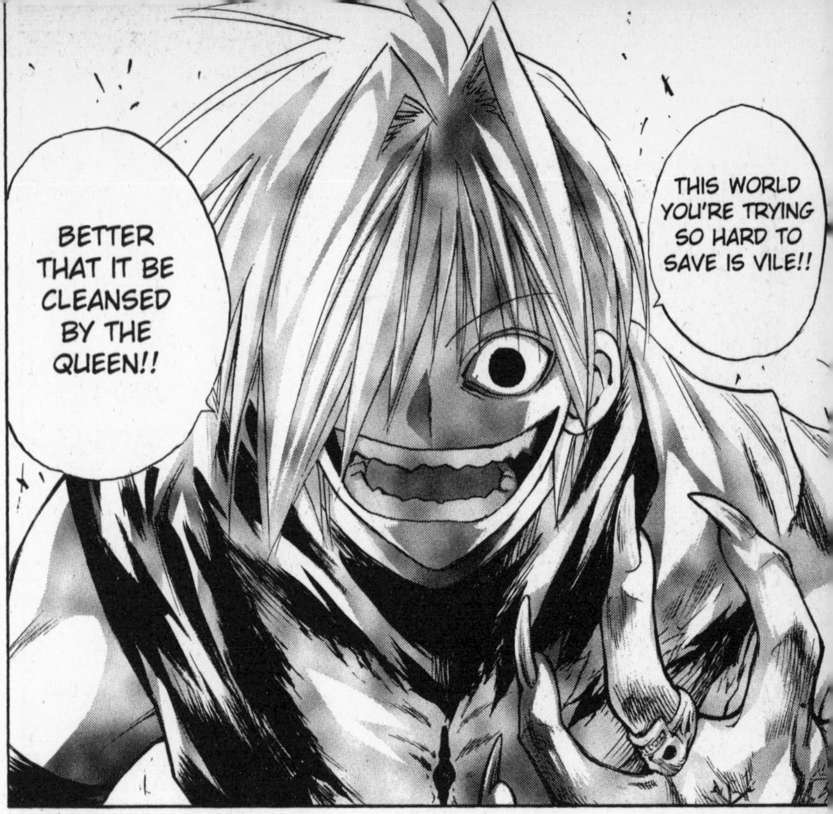
THIS WORLD YOU'RE TRYING SO HARD TO SAVE IS VILE!!
BETTER THAT IT BE CLEANSED BY THE QUEEN!!
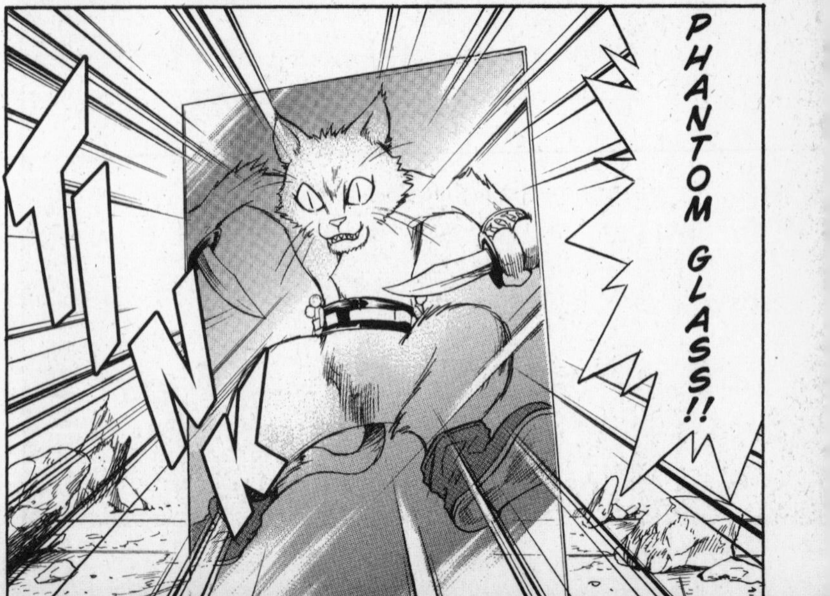
PHANTOM GLASS!!
TINK

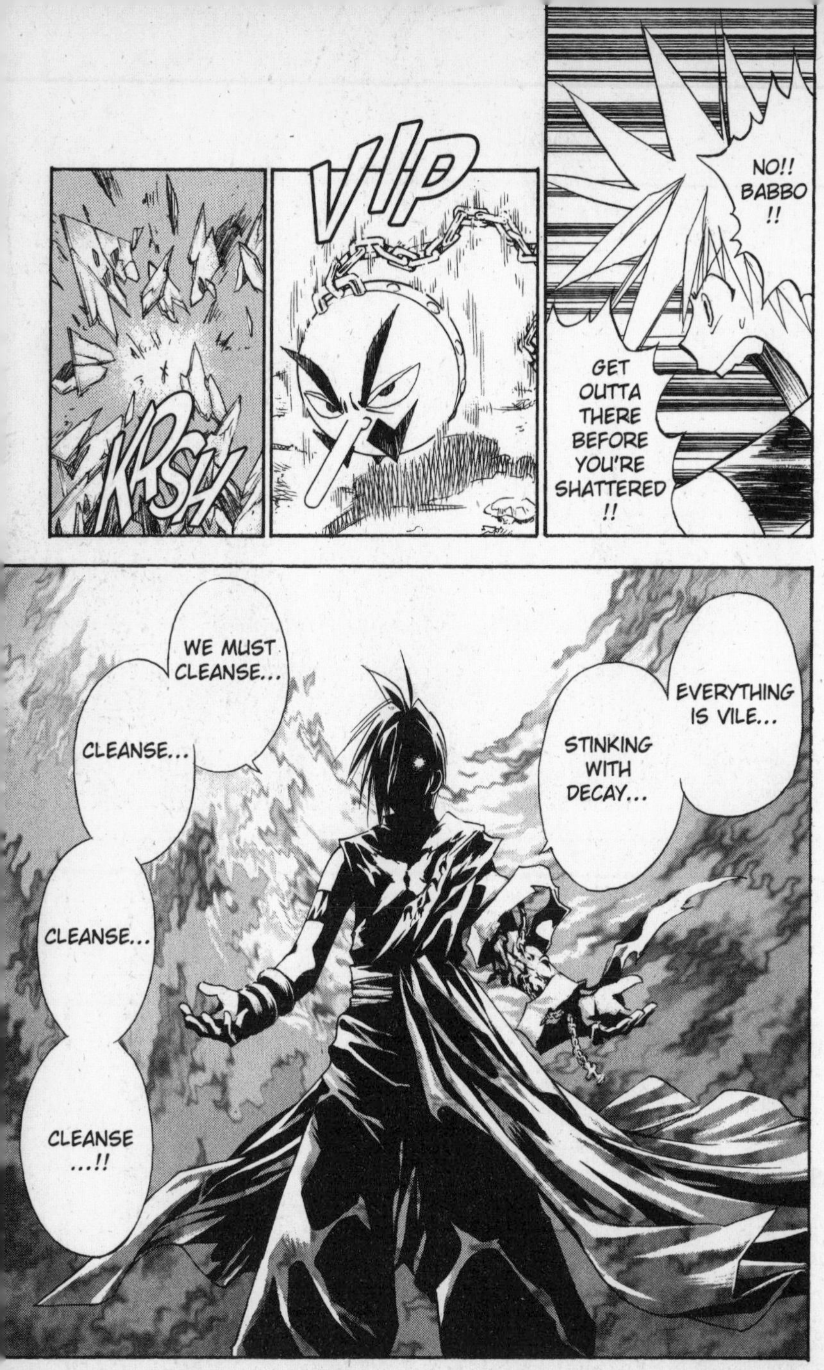
NO!! BABBO !!
GET OUTTA THERE BEFORE YOU'RE SHATTERED !!
VIP
KRSH
EVERYTHING IS VILE...
STINKING WITH DECAY...
WE MUST CLEANSE...
CLEANSE...
CLEANSE...
CLEANSE ...!!

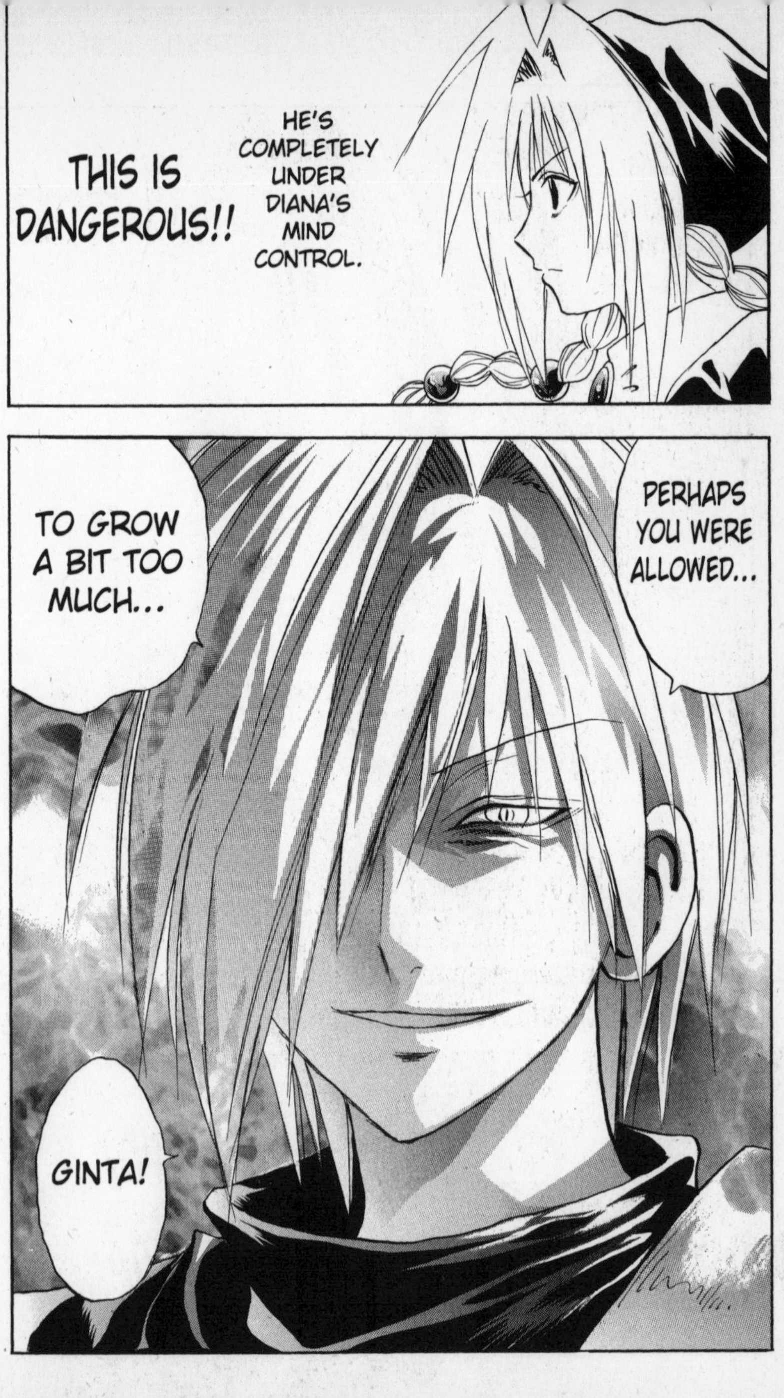
HE'S COMPLETELY UNDER DIANA'S MIND CONTROL.
THIS IS DANGEROUS!!
PERHAPS YOU WERE ALLOWED...
TO GROW A BIT TOO MUCH...
GINTA!

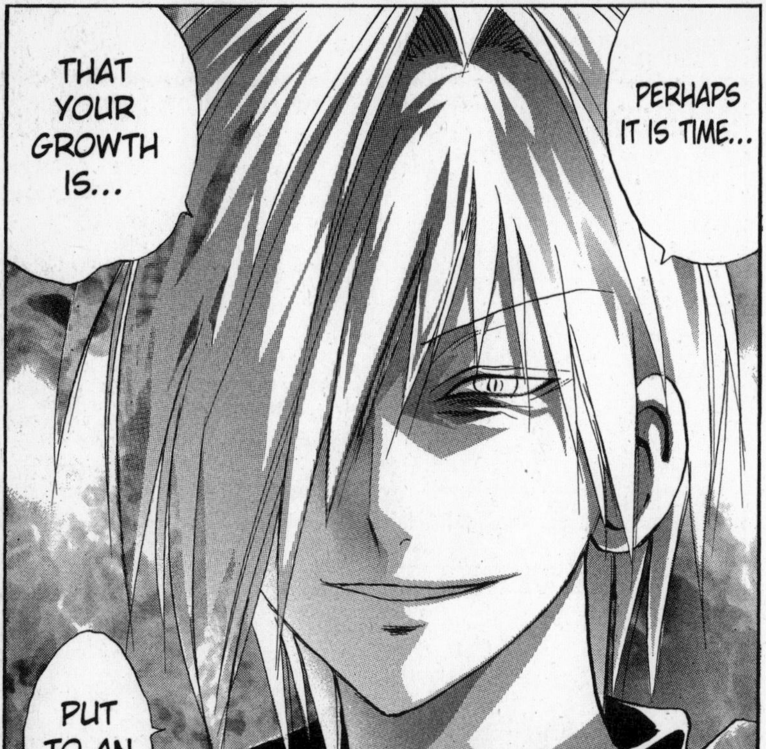
PERHAPS IT IS TIME...
THAT YOUR GROWTH IS...
PUT TO AN END!
AKT.148/
FINAL BATTLE OF THE WAR GAMES
GINTA VS. PHANTOM ⑤
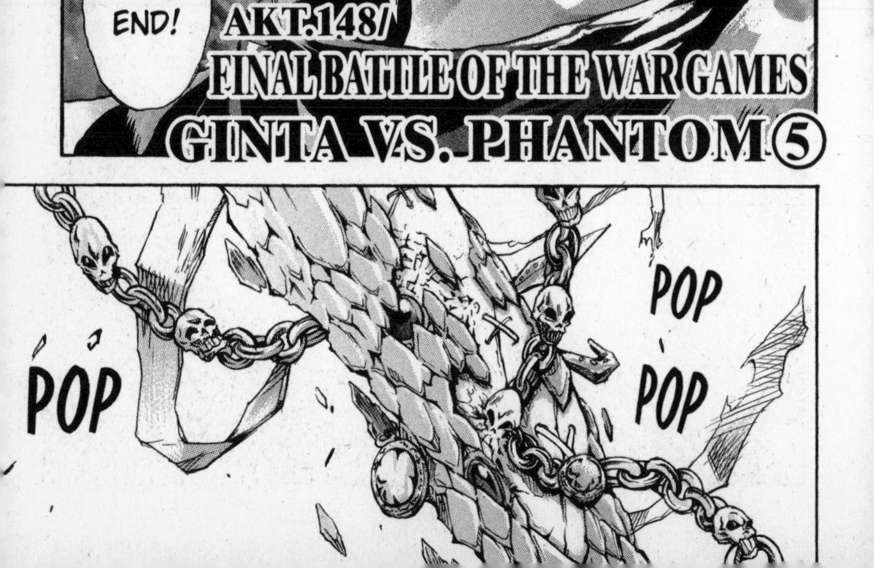
POP
POP
POP

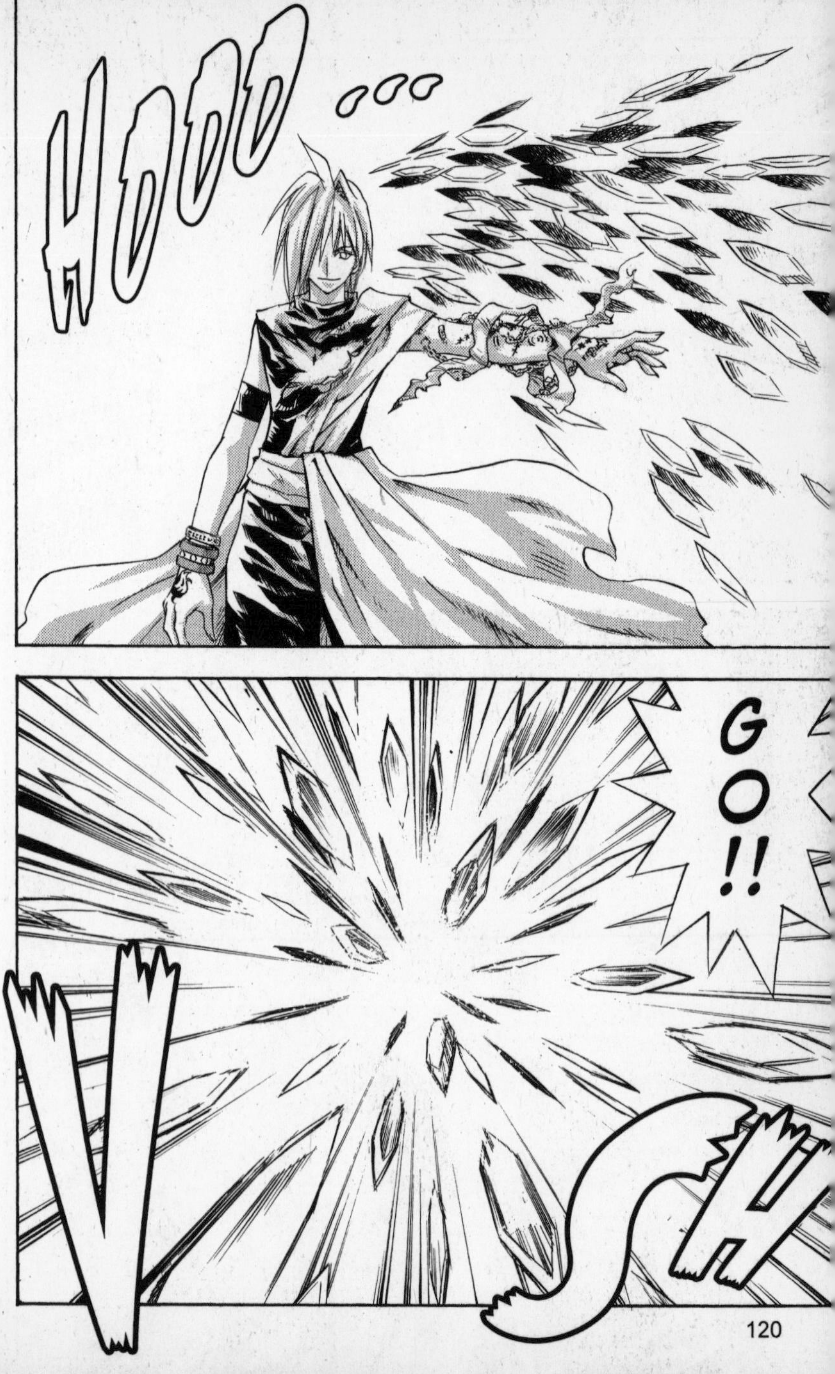
HOOO...
GO!!
VSH

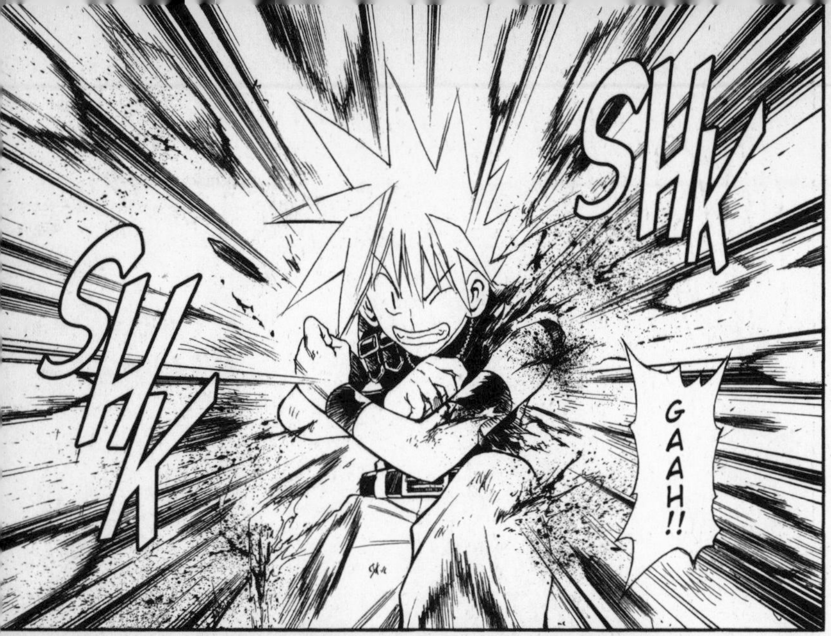
SHK
GAAH!!
SHK

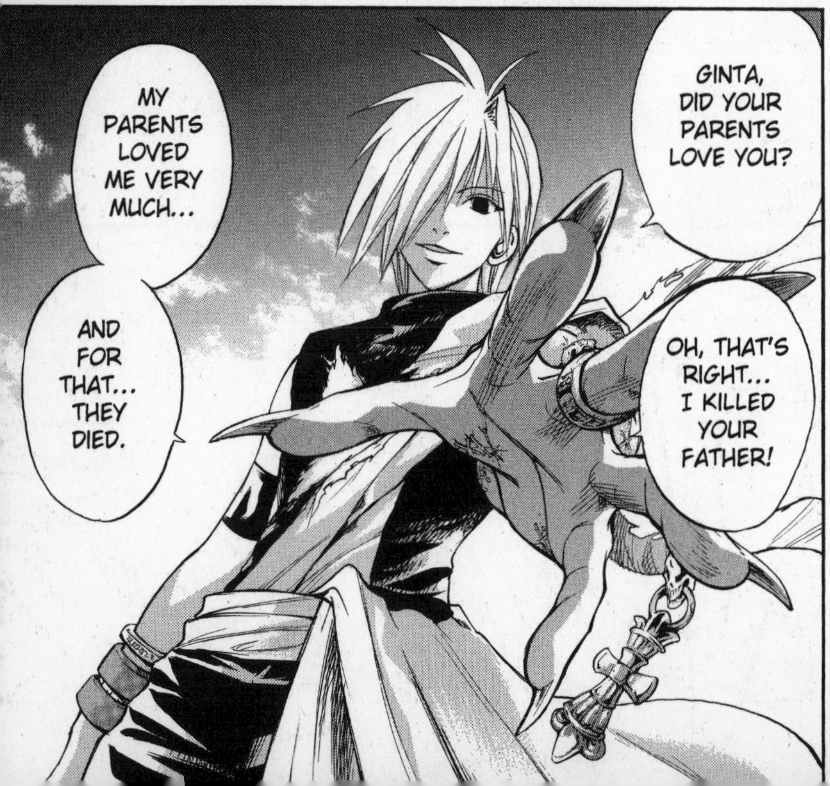
GINTA, DID YOUR PARENTS LOVE YOU?
OH, THAT'S RIGHT... I KILLED YOUR FATHER!
MY PARENTS LOVED ME VERY MUCH...
AND FOR THAT... THEY DIED.

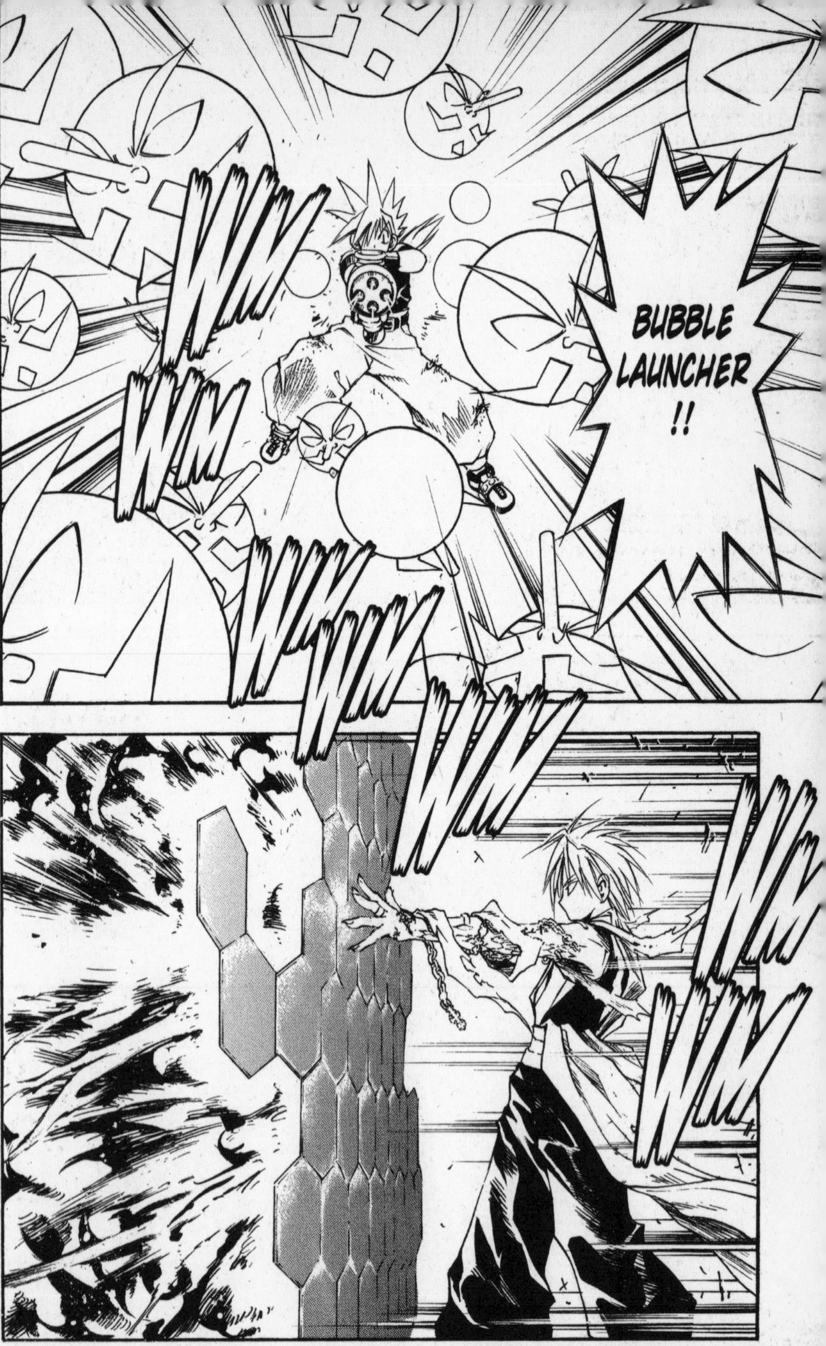
BUBBLE LAUNCHER !!

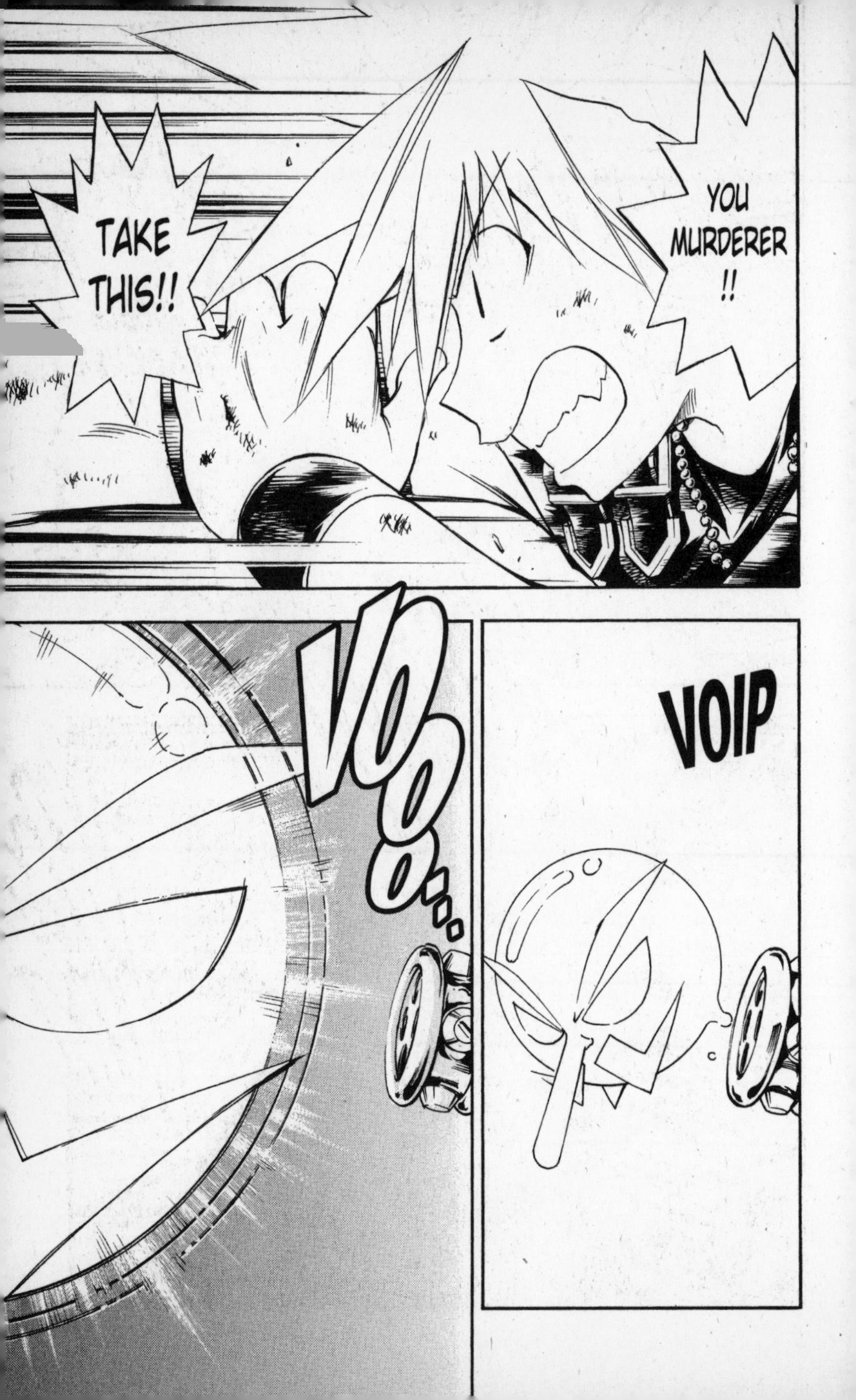
YOU MURDERER!!
TAKE THIS!!
VOIP
VOOO...

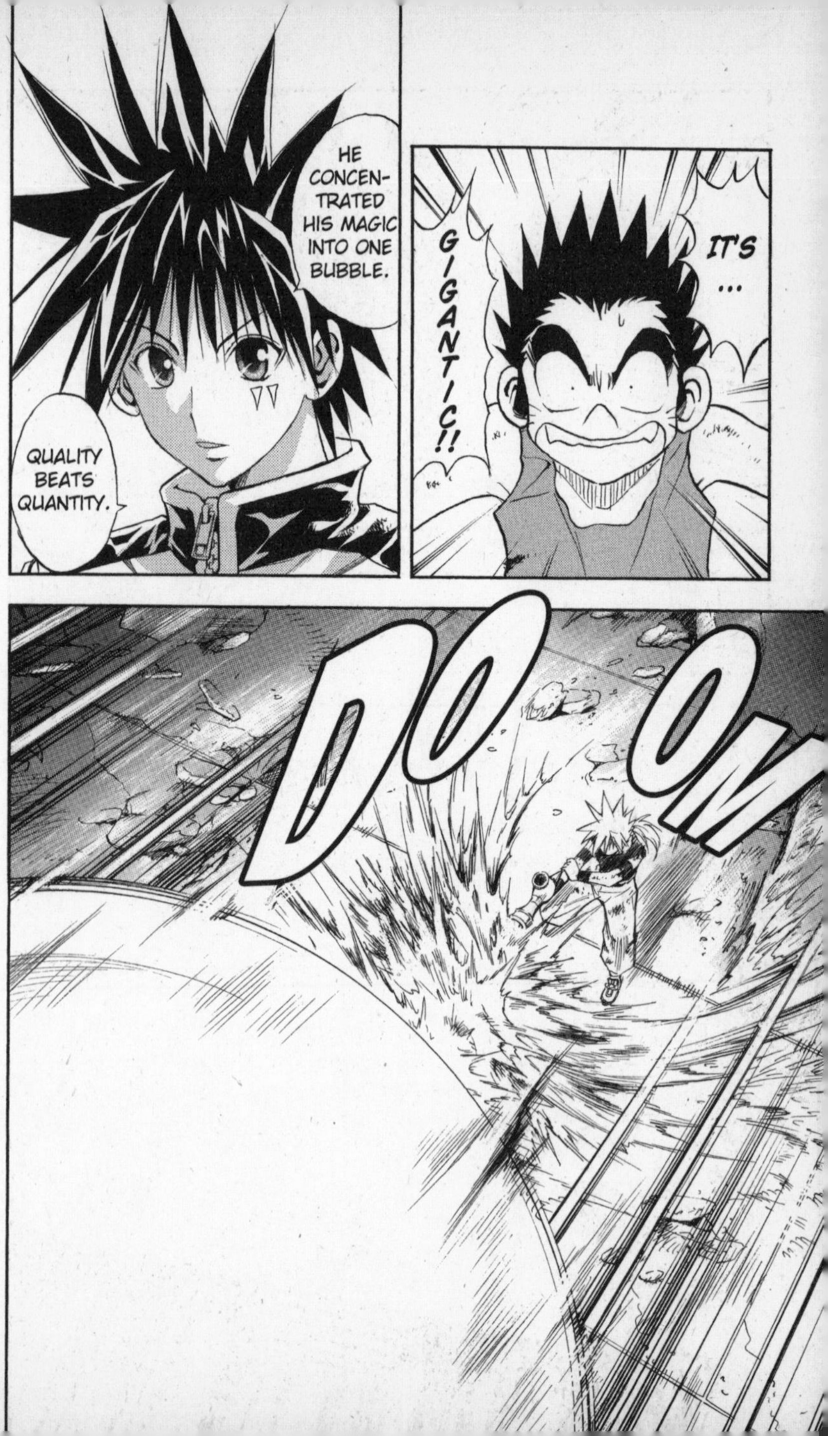
IT'S ...
GIGANTIC!!
HE CONCEN-TRATED HIS MAGIC INTO ONE BUBBLE.
QUALITY BEATS QUANTITY.
DOOM

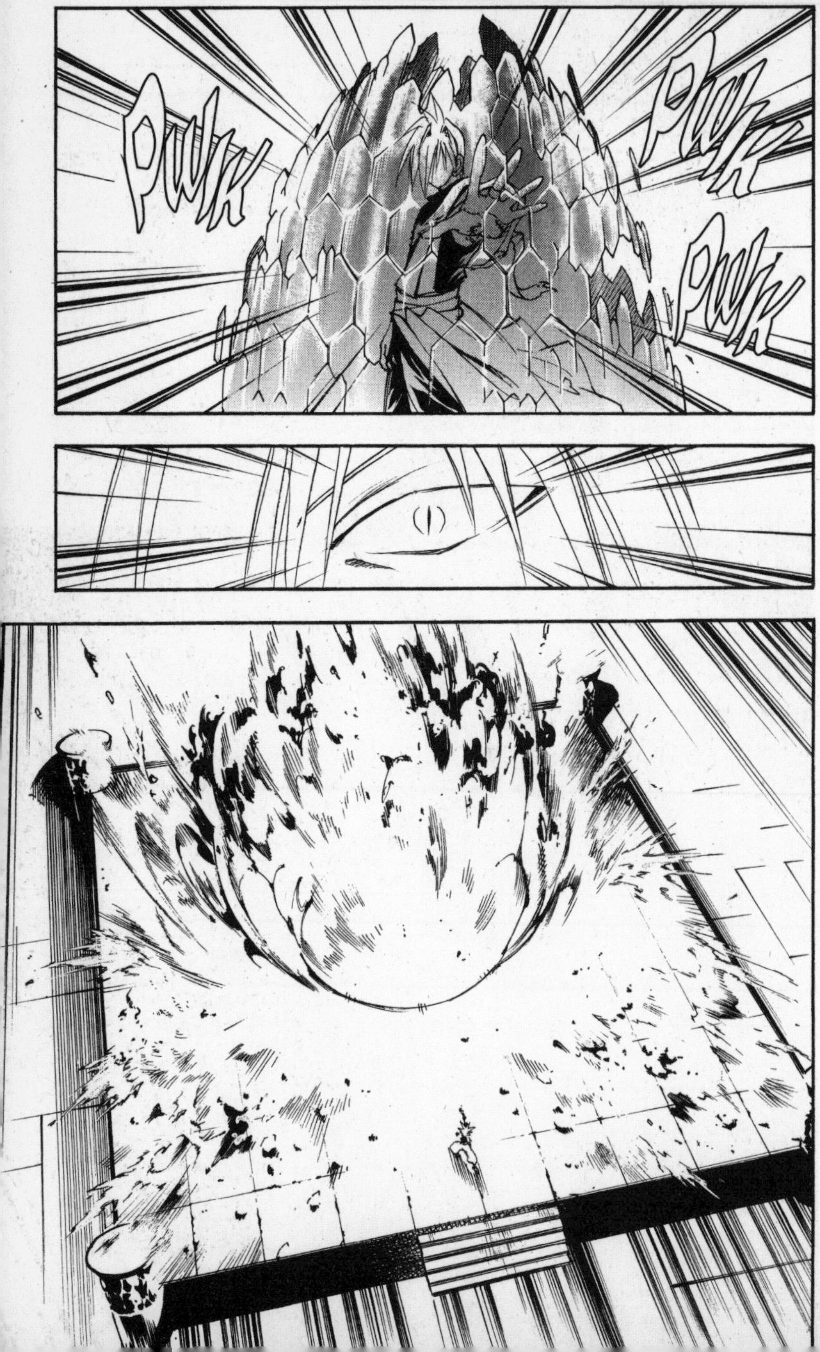
PWK
PWK
PWK

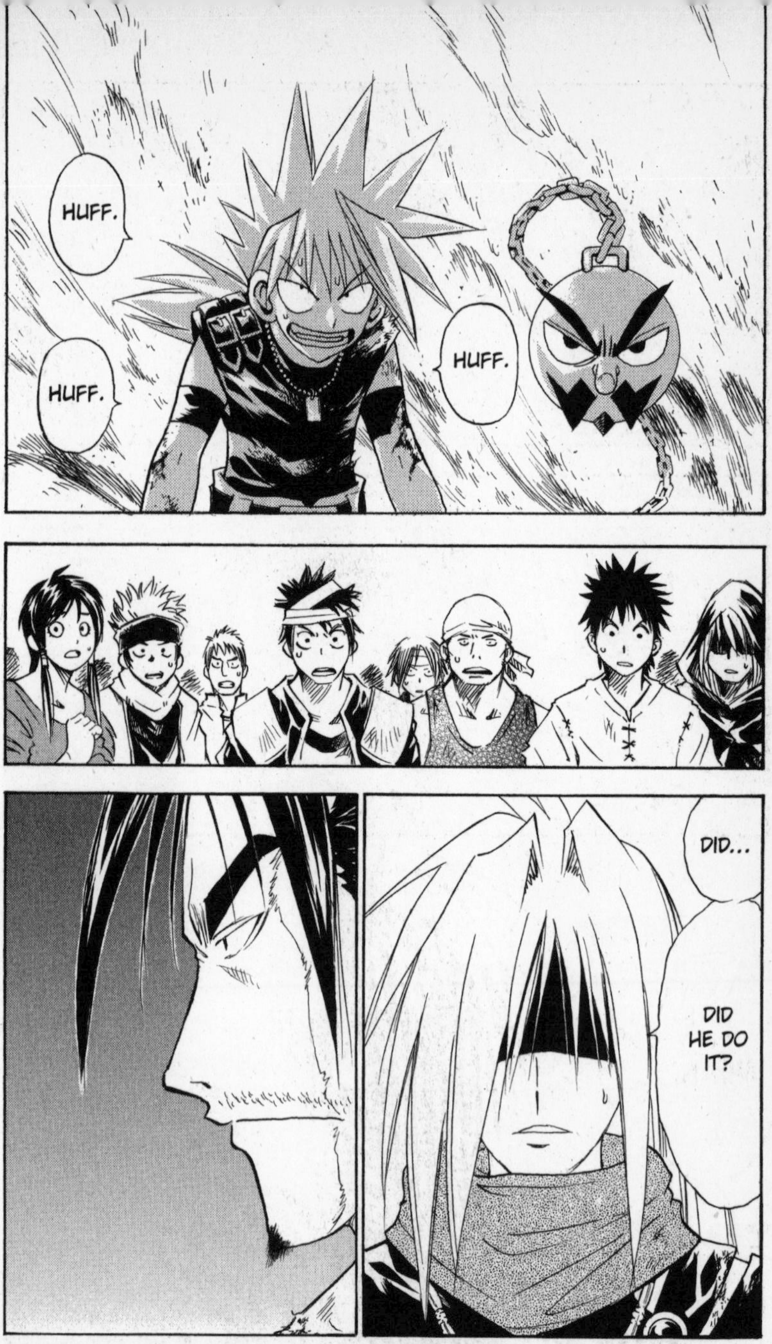
HUFF.
HUFF.
HUFF.
DID...
DID HE DO IT?

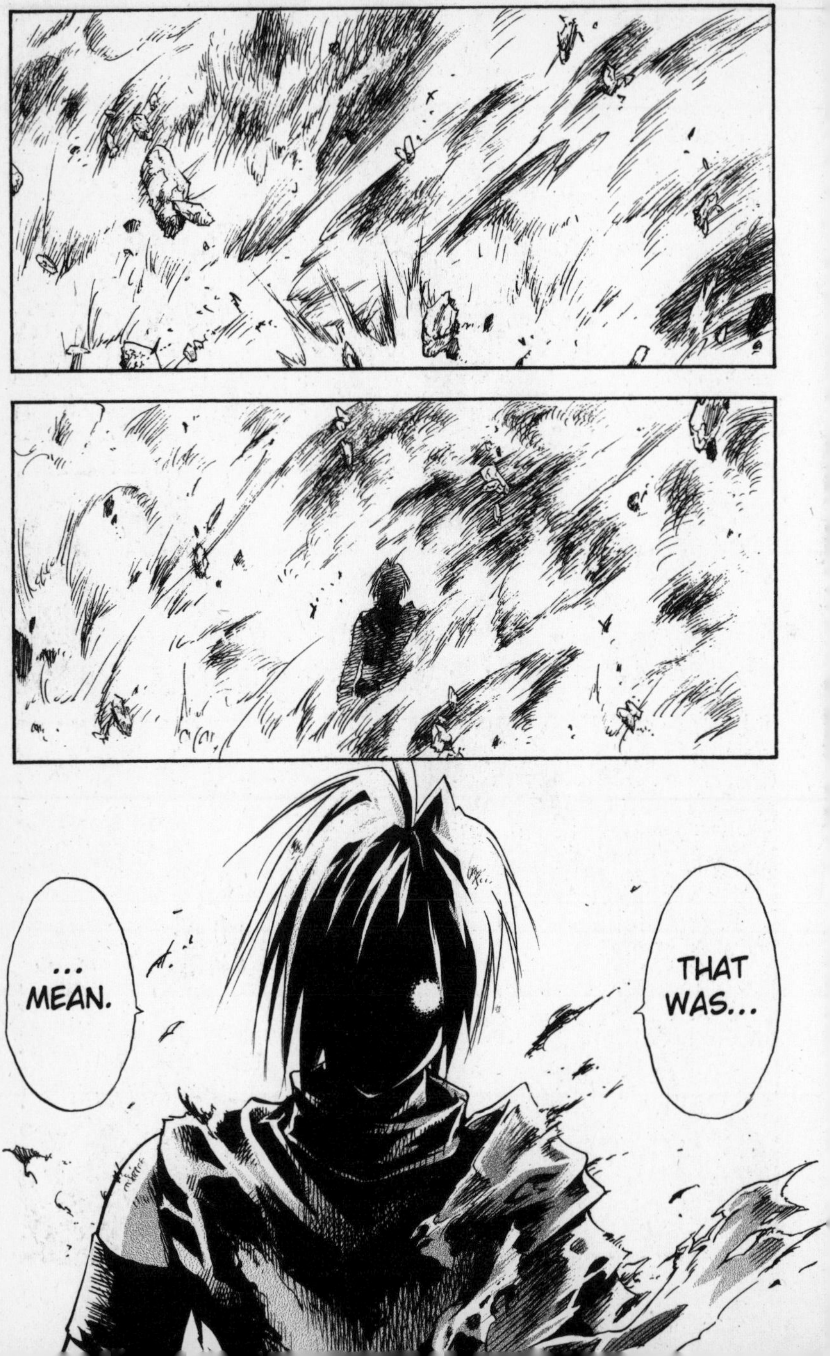
THAT WAS...
... MEAN.

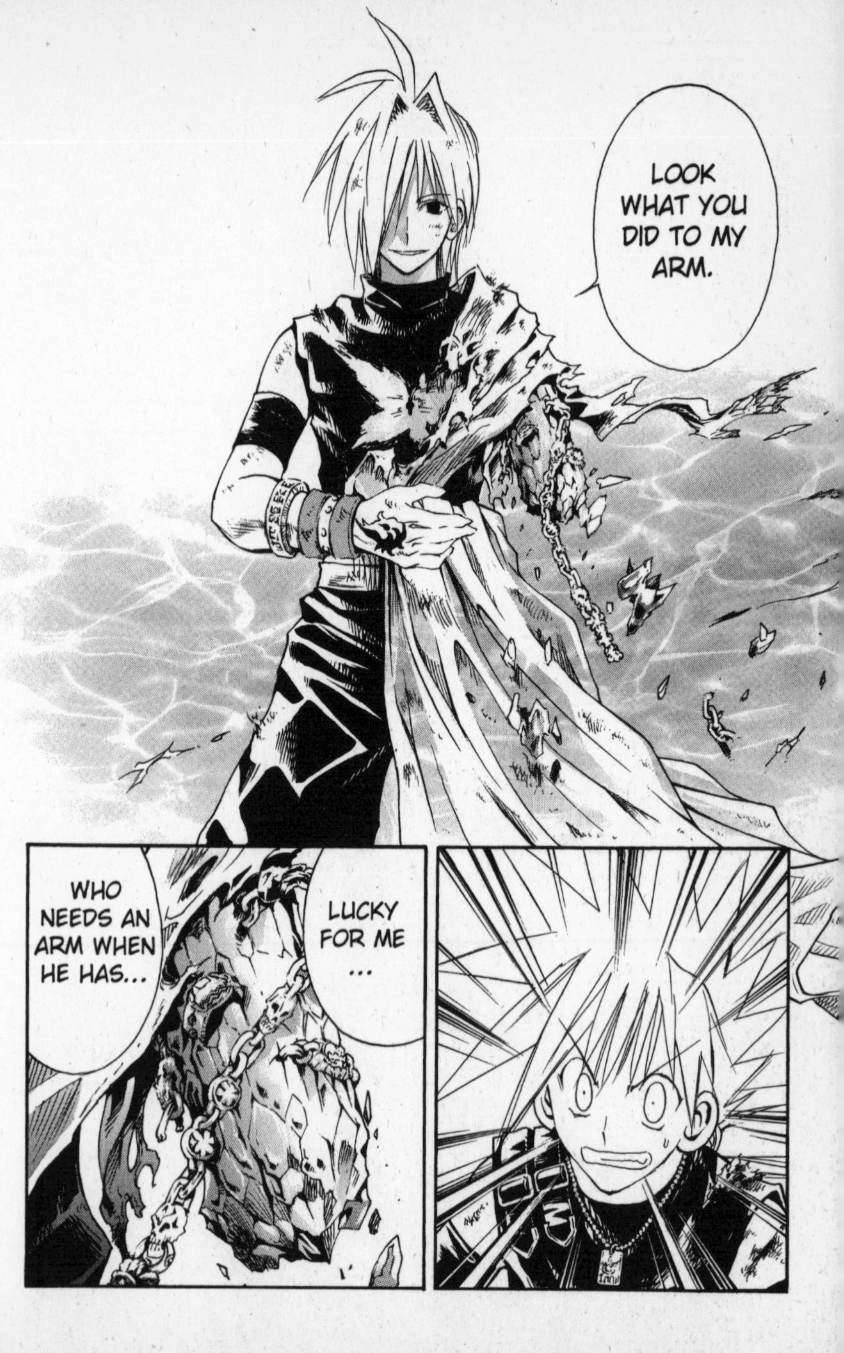
LOOK WHAT YOU DID TO MY ARM.
LUCKY FOR ME ...
WHO NEEDS AN ARM WHEN HE HAS...

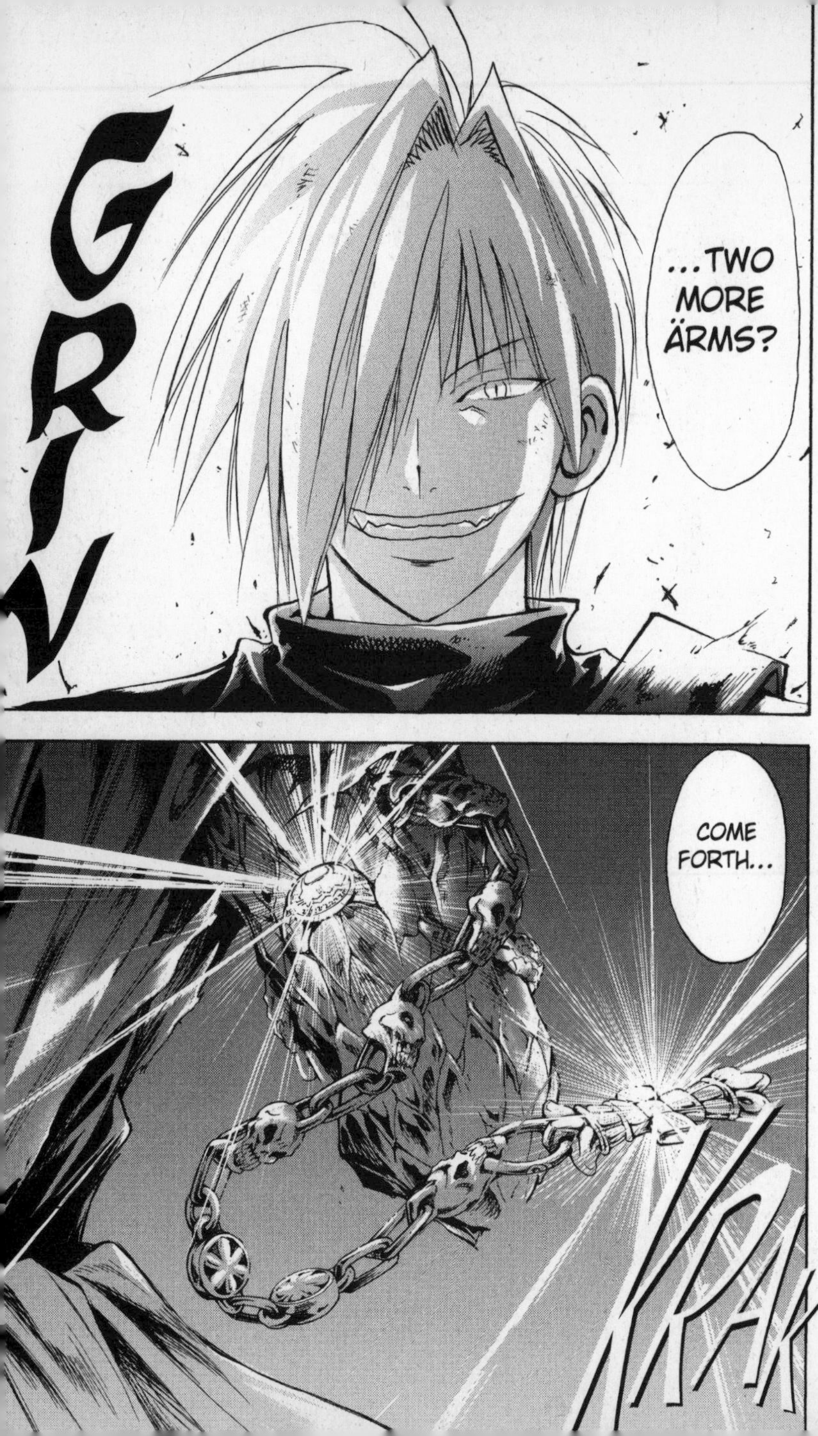
...TWO MORE ÄRMS?
GRIN
COME FORTH...
KRAK

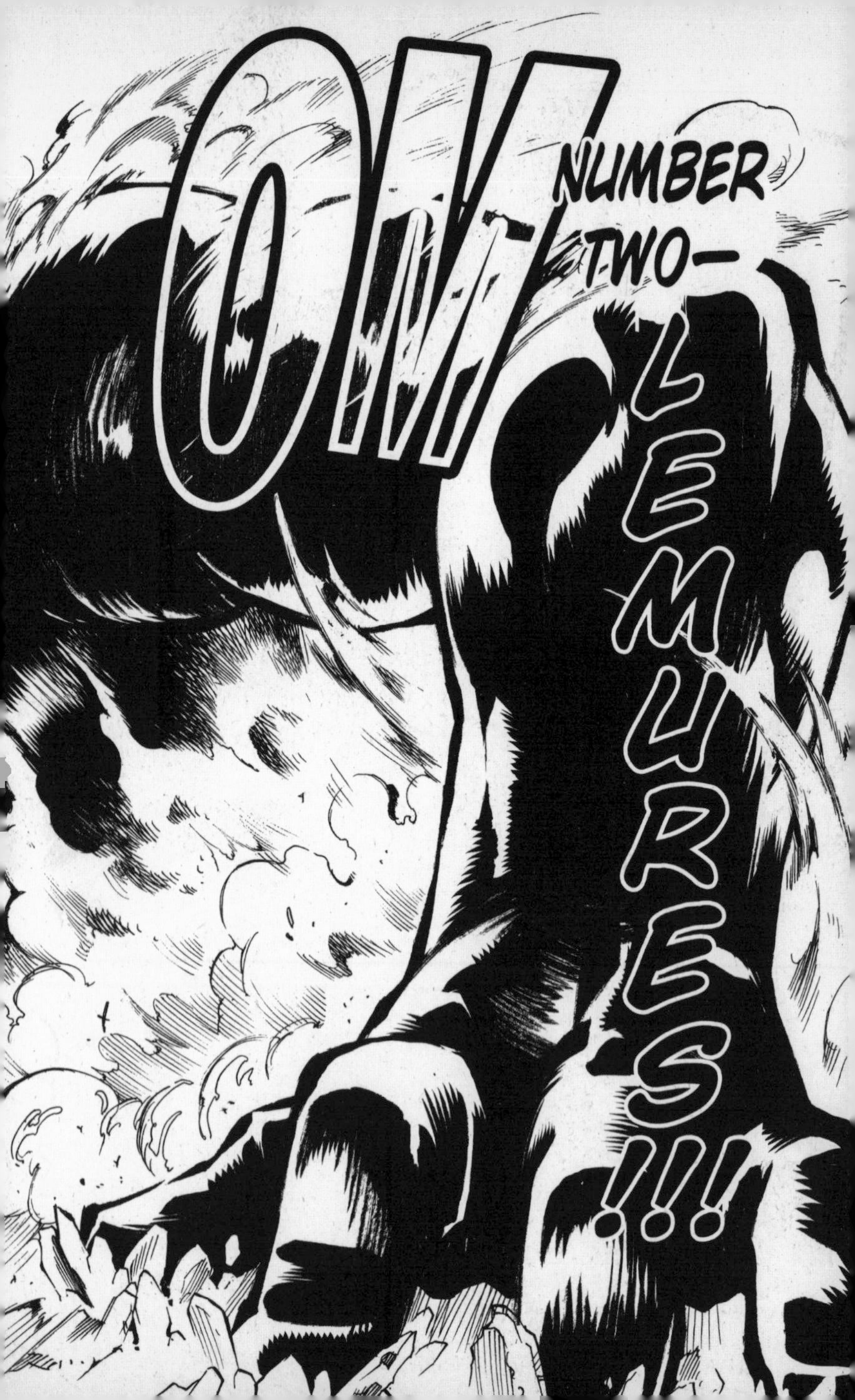
ON
NUMBER TWO—
LEMURES!!!

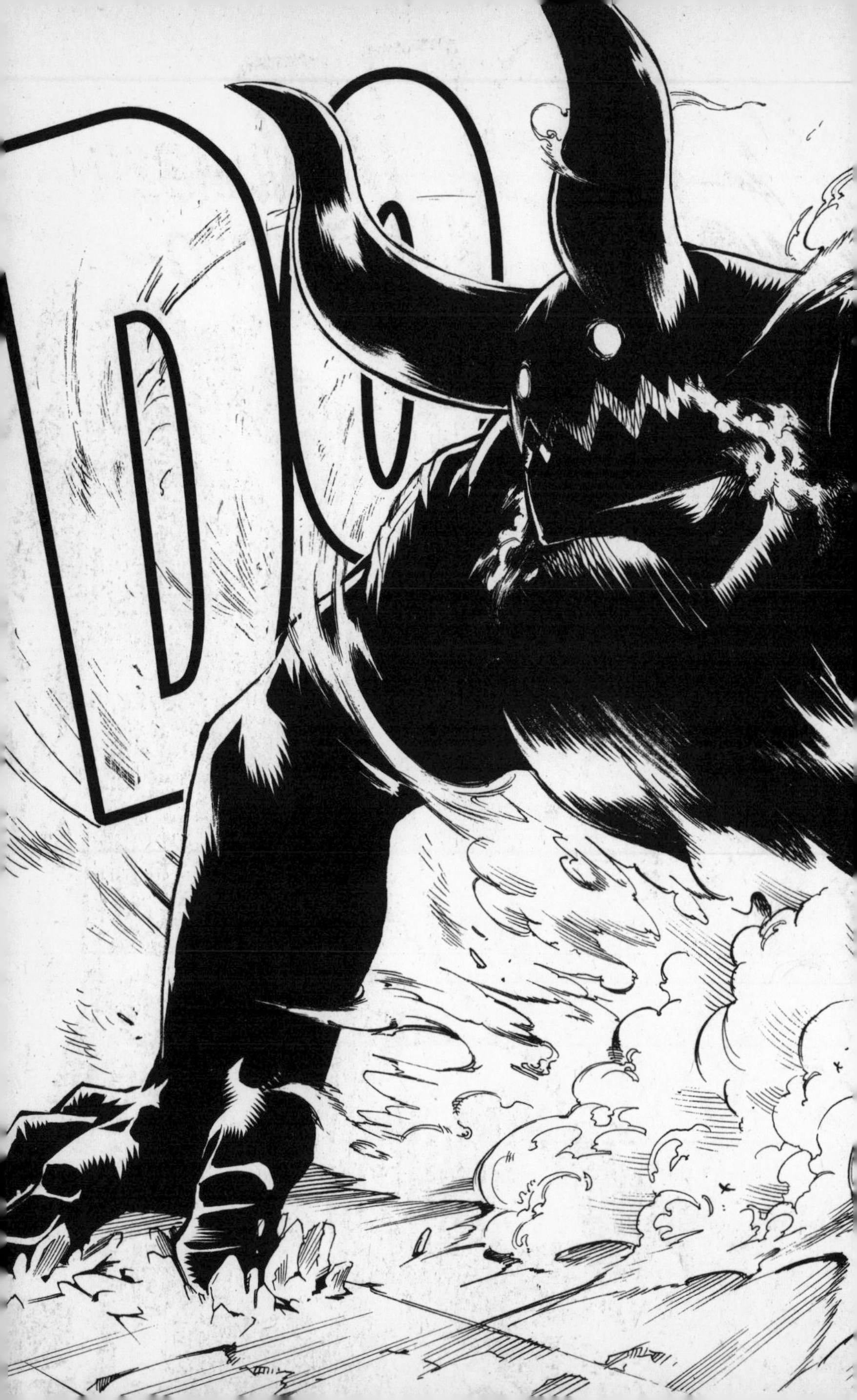
DO

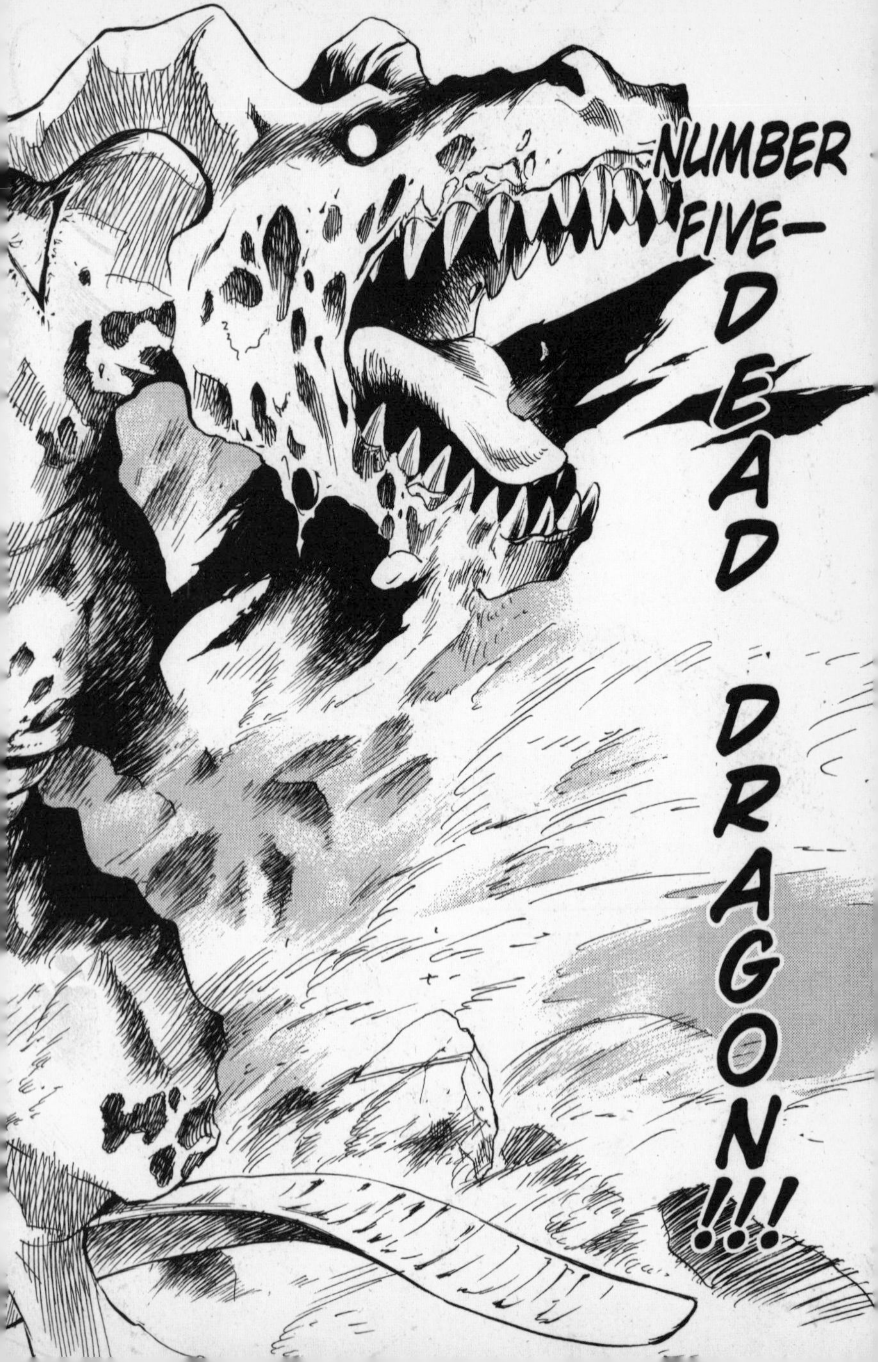
NUMBER FIVE—
DEAD DRAGON!!!

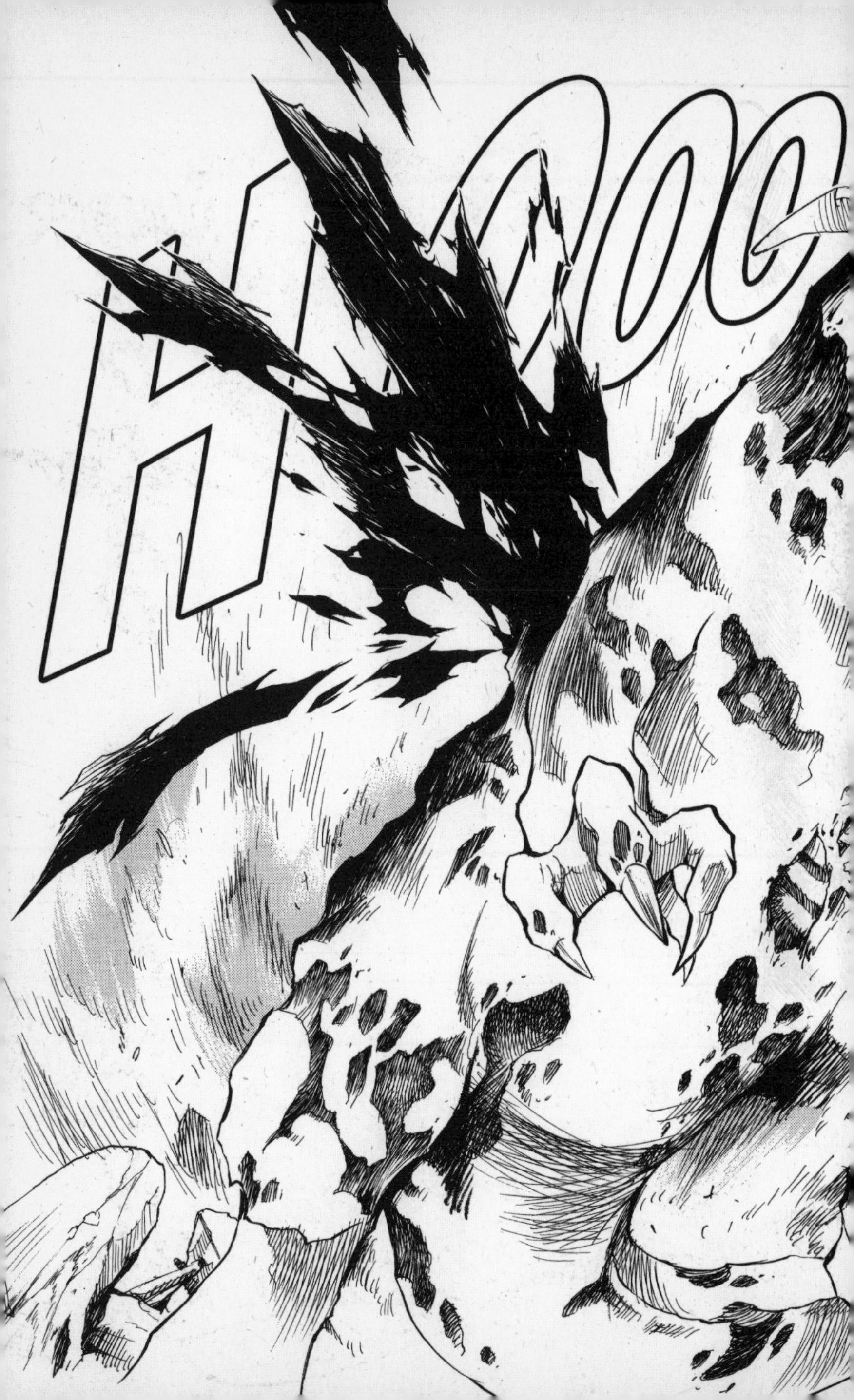
HOOOO

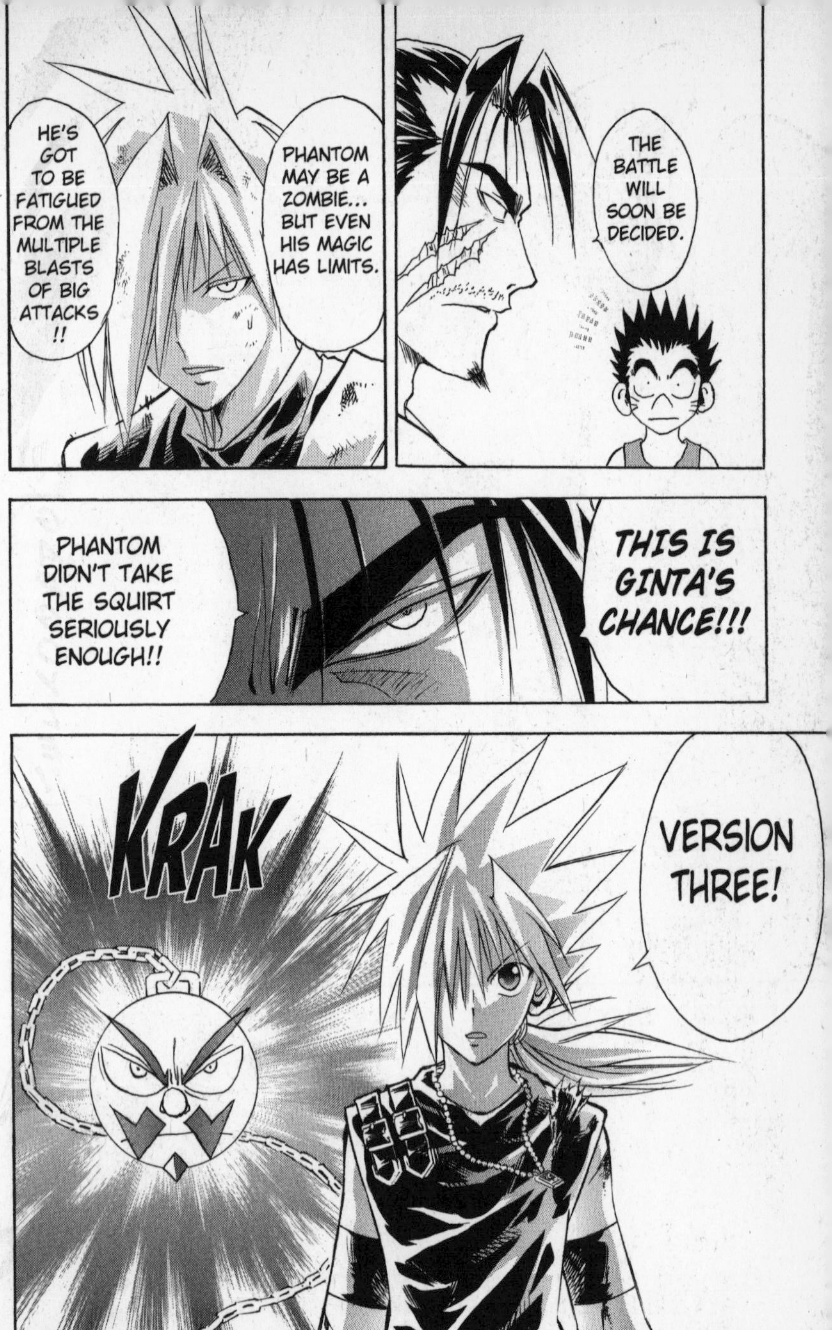
THE BATTLE WILL SOON BE DECIDED.
PHANTOM MAY BE A ZOMBIE... BUT EVEN HIS MAGIC HAS LIMITS.
HE'S GOT TO BE FATIGUED FROM THE MULTIPLE BLASTS OF BIG ATTACKS !!
THIS IS GINTA'S CHANCE!!!
PHANTOM DIDN'T TAKE THE SQUIRT SERIOUSLY ENOUGH!!
VERSION THREE!
KRAK

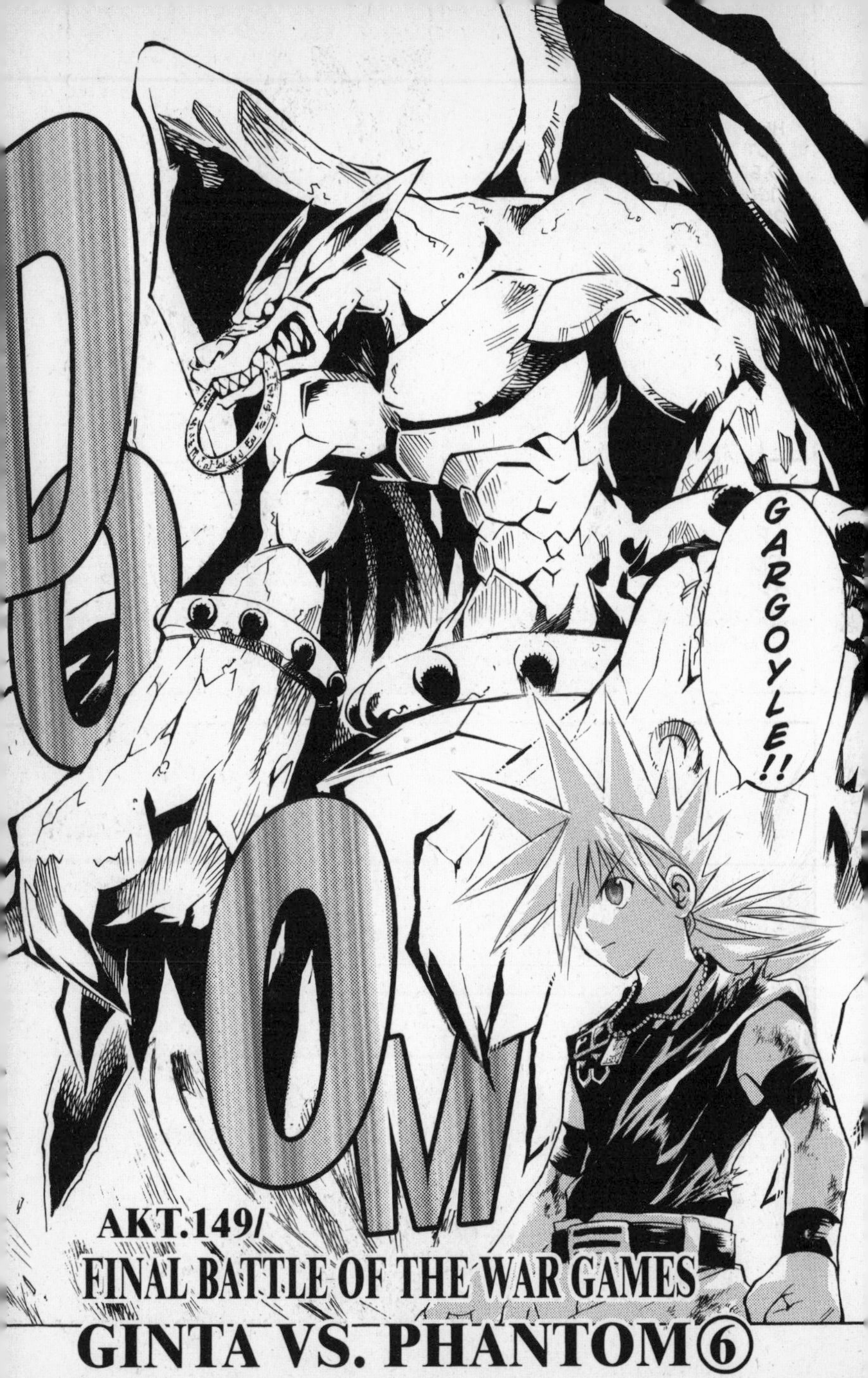
DOOM
GARGOYLE!!

AKT.149/ FINAL BATTLE OF THE WAR GAMES

GINTA VS. PHANTOM ⑥

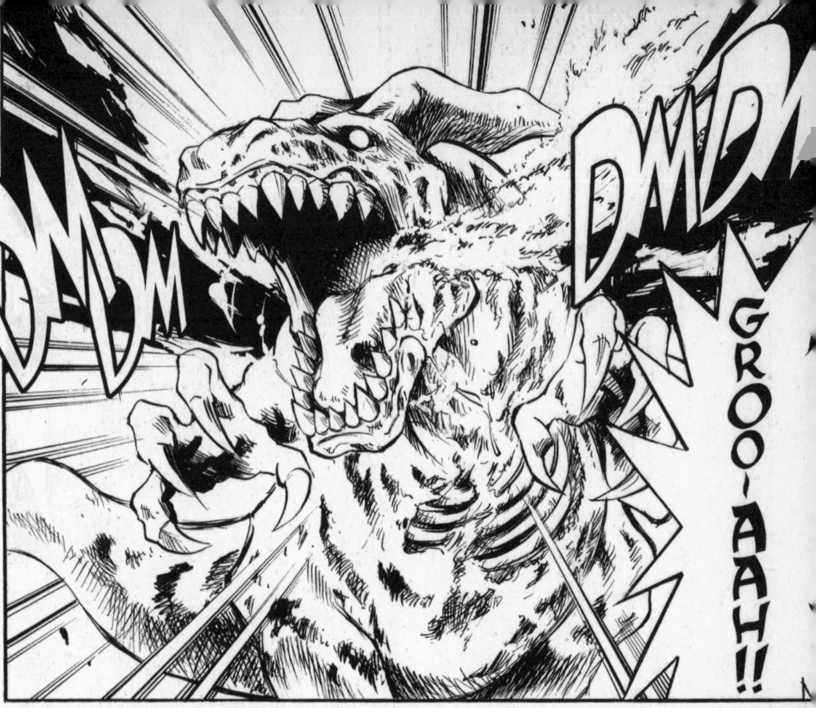
GROO-AAH!!
DMDM

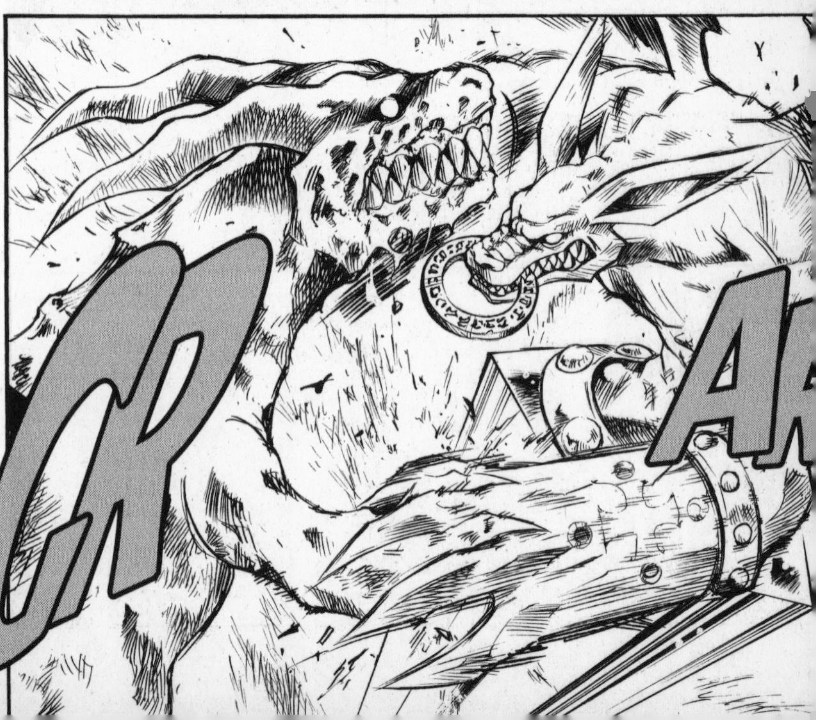
CH

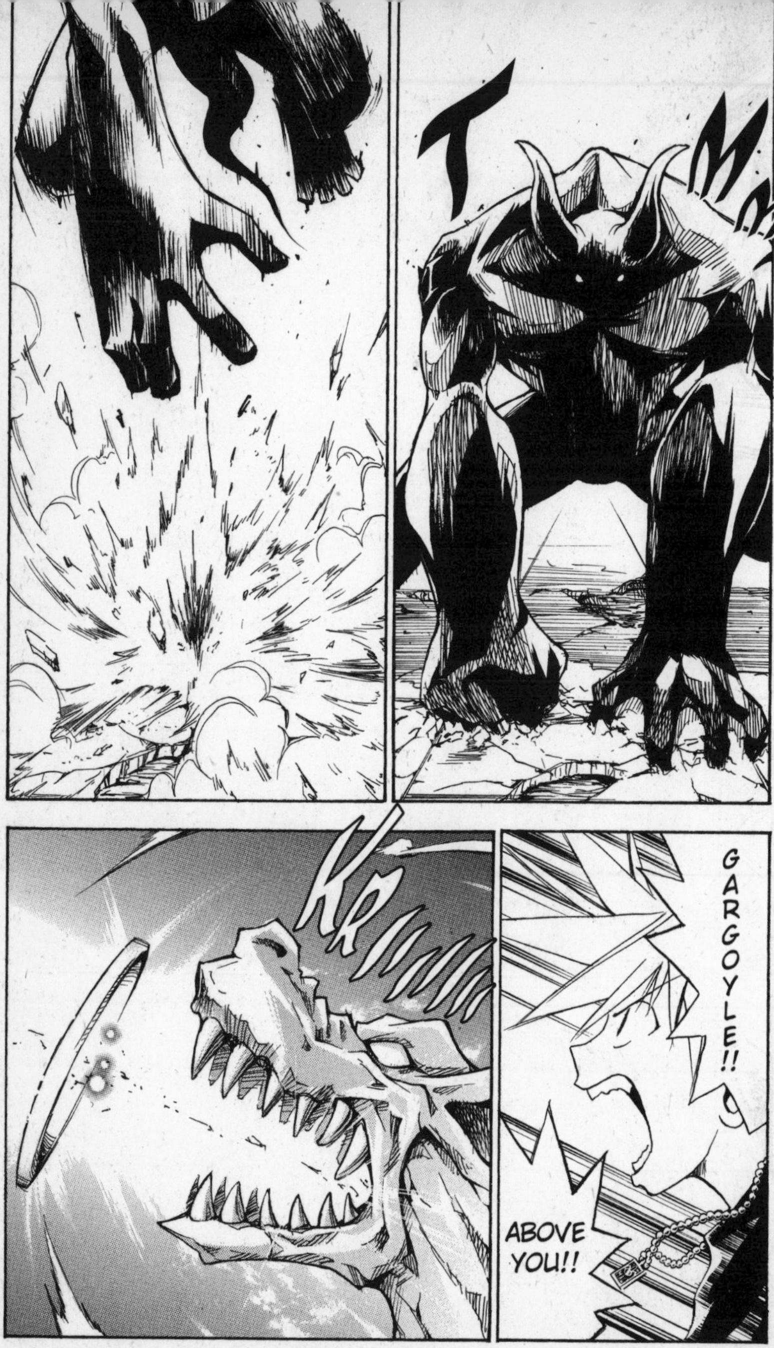
GARGOYLE!!
ABOVE YOU!!

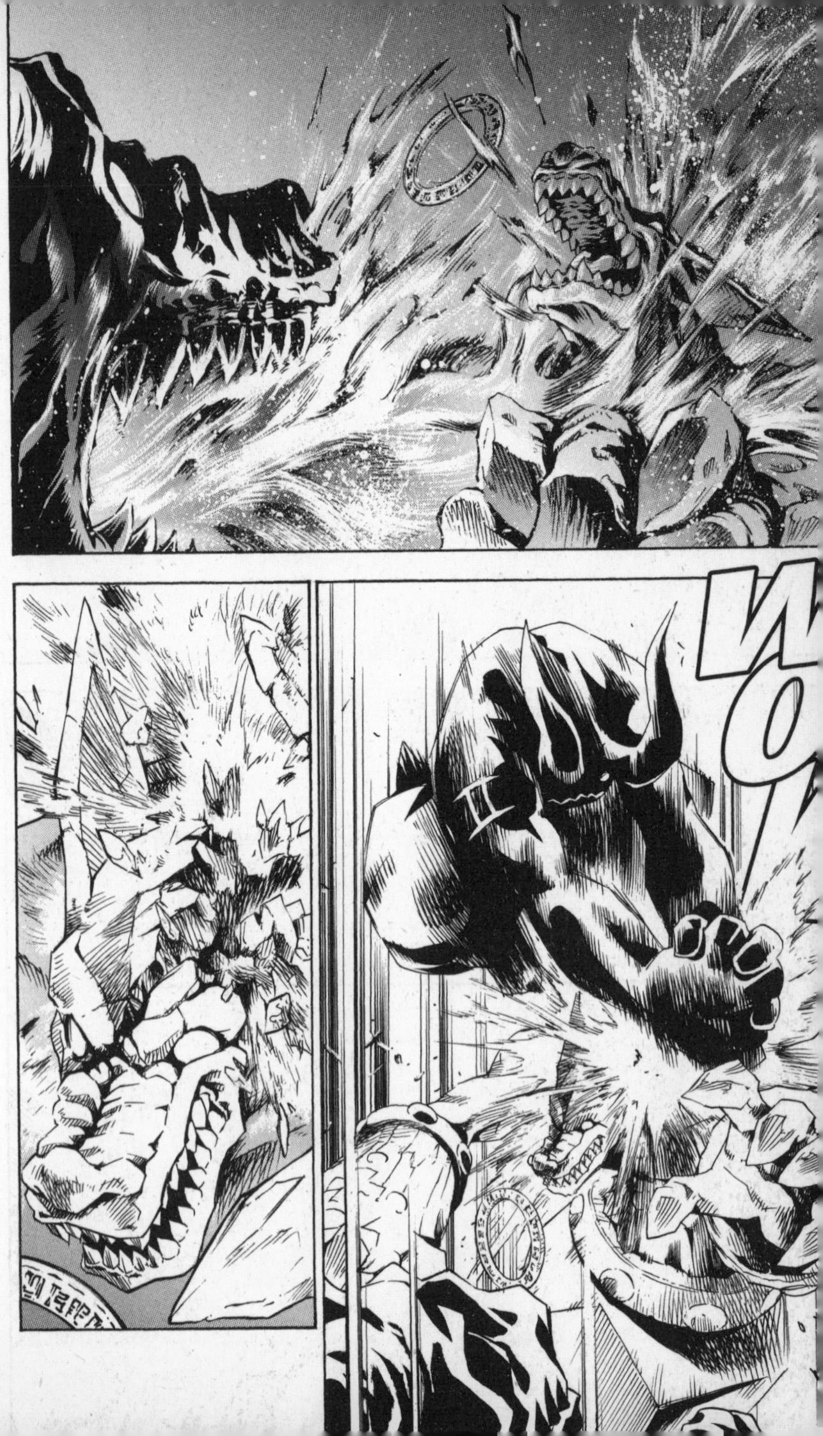

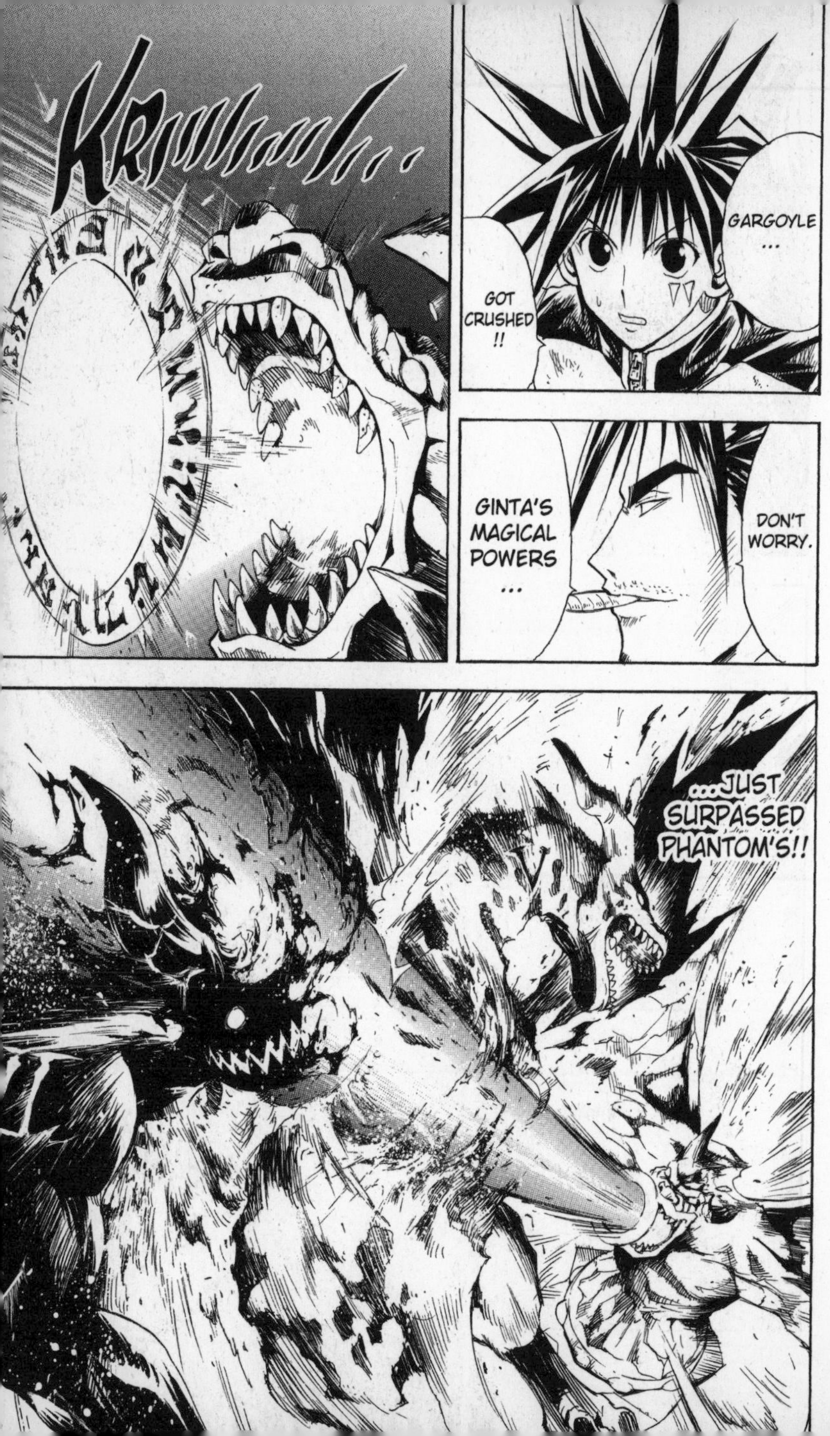
GARGOYLE ...
GOT CRUSHED !!
DON'T WORRY.
GINTA'S MAGICAL POWERS ...
...JUST SURPASSED PHANTOM'S!!

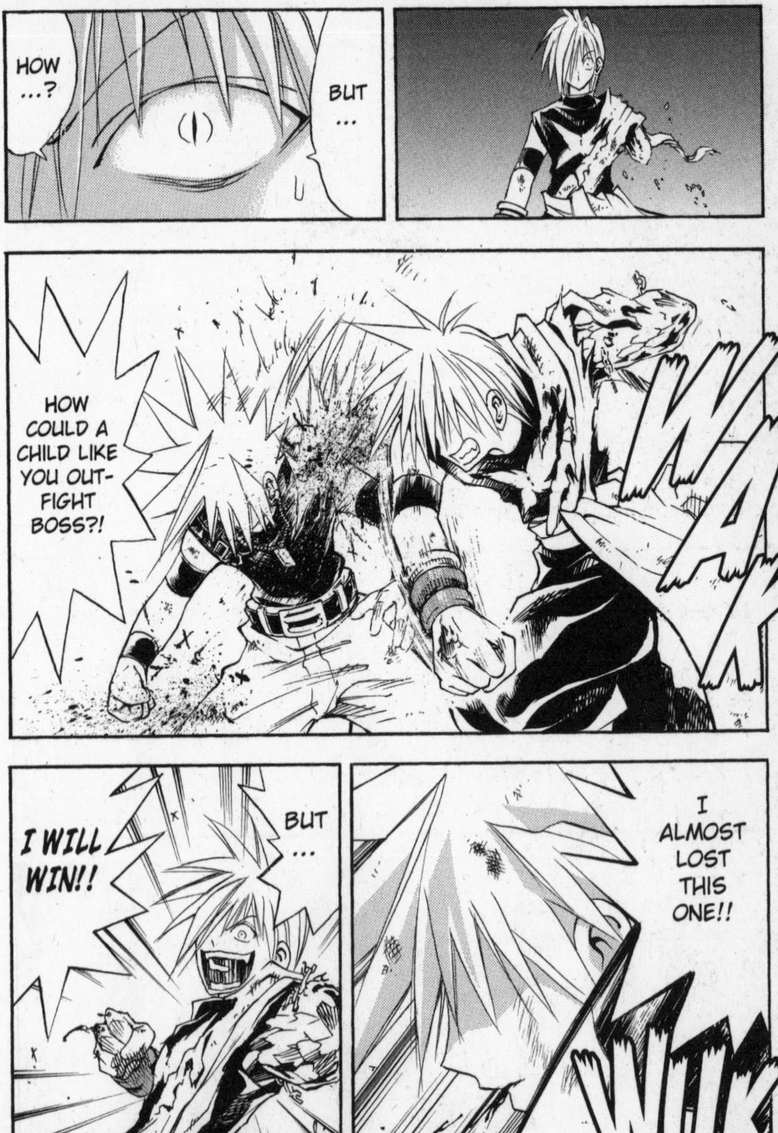
BUT ...
HOW ...?
WAK
HOW COULD A CHILD LIKE YOU OUT-FIGHT BOSS?!
I ALMOST LOST THIS ONE!!
WUK
BUT ...
I WILL WIN!!

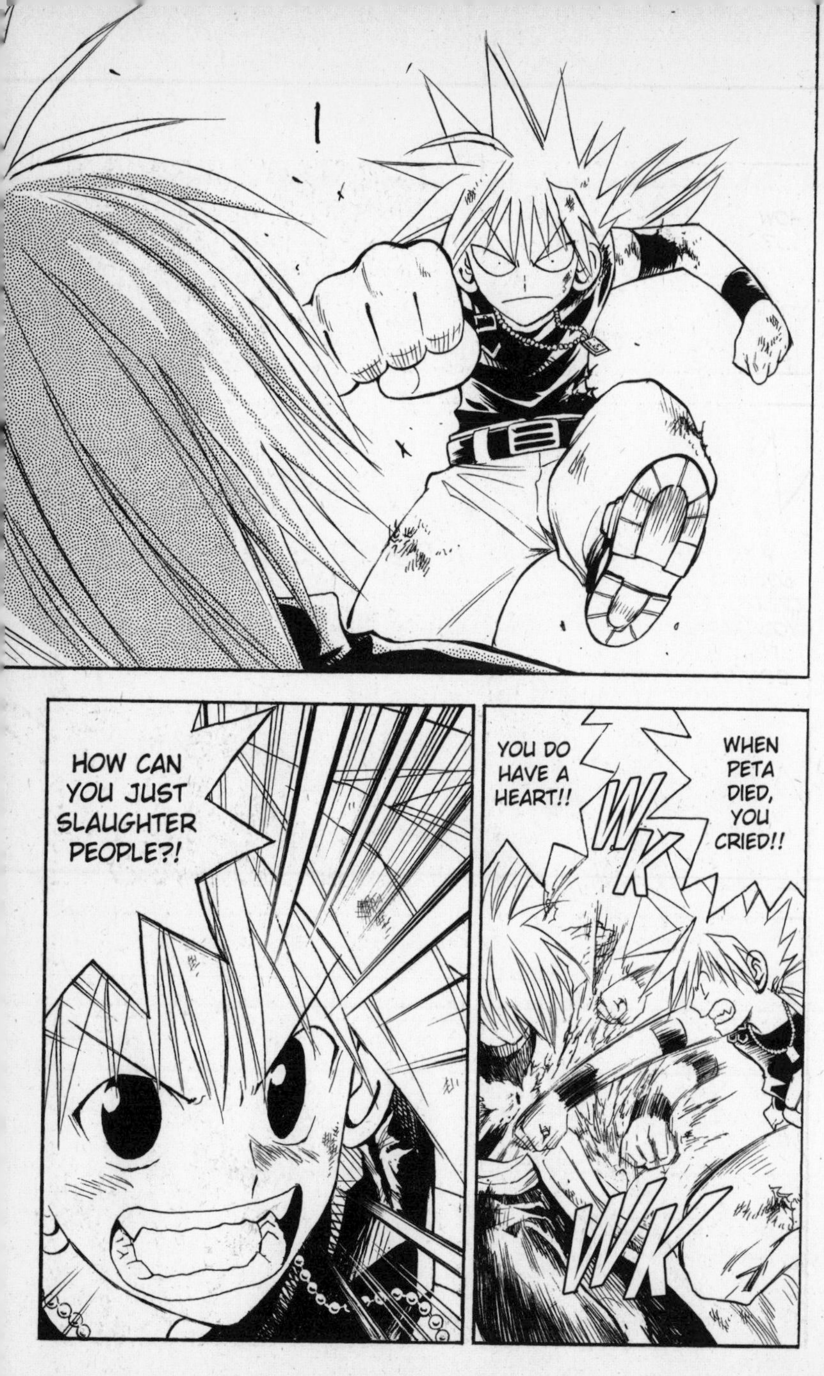
WHEN PETA DIED, YOU CRIED!!
YOU DO HAVE A HEART!!
WK
WK
HOW CAN YOU JUST SLAUGHTER PEOPLE?!

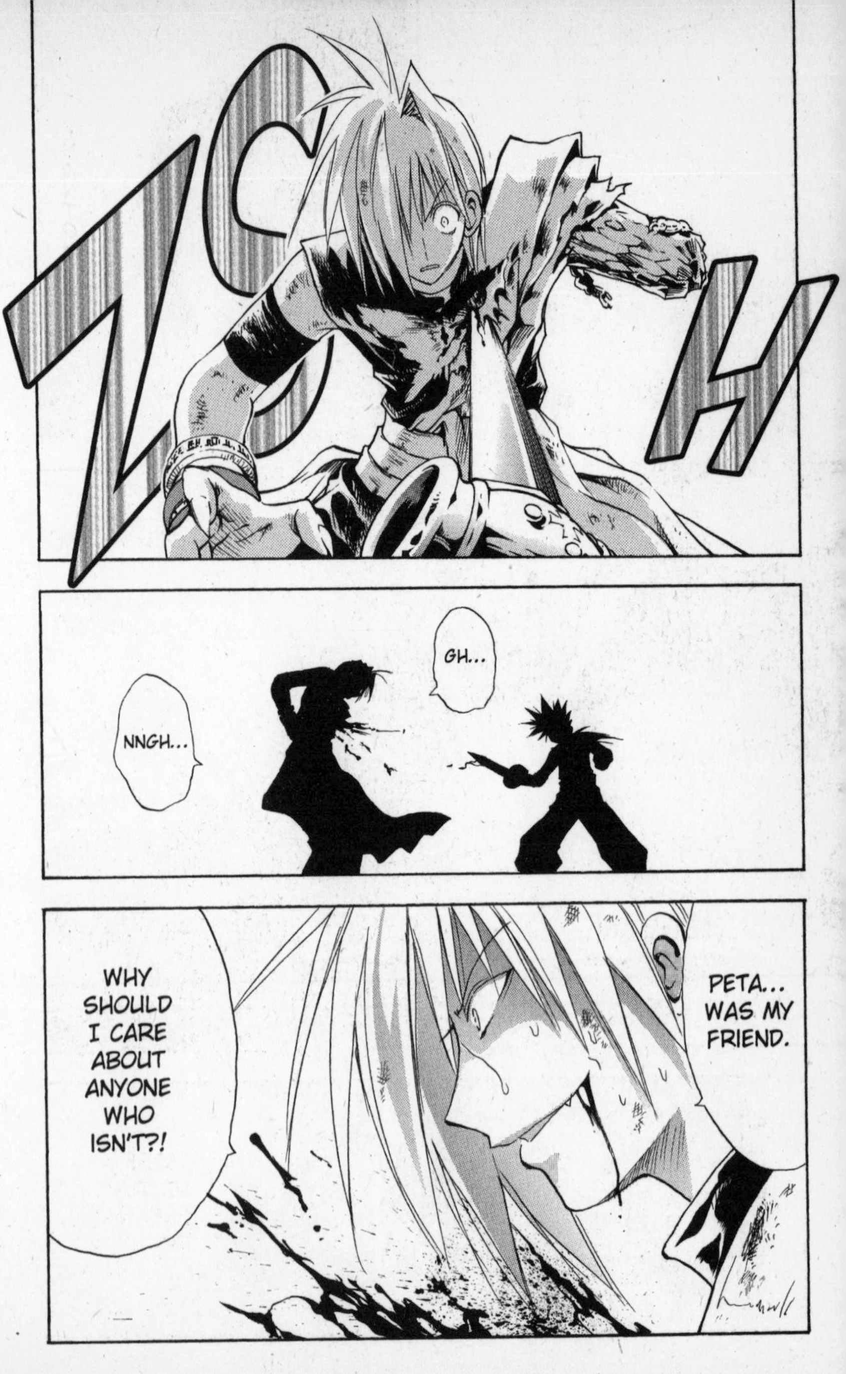
ZCH
GH...
NNGH...
PETA... WAS MY FRIEND.
WHY SHOULD I CARE ABOUT ANYONE WHO ISN'T?!

PHANTOM...

I AM PHANTOM, FIRST AMONG KNIGHTS!!

I BRING MÄR HEAVEN THE GIFT OF HELL!!

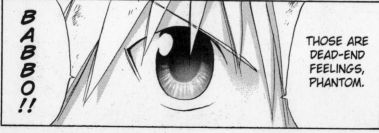

BABBO!!

THOSE ARE DEAD-END FEELINGS, PHANTOM.

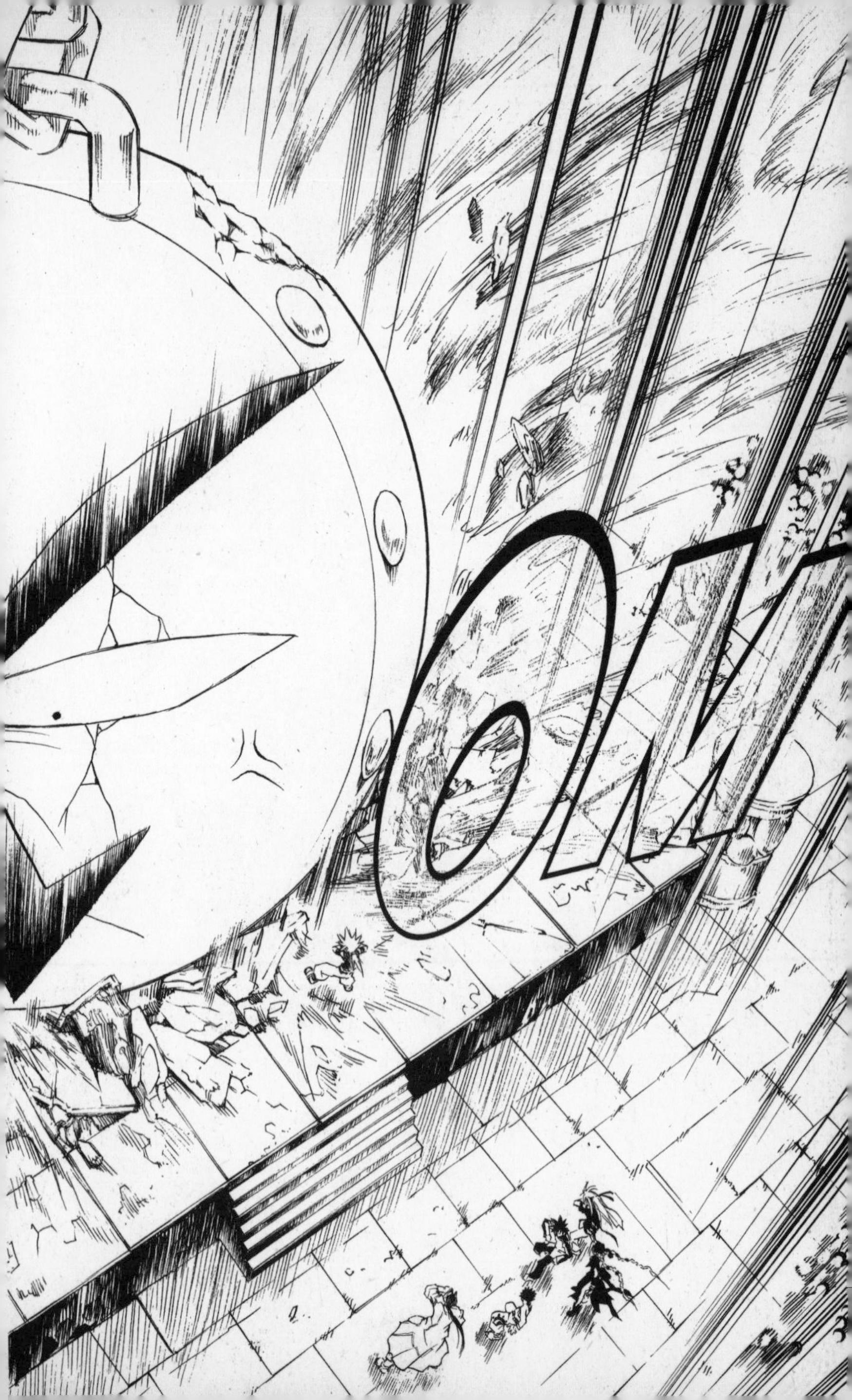
OM

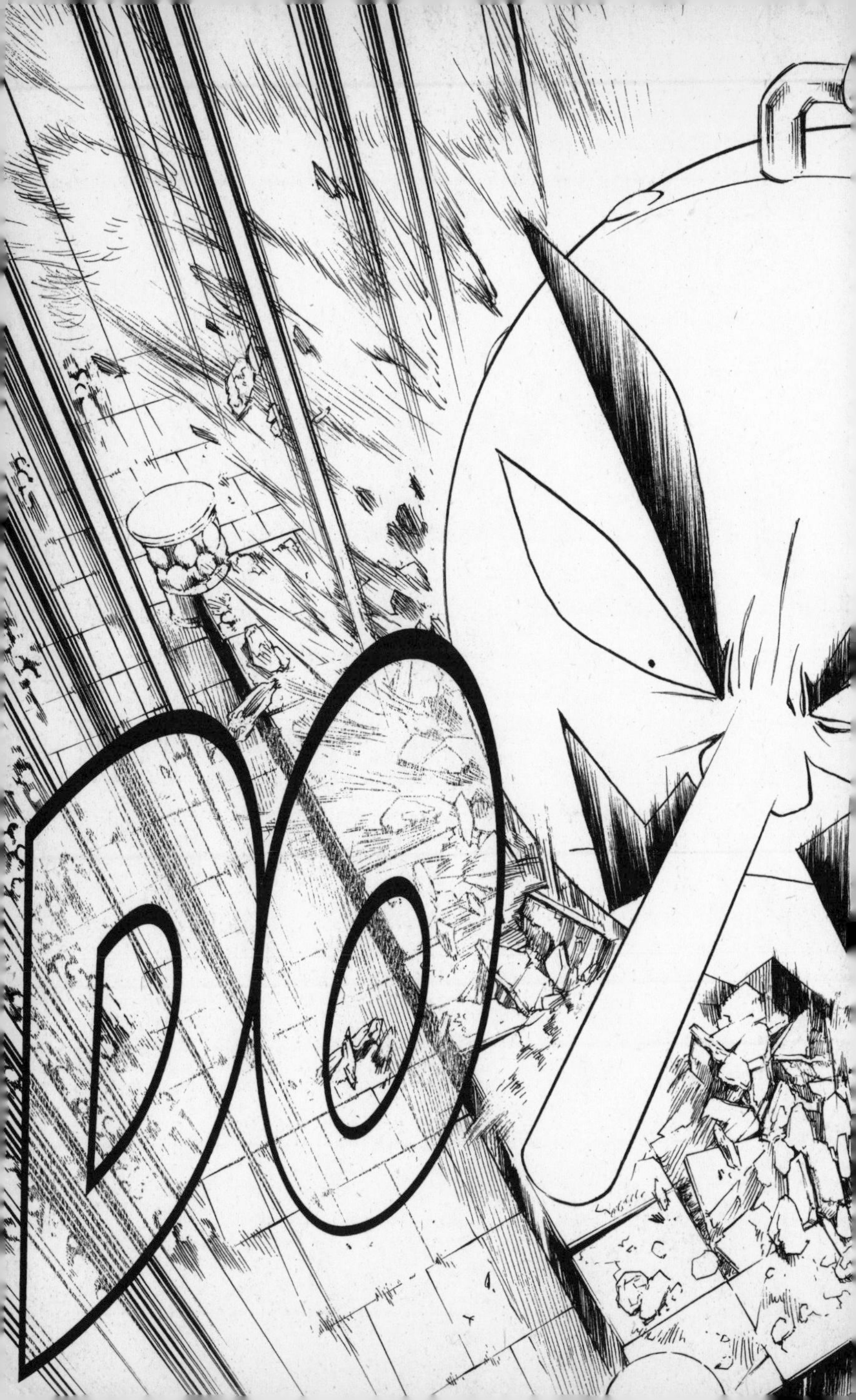
DO

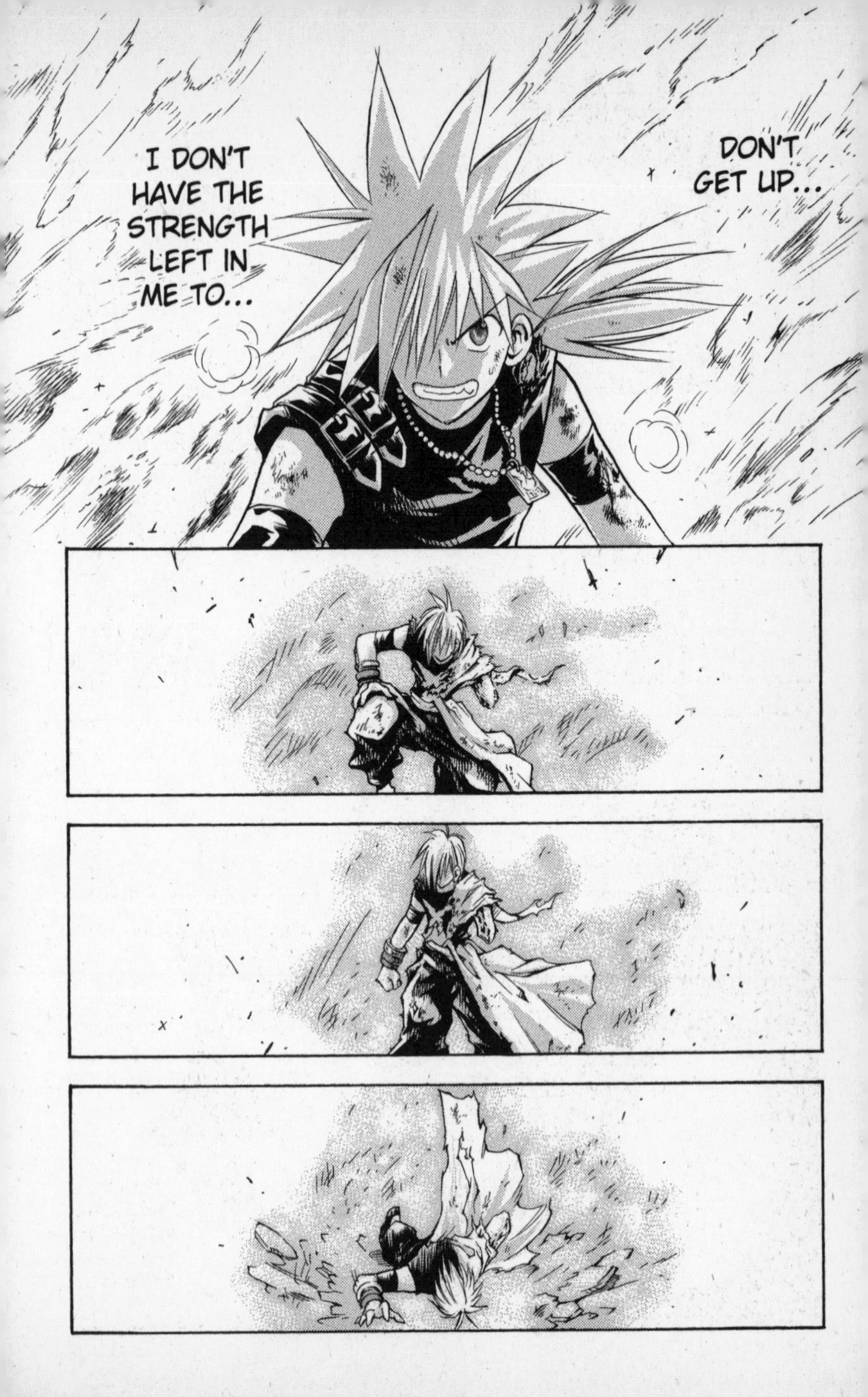
DON'T GET UP...
I DON'T HAVE THE STRENGTH LEFT IN ME TO...

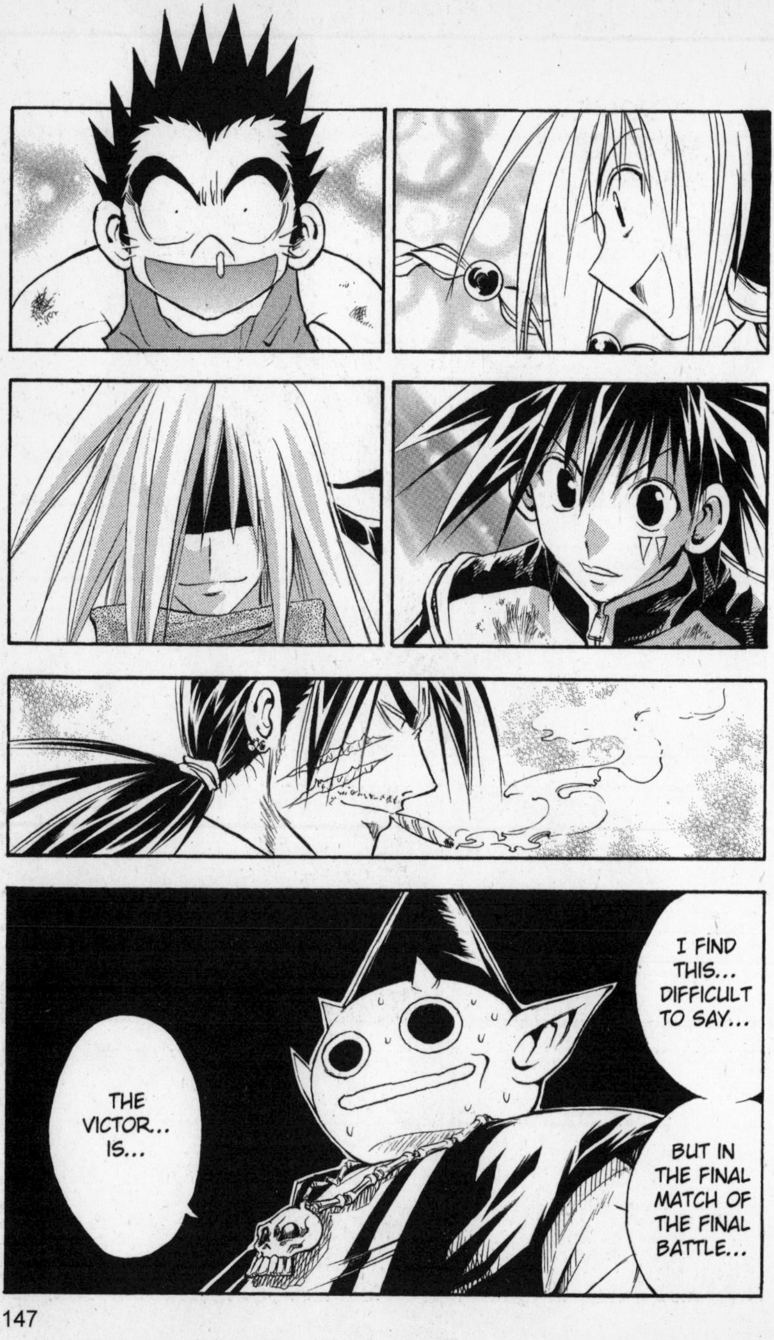
I FIND THIS... DIFFICULT TO SAY...
BUT IN THE FINAL MATCH OF THE FINAL BATTLE...
THE VICTOR... IS...

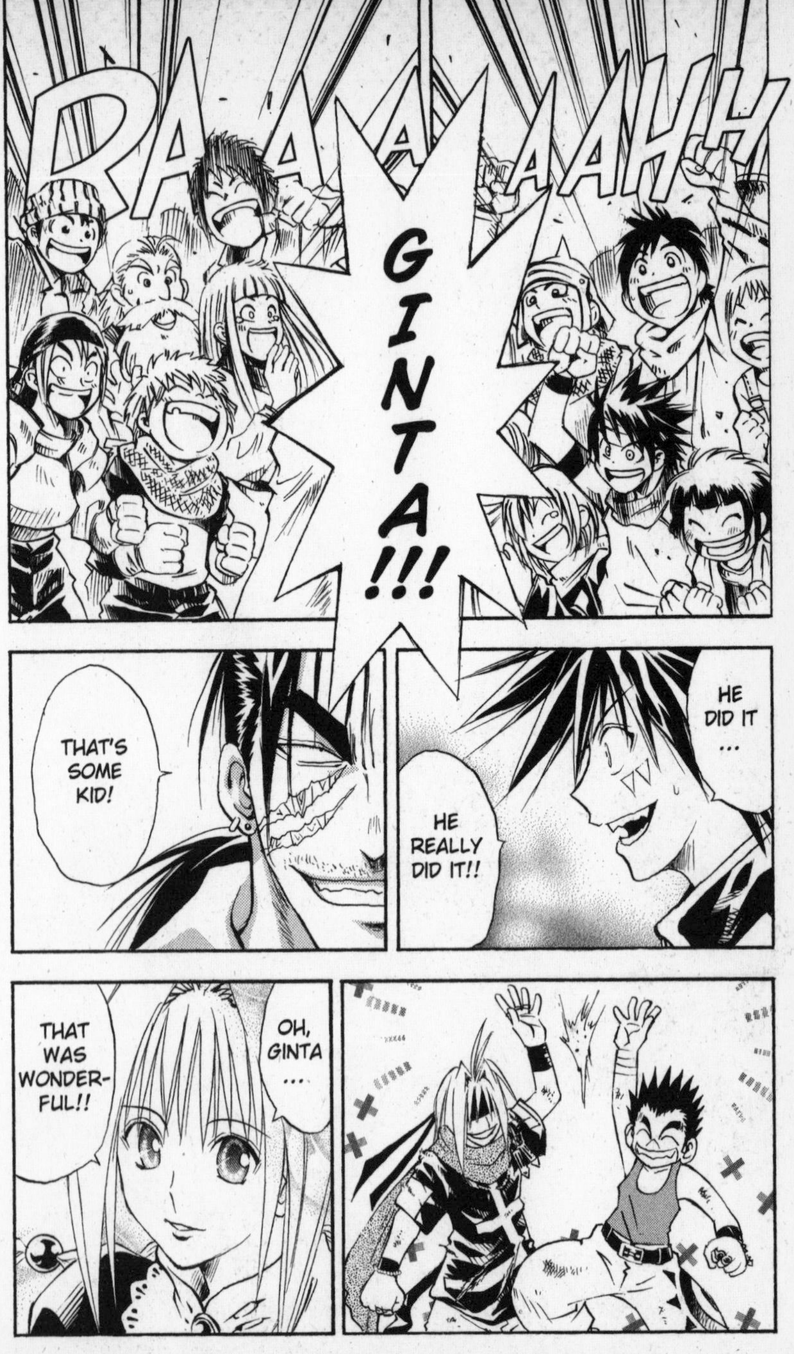

RAAAAAHH
GINTA!!!
HE DID IT ...
HE REALLY DID IT!!
THAT'S SOME KID!
OH, GINTA ...
THAT WAS WONDERFUL!!

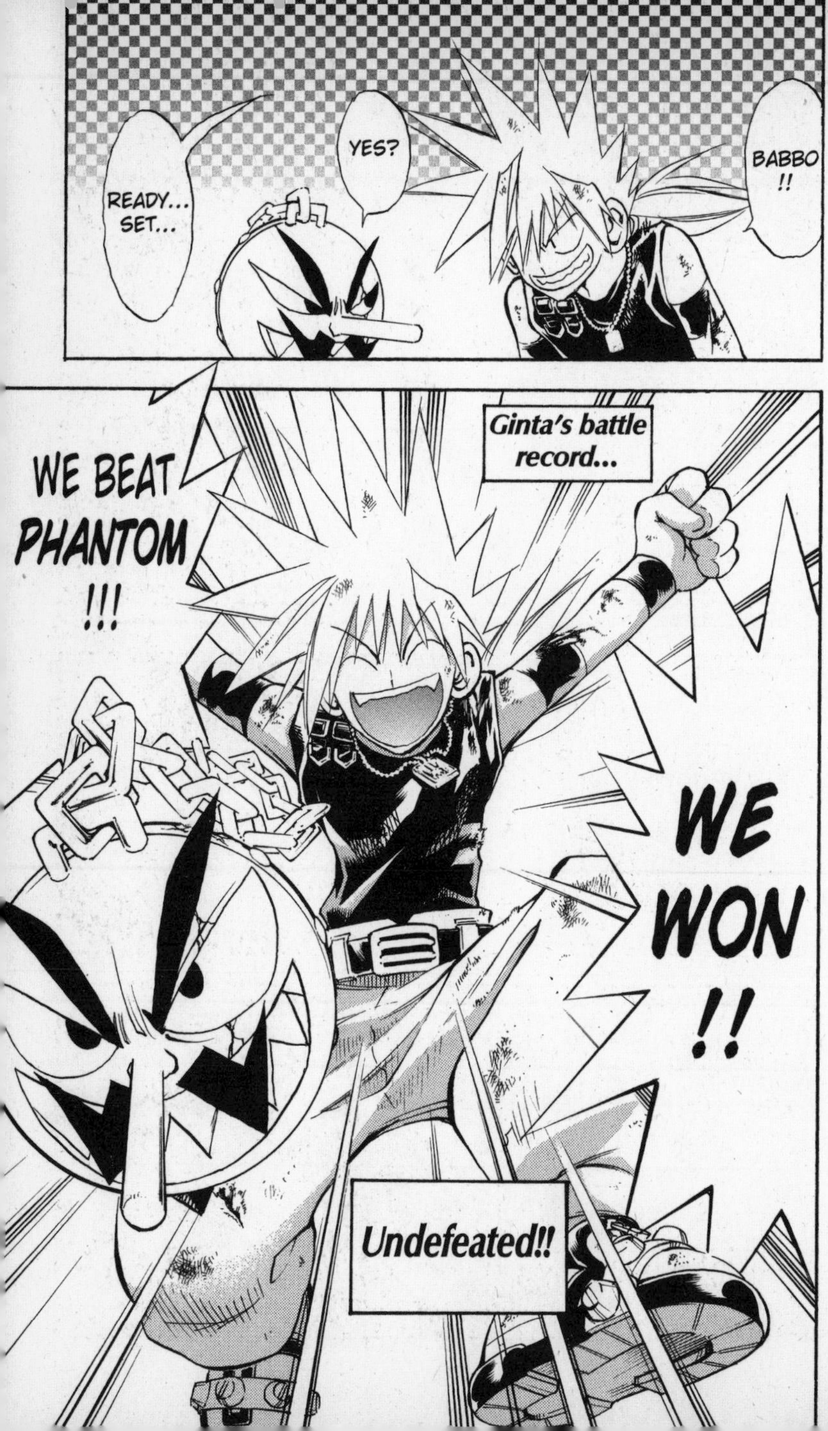
BABBO!!
YES?
READY... SET...
Ginta's battle record...
WE BEAT PHANTOM!!!
WE WON!!
Undefeated!!

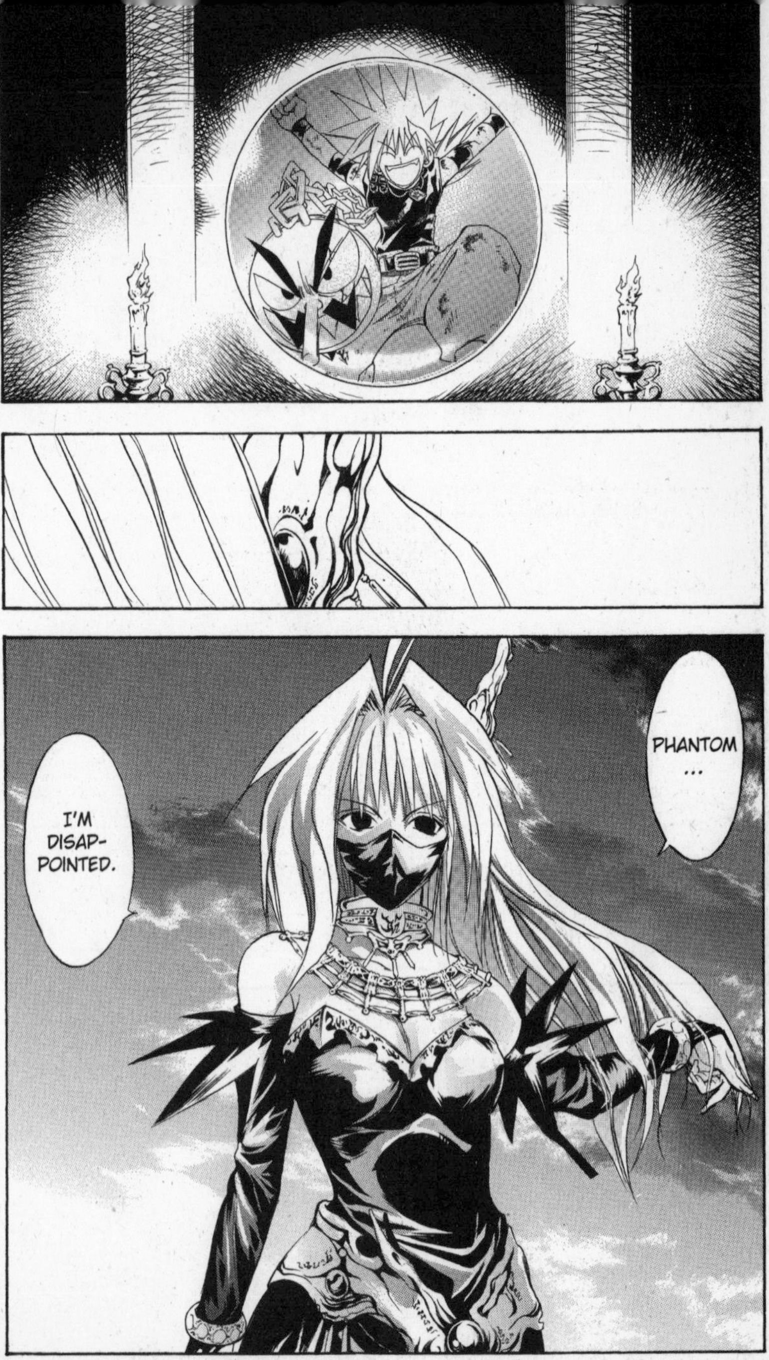
PHANTOM ...
I'M DISAP-POINTED.

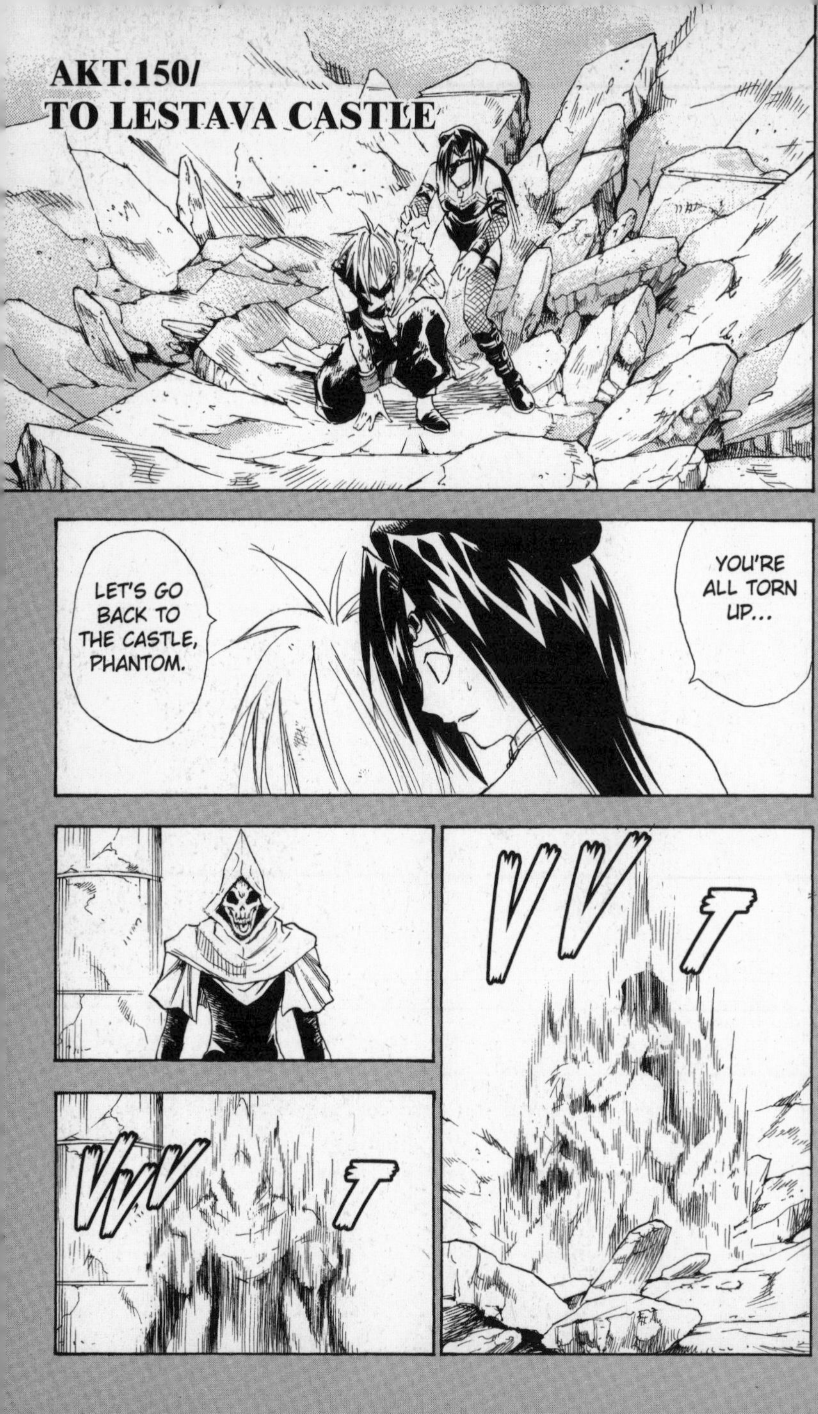
AKT.150/
TO LESTAVA CASTLE
YOU'RE ALL TORN UP...
LET'S GO BACK TO THE CASTLE, PHANTOM.
VVVT
VVVT

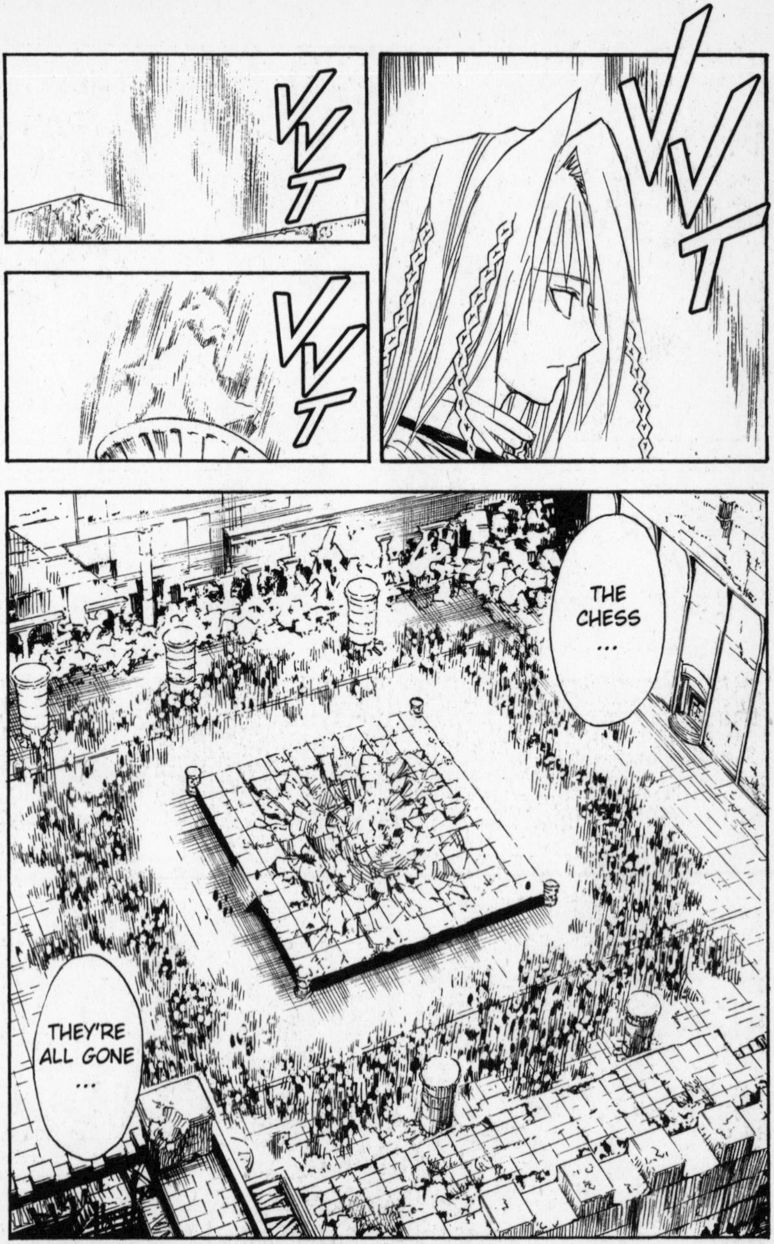
VVT
VVT
VVT
THE CHESS ...
THEY'RE ALL GONE ...

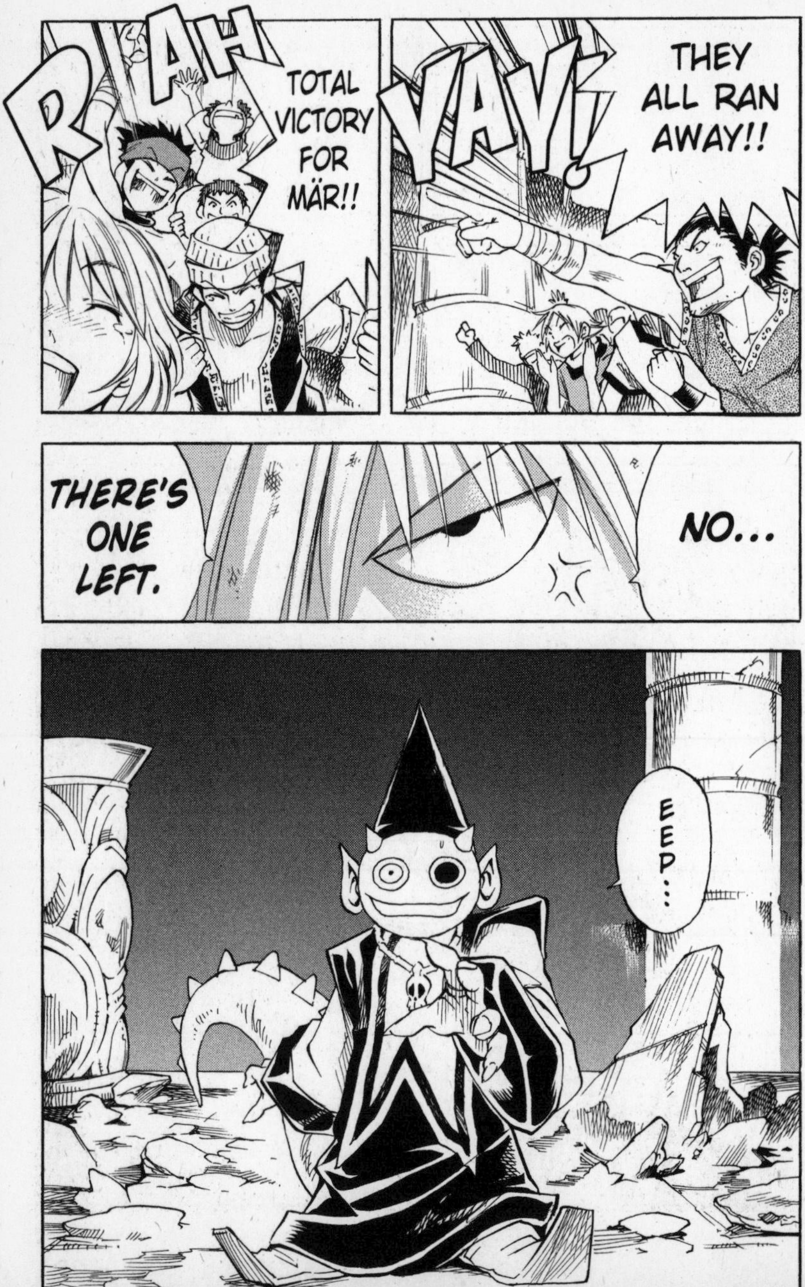
YAY!
THEY ALL RAN AWAY!!
RAH
TOTAL VICTORY FOR MÄR!!
NO...
THERE'S ONE LEFT.
EEP...

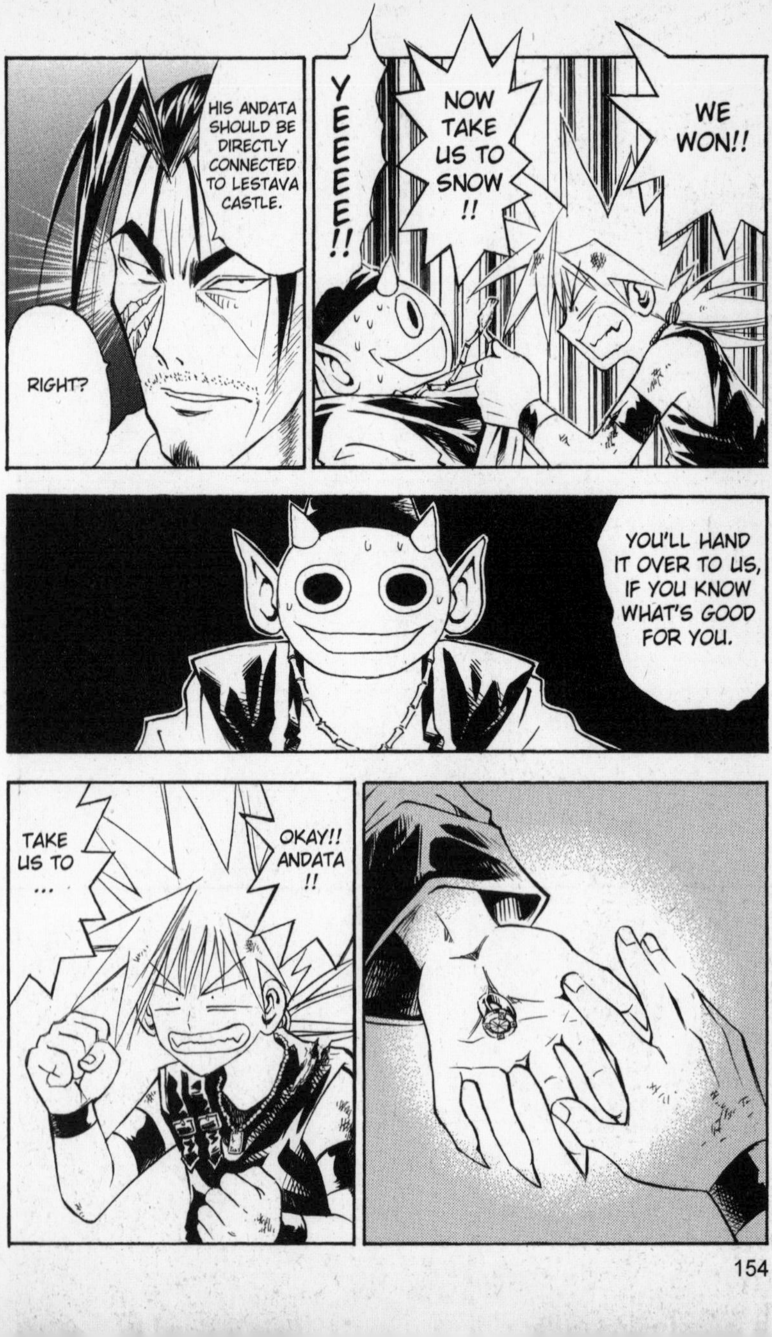
WE WON!!
NOW TAKE US TO SNOW !!
YEEEE!!
HIS ANDATA SHOULD BE DIRECTLY CONNECTED TO LESTAVA CASTLE.
RIGHT?
YOU'LL HAND IT OVER TO US, IF YOU KNOW WHAT'S GOOD FOR YOU.
OKAY!! ANDATA !!
TAKE US TO ...

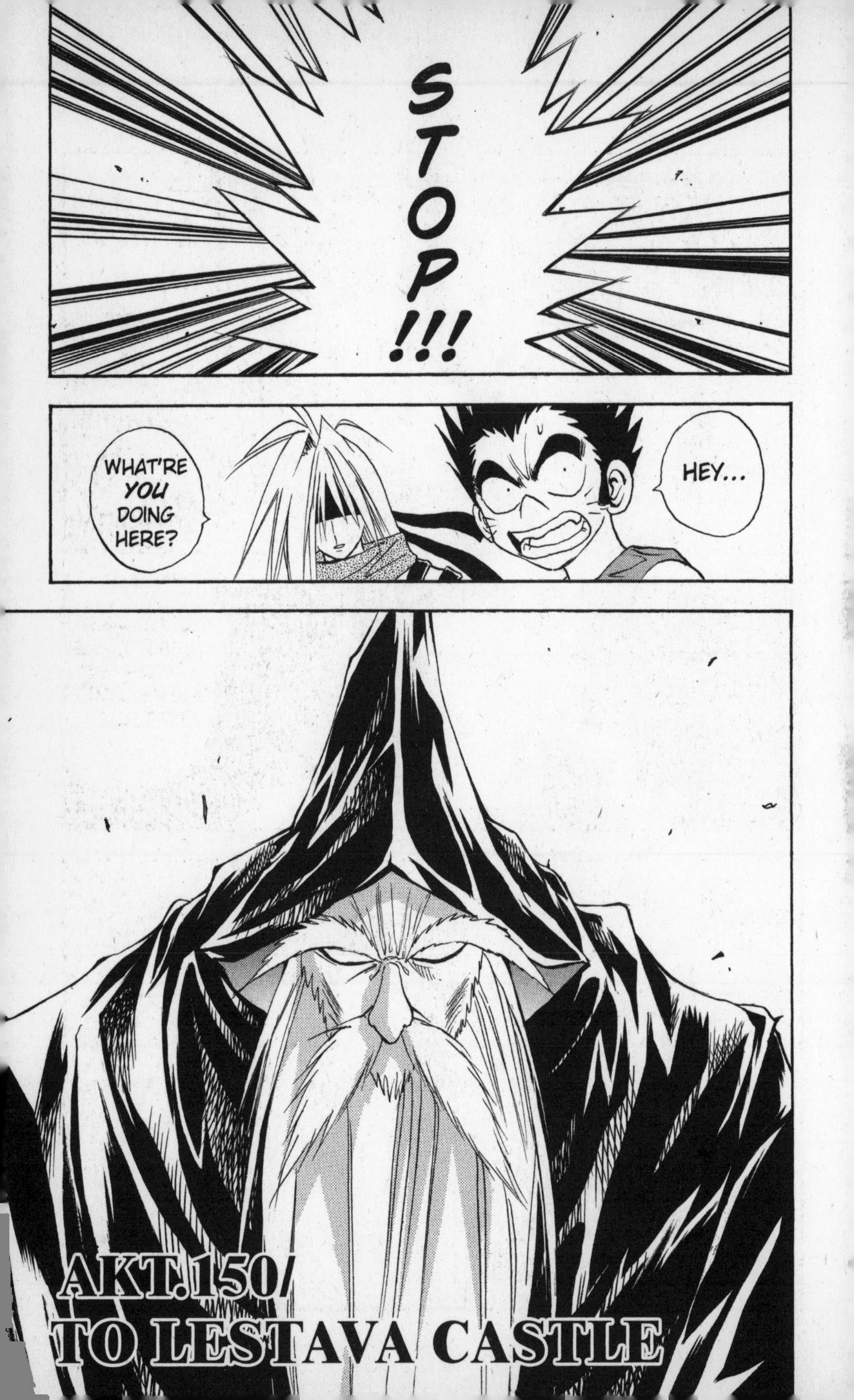
STOP!!!
HEY...
WHAT'RE YOU DOING HERE?
AKT.150/
TO LESTAVA CASTLE

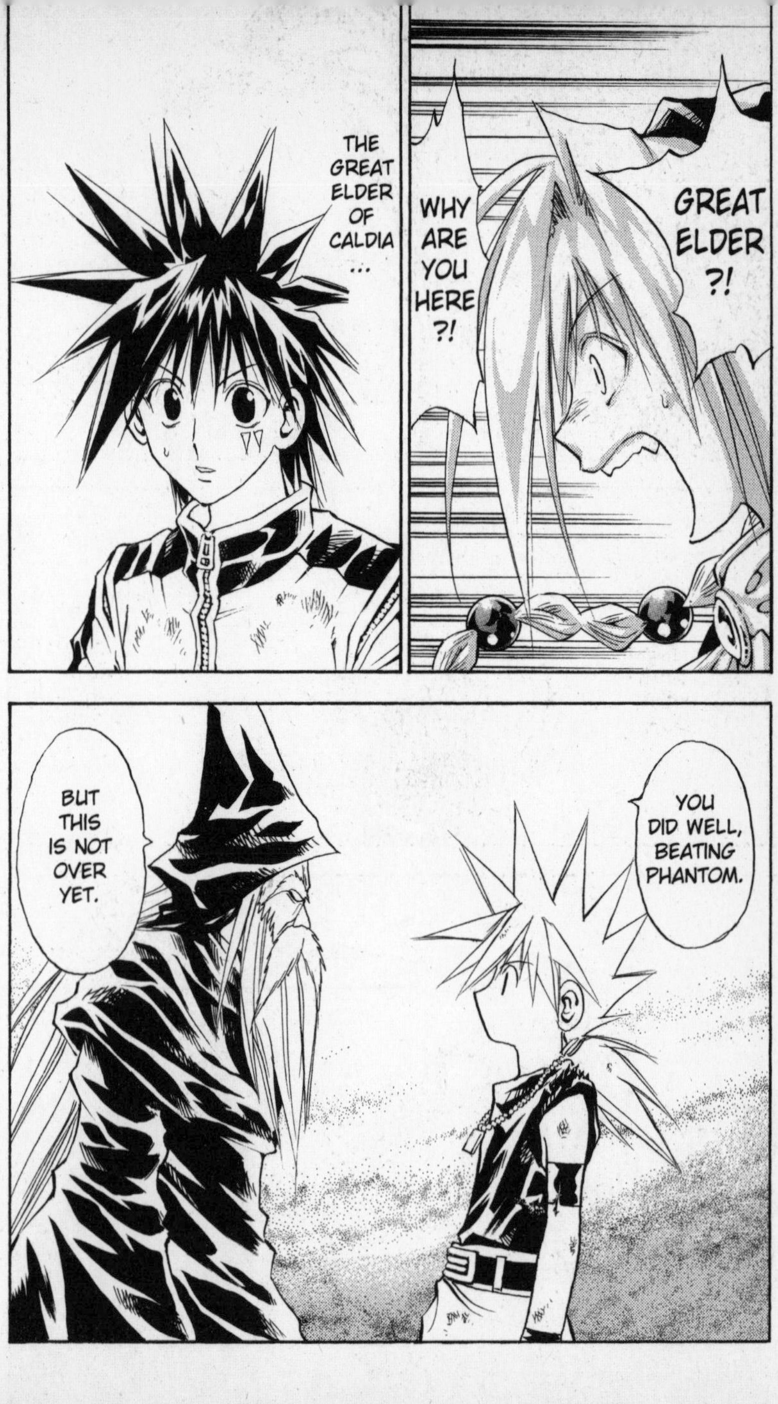
GREAT ELDER ?!
WHY ARE YOU HERE ?!
THE GREAT ELDER OF CALDIA ...
YOU DID WELL, BEATING PHANTOM.
BUT THIS IS NOT OVER YET.

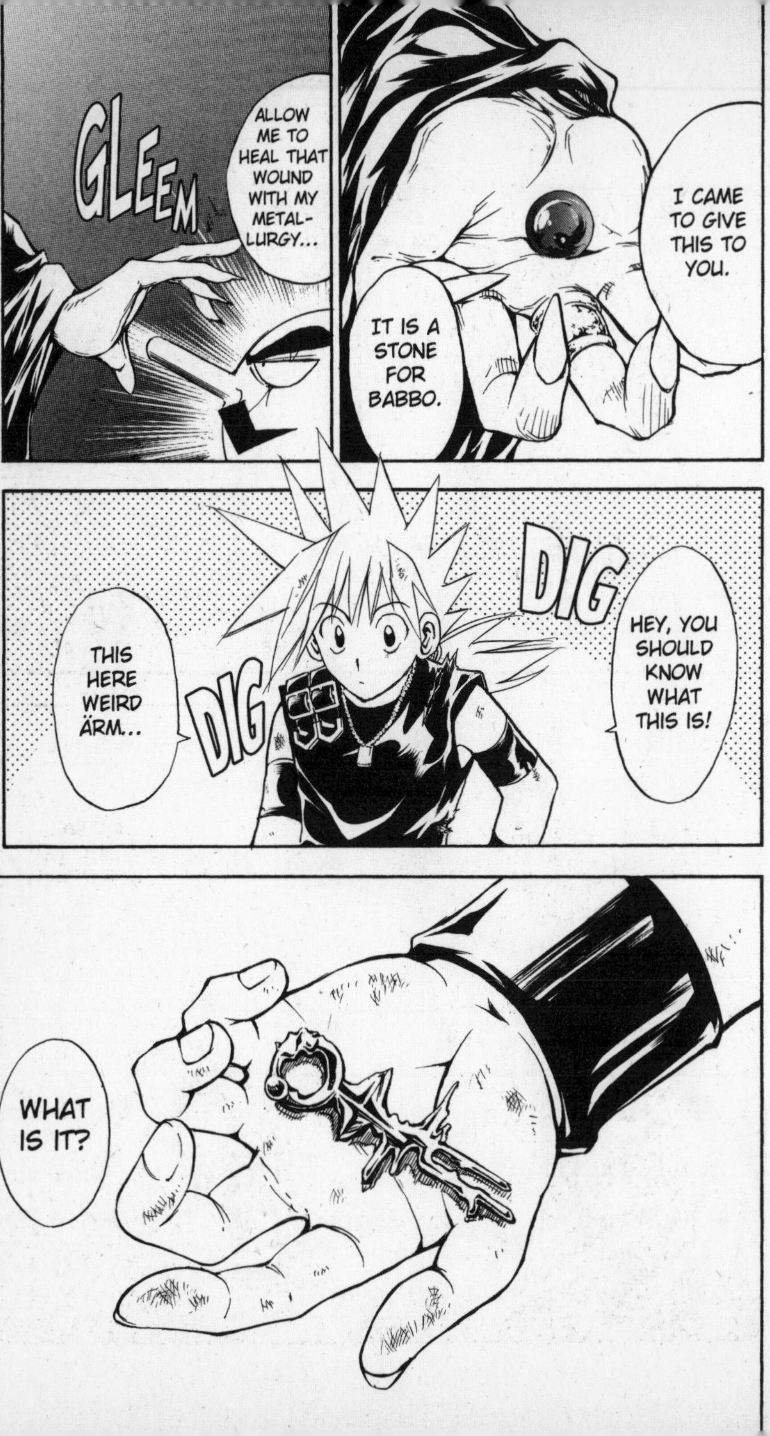
I CAME TO GIVE THIS TO YOU.
IT IS A STONE FOR BABBO.
ALLOW ME TO HEAL THAT WOUND WITH MY METAL-LURGY...
GLEEM
DIG
HEY, YOU SHOULD KNOW WHAT THIS IS!
THIS HERE WEIRD ÄRM...
DIG
WHAT IS IT?

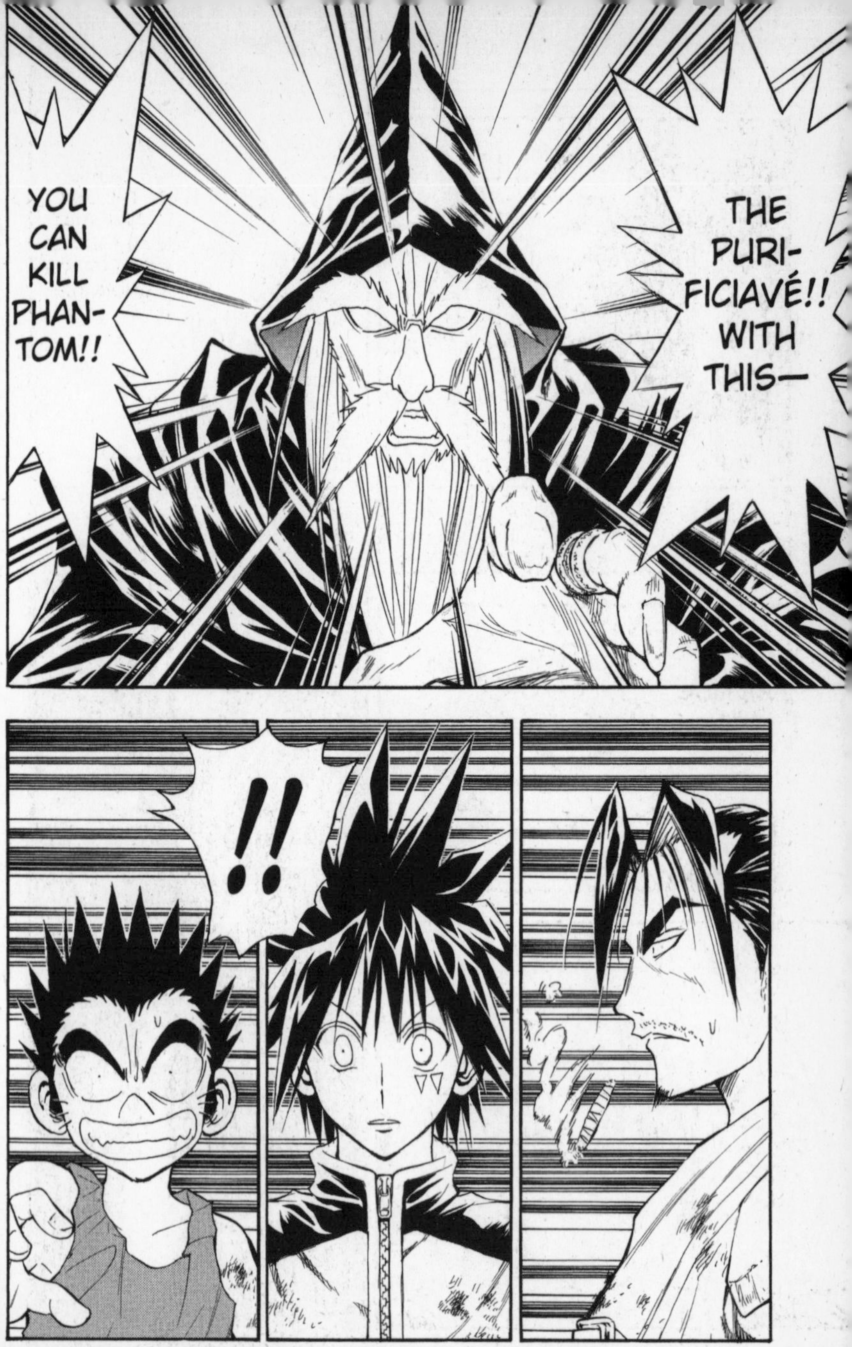
THE PURI-FICIAVÉ!! WITH THIS—
YOU CAN KILL PHAN-TOM!!
!!

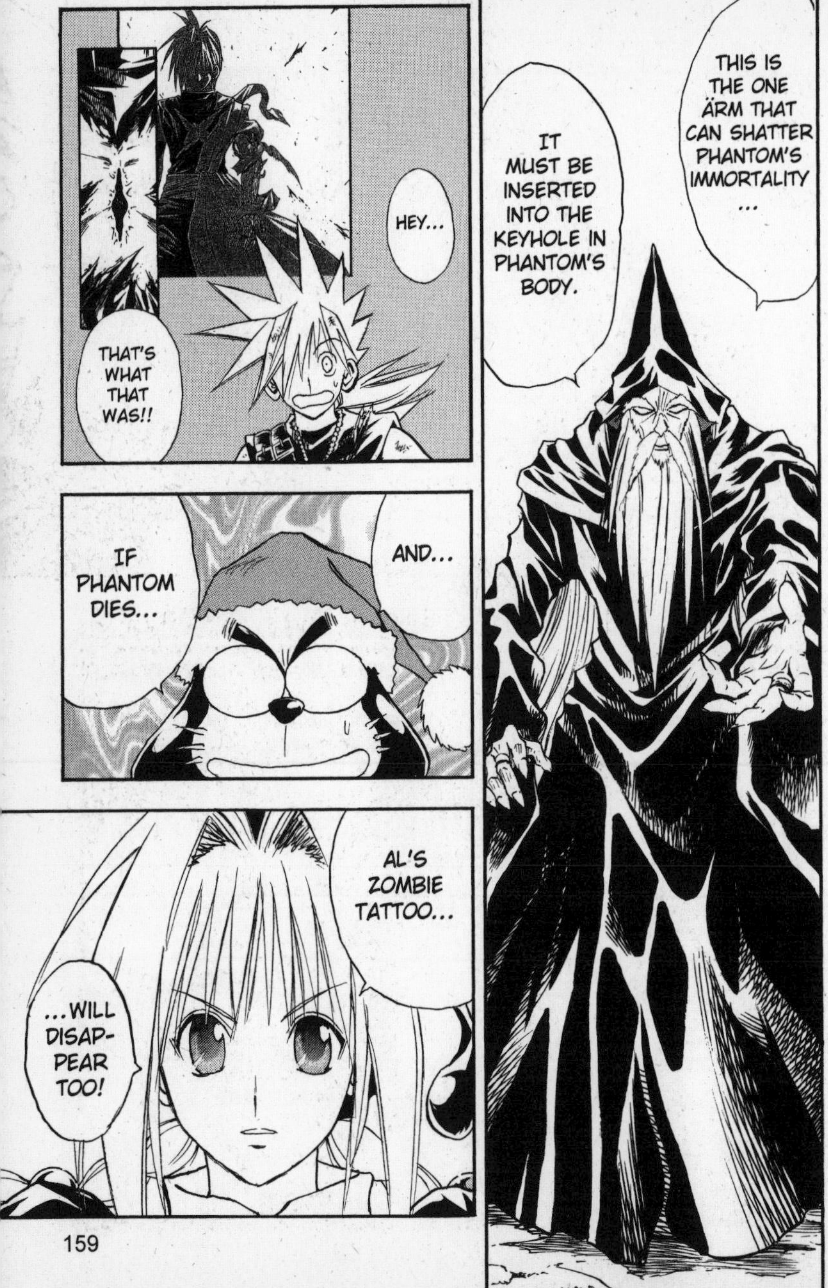
THIS IS THE ONE ÄRM THAT CAN SHATTER PHANTOM'S IMMORTALITY ...
IT MUST BE INSERTED INTO THE KEYHOLE IN PHANTOM'S BODY.
HEY...
THAT'S WHAT THAT WAS!!
AND...
IF PHANTOM DIES...
AL'S ZOMBIE TATTOO...
...WILL DISAP-PEAR TOO!

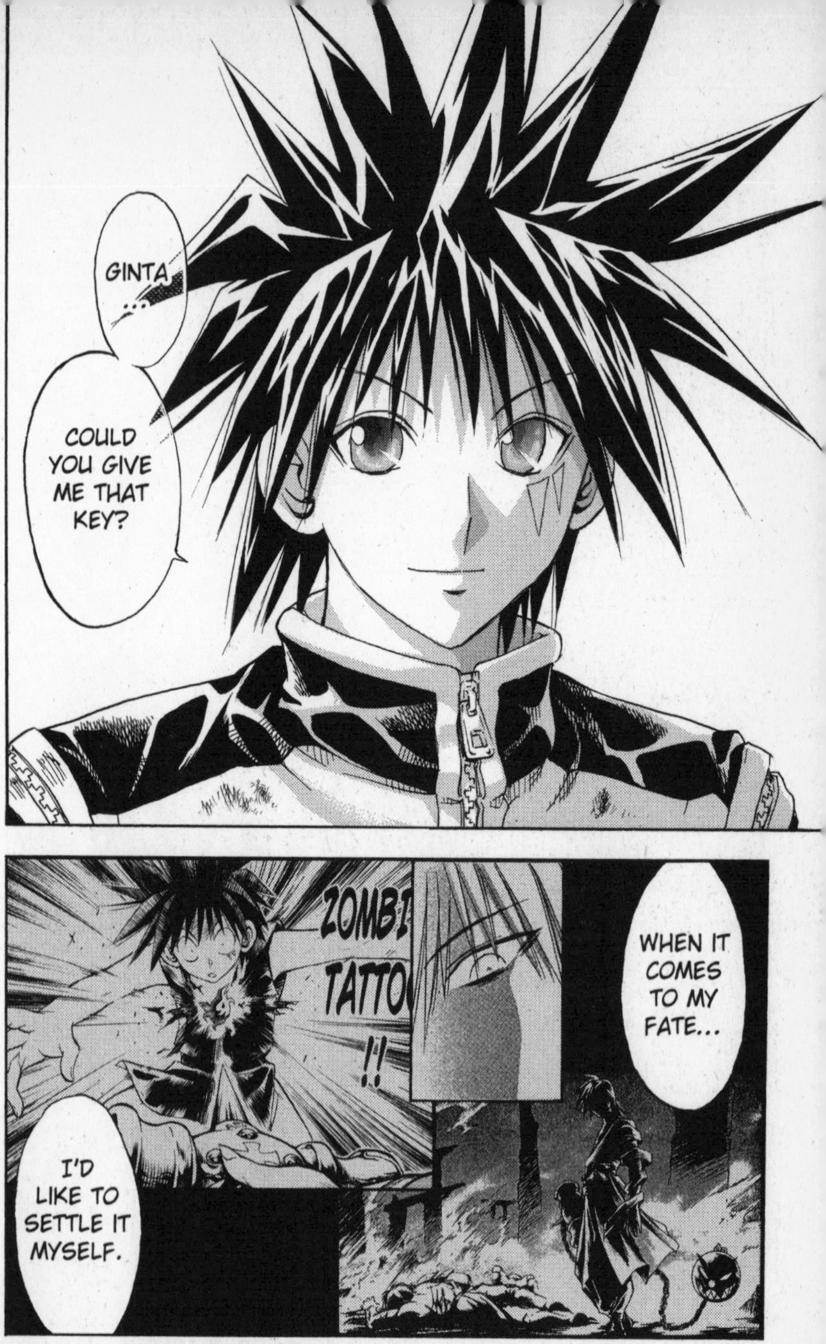
GINTA ...
COULD YOU GIVE ME THAT KEY?
WHEN IT COMES TO MY FATE...
ZOMBI TATTO !!
I'D LIKE TO SETTLE IT MYSELF.

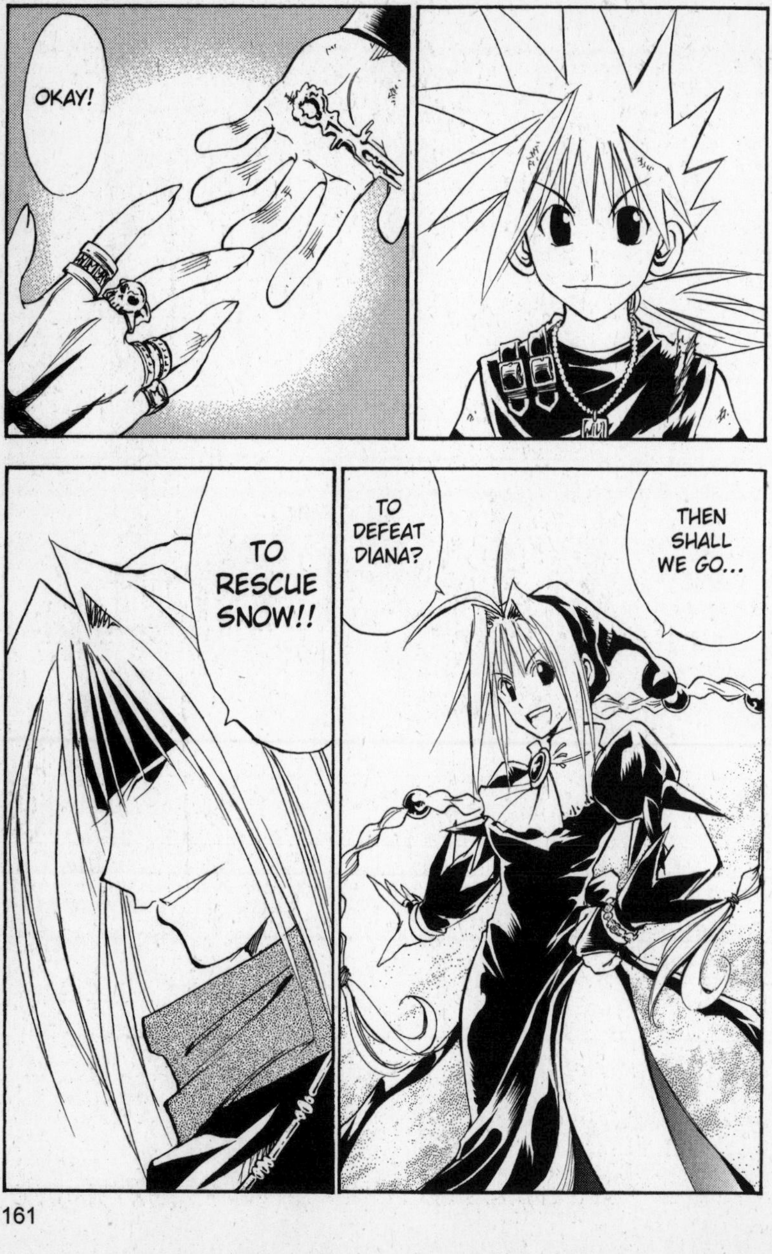
OKAY!
THEN SHALL WE GO...
TO DEFEAT DIANA?
TO RESCUE SNOW!!

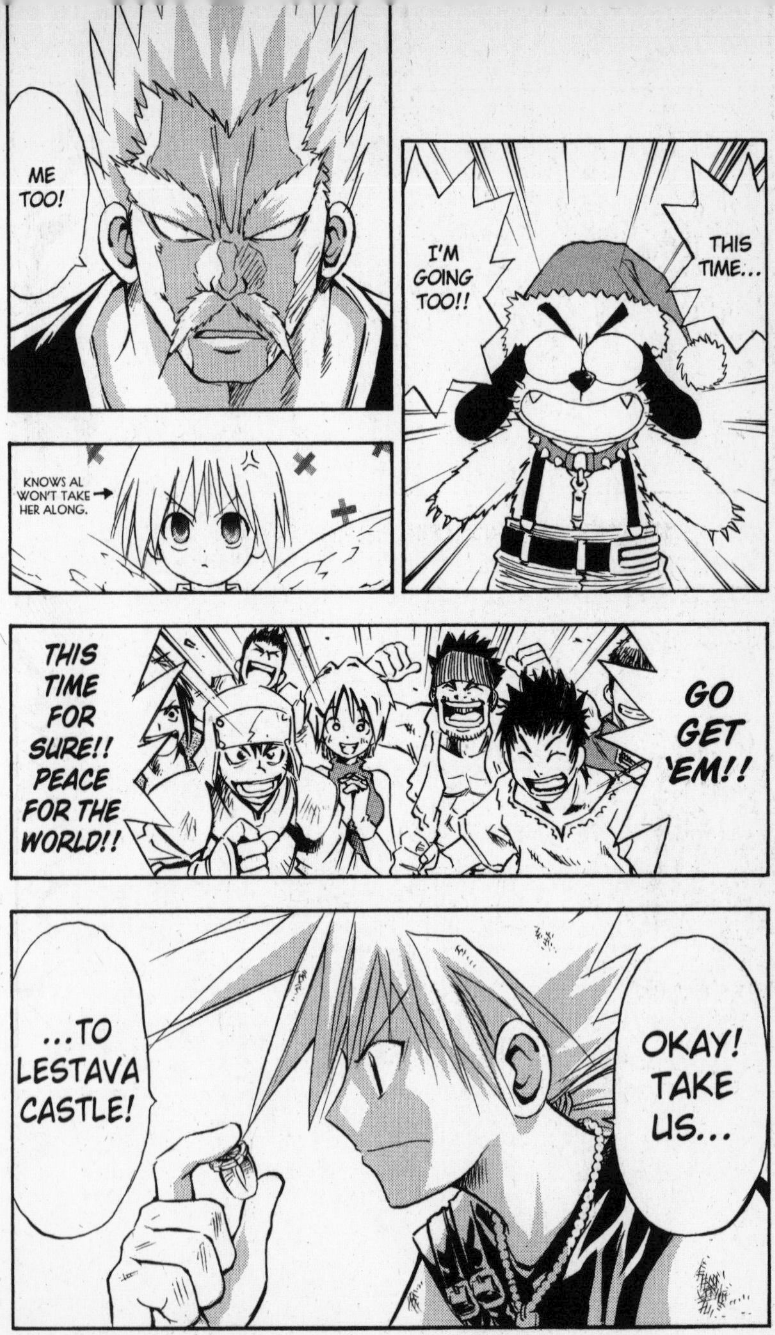

THIS TIME...
I'M GOING TOO!!
ME TOO!
KNOWS AL WON'T TAKE HER ALONG.
GO GET 'EM!!
THIS TIME FOR SURE!! PEACE FOR THE WORLD!!
OKAY! TAKE US...
...TO LESTAVA CASTLE!

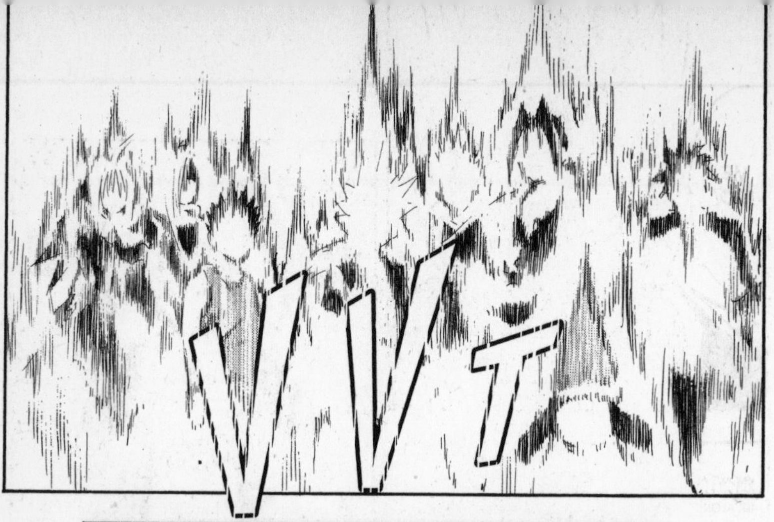
VVT
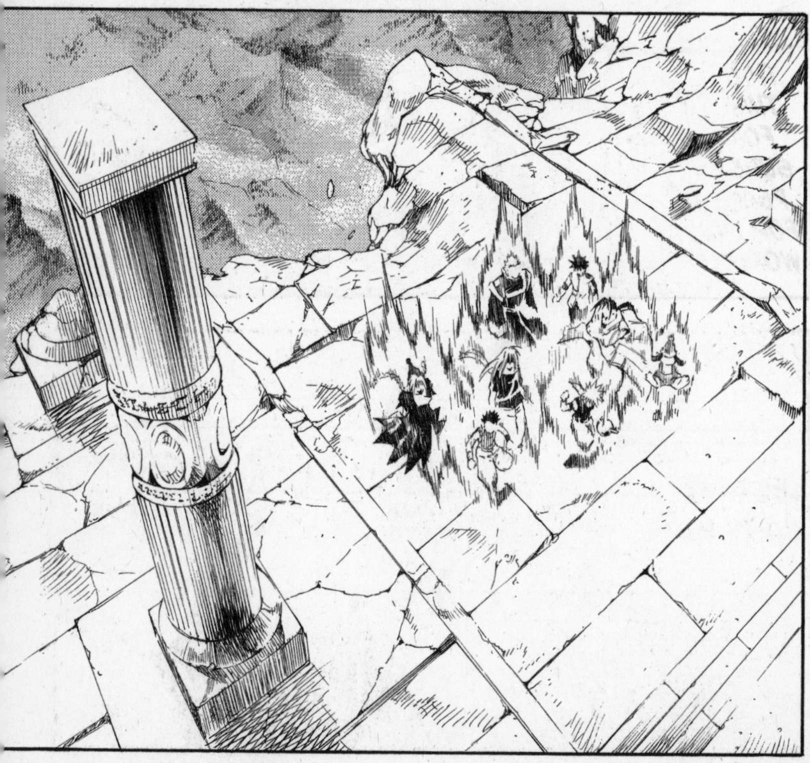

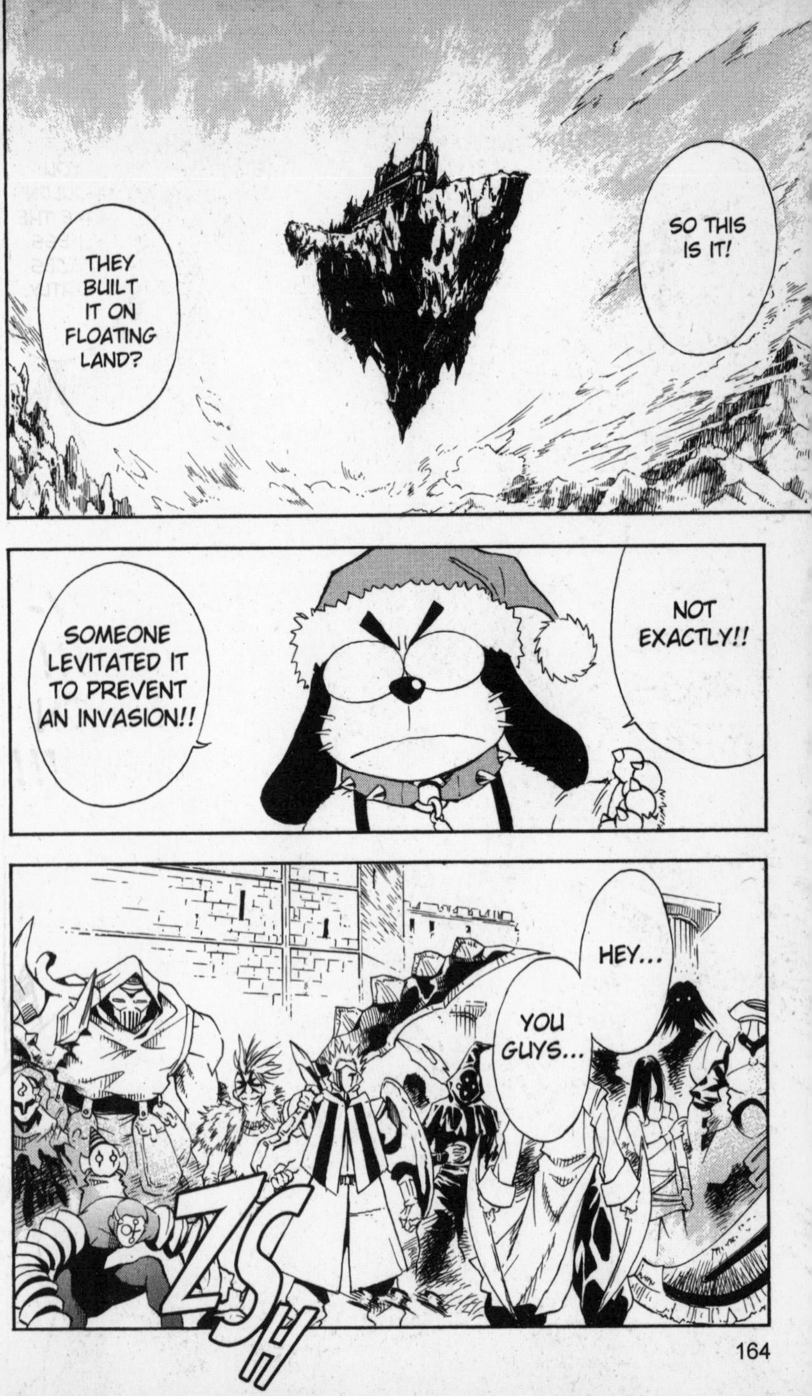
SO THIS IS IT!
THEY BUILT IT ON FLOATING LAND?
NOT EXACTLY!!
SOMEONE LEVITATED IT TO PREVENT AN INVASION!!
HEY...
YOU GUYS...
ZSH

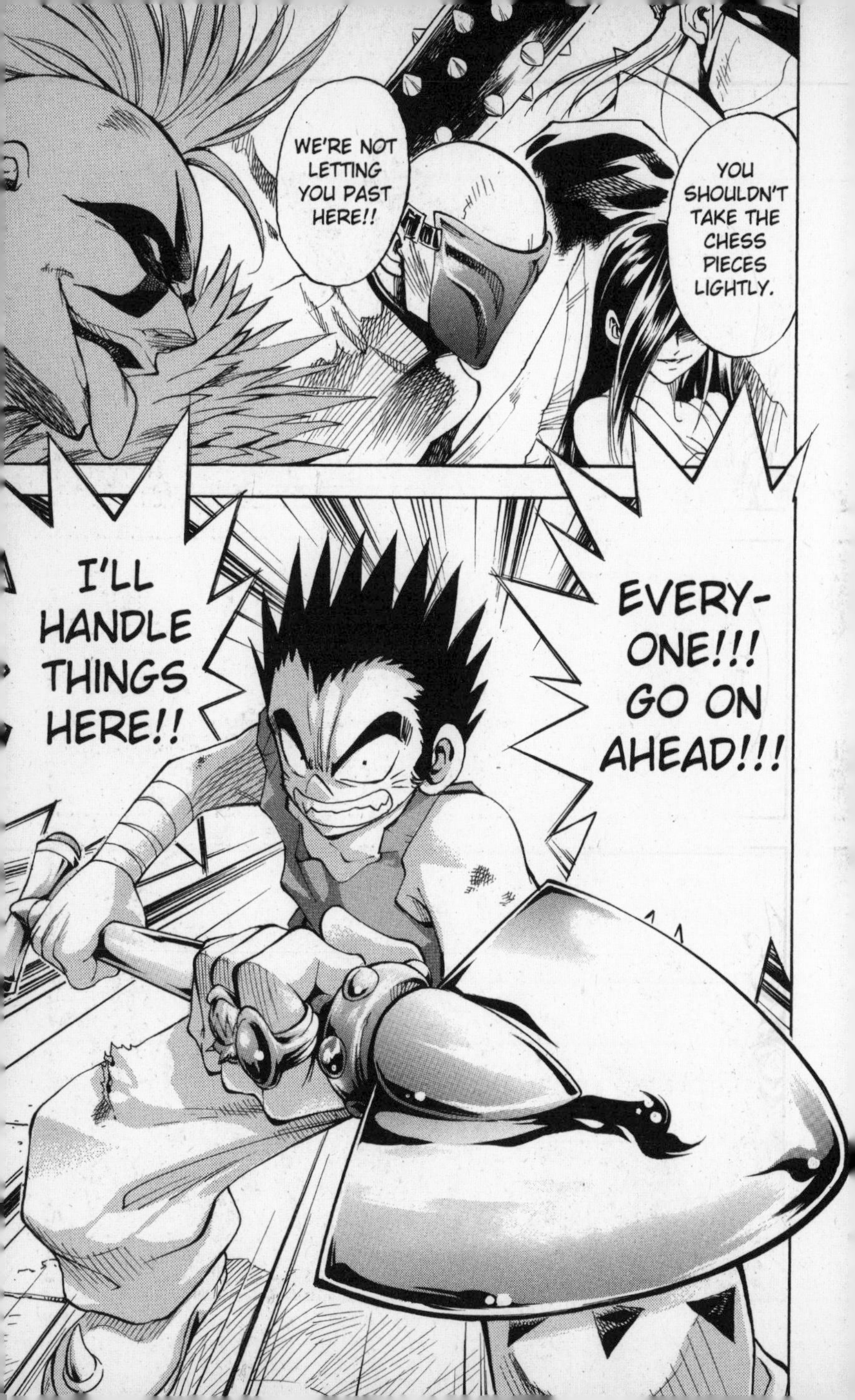
YOU SHOULDN'T TAKE THE CHESS PIECES LIGHTLY.
WE'RE NOT LETTING YOU PAST HERE!!
EVERY-ONE!!! GO ON AHEAD!!!
I'LL HANDLE THINGS HERE!!

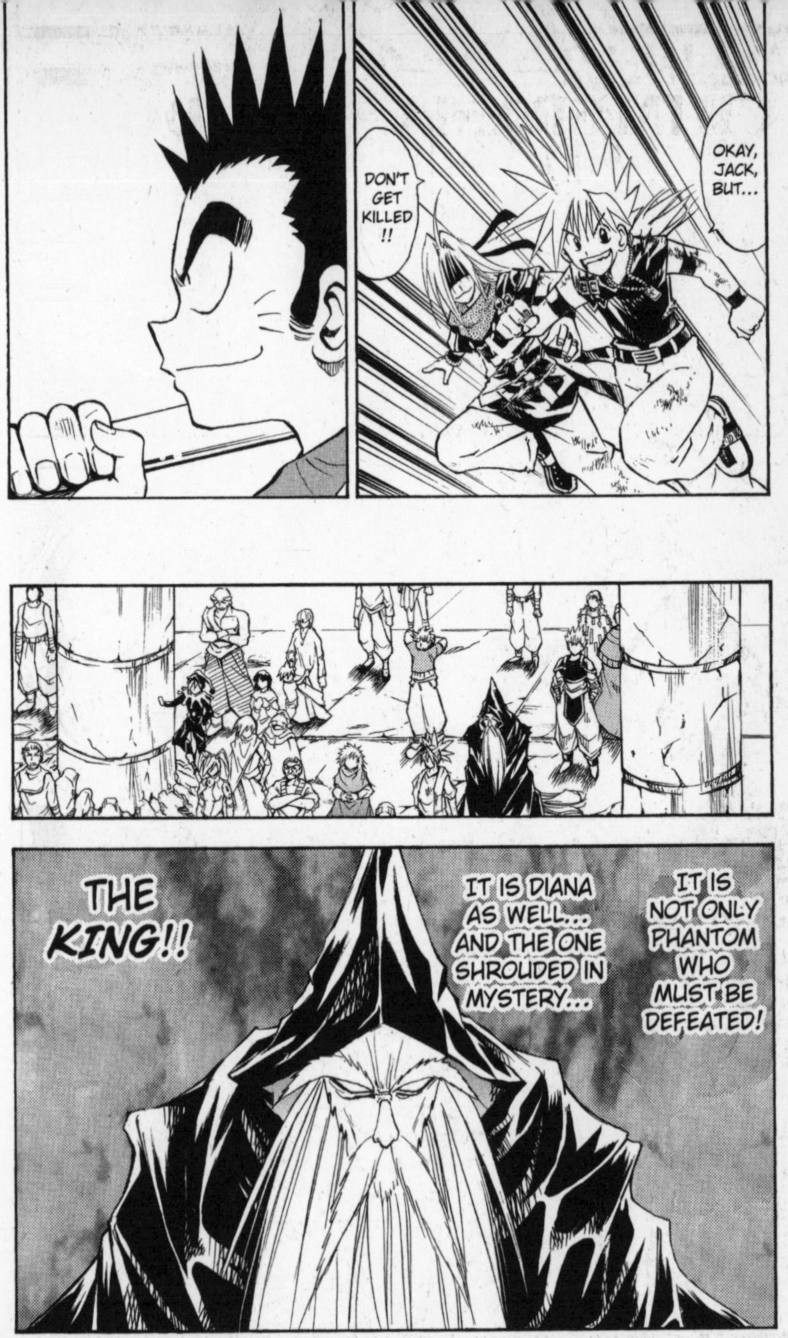
OKAY, JACK, BUT...
DON'T GET KILLED!!
IT IS NOT ONLY PHANTOM WHO MUST BE DEFEATED!
IT IS DIANA AS WELL... AND THE ONE SHROUDED IN MYSTERY...
THE KING!!

AKT.151/ CHIMERA, IAN & GIDO

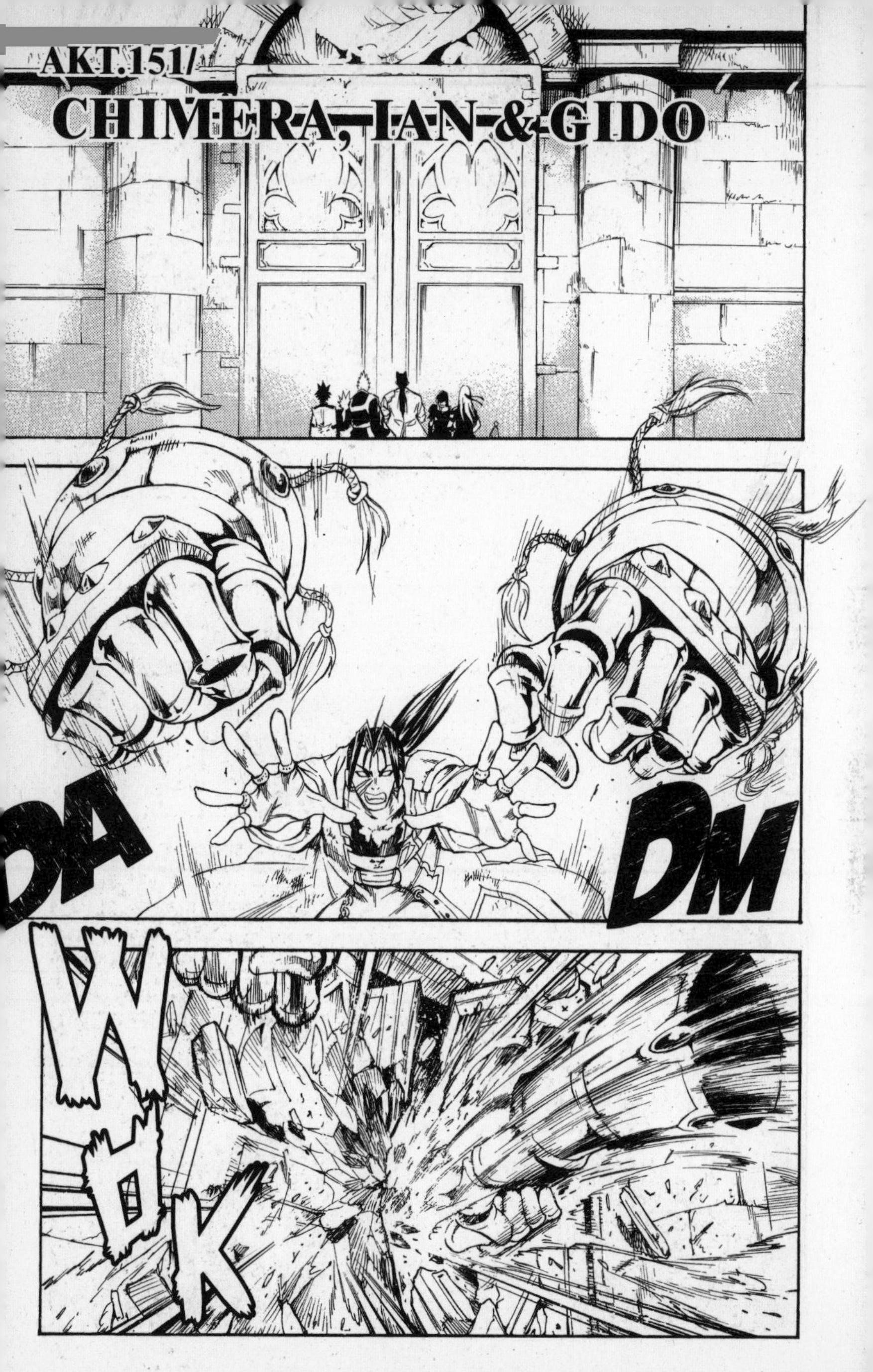
DM
DA
WOK

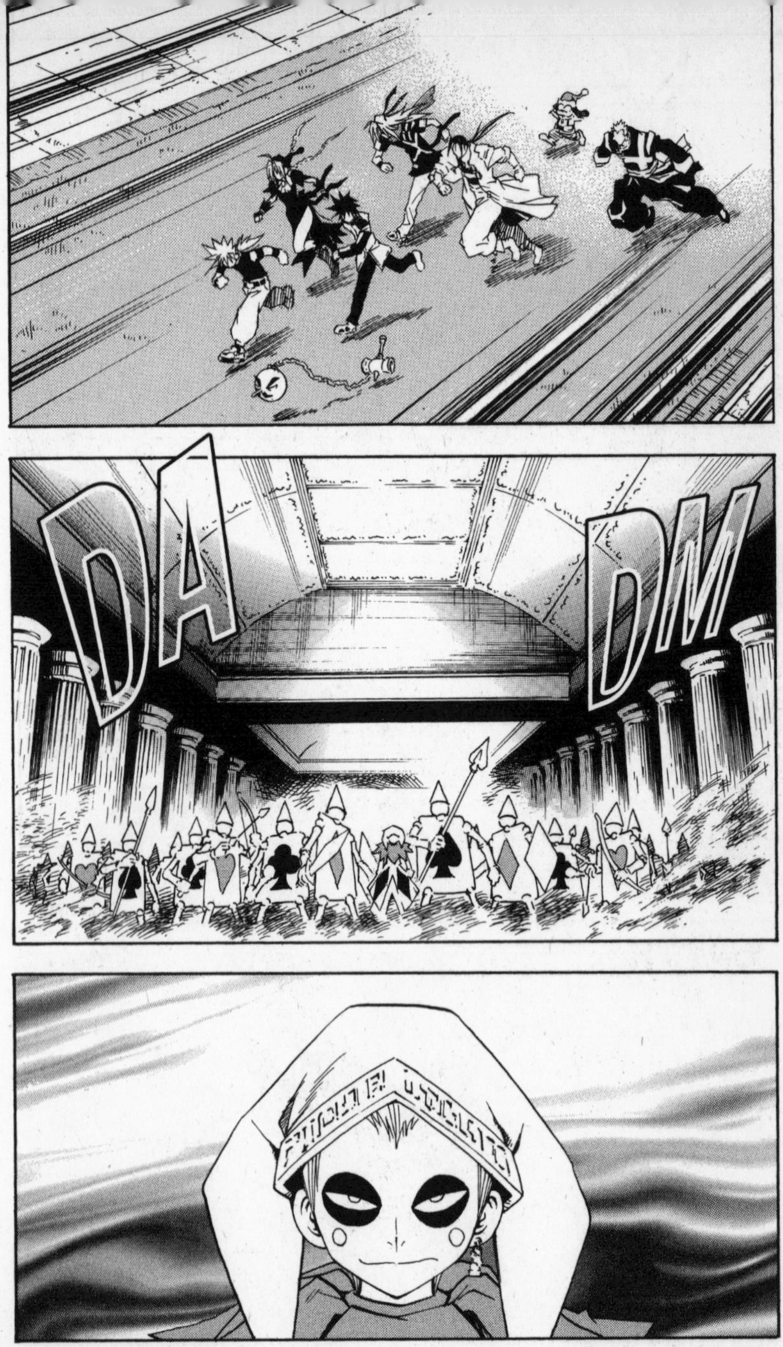
DA DM

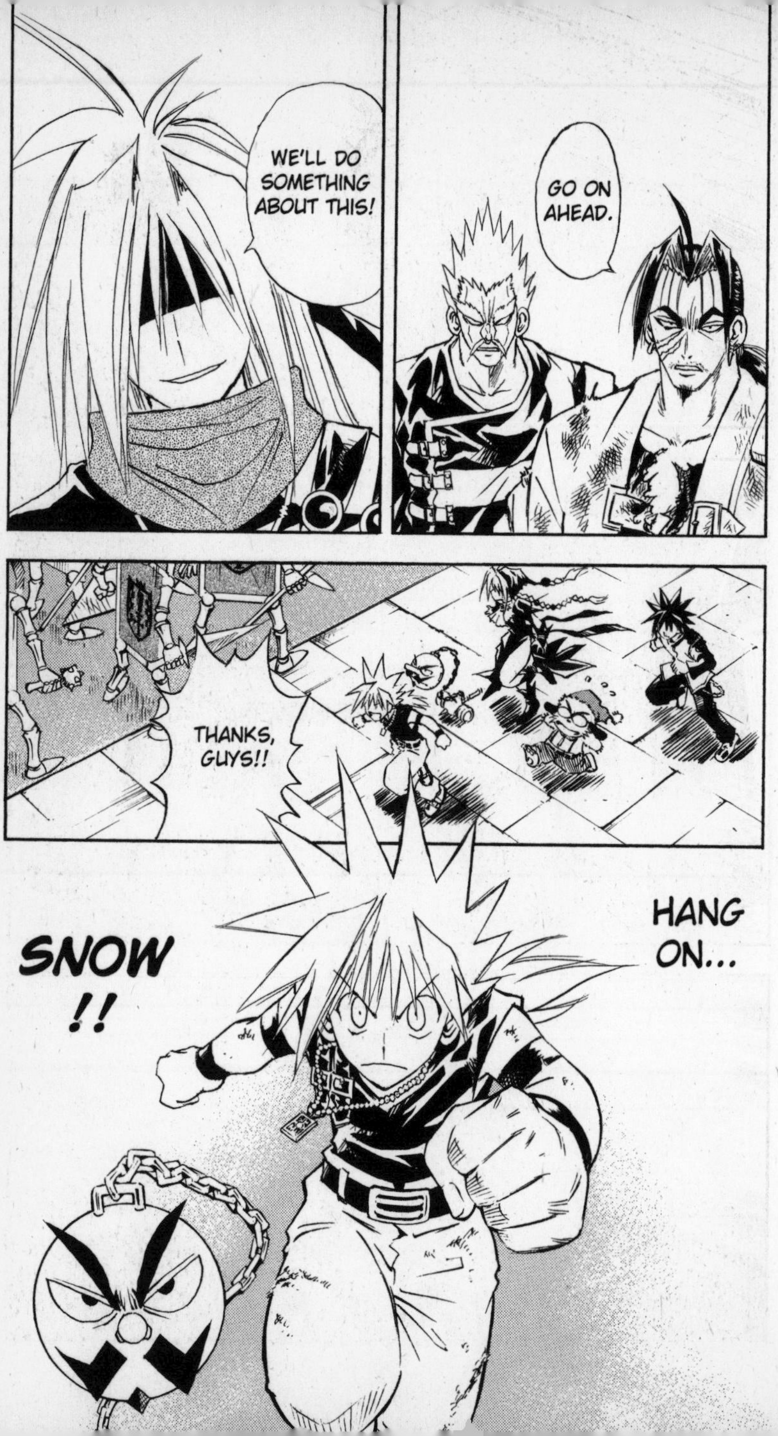
GO ON AHEAD.
WE'LL DO SOMETHING ABOUT THIS!
THANKS, GUYS!!
HANG ON...
SNOW !!

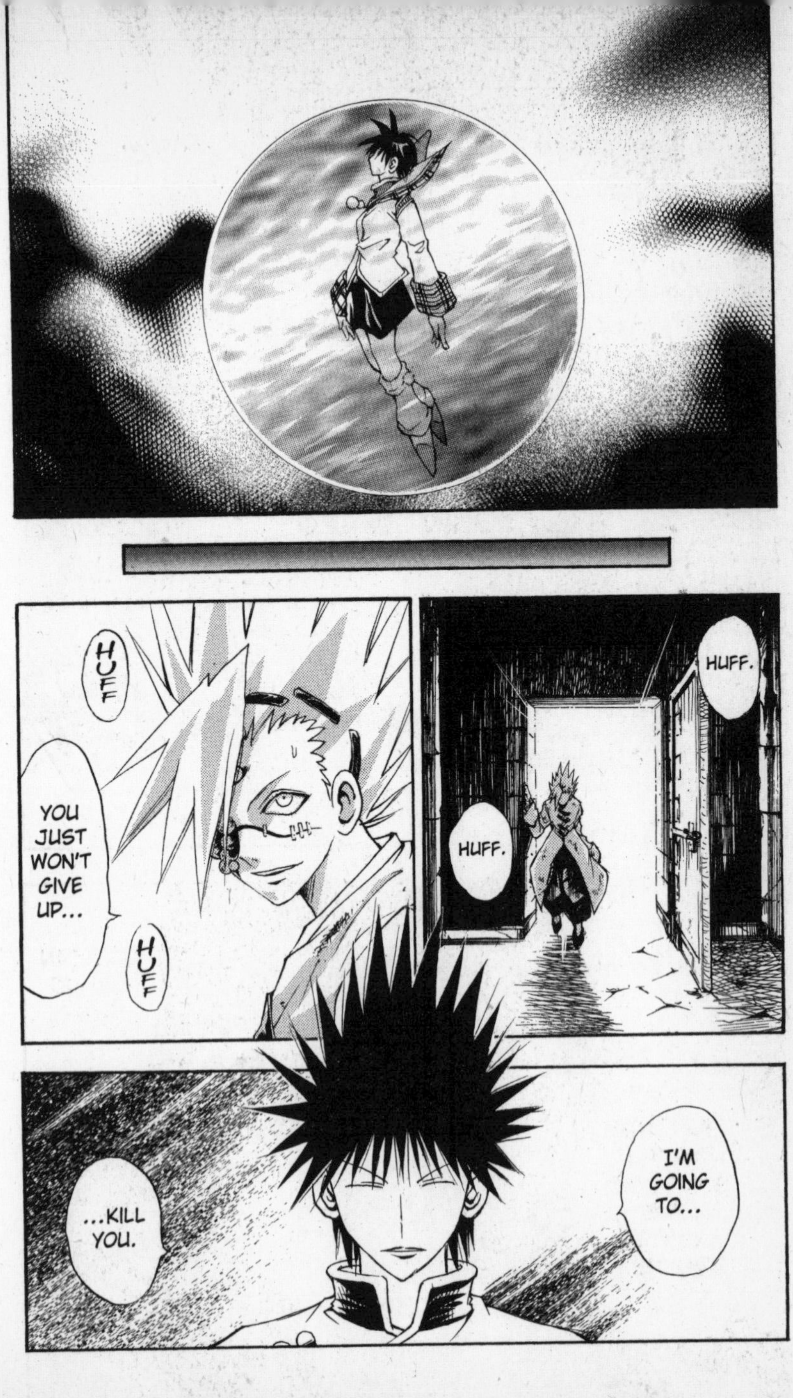
HUFF.
HUFF.
HUFF
YOU JUST WON'T GIVE UP...
HUFF
I'M GOING TO...
...KILL YOU.

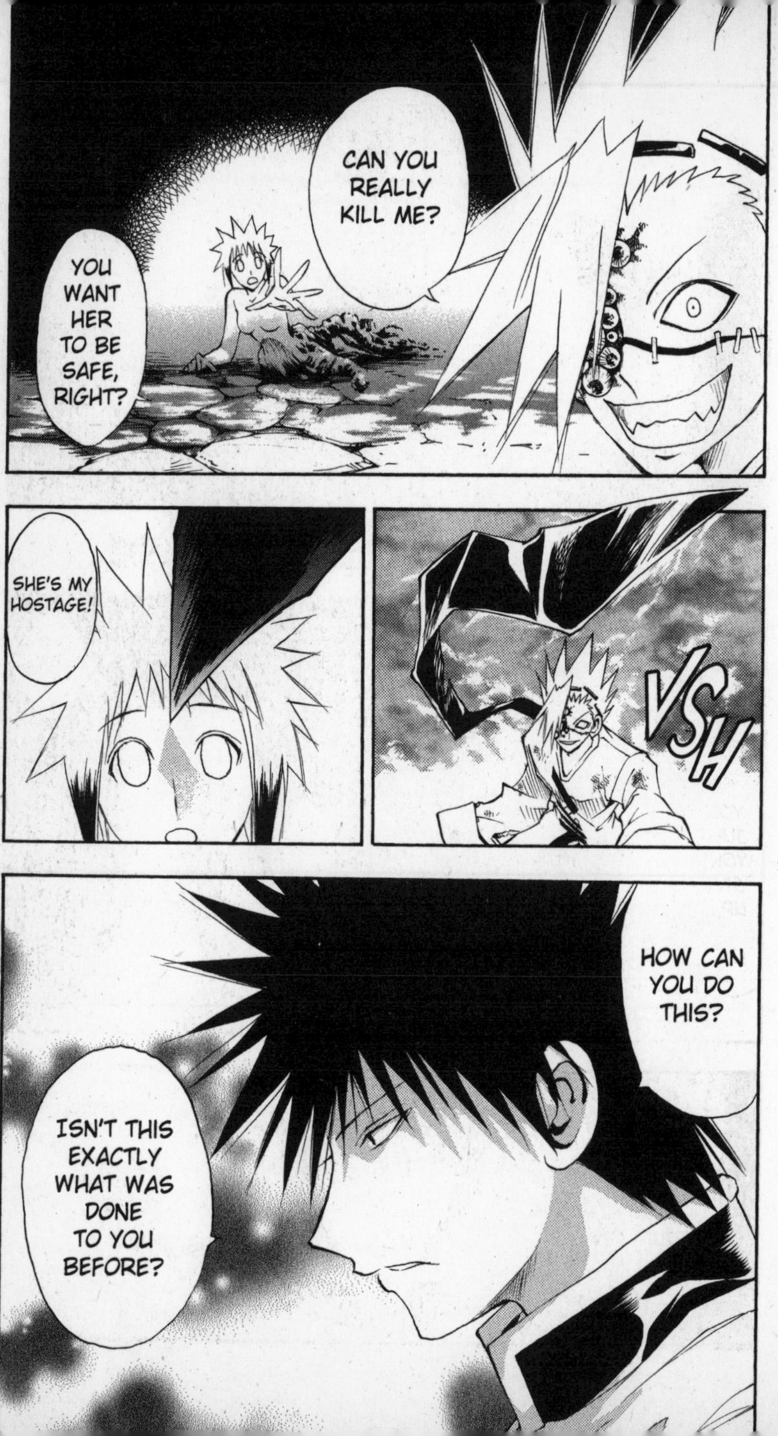
CAN YOU REALLY KILL ME?
YOU WANT HER TO BE SAFE, RIGHT?
VSH
SHE'S MY HOSTAGE!
HOW CAN YOU DO THIS?
ISN'T THIS EXACTLY WHAT WAS DONE TO YOU BEFORE?

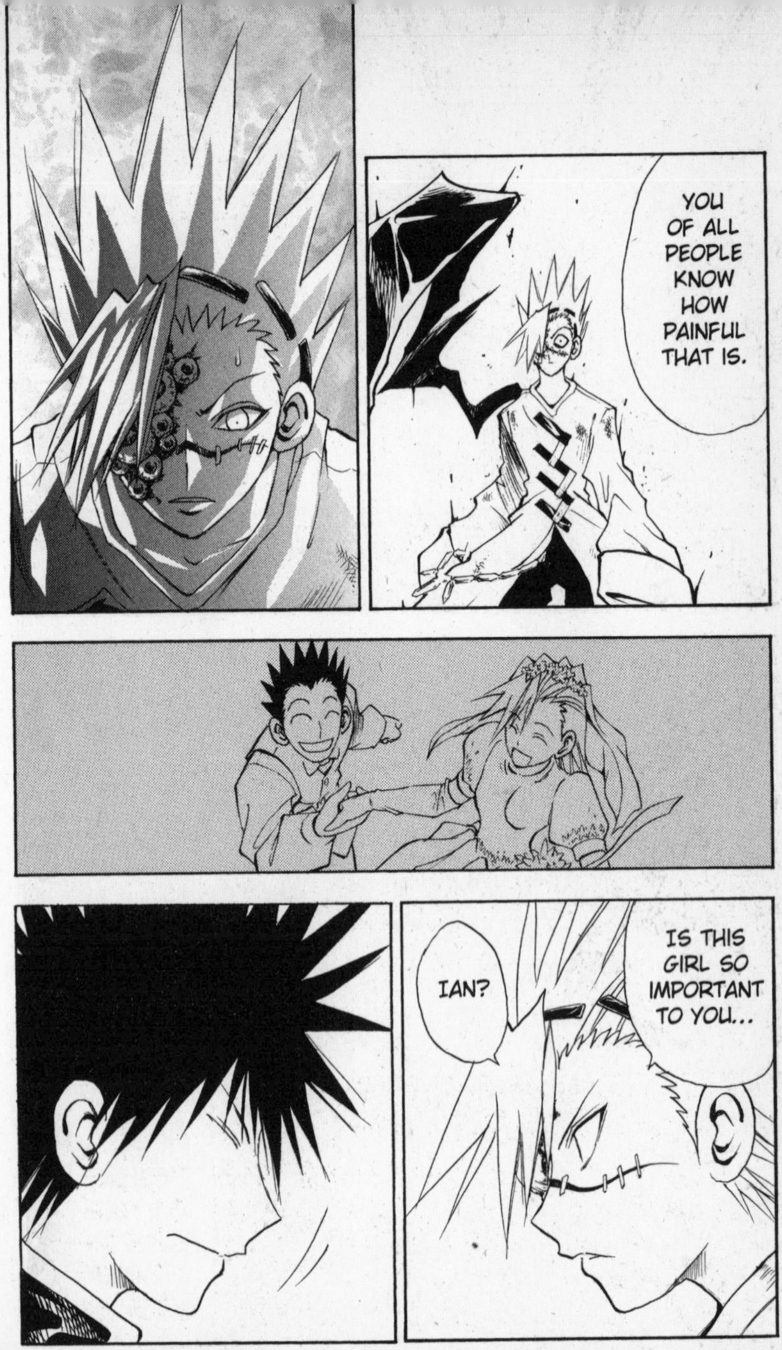
YOU OF ALL PEOPLE KNOW HOW PAINFUL THAT IS.
IS THIS GIRL SO IMPORTANT TO YOU...
IAN?

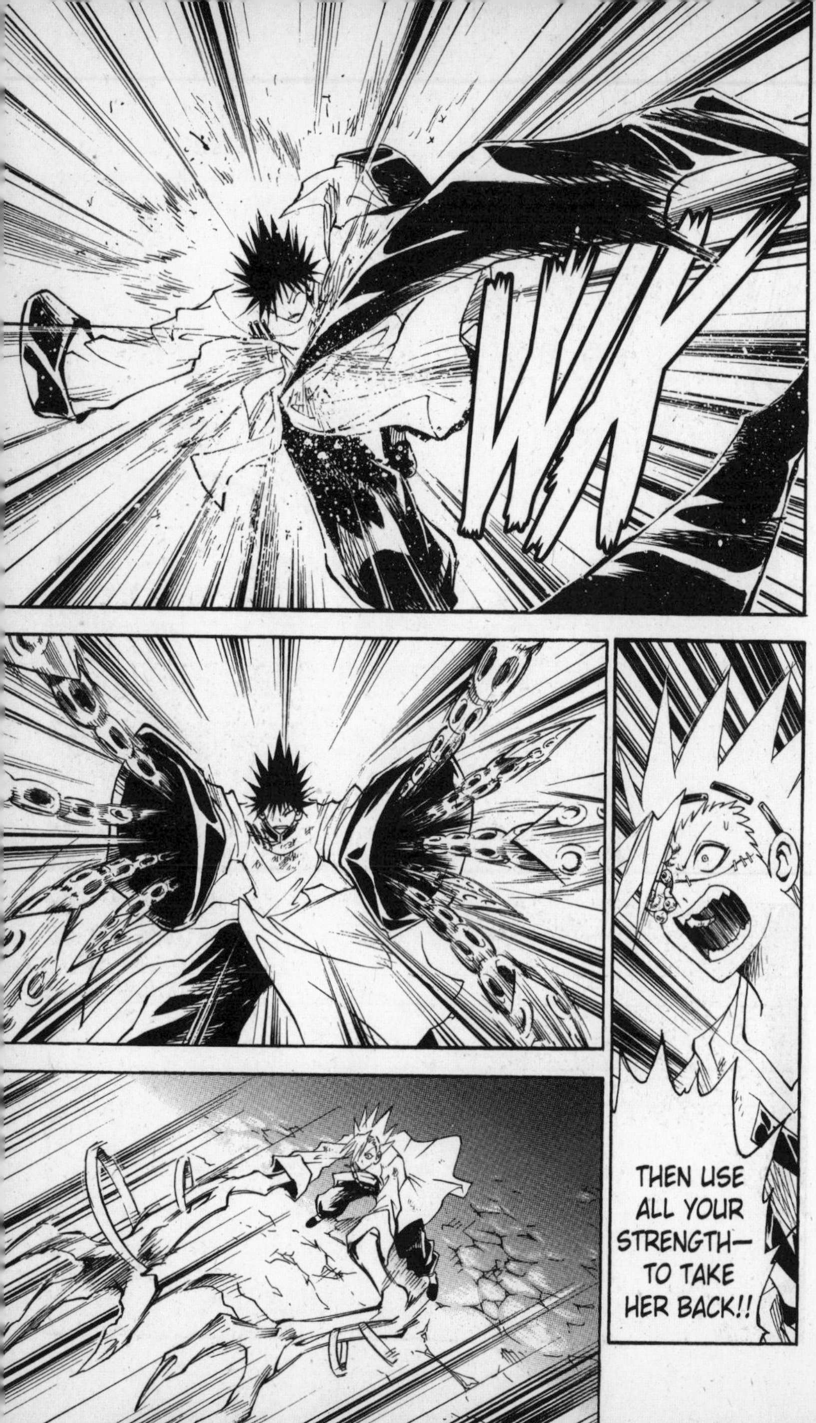
WAK
THEN USE ALL YOUR STRENGTH— TO TAKE HER BACK!!

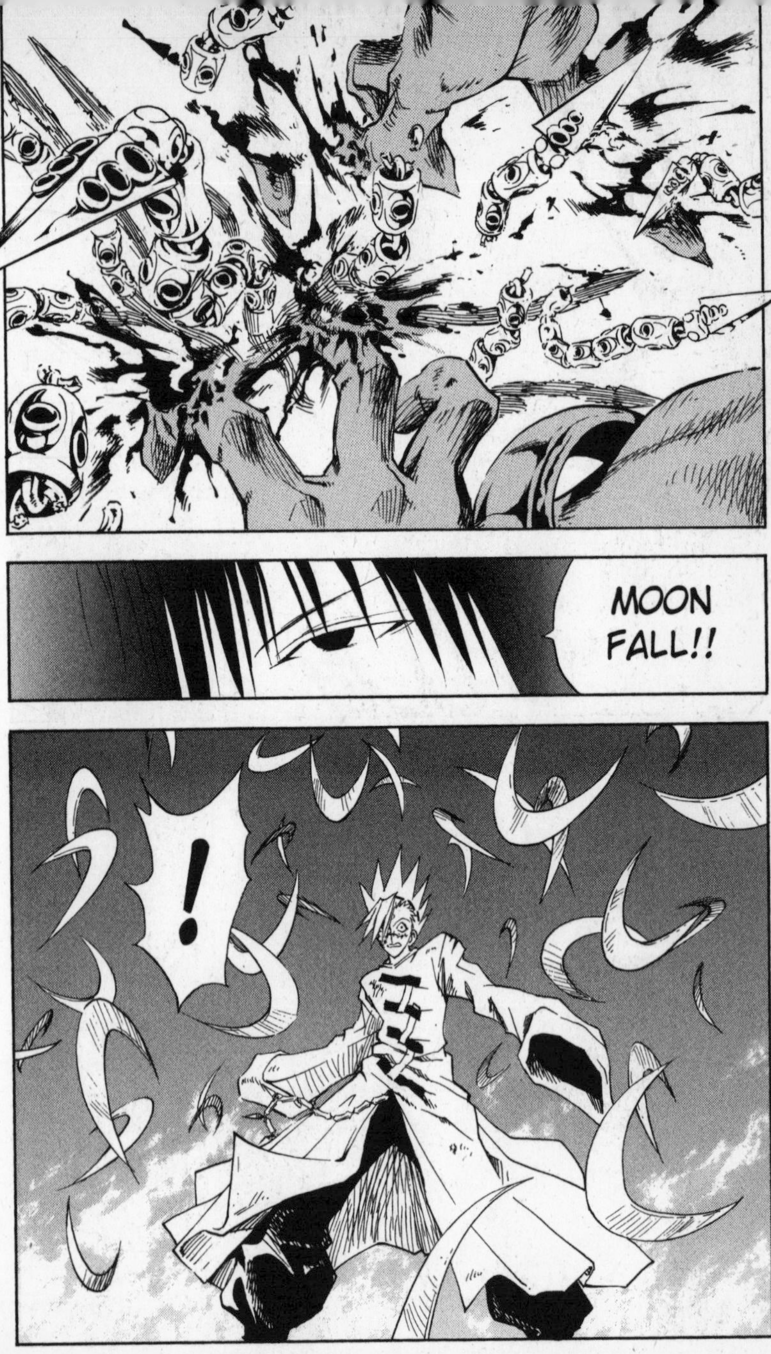
MOON FALL!!
!

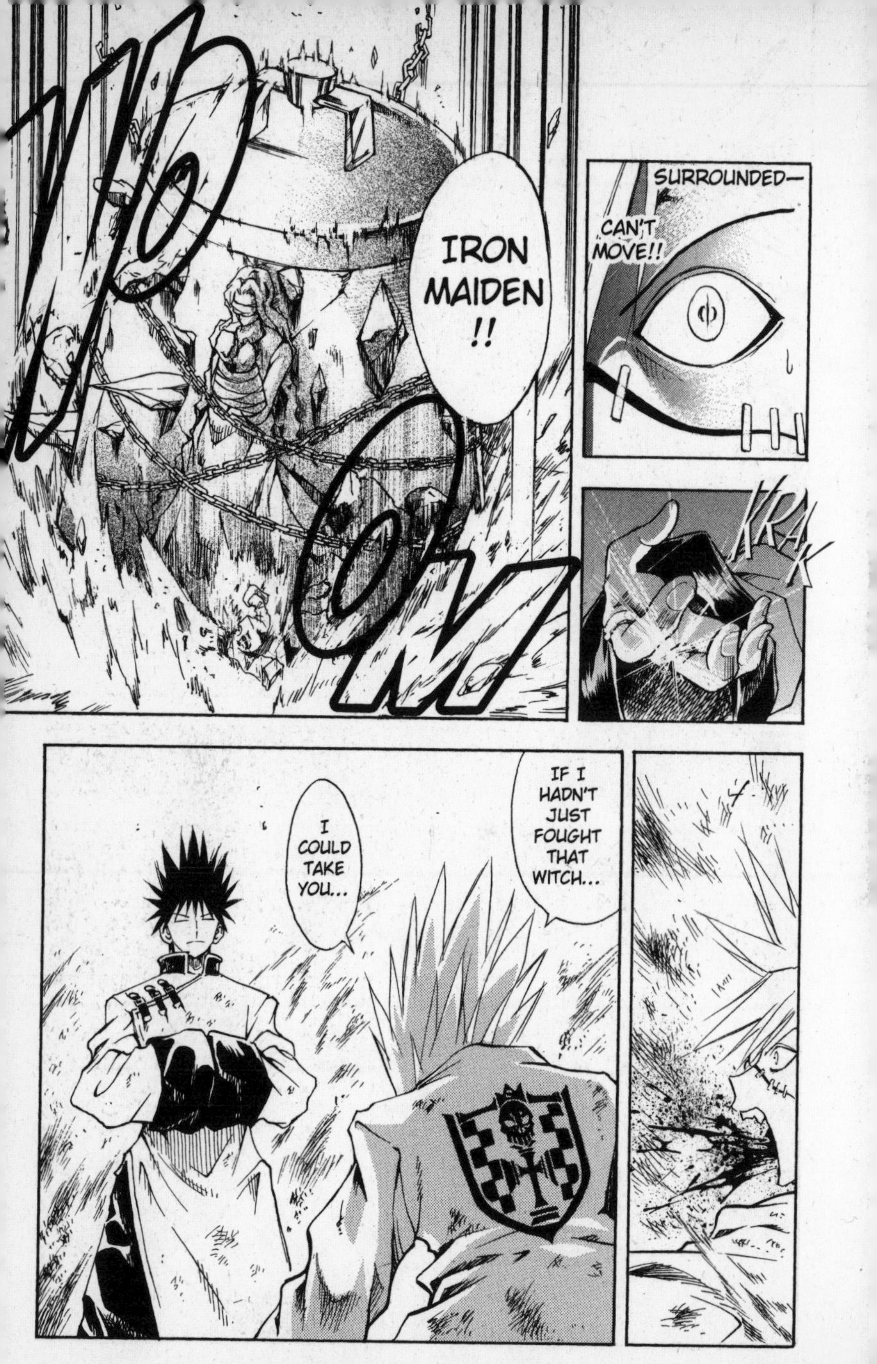
SURROUNDED—
CAN'T MOVE!!
KRAK
IRON MAIDEN!!
IF I HADN'T JUST FOUGHT THAT WITCH...
I COULD TAKE YOU...

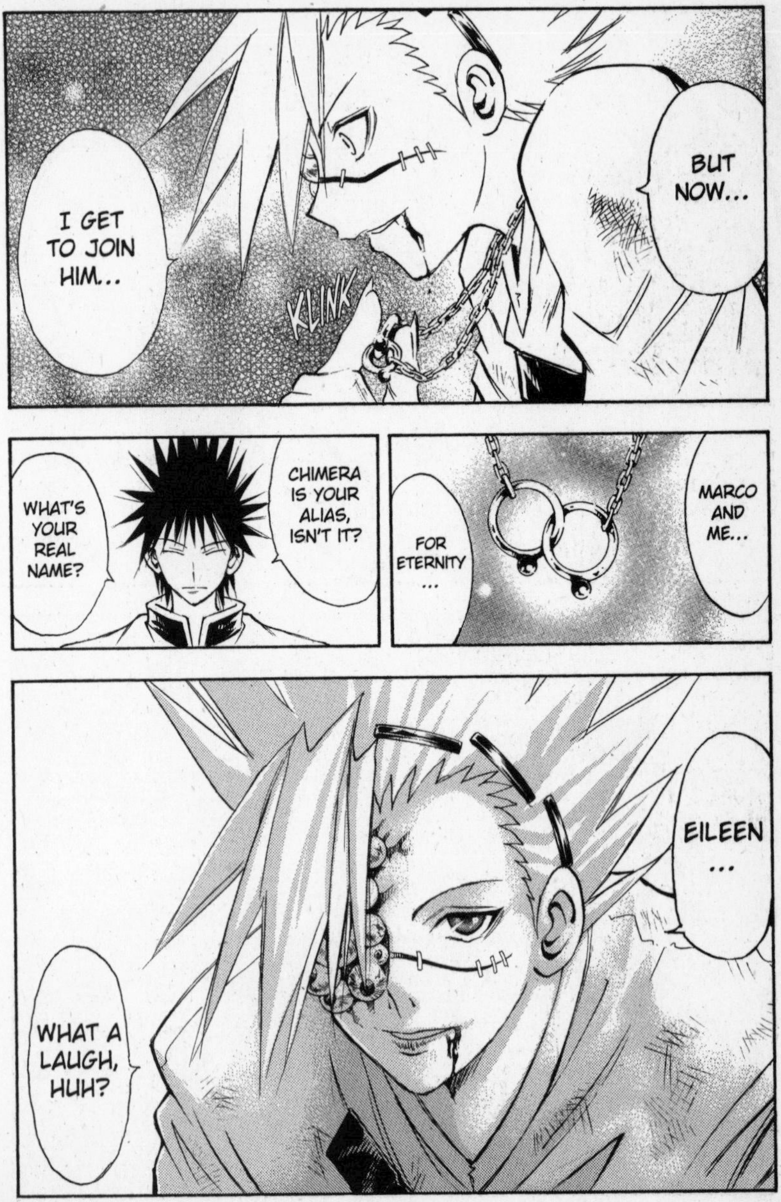
BUT NOW...
KLINK
I GET TO JOIN HIM...
MARCO AND ME...
FOR ETERNITY...
CHIMERA IS YOUR ALIAS, ISN'T IT?
WHAT'S YOUR REAL NAME?
EILEEN...
WHAT A LAUGH, HUH?

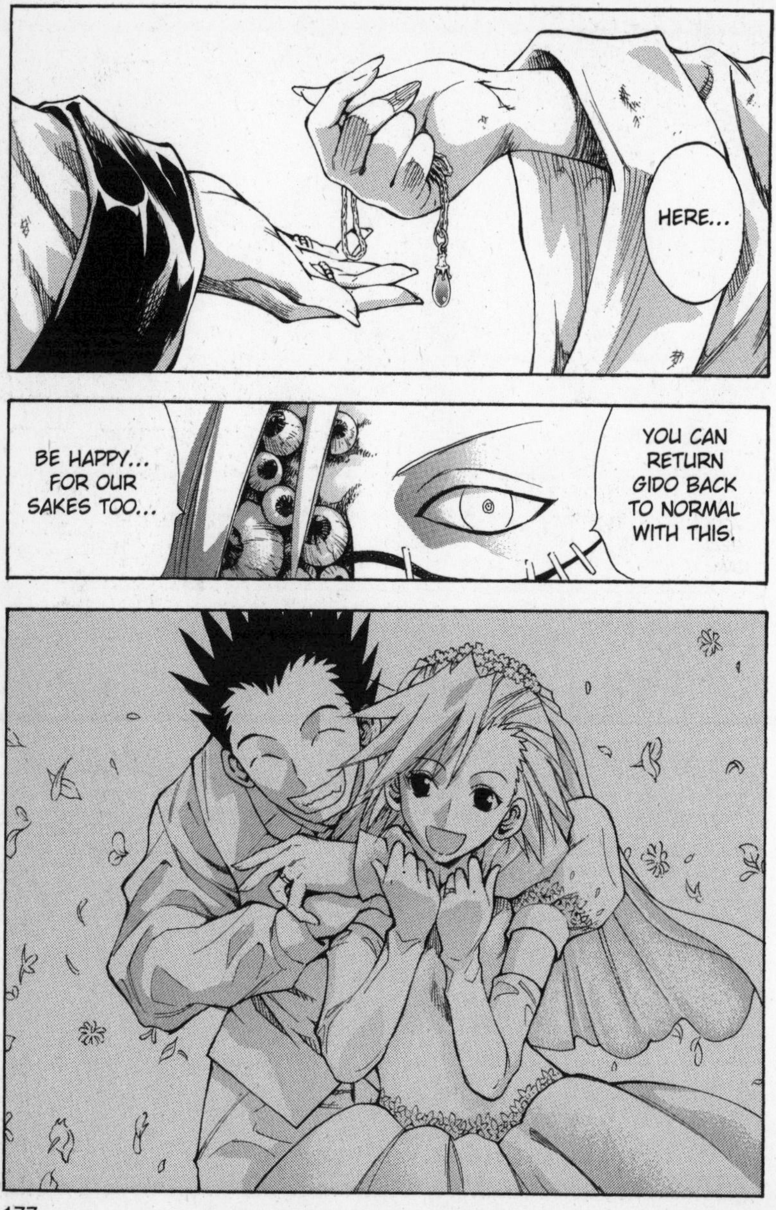
HERE...
YOU CAN RETURN GIDO BACK TO NORMAL WITH THIS.
BE HAPPY... FOR OUR SAKES TOO...

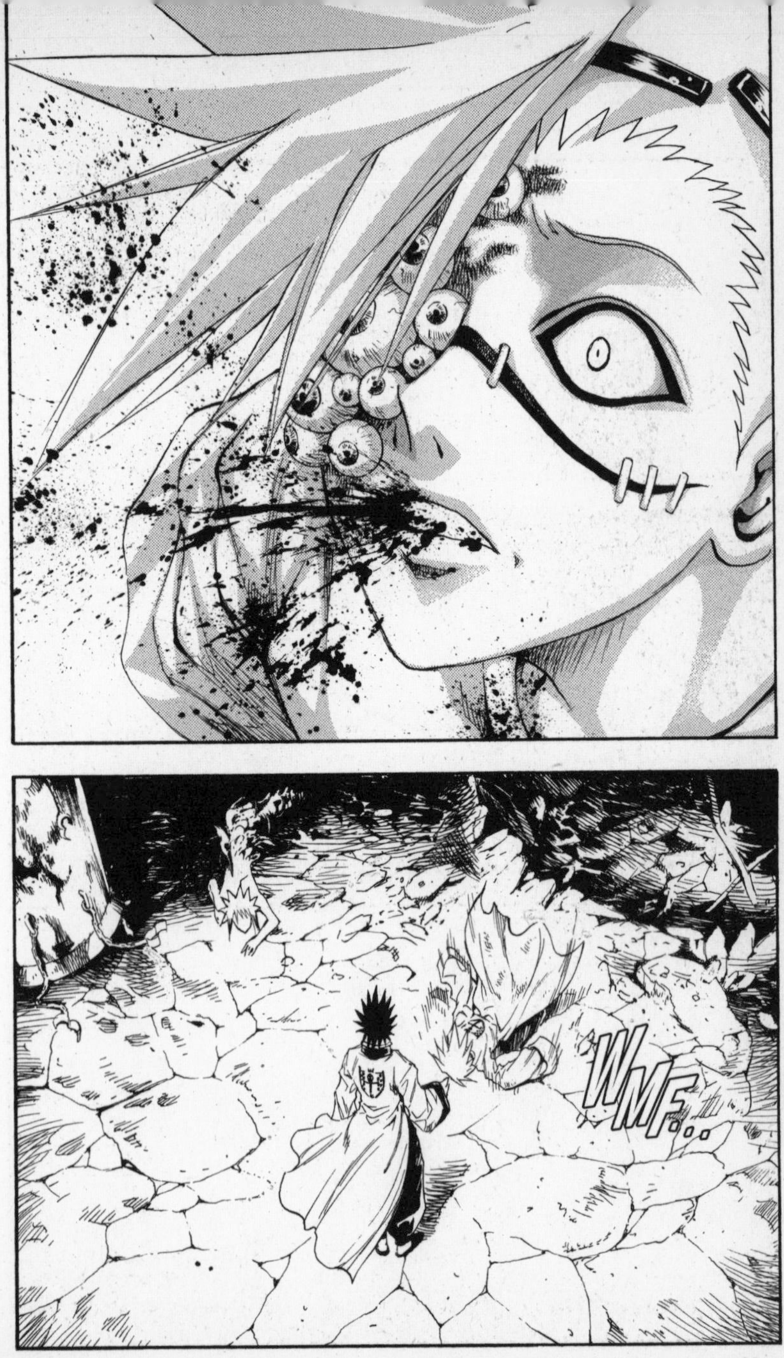
WMF...

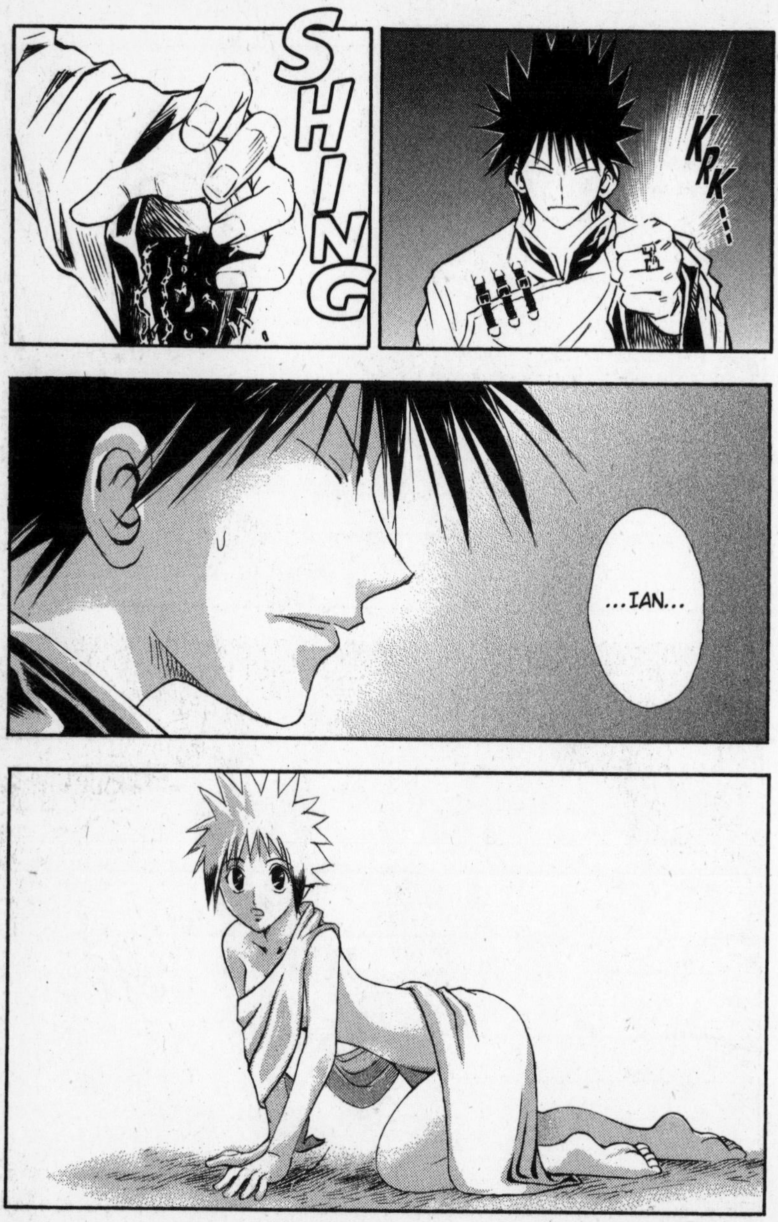
KRK...
SHING
...IAN...

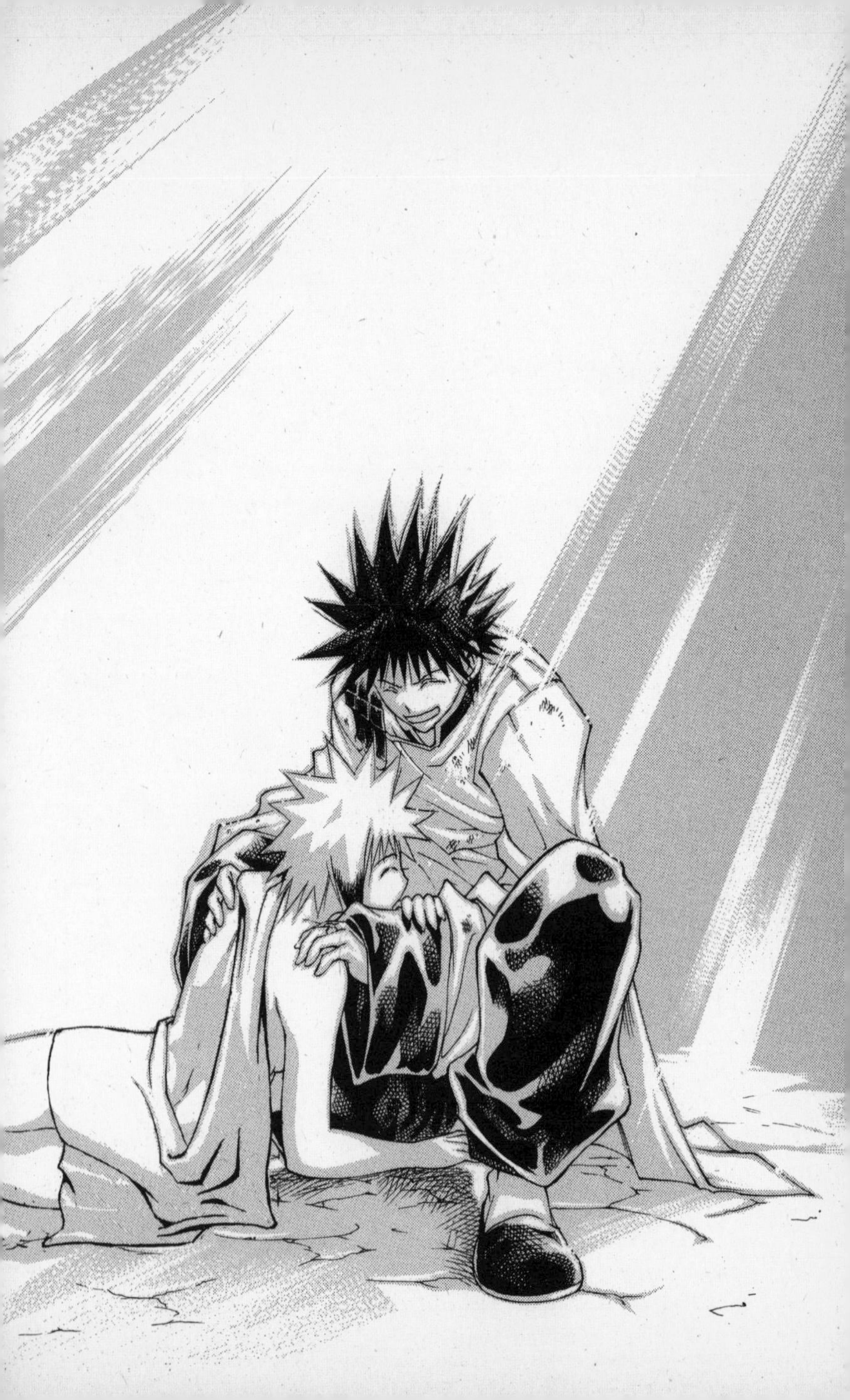

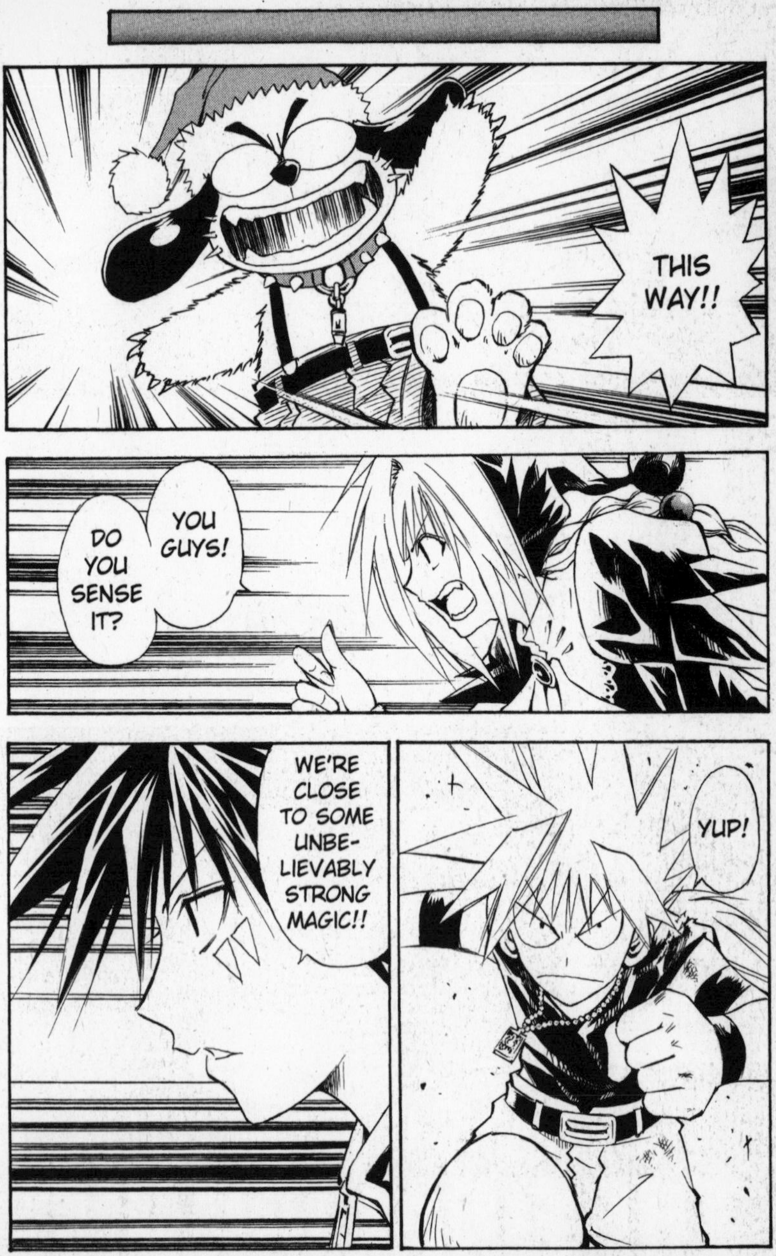
THIS WAY!!
YOU GUYS!
DO YOU SENSE IT?
YUP!
WE'RE CLOSE TO SOME UNBE-LIEVABLY STRONG MAGIC!!

MÄR Volume 14 – The End

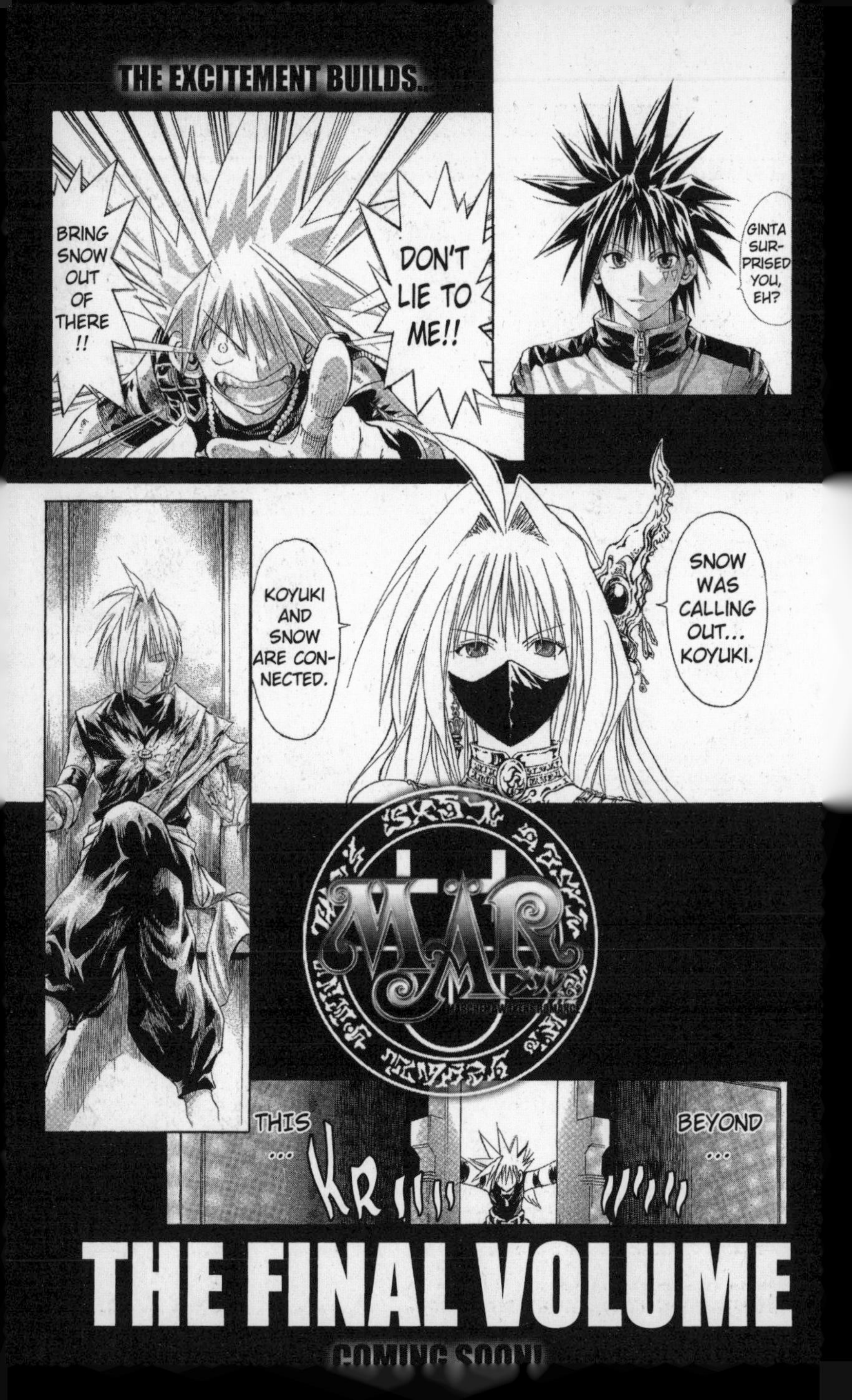
THE EXCITEMENT BUILDS...
GINTA SURPRISED YOU, EH?
DON'T LIE TO ME!!
BRING SNOW OUT OF THERE!!
SNOW WAS CALLING OUT... KOYUKI.
KOYUKI AND SNOW ARE CONNECTED.
MÄR
BEYOND ...
THIS ...
THE FINAL VOLUME
COMING SOON!

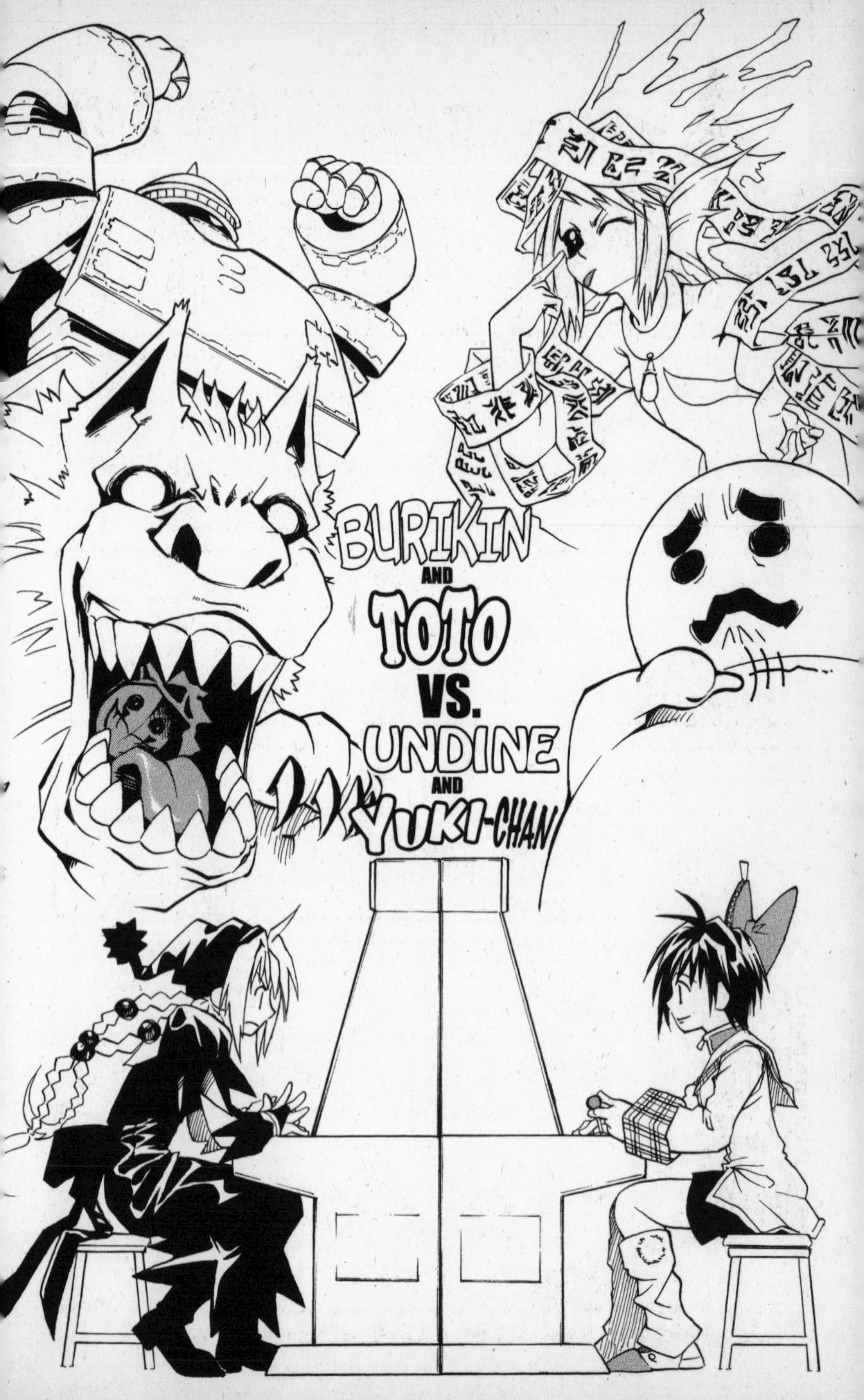
BURIKIN
AND
TOTO
VS.
UNDINE
AND
YUKI-CHAN

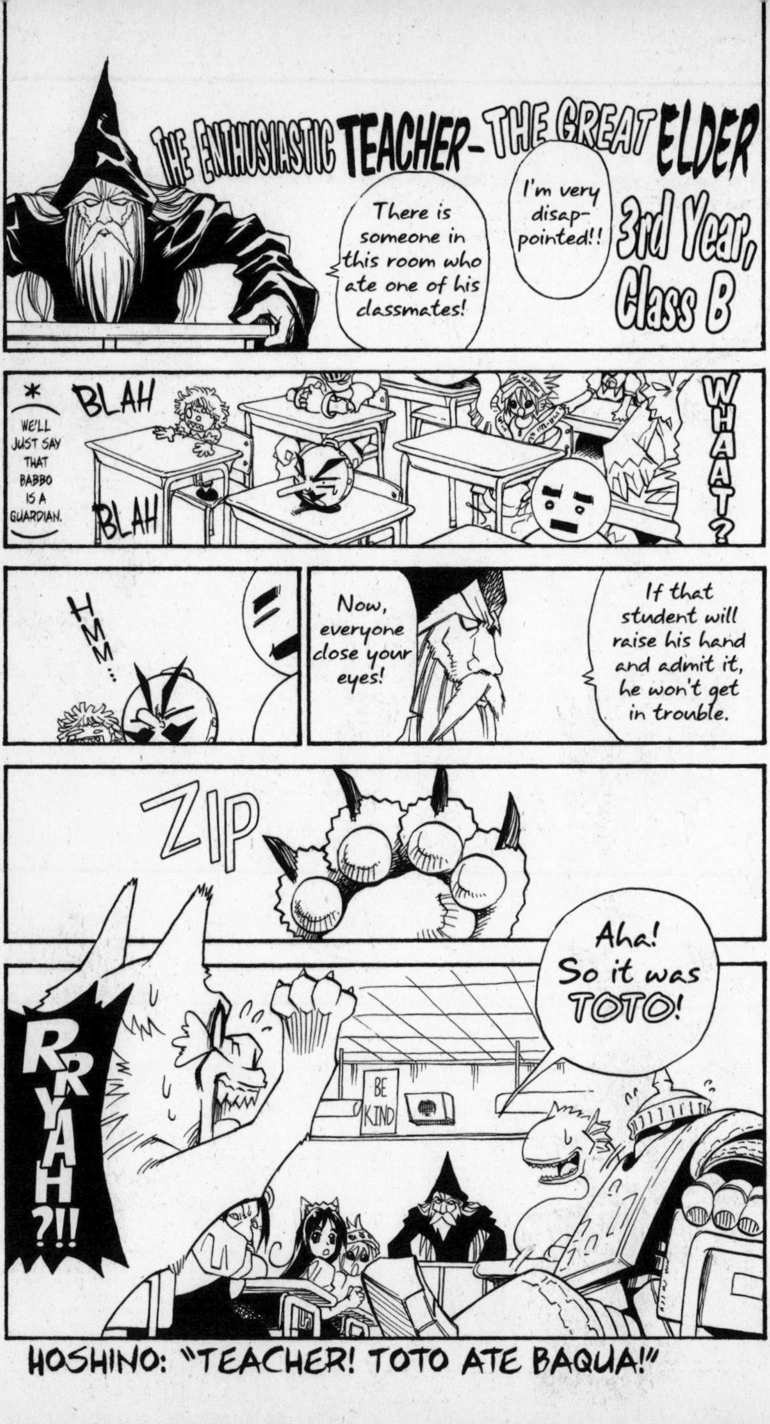
THE ENTHUSIASTIC TEACHER – THE GREAT ELDER
3rd Year, Class B
I'm very disap-pointed!!
There is someone in this room who ate one of his classmates!
WHAAAT?
BLAH
BLAH
* WE'LL JUST SAY THAT BABBO IS A GUARDIAN.
If that student will raise his hand and admit it, he won't get in trouble.
Now, everyone close your eyes!
HMM...
ZIP
Aha! So it was TOTO!
BE KIND
RRYAH?!!

HOSHINO: "TEACHER! TOTO ATE BAQUA!"

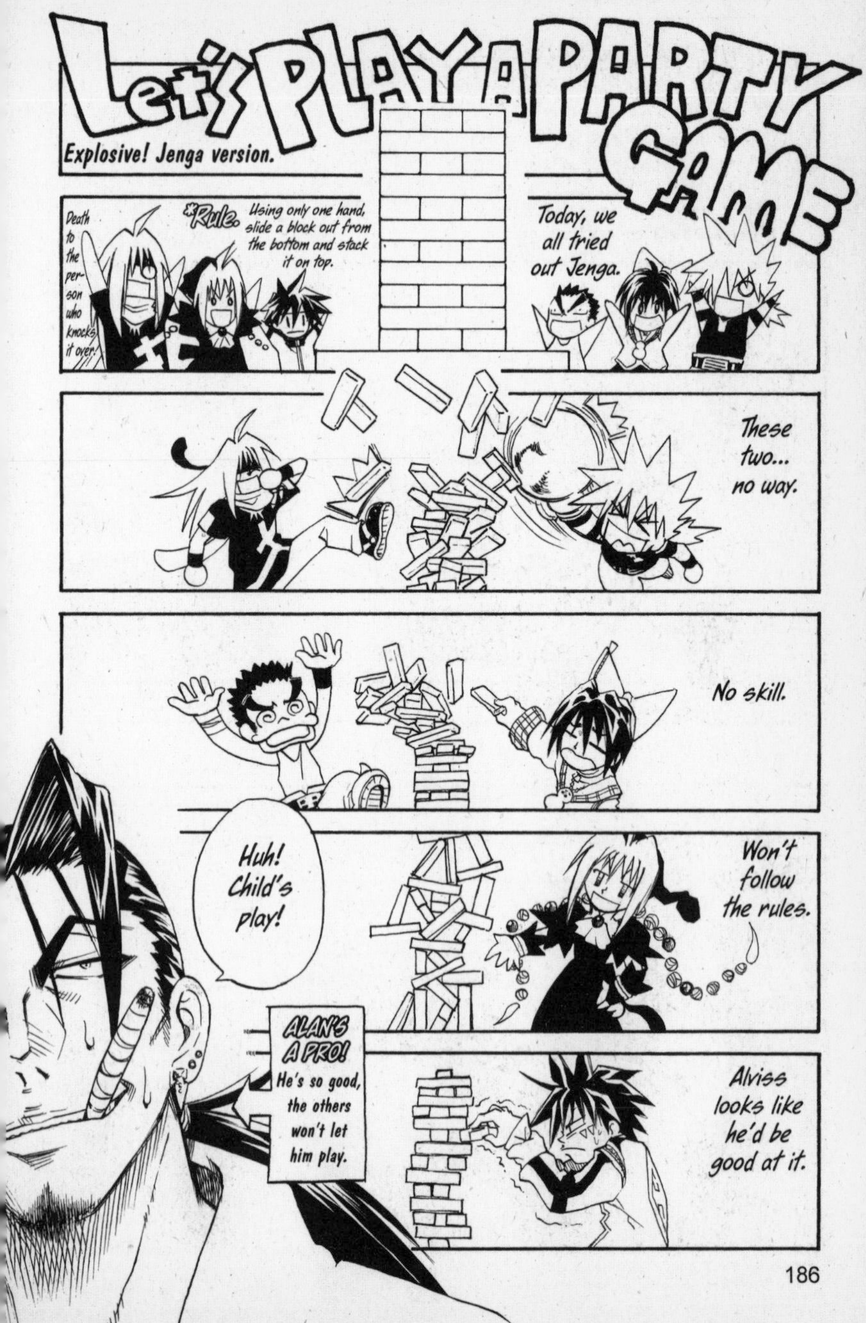
Let's PLAY A PARTY GAME
Explosive! Jenga version.
Today, we all tried out Jenga.
*Rule. Using only one hand, slide a block out from the bottom and stack it on top.
Death to the person who knocks it over!
These two... no way.
No skill.
Won't follow the rules.
Huh! Child's play!
Alviss looks like he'd be good at it.
ALAN'S A PRO!
He's so good, the others won't let him play.

WHAT'S DIFFERENT?

There are eight differences between the top and bottom pictures.
("The thickness of the frame" or "the lines are different" doesn't count!)
Can you find them all?

By: G・B

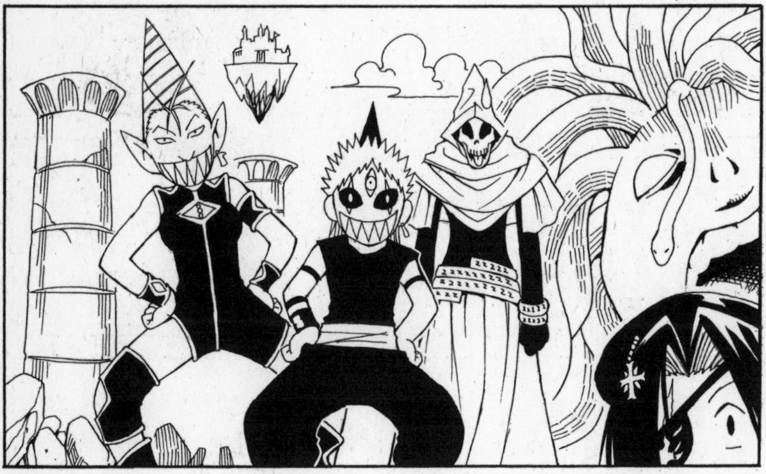

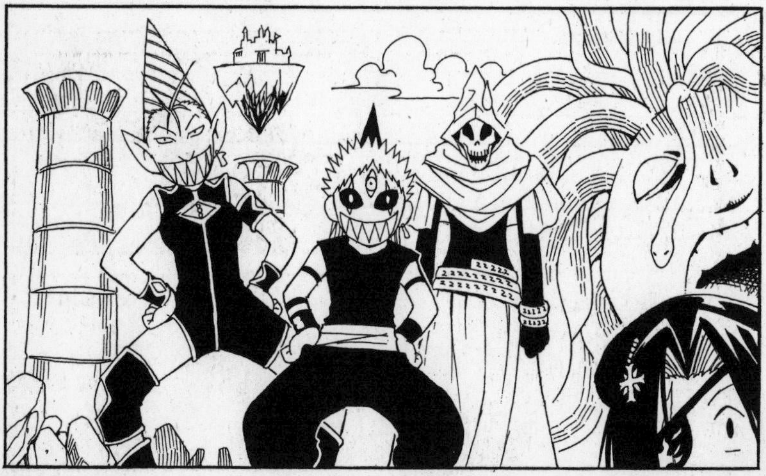

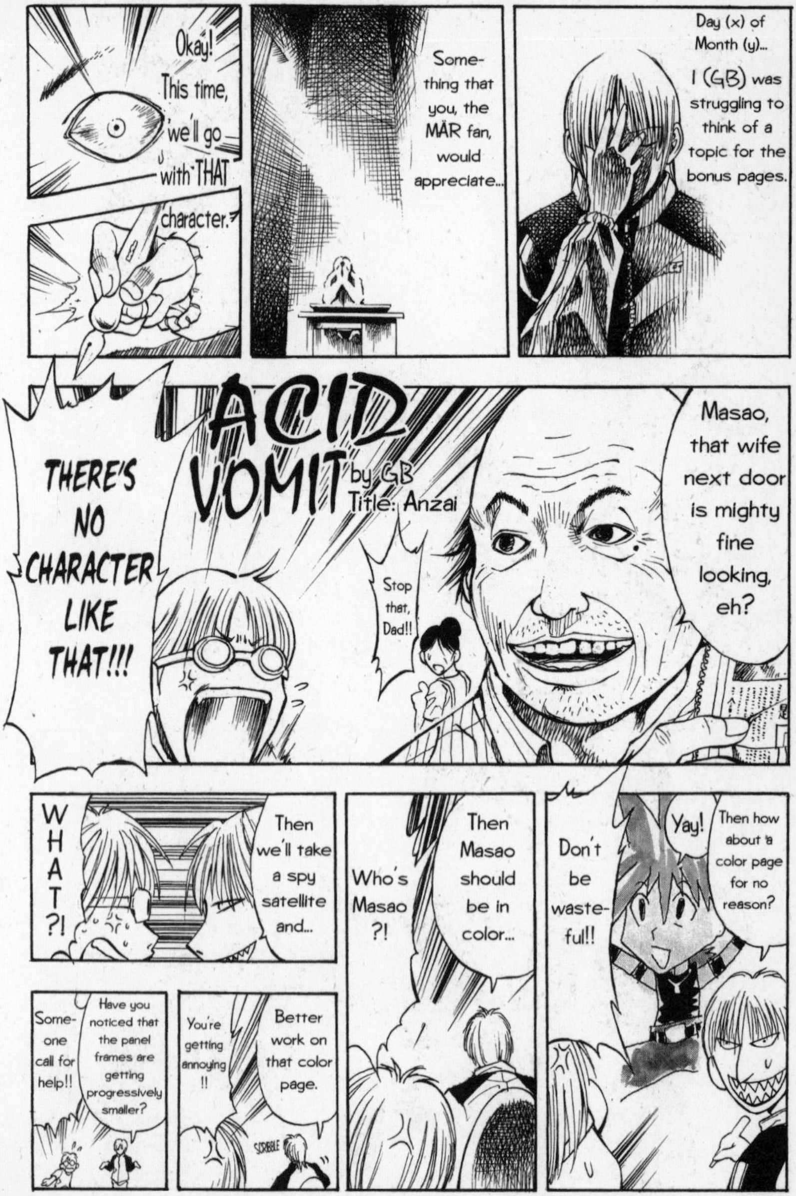
Day (x) of Month (y)... I (GB) was struggling to think of a topic for the bonus pages.
Some-thing that you, the MÄR fan, would appreciate...
Okay! This time, we'll go with THAT character.
ACID VOMIT by GB Title: Anzai
Masao, that wife next door is mighty fine looking, eh?
Stop that, Dad!!
THERE'S NO CHARACTER LIKE THAT!!!
Then how about a color page for no reason?
Yay!
Don't be waste-ful!!
Then Masao should be in color...
Who's Masao ?!
Then we'll take a spy satellite and...
WHAT?!
Better work on that color page.
You're getting annoying !!
SCRIBBLE
Have you noticed that the panel frames are getting progressively smaller?
Some-one call for help!!

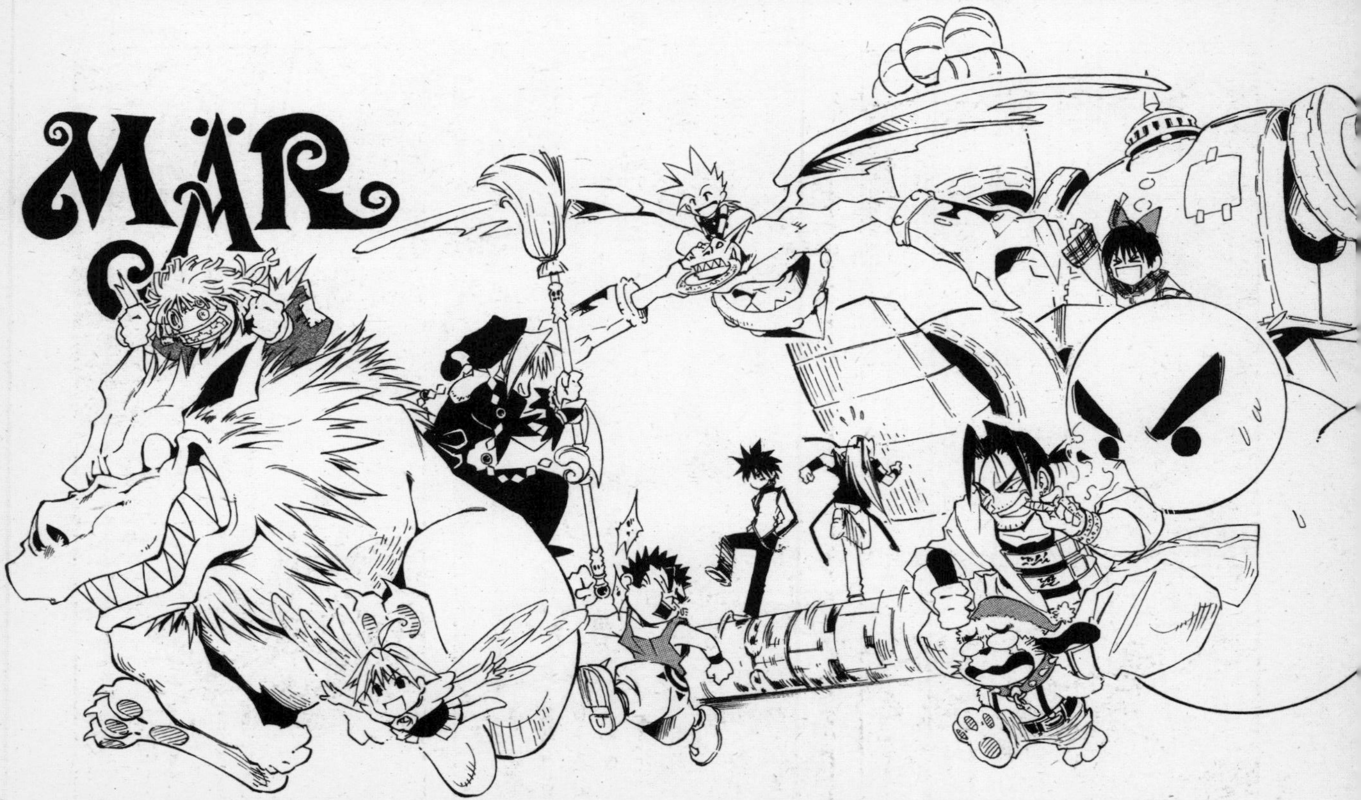
MÄR

QUESTION FOR AN OTAKU

By Hechita

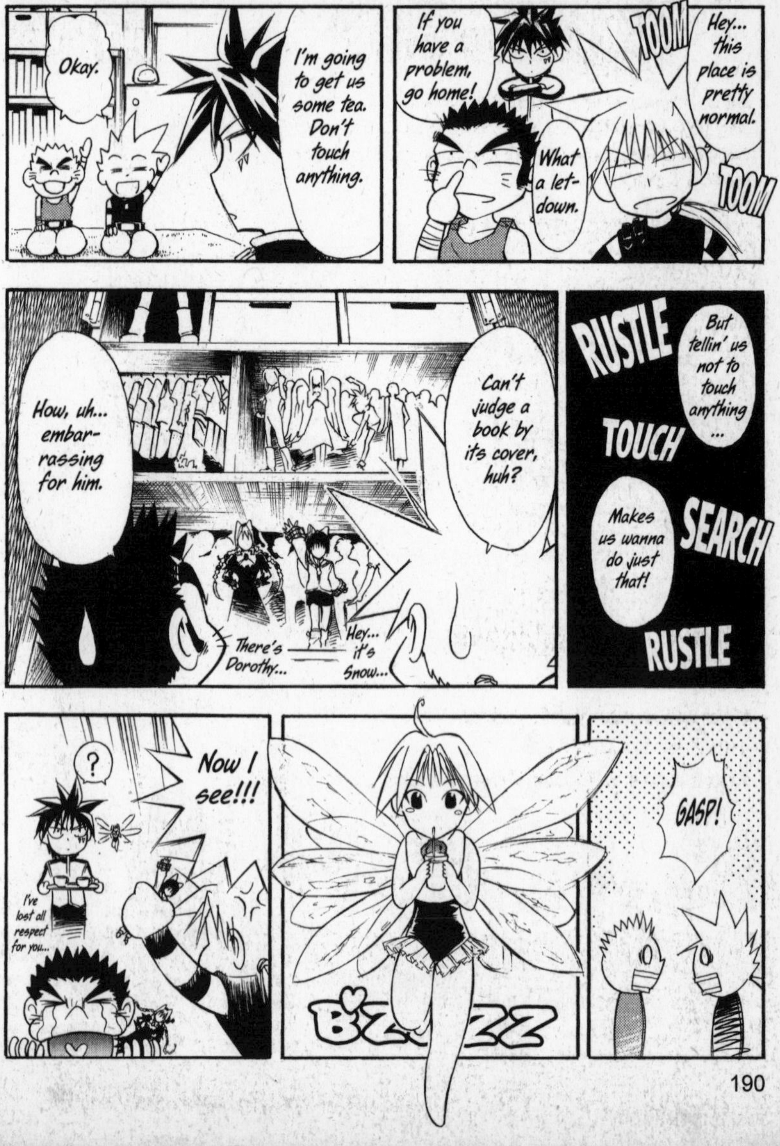
TOOM
Hey... this place is pretty normal.
TOOM
If you have a problem, go home!
What a let-down.
I'm going to get us some tea. Don't touch anything.
Okay.
RUSTLE
But tellin' us not to touch anything...
TOUCH
SEARCH
Makes us wanna do just that!
RUSTLE
Can't judge a book by its cover, huh?
How, uh... embarrassing for him.
Hey... it's Snow...
There's Dorothy...
GASP!
B'ZZZ
Now I see!!!
?
I've lost all respect for you...